MASSACHUSETTS GENEALOGICAL RESEARCH

by

George K. Schweitzer, Ph.D., Sc.D.
407 Regent Court
Knoxville, TN 37923

Wordprocessing by
Anne M. Smalley

My thanks go out to many people who have assisted in the production of this volume, but I want to take special notice of three. First, I am grateful to William H. Schoeffler, a widely-acknowledged expert on New England genealogical research, for reading the manuscript, making numerous helpful suggestions, and saving me from several errors. Second, I am grateful to Mrs. Anne M. Smalley for her computer skills and her pleasant patience in doing the word processing of the material. Third, I continue in my gratitude to my wife Verna L. Pratt Schweitzer for her love and forbearance.

ISBN 0-913857-12-2

TABLE OF CONTENTS

Chapter 1

MASSACHUSETTS BACKGROUND

1. MA geography

The state of Massachusetts (hereafter abbreviated MA), one of the thirteen original colonies, is located in the northeastern region of the eastern seaboard of the US. In shape its major portion resembles a rectangle, about 130 miles long and 50 miles high (see Figure 1). In the northeast there is a slight protrusion, Cape Ann, and in the southeast there is a large protrusion, the Cape Cod peninsula, which curves eastward, then northward about 60 miles into the Atlantic Ocean. Off the southeastern coast rest two large islands, Martha's Vineyard and Nantucket, and the much smaller island group called the Elizabeth Islands. MA is bounded on the north by VT and NH, on the east by the Atlantic Ocean, and on the south by the Atlantic Ocean, RI, and CT, and on the west by NY. Figure 2 depicts the major rivers of MA. The Merrimack River coming out of NH drains northeastern MA, while the Charles River and the Neponset River drain central eastern MA. Moving southward in southeastern MA is the Taunton River. The Blackstone River flows southeasterly from central MA. The western third of the state is separated by the Connecticut River which comes from the north, flows across MA, then enters CT. In MA, it is fed by two major tributaries, the Deerfield joining it in the north, and the Chicopee in the south. Northwestern MA is emptied by the northward-flowing Hoosick River, and the southward-moving Housatonic River drains the central and southern region of western MA.

Figure 3 shows the population centers and sites of MA, including the major cities (with populations in thousands) of Boston (563K), Worcester (162K), Springfield (152K), New Bedford (98K), Cambridge (95K), Brockton (95K), Fall River (93K), Lowell (92K), Quincy (84K), Somerville (77K). The six major land regions of MA are set forth in Figure 4. The Coastal Lowlands are found in the eastern third of the state and the offshore islands. The area has low hills, small lakes and ponds, and short rivers. Along the coast are many good harbors, including Boston, Fall River, Gloucester, and New Bedford, all still being used extensively, and some others which are not as active as they once were: Lynn, Marblehead, Newburyport, Plymouth, Provincetown, Salem. The Eastern Upland occupies the central third of MA, rising to about 1000 feet, then sloping gradually down to the CT River. The CT Valley which runs along the CT River is about 20 miles wide, and is good farming land because of its rich soil and relatively mild climate. West of the CT Valley for about 30 miles is the Western Upland, in which the land rises from the CT Valley to over 2800 feet in places, a region also called the Berkshire Hills. Then there is a slim valley, known as the Berkshire Valley, which is only about 10

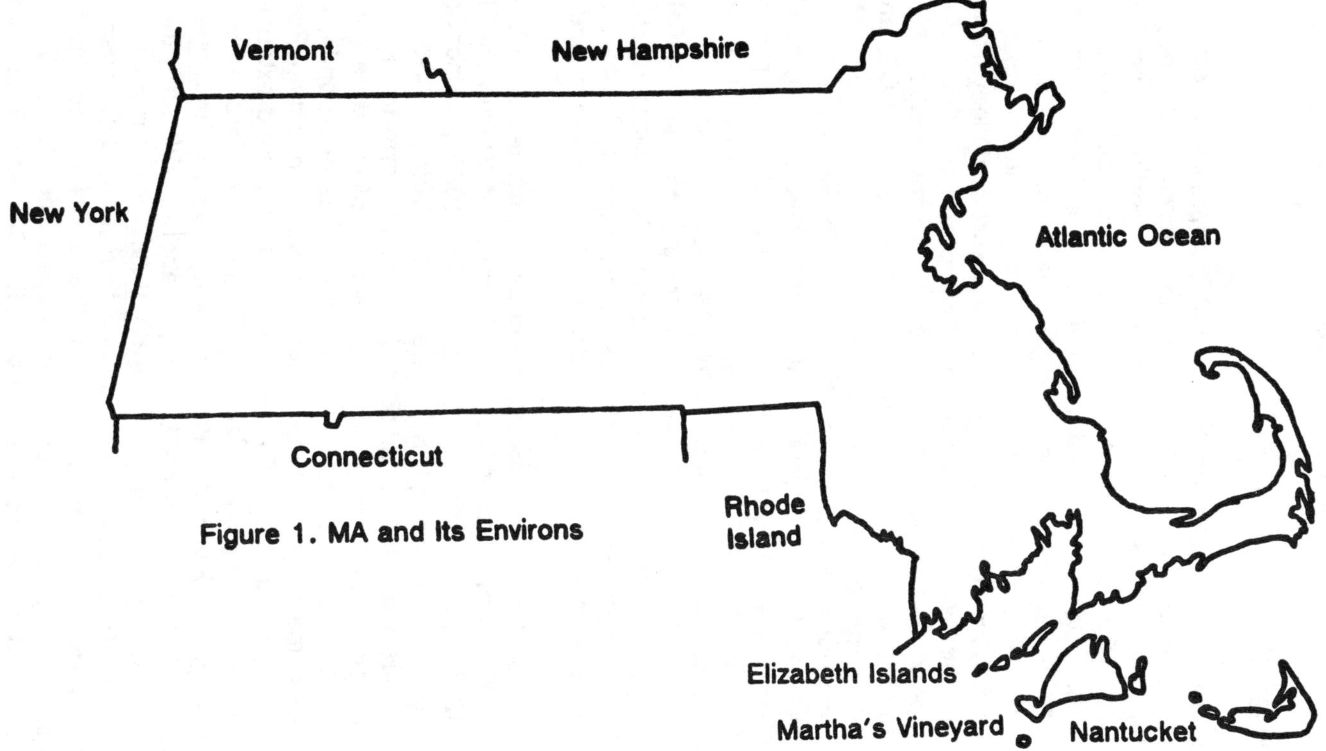

Figure 1. MA and Its Environs

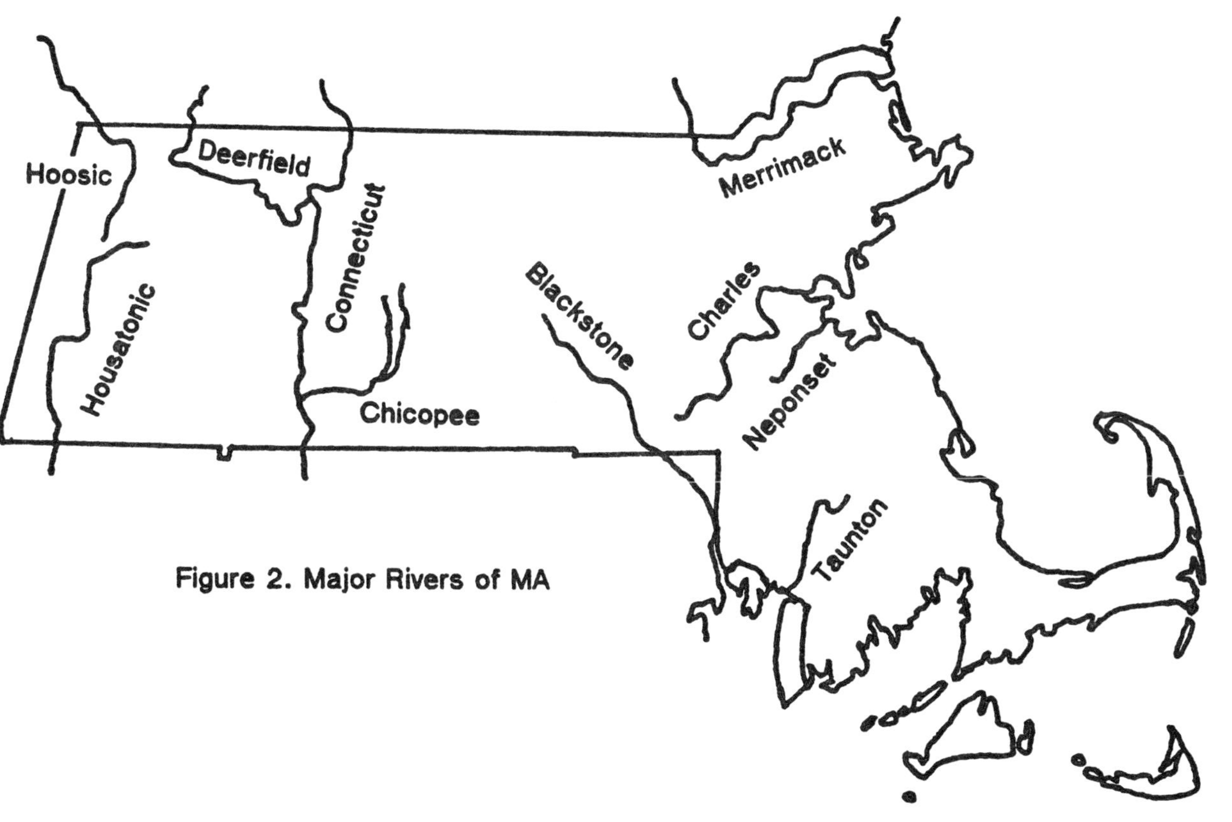

Figure 2. Major Rivers of MA

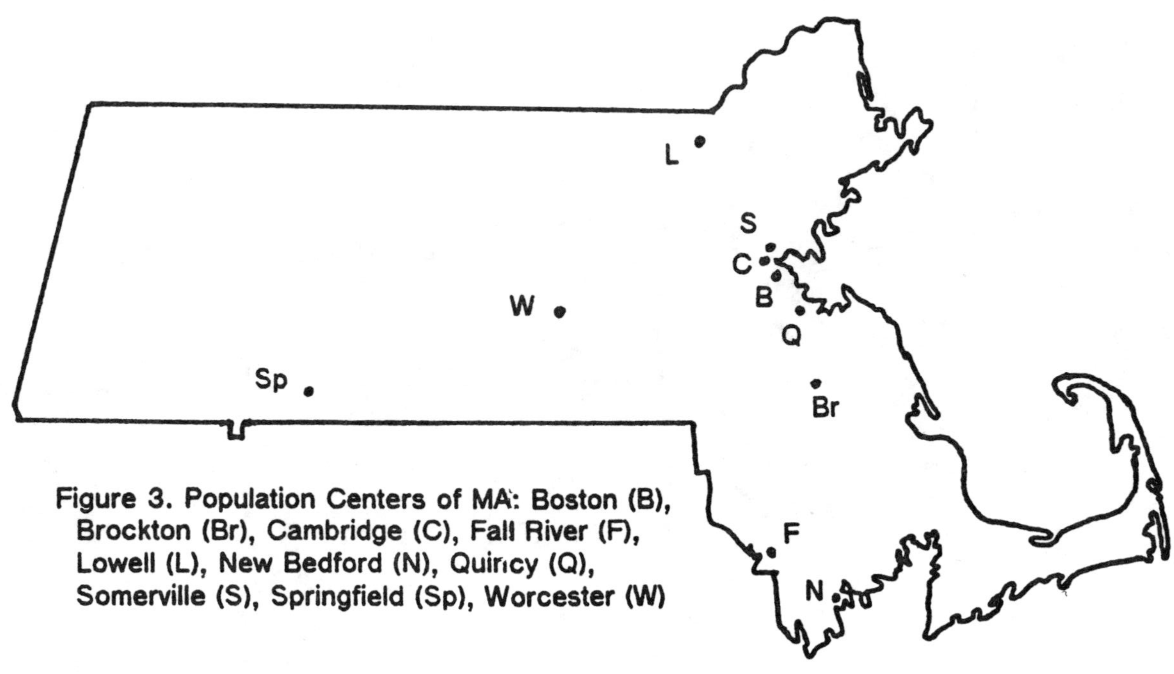

Figure 3. Population Centers of MA: Boston (B), Brockton (Br), Cambridge (C), Fall River (F), Lowell (L), New Bedford (N), Quincy (Q), Somerville (S), Springfield (Sp), Worcester (W)

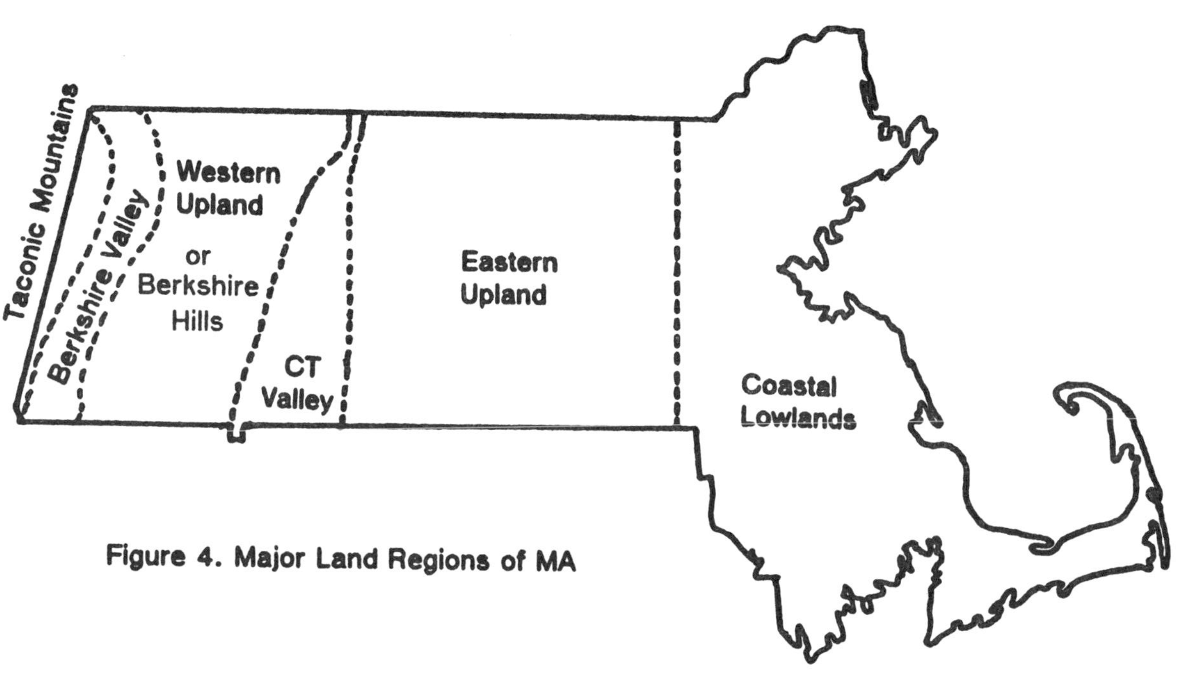

Figure 4. Major Land Regions of MA

miles wide, and is good country for dairy farming. Running along the western edge of MA, over at the NY border, are the Taconic Mountains, the highest peak in them rising to over 3400 feet.

2. Plymouth Colony, 1620-92

In 1588 the Spanish Armada was defeated by English naval forces. This victory marked the replacement of Spain as master of the seas by England. This change in power permitted England to begin colonization as they supplanted the Spanish in the northern areas of the New World. Many explorers investigated the coast of New England, numerous fishing fleets worked the nearby waters, and several unsuccessful attempts at colonization were made in the first two decades of the 1600s. The successful settlement of the area that is now MA resulted from a conjunction of the English desire to plant colonies with two other events. One was a party of colonists who drifted off course in 1620, and the other was a plague in 1615-7 which severely decreased the number of MA Indians.

In the late 1500s, a party called the Puritans developed in the Church of England, which was the national church. They practiced a very conservative faith viewing the literally-interpreted Bible as the to-be-strictly-enforced law of God for individuals, the church, and the state. The Puritans tried to reform the church, were listened to for a time, but in 1604 were rebuffed and came under condemnation, and then persecution. In 1608, a group of Puritans who had separated from the Church of England to set up their own congregations went to Holland. Then, in 1620, they obtained financial backing from London, sailed from Holland, picked up other Puritans and some non-Puritans in Plymouth, England, then headed for VA to settle.

Blown off course by gales, they arrived at Cape Cod, and following a month's exploration, the 102 people established a colony at Plymouth. After being almost halved in number by hardships in the first year, the colony began to grow slowly with a few new settlers coming in each year, so that by 1630, Plymouth numbered 390. In 1621, the governor had received a patent to the area, this was renewed in 1630, and in 1640 was turned over to the freemen (voters). The patent defined the colony as consisting of what today are the counties of Barnstable, Bristol, and Plymouth in MA, and the eastern sections of Newport and Providence Counties plus all of Bristol County in RI. As the population continued to expand (1020 in 1640, 1566 in 1650, 1980 in 1660), colonists established other towns in the area: Scituate (1633), Hingham (1635), Duxbury (1637), Sandwich (1638), Barnstable (1638), Taunton (1639), Yarmouth (1639), Marshfield (1640), Hull (1644), Rehoboth (1645), Eastham (1646), Dartmouth (1652), Bridgewater (1656), Swansea (1668), Middleborough (1669), Freetown (1683), and Rochester (1686).

The colony was governed by a legislature of the freemen called the General Court. They elected the governor and his assistants, made laws, set up courts, appointed officials, distributed land, and levied taxes. In the out-lying towns, town meetings handled local affairs and sent representatives to the General Court (Legislature) in Plymouth. Up to 1636, the General Court handled all trials, but during 1636-85, three other courts came to operate: Court of Assistants (1636-), Court of Admiralty (1636-), and Selectmen's Courts in the towns (1661-). Plymouth Colony at first tried to function with common property, but failed, after 1623 permitting settlers to have individual plots of land. In the newly-formed towns, lands were distributed by the town government and/or by settlement companies called proprietors. Farming, cattle-raising, and fur trading were the major means of subsistence. In 1643, Plymouth Colony entered the New England Confederation, a loose relationship with the colonies of MA Bay, CT, and New Haven for the settlement of boundary and jurisdictional disputes and for mutual defense. As of 1675, further small increases in population having occurred (5333 in 1670), Indian attacks were launched against all the New England colonies. This hostile action was partly a result of the push of New Englanders into Indian lands. The war, named King Philip's War after the Indian leader, brought much destruction and death to both sides, with the colonists subduing the Indians in the south in 1676, but not until 1678 in the north. Increased population (6400 in 1680) brought about the establishment of three counties in 1685: Barnstable, Bristol, Plymouth, and a county seat was designated in each.

The following year (1686) saw the suspension of the previous colonial governments in the region and the setting up of the Dominion of New England, combining Plymouth with all the other New England colonies, and later adding NY and NJ, with headquarters at Boston. The governmental structure, including the courts, was reorganized and tighter controls over the colonists and their activities were put in place. Predictably, the new arrangement was strongly opposed, and following the English Revolution, it was abandoned in 1689. Plymouth Colony reverted to its previous self-government. Under a new charter of 1691, Plymouth, the islands south of Cape Cod (formerly parts of NY), MA Bay, ME, and Nova Scotia were combined as the Province of MA Bay in New England. The year before this, Plymouth Colony numbered 7424 persons, while MA Bay Colony had 49,504 inhabitants. The difference in populations reflects the dependence of Plymouth upon Boston (in MA Bay) as a trade center, the harbor in Boston being far better than any in Plymouth Colony.

3. <u>MA Bay Colony</u>, 1630-92

A small group of settlers came through Plymouth in 1622 and went up into the MA Bay area where they started a plantation at Weymouth. A number of other MA Bay sites were occupied by small groups in the next few years. Then, in 1628, a petition for a grant of land in MA Bay by some Puritans was approved. Shortly thereafter, a shipload of 350 settlers came and established Salem. A royal act of 1629 created the MA Bay Company, and the government of the colony was transferred in 1630 to MA, setting the colony virtually free of English control. Along with the transfer of the charter and government to MA Bay came 1500 people who moved through Salem to establish Charlestown, then to set up Boston. As a result of increasing persecution of Puritans in England, many immigrants came to MA Bay every year for the next 10 years, so that by 1640 the population had reached 8932. By 1650 it had risen to 14,037, and by 1660 it had gone to 20,082, even though Puritan persecution in England had ceased about 1640. The increased population was accommodated by the formation of new towns in the MA Bay region and by migration beyond the region. New towns in the 1630s with their dates of origin included Dorchester (1630), Medford (1630), Roxbury (1630), Watertown (1630), Cambridge (1631), Marblehead (1633), Ipswich (1634), Concord (1635), Lynn (1635), Newbury (1635), Weymouth (1635), Dedham (1636), Rowley (1639), Salisbury (1639), and Sudbury (1639). These expansions, coupled with Indian-English trader hostility, provoked the Pequot War in 1637, because the settlers were pushing into the territory of these Indians. In that conflict, which was borne largely by CT colonists, the Pequots were defeated and driven out, there being several hundred deaths and property loss on both sides. In the 1640s, these new towns were set up: Haverhill (1641), Springfield (1641), Gloucester (1642), Woburn (1642), Wenham (1643), Andover (1646), and Malden (1649). Further towns were carved out of new land and were formed by splitting off existing towns.

The government of the MA Bay Colony, operating almost free of England, was vested in a General Court made up of orthodox Puritan freemen, a governor, a deputy governor, and assistants to the governor. They had complete power to make laws, establish courts, choose officials, and to govern all individuals coming to the colony. They set stringent religious tests for admission to the company of freemen and suppressed all religious and political dissent, with the clergy effectively functioning as a ruling class in a Biblical theocracy. The courts were given a three-tier structure with the Court of Assistants at the upper level, Inferior Quarter Courts which shortly became County Courts at the intermediate level, and Magistrates Courts at the lower or town level. Land was granted to groups of faithful believers (called proprietors) who would start new towns, and would responsibly assign or sell the land to persons properly qualified to contribute constructively to the community. The early settlement of MA thus consisted of a growing cluster of towns, each successive town usually being built adjacent or not too far from an existing town. The local government of each town rested in a town meeting in which every church member had a vote. A few persons were banished and many more left because of religious and political dissent to establish or to join other colonies: CT (1636), RI (1636), NH (1638), ME (1652).

Early MA Bay had a sizable educated population; as of 1640 approximately one out of every 250 inhabitants was an Oxford or Cambridge graduate. The first secondary school in the colonies was opened in 1635, the first college, Harvard, was established in 1636, and the first newspaper, printing press, and library were located in MA. In 1642, training for underprivileged boys was mandated, and in 1647 provisions for elementary schools were made. Meanwhile, in 1643, to handle the expanding number of towns, four counties (shires) were created: Essex, Middlesex, Suffolk, and Norfolk. The latter is known as Old Norfolk County, which included some towns now in NH (and should not be confused with present-day Norfolk County, which dates from 1793). When NH became a royal colony in 1679/80, Old Norfolk was phased out and its towns were partitioned between NH and Essex County of MA. In that same year of 1643, MA Bay entered into the previously-mentioned New England Confederation which coordinated the colonies' defense against Indians and the Dutch of NY. One of the incitements to this Confederation was the Pequot War of 1637. A more devastating Indian War, King Philip's War, was fought 1675-8. Philip, the Indian leader, was eventually defeated in RI in 1676, but sporadic Indian attacks continued north of there until 1678. The war was very costly in MA in loss of property and life; 12 towns and over 600 houses were destroyed and more than 600 colonists perished. The movement of the frontier was stopped and even pushed back by reason of destroyed towns.

In 1660, the monarchy in England was restored after a 20-year period of Revolution, and the British government decided to exercise stricter control over its colonies, especially MA, about which they had received adverse reports. In 1664 and again in 1676 an investigating committee brought back information regarding denials of religious freedom, persecutions, and refusals to obey English law by MA Bay. The year 1679 saw the removal of NH from MA, the newly established area becoming a royal colony. When satisfactory changes were not made in MA, the charter of the MA Bay Company was finally revoked in 1684. The colonial government continued to function until 1686, when MA Bay was combined with the other New England colonies, and later with NY and NJ, into the Dominion of New England. A royal governor, who reorganized the government, was sent from London. However, this arrangement ceased in 1689 when the monarchs in England changed, and MA Bay reverted to its previous governmental structure. In 1691, MA Bay received a new charter in which MA Bay, Plymouth, the islands south of Cape Cod (formerly in NY), and ME were all combined as the Province of MA Bay in New England. This new charter abolished church membership as a prerequisite for voting and thus brought to an end the theocratic form of government. The grip of this religiously exclusive regime upon the people had been gradually weakening since about 1650 as more and more individuals resisted the strict and sometimes harsh control of their lives and the lives of others. MA was now to be a civil commonwealth rather than a Puritan theocracy. Even so, the Congregational (Puritan) Church remained the predominant denomination with the great majority of church-affiliated people belonging to it.

Special attention should be directed to the important migrations of MA people to establish other colonies and settle new regions. Included are the following, with beginning dates shown in parentheses: CT (1636), RI (1636), NH (1638), Long Island (1639), Nantucket (1659). MA settlers continued to move into these areas during the entire 17th century (1600s). Please recognize also that what is now ME remained a province of MA until 1820. Its settlement, though beginning in 1622, was very slow, with persons from the MA Bay Colony moving to its coastal sites, the interior remaining largely under Indian control until well into the 1700s. Practically all those coming to MA during these colonial years were English Protestants, most early ones being dissenters, with fewer coming later on. A few representatives of other groups came: Irish seamen, Scottish (1650-1), Huguenots (1685-), Scots-Irish (1690-).

4. The provincial period, 1692-1775

MA Bay brought to the new province five counties (Essex, Hampshire, Middlesex, Suffolk, York) and 55 towns, which were combined with Plymouth Colony, which contributed three counties (Barnstable, Bristol, Plymouth) and 17 towns. The population of this new province was about 57,000 with Plymouth Colony having given about 7500. The new government now consisted of a governor, a lieutenant governor, a board of councillors, and the General Court (Legislature). The three tiers of courts were kept with some alterations. At the top was the Superior Court of Judicature, at the intermediate level were several county courts (Inferior Courts of Common Pleas, Courts of General Sessions, Judges of Probate), and at the lower level were Justice of the Peace Courts. For four years (1697-1701), NY was once again united with MA, but as before, the joint government did not endure.

The provincial period (1692-1775) was one marked by two major series of events: (1) intermittent wars between the colonies on the east coast and the French and Indians who were in the back country and Canada, and (2) sizable growth with northward and westward settlement movements occurring in between these conflicts. During most of the period which is now being discussed, England and France were at war. The frontiers of MA, especially in ME, figured heavily in the conflict because of their proximity to the French in Canada and in the back country. The four wars between England and France which affected MA were King William's War (1689–97), Queen Anne's War (1701–13), King George's War (1744–8), and the French and Indian War (1756–63). The periods in between these wars were often not ones of peace, but times of sporadic acts of hostility amid an armed truce. None of these wars settled very much except the second and the last. Some of the Indians along the military interface sided with the English colonies, and some with the French. In King William's War (1689–97), the French and their Indian allies raided along the ME coast and down the back country to Haverhill, MA. Personnel from MA participated in an expedition in 1690 which temporarily captured Port Royal in Acadia, and in an unsuccessful 34-ship effort to take Quebec.

After a brief period of lessened activity, Queen Anne's War (1701–13) began. The French and Indians again attacked exposed frontier areas and the English retaliated with actions against Canada. Notable gains were realized by the English in that they took Acadia, Newfoundland, and much territory around Hudson Bay. MA was now protected to a considerable degree, and rapid expansion to the west and north followed. For four decades there had been terror on the frontier, and many villages had been destroyed, then replanted, several times. The thirty-year lull after 1713 was one of expansion in settlement, trade, commerce, and stability. A number of Scots-Irish were among the many immigrants who took advantage of this new situation. The area which is now Worcester County filled rapidly, the small population of the CT River Valley was increased, and then parts of the lands now called Berkshire County were settled. Many CT people accompanied MA settlers into this latter region. As the movement progressed, the MA policy of creating orderly church-dominated towns was slowly given up. Speculators began buying land from town proprietors, and then the legislature gradually succumbed to the wiles of the speculators to whom they gave or sold town sites. Beginning in 1727, towns were also set aside for Indian and French war veterans and their heirs. During 1692–1748 sixty-eight new towns were chartered. Not much good land was left east of the CT River, and almost one-third of that west of the river had been taken up. Settlements had spread far enough that the old river routes and the Indian trails were no longer adequate, so many roads, bridges, and ferries were built. The population had risen as shown here, with thousands of inhabitants given in parentheses: 1700 (56K), 1710 (62K), 1720 (91K), 1730 (114K), 1740 (152K), 1750 (188K). Toward the end of the lull, in the 1740s, sizable migrations from southeastern MA to Dutchess County, NY, occurred.

In 1744, King George's War (1744–8) found England and France once again battling over North American colonial possessions. Urged on by the French, Indians brought suffering to the MA frontier, resulting in a considerable number of deserted towns. MA troops were heavily involved in an expedition which took the very important French fort at Louisburg (the gateway to Canada) in Nova Scotia. A treaty of 1748 was nothing but an armed truce, with both sides preparing for renewal of combat, and with the British returning Louisburg to France. Hence, almost no new towns were established in the decade following 1744. The final and decisive war in this four-war series was the French and Indian War (1756-63), with armed conflict actually beginning in 1754 in western PA. Again, the impact on MA was sufficient (with Indians sweeping down the Champlain Valley into MA) that no new towns were planted until the end of the war. With the fall of Quebec in 1759 and of Montreal in 1760, the war effectively ended in America, even though it continued in Europe. Three years later, when a treaty was finally agreed on, Britain was given all of Canada and all of the back country up to the MS River. Beginning in 1760, when hostilities ceased in the colonies, practically all unappropriated lands in central and western MA were rapidly occupied. By 1768, all of MA had been laid out in towns, and all of them had been disposed of and at least partially occupied. All further towns, as had some previous ones, resulted from splitting of existing of towns.

During this period after the defeat of the French and the subdual of hostile Indians (1760-), many MA people migrated. The inhabitants of eastern MA tended to go to ME, those of central MA to NH, and those of western MA to VT. The British government forbid settlement beyond the Appalachian Mountains, but even though some people disregarded the regulation, there was no large movement into that vast area. The 1760 population of MA was 222K (about 20K in what is now ME), and in 1770, it was 266K (with about 31K in ME). As previously, the majority of immigrants were English Protestants.

5. The Revolutionary period, 1763-80

Following the termination of the French and Indian War (1763), Britain found herself severely in debt, and began to tighten up her trade and taxation policies in the American colonies. Having become used to an independence fostered by previous British disinterest, the colonies strongly resented the new taxes and the restrictive trade regulations. In addition, the British had decided to exercise closer supervision of the colonial governments and had forbidden settlers to move into the newly acquired territories beyond the Appalachian Mountains. In 1764, Parliament passed an act which curtailed the lucrative trade with French and Spanish colonies, and in 1765, an act collecting revenue on all legal and commercial documents was put in force. Protesting mobs hit the Boston streets, harassed the British officials, and did some property damage. A general boycott of English goods followed, with similar boycotts in Philadelphia and New York. In 1766, the regulations were relaxed and things returned to normal.

However, in 1767, a series of revenue measures levying duties on several items which were being imported in the colonies again stirred MA and other colonies into heated resentment. Mobs again ranged through Boston, and merchants refused to buy English imports. The British responded by sending in several regiments of troops to preserve the peace. MA people continued their protests, asserting that they should not be taxed unless they were permitted representation in Parliament, or unless they could set and raise their own taxes. In 1770, when some Bostonians taunted and assailed a British sentry, Royal troops fired into the harassers, killed three, and mortally wounded two. Boston patriots set up committees of correspondence with other MA towns, and soon extended the communications network to other colonies. These committees encouraged protest, organized boycotts, and kept in touch with each other. The repeal of most of the oppressive revenue acts in 1770 led to about three years of prosperity, although anti-British incidents continued.

Then, in 1773, another cycle of protests, boycotts, and violence was set in motion by a new regulation which gave the East India Company a monopoly on the very profitable tea trade. Merchants, shippers, and tea smugglers were all threatened financially, plus beset with fear that the British would award other such monopolies. In protest, disguised tradesmen boarded three tea ships in Boston Harbor and dumped their cargo overboard. The British government in 1774 hastily passed acts closing the Port of Boston to trade, amending the charter with severe restrictions, and inflicting penalties on MA. Other colonies pledged support to MA, and the first Continental Congress was proposed, called, and met in Philadelphia. The situations in late 1774 and early 1775 deteriorated, with the MA assembly moving to Concord and organizing as an independent provincial congress. British garrisons controlled only the main towns, and the countryside gradually became overtly rebellious. Militia were drilled, and arms, ammunition, equipment, and supplies were stockpiled.

On 19 April 1775, the British acted, sending a contingent of 700 troops to Concord to destroy a depot of arms and ammunition. After a brief skirmish in Lexington which resulted in 9 American casualties, the British destroyed the stores at Concord. As they returned to Boston, they were hounded by patriots who subjected them to steady gunfire resulting in 273 British casualties. News was spread rapidly, and soon sympathizers in the other colonies were preparing to join the fray. Militia from the towns of MA now poured into Cambridge (opposite Boston), and troops from neighboring colonies joined them, shutting the Royal Army up in Boston. The provincial troops fortified Breed's Hill and the British attacked them, driving them back slowly, at a terrible cost in British lives.

The American forces withdrew only a short distance, and when Washington arrived in July 1775, they surrounded Boston. In the early spring of 1776, the rebels placed cannons (captured at Ticonderoga) above the city, and began bombarding. The British, unable to withstand the attack, withdrew in March 1776, taking with them many Loyalist (Tory) citizens.

The state of MA had won its independence; no further battles were fought on its territory. However, the war raged on in the other colonies, at first in the middle colonies, then moving into the south, finally effectively ending in 1781. In every campaign of the war except during 1779-80, MA fielded more soldiers than any other colony. Almost 60,000 fought in the Continental Army, and over 15,000 militia actively participated. MA also sent very large amounts of supplies to American forces, and her ships captured many British vessels. Since 1774, MA had been governed by a provisional legislature (provincial congress). A state constitutional convention of 1778 drew up a document which was ratified by the people in 1780, and is still in place today. The MA constitution, with its checks and balances, its strong executive branch, and its bill of rights, strongly influenced the character of the US Constitution. The state of MA was markedly altered by the war. Many of its pre-war leaders were Tories (Loyalists) and left the state, along with numerous Loyalist common people. A new class of leaders took their place, these being people along the coast who drew their wealth from the sea trade. MA residents suffered not only when the war was being fought in the state, but during all its years. There were many men killed or disabled, inflation and high taxation dogged farmers and tradesmen, and there was widespread profiteering. In 1780, with the MA population at 317,760, the state government was put in place with the election of the first governor.

6. <u>The early commonwealth</u>, 1780-1815

As the Revolutionary War wound down (1780-3), sizable numbers of MA citizens moved into VT, NH, and ME. However, these migrations were soon eclipsed by the increasing numbers who moved into PA, NY, and OH during 1780-1815. In 1784, MA, following the examples of VA and NY, ceded to the US all lands west of NY which she had previously claimed. However, the Commonwealth of MA reserved a claim to the western portion of NY, which NY acknowledged. NY was given sovereignty over the entire area, but the lands belonged to MA to sell. During 1788-91, MA sold the land to several speculators, and by 1805, the region was beginning to pass beyond the frontier stage. The year 1785 saw the MA governor raise taxes, during a severe general economic depression, in order to pay off the state's war debt. The farmers in western MA, already in debt and on the edge of poverty, organized a rebellion in which large numbers obstructed the collection of taxes, refused to pay debts which officials were trying to collect, and closed down the courts in several counties. The governor called out the state militia, which repulsed their attempt to take over a state arsenal, pursued them, routed them, took prisoners, then subdued several contingents of them at various places in the western counties.

In 1788, MA ratified the US Constitution and thus entered the Union. By this time, the religious and political unity of MA had moved strongly toward a pluralism. Government was becoming more democratic and less aristocratic as more common people participated in the process. Religious diversity had come to be represented by groups as different as evangelical revivalistic Baptists and rationalistic deistic Unitarians, both having claimed people who were once Congregationalists or whose parents were. The commerce of the Commonwealth expanded almost explosively, the major activities being the production and sale of fish and whale products, the building of ships, and the running of ships in world-wide trading activities, as far away as China and India. In practically every major port of the world, ships of MA began to appear. Then, in 1793, England and France declared war on each other, which permitted MA to take over much of the trade that these two powerful seafaring nations had almost completely controlled. Wealth flowed into MA, and a state-wide prosperity resulted. MA sold everything it could produce, in the many places where it traded, and to the two warring nations. Full employment was realized, in fact, there was a labor shortage, the population grew rapidly, and the state experienced dynamic economic growth.

MA shipowners who risked sending their vessels into European waters reaped enormous profits from the British and the French. But, the two warring countries began stopping and attacking ships carrying supplies to their enemy's ports. Fearing that such attacks on American ships might force the US into war, the President persuaded Congress in 1807 to pass a law halting exports to foreign countries and prohibiting US ships from going to foreign ports. Overnight, the sea-based economy of MA came to abrupt disaster, and the state went rapidly into a depression. In 1809, the law was altered to forbid trade with only France and England, but MA shipping only partly recovered. A year later, all restrictions on American commerce were repealed, and trade especially with France who invited it, was resumed. So were British harassments of American ships.

The rising tide of American hostility toward Britain's actions against American ships and indications that Britain was inciting Indians to attack frontier settlements led to a declaration of war against Britain in 1812. The declaration of the War of 1812 was opposed by MA, because they rightly believed such a war would bring trade to a standstill, which it did. Americans were driven off the seas by a vastly superior British navy. MA, out of its resentment, only partly supported the war, giving meager funding, forbidding her militia to leave the state, celebrating English victories over France, and threatening to secede in a Convention of New England states held in 1814. Even so, MA supplied many seamen for the US Navy. The only part of MA that Britain invaded was ME. In the curtailments of MA trade, which began in 1807 and extended until the War ended in late 1814, the people of MA made some beginnings in industrialization. Small home industries were started and expanded, mills were built and enlarged, and a textile factory was established.

During the years just after the Revolutionary War, MA people had moved north into the unoccupied and sparsely settled parts of ME, NH, and VT. They also began moving west, following the Mohawk Valley into western NY and moving into northern and western PA, arriving in the latter area via the old Braddock Road. By 1786 they were showing up in southern OH, and soon thereafter in the northeastern section of the state, then in the central area.

7. The industrial changeover, 1815-61

In MA, the period after the War of 1812 (1815-61) was characterized by two major movements: industrialization and reform. The trade restrictions just before and during the war had forced MA people to seek another means of earning money. They turned to manufacturing, and when the war ended, activity in this area increased rapidly. The first industry to become widespread in the state was textile production, but manufacturing of paper, shoes, and metal products soon followed. There was abundant labor available to do the work because MA agriculture was rapidly declining. The MA farmers could not compete with the cheap produce which was being sent in from western farms. This was particularly the case after 1825, when the Erie Canal was opened, and began providing very inexpensive transportation. Rural decay in MA started to set in, as numerous farms were abandoned. In addition to joining the manufacturing labor force, farmers in large numbers also migrated west. Meanwhile, on the coast, shipbuilding, whaling, and marine shipping flourished.

The reform spirit moved rapidly also, one of its first results being the release of ME to become a separate state in 1820. A constitutional convention of that same year removed the property qualifications for voting and eliminated religious tests for office holders. Then, in 1833, the state completely separated the Congregational Church and the government, making into law what had already occurred in practice. Reform movements for humanitarian care of the mentally-ill, universal education, abstinence, and abolition of slavery were widely supported. Amidst all this progressive action, there came a movement which had distressing proportions. In the 1840s and 1850s a large steady stream of Irish immigrants moved into MA. Most of them took factory jobs in the cities, and soon the Irish came to be the major group in many of these cities. Some of the older residents of the commonwealth became alarmed at this, and crusaded for laws to limit immigration and to check the mounting influence of the Catholic Church. The Mexican War of 1846-8 was opposed by MA, but one regiment of troops was raised for service.

After the War of 1812, MA emigrants moved into northern IN (1816-40), northern IL (1825-50), southern MI (1830-50), and south-eastern WI (1835-55). After 1840, MA was contributing settlers to states across the MS River, particularly IA and MN. And some were starting to cross the Rocky Mountains to help begin populating OR and WA. Over these years, MA sent many pioneers to ME, NH, VT, NY, OH, IL, MI, and WI, with fewer to PA and IN. The major factor which sent them to the frontier was fertile and inexpensive land, which gave them a chance to better themselves economically. Not only were MA families attracted by land in the west, they were also often driven away from MA by adverse social, economic, religious, and political differences in which their freedoms and/or welfare were threatened. In 1850, the number of MA natives in the major states that had received them were (K stands for thousands): NY(56K), OH(19K), NH(18K), ME(17K), VT(15K), CT(11K), RI(11K), IL(9K), MI(8K), WI(6K), CA(5K), and IN(3K).

8. The Civil War and after, 1861-

Prior to 1860, compromises between the many differences which separated the northern states and southern states were worked out, chiefly by moderates in the Congress. Many people in MA did not fall into this category, since there had been a very active abolitionist movement centering in Boston from the 1830s onward. The movement spread rapidly over the north, and many of its adherents participated in the underground railroad to transport escaping slaves to freedom in Canada. Some MA anti-slavery advocates also organized and sent settlers into the Territory of KS hoping that they could populate it with voters who would bar slavery. By 1856, MA had swung its political allegiance to the newly-formed Republican Party with its anti-slavery principles. From this time on, the north-south compromises became increasingly unsatisfactory, particularly to the south, and as 1860 was approached, the potential for war loomed large. When Lincoln was elected in that year, southern states began seceding, and by April 1861, seven of them had left the Union (SC, AL, FL, GA, LA, MS, TX). When the US Fort Sumter in Charleston, SC, harbor fell to Confederate forces, Lincoln called for troops to defend the north, and four other southern states seceded (NC, VA, AR, TN). The two sides, Union and Confederate, mobilized their men and resources, and four years of horrible conflict began.

The battles of the war were fought south and southwest of MA, no action occurring upon her soil. However, the state played an exceptionally important role in the Civil War. When Lincoln called for troops, MA was the first state to respond, and throughout the war, MA raised troops in excess of every federal call. Over 125,000 men served in the army, nearly 14,000 dying in service. MA troops were the first to receive hostile enemy fire, this occurring in Baltimore as the soldiers were moving to secure Washington, DC. The state built, equipped, and manned many naval vessels for the Union, furnishing more than 20,000 men for the navy. The extensive industrial facilities of MA were placed in service to supply arms, equipment, and materials for the war effort, and large sums of money were raised. The end of the War Between the States marked the essentially complete change of MA to an industrial economy.

The post-war years saw a slow decline in agriculture, shipping, and whaling, and an almost explosive growth in the manufacturing industries. Textile mill activity (both wool and cotton) expanded, leather (boots and shoes) and metal product (machinery) manufacture grew rapidly, and the cities in which these industries were located increased in population. To provide the labor, immigrants by the thousands poured in: Italians, Poles, Russians, French Canadians, Portuguese, and Eastern Europeans. The majority were Catholic, and this worked a marked change in the religious constituency of the commonwealth, with it soon becoming predominantly Catholic. Less than satisfactory working conditions for the increasing numbers of laborers were the order of the day, but changes slowly began to occur. In 1874, a law was passed which regulated working hours for women and children. Trade unions grew, industrial strife was broadspread in the later 1800s, and reform organizations were very active. As a result, many gains for the workers developed. By 1885, the MA General Court (Legislature) had chartered 23 cities, and they contained 60 percent of the people.

MA furnished about 12,000 soldiers and sailors to the Spanish-American War in 1898. By 1920, MA had become almost completely an industrial state. In this year, only about 120,000 people lived on farms with more than 700,000 employed in manufacturing. The tremendous influx of people from overseas can be seen by realizing that in 1907 over 70 percent of the commonwealth's population were either immigrants or had at least one immigrant parent. After World War I (1914-8), an economic recession weakened the MA textile and leather industries, which were further damaged a decade later by the great depression (1929-39). Other industries suffered, but not so severely. The years of World War II (1941-5) brought considerable economic recovery, as MA revitalized her industrial capabilities to provide materials and equipment for the war effort in her factories and shipyards.

9. MA Counties, Towns, and Cities

As of the present, the Commonwealth of MA is made up of 14 counties and 351 subdivisions called towns or cities. Figure 5 shows the county locations: Barnstable, Berkshire, Bristol, Dukes, Essex, Franklin, Hampden, Hampshire, Middlesex, Nantucket, Norfolk, Plymouth, Suffolk, and Worcester. Figure 6 presents the 15 towns of Barnstable County: Barnstable, Bourne, Brewster, Chatham, Dennis, Eastham, Falmouth, Harwich, Mashpee, Orleans, Provincetown, Sandwich, Truro, Yarmouth. The 32 towns/CITIES of Berkshire County are depicted in Figure 8 (CITIES in all CAPITALS): Adams, Alford, Becket, Cheshire, Clarksburg, Dalton, Fremont, Florida, Great Barrington, Hancock, Hinsdale, Lanesborough, Lee, Lenox, Monterey, Mount Washington, New Ashford, New Marlboro, NORTH ADAMS, Otis, Peru, PITTSFIELD, Richmond, Sandisfield, Savoy, Sheffield, Stockbridge, Tyringham, Washington, West Stockbridge, Williamstown, Windsor.

Figure 9 displays the 20 towns/CITIES which make up Bristol County: Acushnet, ATTLEBORO, Berkley, Dartmouth, Dighton, Easton, Fairhaven, FALL RIVER, Freetown, Mansfield, New Bedford, North Attleboro, Norton, Raynham, Rehoboth, Seekonk, Somerset, Swansea, Taunton, Westport. The 7 towns of Dukes County and the single town of Nantucket County (Nantucket) are shown in Figure 7: Chilmark, Edgartown, Gayhead, Gosnold, Nantucket, Oak Bluffs, Tisbury, West Tisbury. The 34 town/CITY subdivisions of Essex County are the subject of Figure 10: Amesbury, Andover, BEVERLY, Boxford, Danvers, Essex, Georgetown, GLOUCESTER, Groveland, Hamilton, HAVERHILL, Ipswich, LAWRENCE, LYNN, Lynnfield, Manchester, Marblehead, Merrimac, Methuen, Middleton, Nahant, Newbury, NEWBURYPORT, North Andover, PEABODY, Rockport, Rowley, SALEM, Salisbury, Saugus, Swampscott, Topsfield, Wenham, West Newbury.

Franklin County is composed of 26 towns as shown in Figure 11: Ashfield, Bernardston, Buckland, Charlemont, Colrain, Conway, Deerfield, Erving, Gill, Greenfield, Hawley, Heath, Leverett, Leyden, Monroe, Montague, New Salem, Northfield, Orange, Rowe, Shelburne, Shutesbury, Sunderland, Warwick, Wendell, Whately. The 23 towns/CITIES of Hampden County are also presented in Figure 11: Agawam, Blandford, Brimfield, Chester, CHICOPEE, East Longmeadow, Granville, Hampden, Holland, HOLYOKE, Longmeadow, Ludlow, Monson, Montgomery, Palmer, Russell, Southwick, SPRINGFIELD, Tolland, Wales, West Springfield, WESTFIELD, Wilbraham.

Hampshire County is made up of 20 town/CITY subdivisions which are displayed in Figure 12: Amherst, Belchertown, Chesterfield, Cummington, Easthampton, Goshen, Granby Hadley, Huntington, Middlefield,

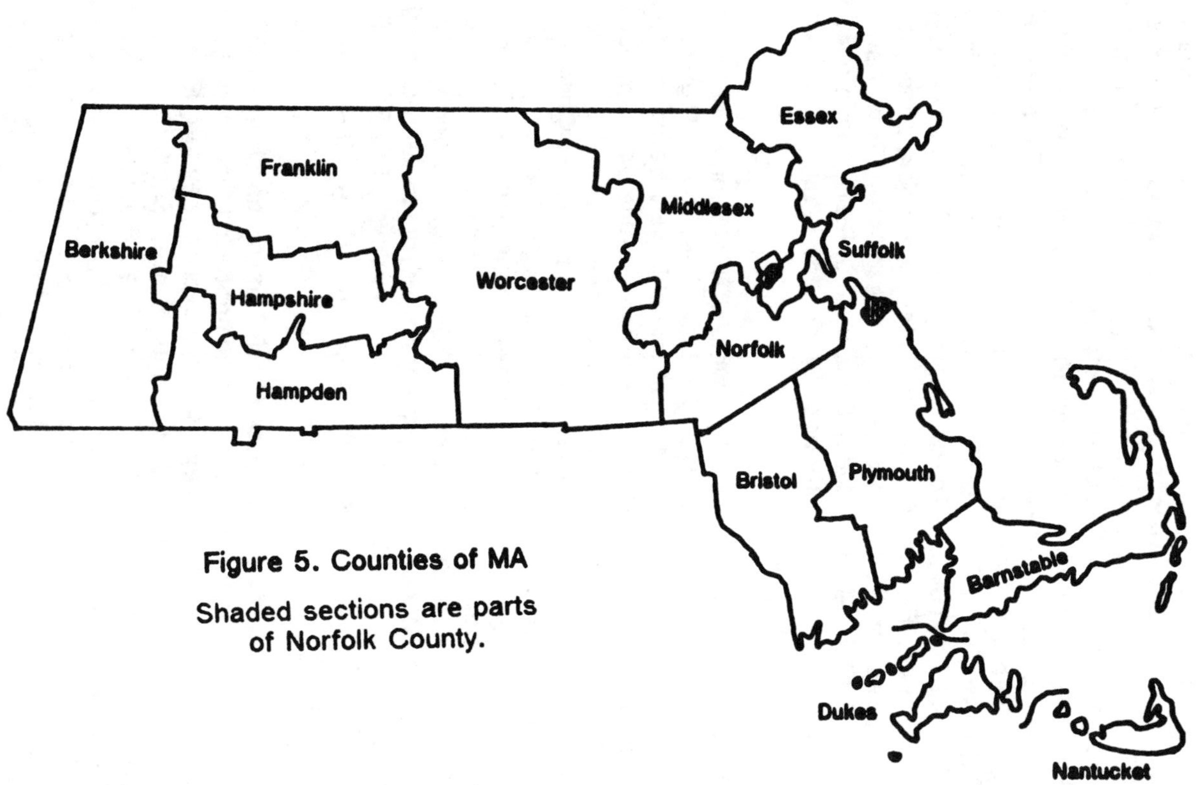

Figure 5. Counties of MA

Shaded sections are parts of Norfolk County.

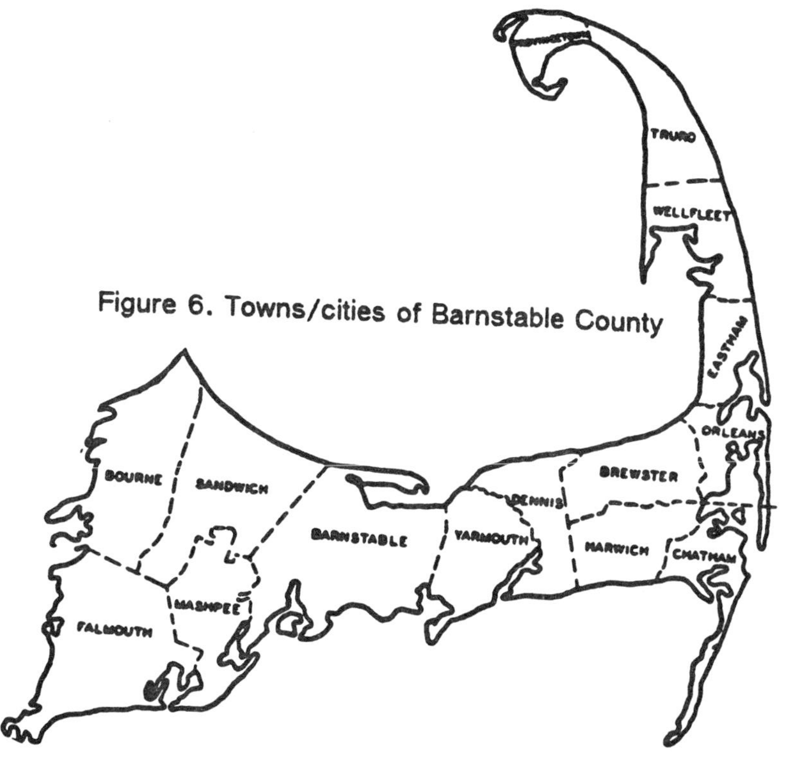

Figure 6. Towns/cities of Barnstable County

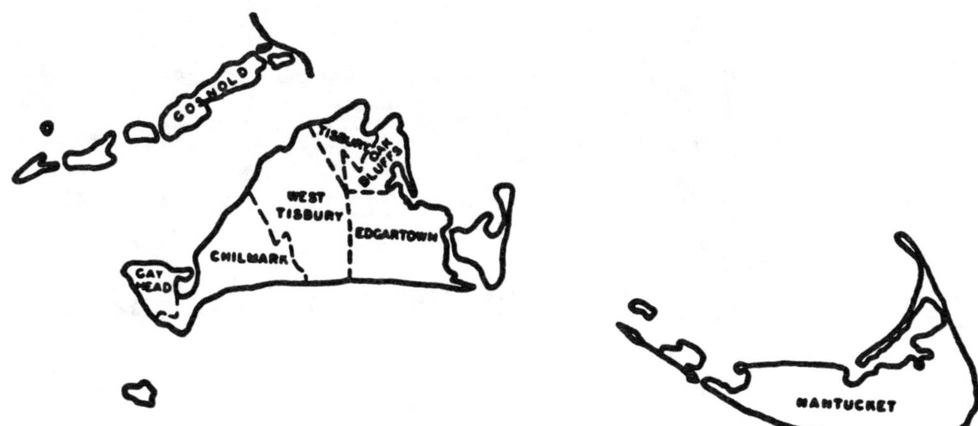

Figure 7. Towns of Dukes and Nantucket Counties

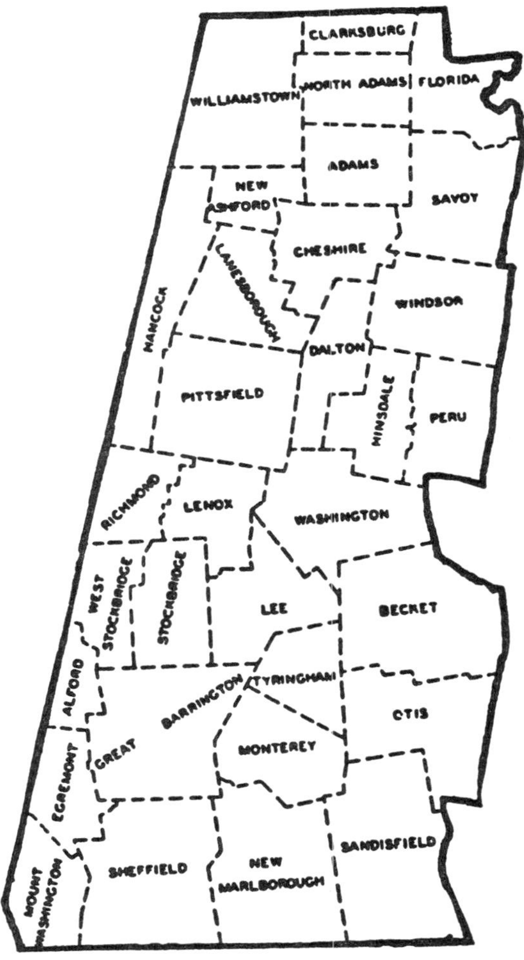

Figure 8. Towns/cities of Berkshire County

Figure 9. Towns/cities of Bristol County

Figure 10. Towns/cities of Essex County

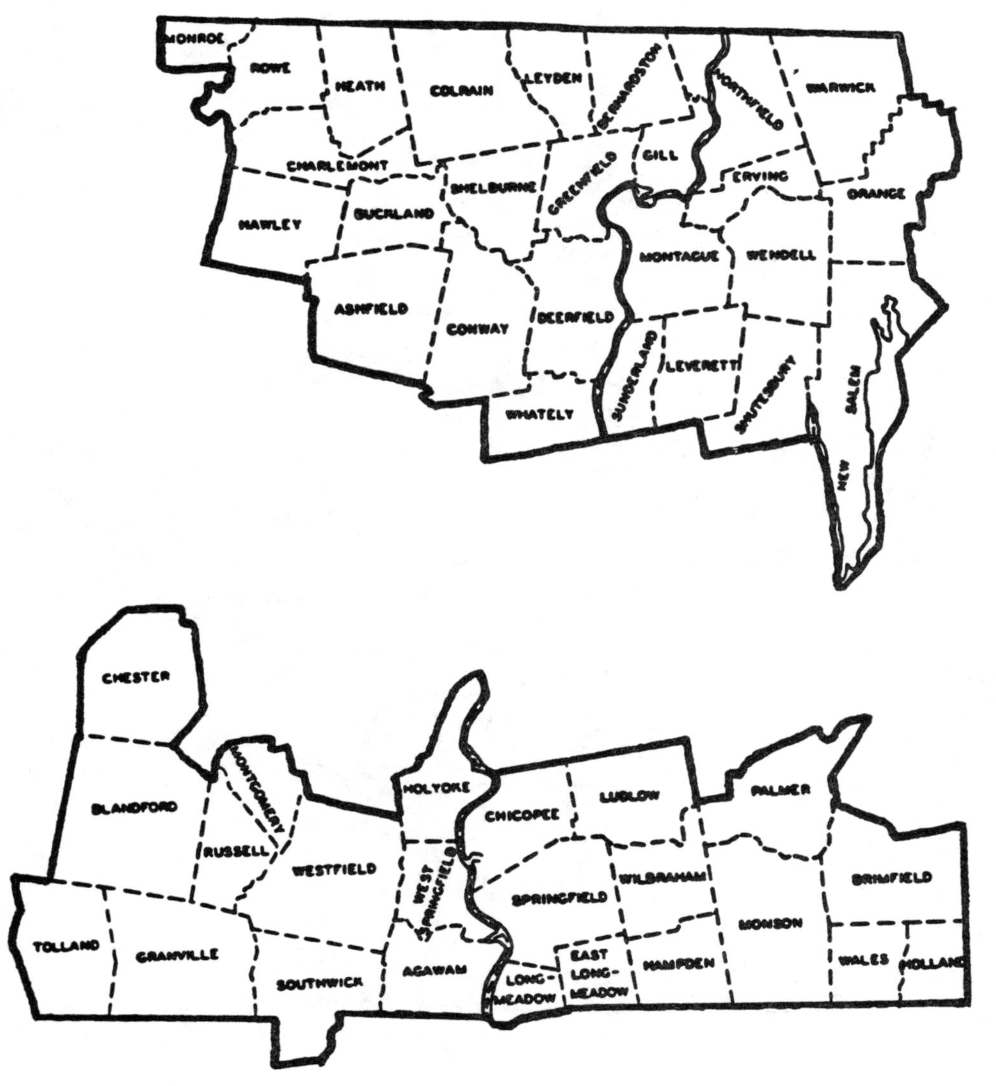

Figure 11. Towns/cities of Franklin (top) and Hampden Counties

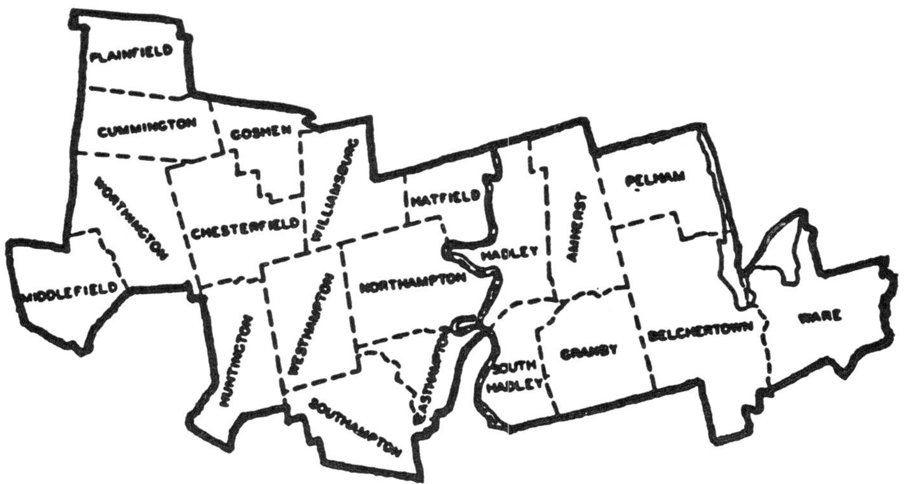

Figure 12. Towns/cities of Hampshire County

NORTHAMPTON, Pelham, Plainfield, South Hadley, Southampton, Ware, Westhampton, Williamsbury, Worthington. The map of Figure 13 details the 54 towns/CITIES of Middlesex County: Acton, Arlington, Ashby, Ashland, Ayer, Bedford, Belmont, Billerica, Boxborough, Burlington, CAMBRIDGE, Carlisle, Chelmsford, Concord, Dracut, Dunstable, EVERETT, Framingham, Groton, Holliston, Hopkinton, Hudson, Lexington, Lincoln, Littleton, LOWELL, MALDEN, MARLBOROUGH, Maynard, MEDFORD, MELROSE, Natick, NEWTON, North Reading, Pepperell, Reading, Sherborn, Shirley, SOMERVILLE, Stoneham, Stow, Sudbury, Tewksbury, Townsend, Tyngsborough, Wakefield, WALTHAM, Watertown, Wayland, Westford, Weston, Wilmington, Winchester, WOBURN.

The 28 towns/CITY of Norfolk County are displayed in Figure 14: Avon, Bellingham, Braintree, Brookline, Canton, Cohasset, Dedham, Dover, Foxborough, Franklin, Holbrook, Medfield, Medway, Millis, Milton, Needham, Norfolk, Norwood, Plainville, QUINCY, Randolph, Sharon, Stoughton, Walpole, Wellesley, Westwood, Weymouth, Wrentham. Also pictured in Figure 14 are the 4 town/CITIES of Suffolk County: BOSTON, CHELSEA, REVERE, Winthrop. For Plymouth County, the map labelled Figure 15 shows the 27 towns/CITIES: Abington, Bridgewater, BROCKTON, Carver, Duxbury, East Bridgewater, Halifax, Hanover, Hanson, Hingham, Hull, Kingston, Lakeville, Marion, Marshfield, Mattapoisett, Middleborough, Norwell, Pembroke, Plymouth, Plympton, Rochester, Rockland, Scituate, Wareham, West Bridgewater, Whitman.

The 60 towns/CITIES of Worcester County are shown in Figure 16: Ashburnham, Athol, Auburn, Barre, Berlin, Blackstone, Bolton, Boylston, Brookfield, Charlton, Clinton, Douglas, Dudley, East Brookfield, FITCHBURG, GARDNER, Grafton, Hardwick, Harvard, Holden, Hopedale, Hubbardston, Lancaster, Leicester, LEOMINSTER, Lunenburg, Mendon, Milford, Millbury, Millville, New Braintree, North Brookfield, Northborough, Northbridge, Oakham, Oxford, Paxton, Petersham, Phillipston, Princeton, Royalston, Rutland, Shrewsbury, Southborough, Southbridge, Spencer, Sterling, Sturbridge, Sutton, Templeton, Upton, Uxbridge, Warren, Webster, West Boylston, West Brookfield, Westborough, Westminster, Winchendon, WORCESTER.

The 351 towns/CITIES of MA have been established since 1620, many resulting from expansions into new territory, and many resulting from splits of older towns. Through the years, some have been abolished, some have changed names, numerous small boundary changes have been made plus a few fairly sizable ones, towns which grew in population have become CITIES, and sometimes towns have been annexed by neighboring towns. Main events of this sort will be listed in individual sections of Chapter 4 in which towns/CITIES will be treated in detail. The best overall consideration of these numerous details will be found in:

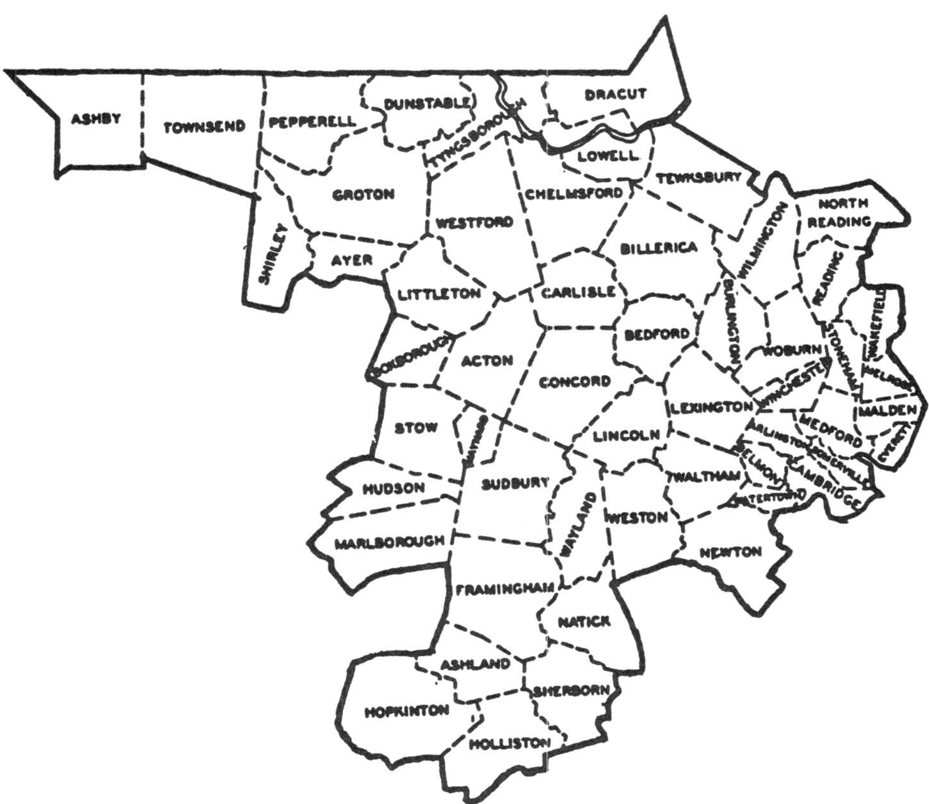

Figure 13. Towns/cities of Middlesex County

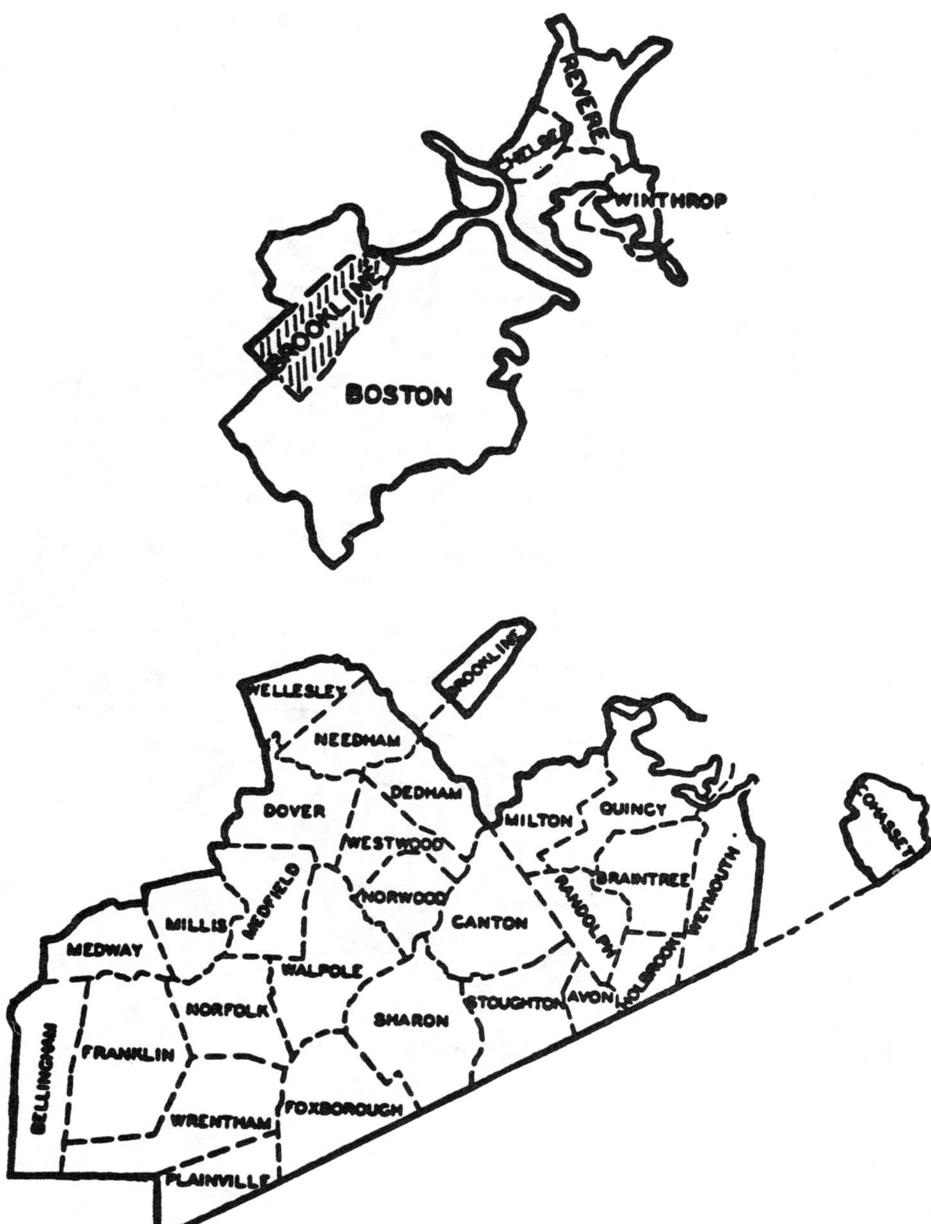

Figure 14. Towns/cities of Suffolk (top) and Norfolk Counties
Please note that Brookline is in Norfolk County.

Figure 15. Towns/cities of Plymouth County

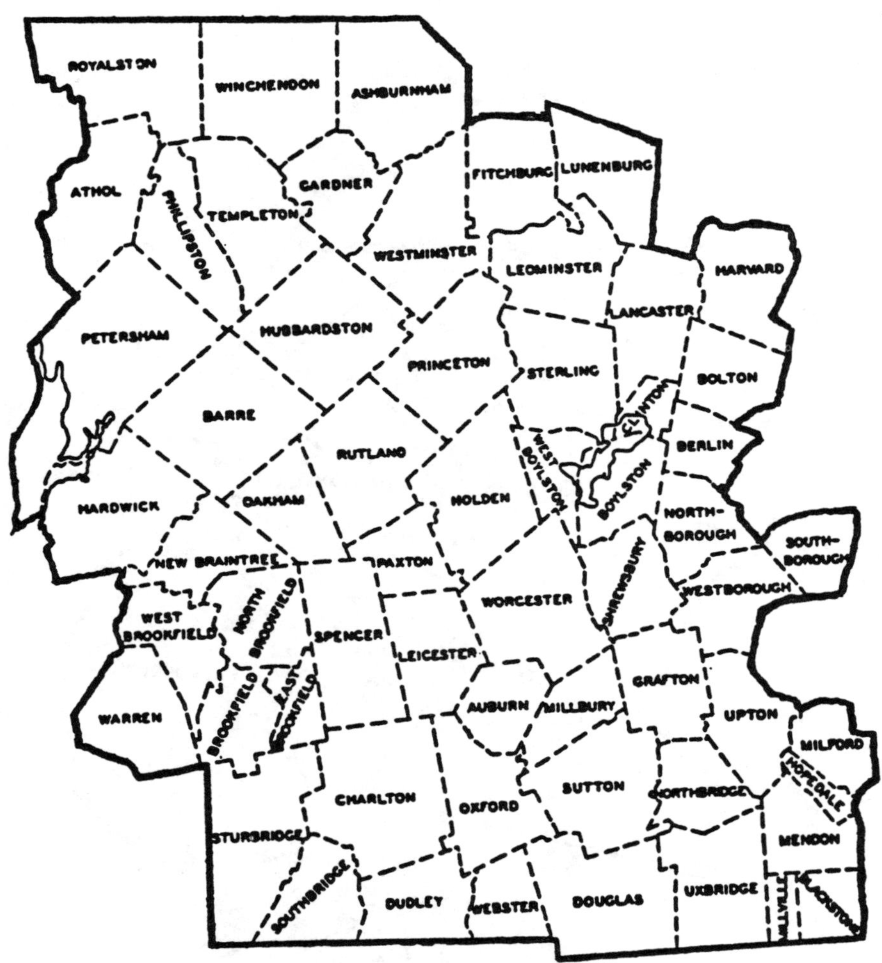

Figure 16. Towns/cities of Worcester County

_Secretary of the Commonwealth of MA, HISTORICAL DATA RELATING TO COUNTIES, CITIES, AND TOWNS IN MA, State Printers, Boston, MA, 1920, 1948, 1966, 1975.

In 1643, 1685, and 1695, groups of towns were gathered to form counties, four counties in 1643, three more in 1685, and two in 1695. Other counties were constituted later, and one became extinct, such that the present 14 were in place by 1812. The history of these cities, towns, and counties will now be viewed in brief to give you an idea of their development.

Plymouth Colony and the Town of Plymouth were established in 1620, and as the population grew new towns were set up around the original settlement. In the immediate vicinity of Plymouth were Scituate (1633), Duxbury (1637), Marshfield (1642), Hull (1644), Bridgewater (1656), and Middleborough (1669). To the west of Plymouth were Taunton (1639), Rehoboth (1645), Dartmouth (1652), Swansea (1668), and Freetown (1683). To the southeast of Plymouth were Barnstable (1638), Sandwich (1638), Yarmouth (1639), and Eastham (1646). In 1685, the towns in the vicinity of Plymouth were made into Plymouth County, those to the west into Bristol County, and those to the southeast into Barnstable County. Then, in 1691, the three counties were annexed to MA Bay Colony.

MA Bay Colony got started with the towns of Salem (1630), Charlestown (1630), Medford (1630), Watertown (1630), and Boston (1630). Towns settled to the north of Boston included Salem (1630), Lynn (1631), Ipswich (1634), Newbury (1635), Rowley (1639), Gloucester (1642), Enon[Wenham] (1643), and Cochichawick[Andover] (1643). Towns established west and northwest of Boston were Charlestown (1630), Watertown (1630), Medford (1630), Cambridge (1631), Concord (1635), Sudbury (1639), Woburn (1642), and Lynn Village[Reading] (1643/4). To the far north (relatively speaking), there came to be the towns of Dover (1623), Exeter (1631), Strawberry Bank[Portsmouth] (1631), Hampton (1635), Salisbury (1640), and Haverhill (1641). To the south of Boston, these towns were set up: Roxbury (1630), Dorchester (1630), Weymouth (1635), Hingham (1635), Dedham (1636), Braintree (1640), and Nantascot[Hull] (1643/4). Boston and the towns to the south were constituted as Suffolk County. The towns to the north of Boston were gathered into Essex County, those towns west of Boston into Middlesex County, and those further north into Old Norfolk County. Old Norfolk County was abolished in 1679, and all its towns went to NH except Salisbury, Haverhill, and Amesbury (split off from Salisbury in 1668), which were taken up into Essex County of MA.

The islands off the south coast of MA belonged to NY prior to 1691 when they were given over to MA. Early towns in the area were Nantucket (1659), Edgartown (1671), Tisbury (1671), and Chilmark (1694). In 1695, the first was taken up as Nantucket County and the others collectively became Dukes County. Hence, as of 1695, what is now the Commonwealth of MA had 9 counties: Barnstable, Bristol, Dukes, Essex, Hampshire, Middlesex, Nantucket, Plymouth, and Suffolk. These represented the fact that much of the eastern half of MA had been settled. The continued westward occupation of the land is represented by the dates of establishment of other counties: Worcester (1731), Berkshire (1761), Franklin (1811), Hampden (1812). And the population growth in the east is reflected by the need for another county there: Norfolk (1793). These county expansions, as you must realize, resulted from increases in the populations and the numbers of towns.

Originally governmental record keeping in MA was done at the town level and the colony level (Plymouth Colony, MA Bay Colony). When counties were established (1643, 1685, 1695), record keeping by the government was done at three levels: town, county, colony. Then when Plymouth and MA Bay Colonies were united, the three-level record keeping was carried on by the towns, counties, and the Province of MA Bay. It must also be recognized that prior to the Revolutionary War MA records were also kept by the British government. When towns grew and became cities, essentially no interruption of record keeping occurred. In addition to governmental records, the most important keepers of records in the early years of MA were the Congregational Churches. However, they were so closely interlocked with the government that often no distinction in the records can be made. The combined government-church structure in MA kept good records from the beginning, usually being very careful to keep vital records (births, marriages, deaths) as well as land, probate, and court records.

The types of records that genealogical researchers in MA will be seeking include national records, colony-state records, county records, town-city records, and private records. Among the important national records are: census, court, immigration, military, naturalization, and tax. Included in the colony-state records are: birth, census, colonial, court, death, divorce, land, marriage, military, naturalization, tax, and will-probate. The major county records which were kept in MA are court, land, marriage, naturalization, and will-probate, and also sometimes notary and vital records (birth, death). The chief sorts of city-town records which are to be found are birth, constable, death, early church, magistrate, marriage, proprietors, rate (tax), town meeting, and townsmen (selectmen). The principal types of private records are atlas, biography, cemetery, church, city directory, city and county history, DAR works, ethnic, gazetteers, genealogical compilations, genealogical and historical periodicals, manuscripts, mortuary, newspaper, and WPA works.

All of the records mentioned in the previous paragraph will be discussed in detail in Chapter 2. You will be told exactly what years they cover, how they may be obtained, what information they contain, and how to discover if they have been published, either in printed or microform medium. Chapter 3 will inform you about the major genealogical repositories (libraries and archives) in and out of MA, and will indicate to you which records are available in each. The fourth chapter lists all the MA counties and towns (cities), and tells you what records are available (in original, published, and microform media). In addition, you are told where the county seats are, when the counties were created, and the county or counties from which each was formed. Similar data regarding the establishment of the towns are presented. These county and town formation data are very important to you because sometimes you will need to trace an ancestor back into a county or town out of which a new county or town came. This occurs when your ancestor lived on a piece of property which was in land split off from an old county or town to form a new unit.

10. Recommended reading

A knowledge of the history of MA and its local regions and jurisdictions is of extreme importance for the tracing of the genealogies of its former inhabitants. This chapter has been a brief treatment of that history. Your next step should be the reading of several of the following, relatively short one-volumed works:

_J. F. Clark, MA, FROM COLONY TO COMMONWEALTH, Windsor Pblns., Northridge, CA, 1987.
_R. D. Brown, MA, A BICENTENNIAL HISTORY, Norton, New York, NY, 1978.
_R. I. Bexler, MA, A CHRONOLOGY AND DOCUMENTARY HISTORY, Oceana Publ., Dobbs Ferry, NY, 1978.
_W. M. Whitehall and N. Kotleer, MA, A PICTORIAL HISTORY, Scribner's Sons, New York, NY, 1976.
_J. Dernos, A LITTLE COMMONWEALTH, Oxford Univ. Press, New York, NY, 1960.
_H. F. Howe, MA, THERE SHE IS, BEHOLD HER, Harper, New York, NY, 1960.
_W. J. Reid and H. G. Regan, MA, HISTORY AND GOVERNMENT OF THE BAY STATE, Oxford Book Co., New York, NY, 1956.
_D. P. Toomey and T. C. Quinn, MA OF TODAY: A MEMORIAL OF THE STATE, Columbia Publ. Co., Boston, MA, 1892.
_G. L. Austin, THE HISTORY OF MA, Russell, Boston, MA, 1884.
_W. J. Comley, COMLEY'S HISTORY OF MA, Comley Bros., Boston, MA, 1879.
_W. H. Carpenter, THE HISTORY OF MA, Lippincott, Philadelphia, PA, 1853.

If you care to go further, or if you wish to explore a particular topic or a particular time span in greater detail, you may wish to employ one or more of the several multi-volumed histories of MA. Among the better ones are:

_A. B. Hart, COMMONWEALTH HISTORY OF MA, Russell and Russell, New York, NY, 1966, 5 volumes.
_W. H. Clark and D. L. Marsh, THE STORY OF MA, American Historical Society, New York, NY, 1938, 4 volumes.
_J. G. Palfrey, A COMPENDIOUS HISTORY OF NEW ENGLAND, Boston, MA, 1873, 5 volumes.
_J. S. Barry, THE HISTORY OF MA, Phillip, Simpson, and Co., Boston, MA, 1856-7, 3 volumes.

For further specialized reading, here are some volumes pertaining to larger regions of MA:

_A. P. Langtry, METROPOLITAN BOSTON, A MODERN HISTORY, Lewis Historical Publishing Co., New York, NY, 1929.
_E. S. Thompson, HISTORY OF PLYMOUTH, NORFOLK, AND BARNSTABLE COUNTIES, Lewis Historical Publishing Co., New York, NY, 1928.
_HISTORY OF THE CT VALLEY IN MA, Everts, Philadelphia, PA, 1879.
_J. G. Holland, HISTORY OF WESTERN MA, Bowles and Co., Springfield, MA, 1855.
_J. H. Lockwood et al., WESTERN MA, A HISTORY, 1636-1925, Lewis Historical Publishing Co., New York, NY, 1926, 4 volumes.
_H. A. Wright, THE STORY OF WESTERN MA, Lewis Historical Publishing Co., New York, NY, 1949.

As is usually the case, a thorough understanding of your ancestor's life and times will require additional reading in state, regional, and local histories, as well as in histories of specialized topics and particular times. Useful volumes for such information can be located in the following reference works:

_J. D. Haskell, Jr., MA, A BIBLIOGRAPHY OF ITS HISTORY, University Press of New England, Hanover, NH, 1976.
_M. Kaufman, J. W. Ilkovic, and J. Carvalho III, A GUIDE TO THE HISTORY OF MA, Greenwood Press, Westport, CT, 1988.
_C. A. Flagg, A GUIDE TO MA LOCAL HISTORY, Salem Press, Salem, MA, 1907.
_M. J. Kaminkow, US LOCAL HISTORIES IN THE LIBRARY OF CONGRESS, Magna Carta Book Co., Baltimore, MD, 1975 ff., 5 volumes.
_P. W. Filby, BIBLIOGRAPHY OF AMERICAN COUNTY HISTORIES, Genealogical Publishing Co., Baltimore, MD, 1985.
_NY Public Library, US LOCAL HISTORY CATALOG, Hall, Boston, MA, 1974, 2 volumes, with BIBLIOGRAPHIC GUIDE TO NORTH AMERICAN HISTORY, Hall, Boston, MA, annual supplements, 1977-.

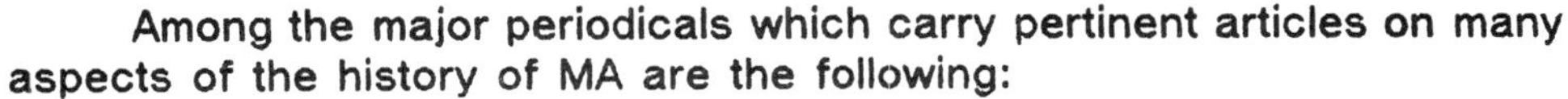

Among the major periodicals which carry pertinent articles on many aspects of the history of MA are the following:

_NEW ENGLAND HISTORICAL AND GENEALOGICAL REGISTER, New England Historic Genealogical Society, Boston, MA, 1847-.

_PROCEEDINGS OF THE MA HISTORICAL SOCIETY, The Society, Boston, MA, 1859-.

_NEW ENGLAND QUARTERLY, New England Quarterly, Inc., Boston, MA, 1928-.

_PUBLICATIONS OF THE COLONIAL SOCIETY OF MA, The Society, Boston, MA, 1895-.

_ESSEX INSTITUTE HISTORICAL COLLECTIONS, The Institute, Salem, MA, 1859-.

_HISTORICAL JOURNAL OF MA, Institute for MA Studies, Westfield, MA, 1972-.

_PROCEEDINGS OF THE AMERICAN ANTIQUARIAN SOCIETY, The Society, Worcester, MA, 1812-.

_WILLIAM AND MARY QUARTERLY, Institute of Early American History and Culture, Williamsburg, VA, 1892-.

_AMERICAN QUARTERLY, Johns Hopkins Univ. Press, Baltimore, MD, 1949-.

_AMERICAN HISTORICAL REVIEW, American Historical Association, Washington, DC, 1895-.

_JOURNAL OF AMERICAN HISTORY, Organization of American Historians, Bloomington, IN, 1914-.

In addition to published sources, such as those cited above, there are many active historical societies and agencies in MA. These are of great value to family historians, since they not only deal in historical materials, but often have genealogical interests also. Detailed listings of these will be found in:

_Bay State Historical League, DIRECTORY OF HISTORICAL AGENCIES IN MA, The League, Boston, MA, latest edition.

_American Association of State and Local History, DIRECTORY OF HISTORICAL AGENCIES IN THE US AND CANADA, The Association, Nashville, TN, latest edition.

Key to Abbreviations

A	=	Agricultural census records
AGLL	=	American Genealogical Lending Library
BPL	=	Boston Public Library
C	=	Civil War Union veterans census
DAR	=	Daughters of the American Revolution
E	=	Early census-like lists
FHC	=	Family History Center(s)
FHL	=	Family History Library
FHLC	=	Family History Library Catalog
I	=	Industrial census records
IGI	=	International Genealogical Index
LGL	=	Large genealogical libraries
LL	=	Local library(ies) in MA
M	=	Mortality census records
MD	=	Mayflower Descendant
MHS	=	MA Historical Society
MSA	=	MA State Archives
NA	=	National Archives
NABB	=	National Archives, Boston Branch
NAFB	=	National Archives, Field Branch(es)
NEHGS	=	New England Historic Genealogical Society
P	=	Revolutionary War pensioner census
R	=	Regular census records
RL	=	Regional library(ies) in MA
S	=	MA state census records
SASE	=	Long, self-addressed, stamped envelope
SLM	=	State Library of MA

Chapter 2

TYPES OF RECORDS

1. Introduction

The commonwealth of Massachusetts (MA) is exceedingly rich in genealogical source material, even though there have been some sizable losses of records. In addition, an astonishing amount of work has been done by many people in accumulating, preserving, photocopying, microfilming, transcribing, abstracting, printing, and indexing records. As mentioned in the previous chapter, there are five main categories of records: town-city governmental records, county governmental records, colony-state governmental records, national governmental records, and private records.

Among the most important genealogical records of MA are the local town-city governmental records (birth, constable, death, early church, justice of peace, magistrate, marriage, proprietors, rate [tax], town meeting, and townsmen [selectmen]). The originals of these records are largely in the towns-cities with the town-city clerks, in town-city archives, in local libraries, and/or in local historical societies. The vital records birth, death, marriage) of many of the towns have been published, many microfilmed by the Family History Library (FHL) in Salt Lake City, UT, and many put on microfiche by the Holbrook Institute and other agencies. As of this writing, fewer than 65 of the 351 towns-cities of MA are not represented by one or more of these. In addition, some of the other town-city records, especially the earlier ones, have been published and/or microfilmed, most of the microfilming having been done by the Family History Library (FHL). The FHL microfilms are available at the FHL, at its over 250 branch Family History Centers (FHC) in the US, and at the MA State Archives (MSA). The published items (books, journal articles, typescripts) are generally available at large genealogical libraries (LGL) in MA, and many of them will be found in large genealogical libraries elsewhere.

County governmental records are also of great importance for MA family researching (court, land, marriage, naturalization, will-probate, and sometimes birth, death, and notary). The originals of the court records are in the MA State Archives (MSA) or in the county (County Clerk, county archives, local libraries, local historical societies). Many of the land and will-probate records and some of the other records, particularly the court and marriage, have been microfilmed by the Family History Library (FHL). And some of the county records, especially early ones, have been published (in books, journal articles, and typescripts). The microfilms are available at the Family History Library (FHL), at each of its branches, called Family History Centers (FHC), and at the MA State Archives (MSA). The published records are available at large genealogical libraries (LGL) in MA, and many are in large genealogical libraries outside MA.

The colony-state governmental records of MA provide a further valuable source of information on your MA progenitors (birth, census, colonial, court, death, divorce, land, marriage, military, naturalization, tax, and will-probate). The original records of this type are in the repository dedicated to their preservation, namely, the MA State Archives (MSA). Some of the records have been microfilmed by the Family History Library (FHL) and are available there and in its Family History Center (FHC) branches. Among these microfilms are these record types: census, court, naturalization, tax, and vital records (birth, death, marriage). In addition, there are numerous published records, especially for the colonial period. The published items can be located in large genealogical libraries (LGL) in MA, with many of them also being in other large genealogical libraries.

The national governmental records relating to MA consist primarily of census, immigration, military, naturalization, and tax records. The originals of most of these exceptionally useful materials are in the National Archives (NA) in Washington, DC. The most valuable of them have been microfilmed by the National Archives (NA), and the microfilm copies are available in the National Archives Field Branches (NAFB), including the Boston Branch (NABB), the Family History Library (FHL), its branch Family History Centers (FHC), many large genealogical libraries (LGL), and from the American Genealogical Lending Library (AGLL) in Bountiful, UT. Some are also available at the MA State Archives (MSA) and the Boston Public Library (BPL).

In addition to the above-mentioned governmental records, there are many private records which are likely sources of data for your MA progenitor(s). Included among them are the following record types: atlases, biographies, cemetery, church, city directories, city and county histories, DAR works, ethnic, gazetteers, genealogical compilations and indexes, genealogical and historical periodicals, manuscripts, mortuary, newspapers, and WPA works. These items take many forms: books, articles, typed records and abstracts, hand-written materials. They will be found in a wide variety of MA places: libraries with genealogy collections, cemetery offices, churches, archives, museums, mortuary offices, and newspaper offices. Many have been microfilmed by the Family History Library (FHL) and can be accessed through their branch Family History Centers (FHC). Especially good holdings of these source materials are in the New England Historic Genealogical Society Library (NEHGS), the State Library of MA (SLM), and the Boston Public Library (BPL).

The best place to go for MA genealogical research is Boston, because of the presence there of several major record repositories. There is the MA State Archives (MSA). They are the official agency for the collection and preservation of MA Colonial Commonwealth records. Among their holdings are published vital record (birth, marriage, death) collections for the pre-1841 period for 290 out of the 351 towns/cities of MA. Some are printed, some microfilms, some microfiche. In addition they have the 1790-1900 federal censuses, the federal special censuses for 1850/60/70, the state censuses of 1855/65, and indexes to many of them. There are also state court records (court of assistants 1630-92, superior court of judicature 1692-1780, court of admiralty 1714-72, supreme judicial court 1780-), and many county court records (county courts 1638-1792, courts of general sessions 1692-1827, courts of common pleas 1692-1859, superior court 1859-, probate 1692-, naturalization 1790-1885). The county court records are by no means complete, the holdings being only for certain counties, certain record types, and certain periods of time [Many remain in the counties]. Further records at MSA are Boston alien passenger arrivals with an index, MA land grants, military records for 1643-1781 (colonial wars, the Revolutionary War, state Revolutionary pensions, state Revolution bounty land grants for land in ME, all indexed), disposition of Loyalist estates, commissary and quartermaster records for the War of 1812, some records of the Adjutant General for the Civil War and the Spanish-American War veterans' pay claims. In addition, you will find there numerous MA Commonwealth records: 1885-1931 naturalizations, legislature records (General Court), Governor's Office, Governor's Council, Secretary, Treasurer, schools, almshouses, and prisons. Other holdings are tax evaluations for 1738-86, the 1798 Federal MA Direct Tax, and town records of various types for some towns (town meetings, selectmens' records, proprietors' records, church, cemetery, genealogy). Finally, there are sizable separate collections of material of all sorts, including vital records, church, court records, deeds, tax, probate, and wills for Plymouth Colony (1620-91), and similar detailed records for the MA Bay Colony (1628-86), for Boston (1630-), and for Suffolk County (1643-).

The second amazingly stocked record repository in Boston is the New England Historic Genealogical Society Library (NEHGS), the oldest genealogical library in the US (1845), and one of the largest. Among its over 400,000 volumes, many of them are books on MA, including published biographical, Bible, cemetery, census, church, colonial, court, immigration, land, military, naturalization, tax, early town, will, probate, and vital records. Also there are published family genealogies, local histories, genealogical collections, genealogical periodicals, newspapers, newspaper abstracts, city directories, atlases, gazetteers, and maps. These books are supplemented by over 2000 microfilm reels with a similar variety of record types. The NEHGS is the repository for an exceptionally large amount of manuscript materials (over one million items): personal papers of notables, diaries, military documents, business and trade records, maritime records, society, organization, and union records, church records, and unpublished genealogical and historical material. The above-mentioned vast collection of published works, microforms, and manuscripts is well supplied with book, card, computer, typescript, and microform indexes, giving broad and easy access to the items making up the collection. Many of their records and numerous other MA materials have been published by the NEHGS in their journal, the New England Historical and Genealogical Register, which was started in 1847. The NEHGS has also put some of their most useful materials on microfilm.

Another important Boston storehouse of MA genealogical research materials is the Boston Public Library (BPL), especially the Social Sciences Department. The book, microform, and manuscript holdings are quite rich. Books include state, regional, local and family histories, biographies, colonial records, town vital records, military records, and census indexes. Among the notable microforms are colonial and state newspapers, indexes to obituaries in several Boston newspapers, genealogical columns of the Boston Evening Transcript, Suffolk County records, Middlesex County and town records, passenger lists for MA ports, US censuses, MA Historical Society records, American Loyalist claims, and British Colonial Office records for MA. Manuscripts are represented by a very large number of personal papers, documents of many sorts, letters, diaries, Revolutionary and Civil War papers, colonial writings, and genealogies. Especially useful for family historians are the records of the City of Boston: City Clerk files, colonial and Revolutionary materials, Civil War records, tax information, passenger lists, and city directories.

Of considerable import to family searchers is the Military Records Section of the MA Adjutant General's Office near Boston in Natick, MA. Their holdings include records of early militia (1776-1820), War of 1812, MA militia (1820-60), Mexican War (1846-8), Civil War (1861-5), the reconstruction (1866-97), and the Spanish American War (1898-9). Although not dealing primarily with genealogy, two other institutions in Boston have good collections which serve the genealogical community: the MA Historical Society and the State Library of MA. The MA Historical Society has the largest manuscript collection dealing with MA history, records of early Boston residents, personal papers of important Bay State and Colony persons, and numerous maps. The State Library of MA (SLM) has newspapers with indexes to many of them, county and town histories, atlases of counties, cities, and towns, maps, and city directories for MA.

There is a sizable collection of books and microfilm copies of MA genealogical materials (federal, colonial, state, county, city, town, non-governmental) in the largest genealogical library in the world, namely, the Family History Library (FHL) of the Genealogical Society of UT, which is located in Salt Lake City, UT. Not only is this very large record group available in Salt Lake City, but the thousands of microfilms can be borrowed through the numerous branch libraries, known as Family History Centers (FHC), located all over the US and beyond. Included among these branches are ones in Weston, Lynnfield, Foxboro, and Worcester. Each branch library has microform copies of the major indexes which list the holdings of the main library in Salt Lake City, and from which record microfilms may be borrowed.

Many records pertaining to MA which were accumulated by the federal government are available in the National Archives (NA) in Washington, DC. These records include the following types: census, military (service, pension, bounty land), naturalization, passenger arrival, court, tax, passport, seamen, and maps. Many of the most useful of these materials have been microfilmed. Some of these microfilms are available in many of the MA libraries mentioned previously, and sizable numbers of them will be found in the eleven National Archives Field Branches (NAFB), one of which is very near Boston, namely the National Archives Boston Branch (NABB) in Waltham, MA. Many of the microfilms may also be borrowed through your local library or individually from AGLL (American Genealogical Lending Library, PO Box 244, Bountiful, UT 84010).

In addition to the above collections, there are MA record collections in a number of large genealogical libraries (LGL) around the country, especially those in states near MA and in states that received sizable numbers of migrants from MA. Such libraries will be found in Fort Wayne, IN, New York City, Washington, DC, Cleveland, Detroit, Chicago, Cincinnati, Madison, WI, Dallas, Los Angeles, and other cities. Other collections, usually with an emphasis on a particular section of MA, are located in several good regional libraries (RL) in MA. Finally, local libraries in county seats, in cities, and in towns often have good materials relating to their own areas. These libraries may be county, city, town, village, or private (such as ones sponsored by local historical or genealogical societies or ones maintained by private endowments). All of the archives, libraries, and repositories mentioned above will be discussed in detail in Chapter 3.

In this chapter, the many types of records which are available for MA genealogical research are discussed. Those records which are essentially national or state-wide in scope will be treated in detail, both governmental and private (non-governmental). Records which are basically county-city-town records (both governmental and non-governmental) will be described and treated generally, since detailed lists of them will be given in Chapter 4, where the major records available for the 14 MA counties and the 351 MA town/CITIES will be presented.

2. Bible records

During the past 200 years it was customary for families with religious affiliations to keep vital statistics on their members in the family Bible. These records vary widely, but among them the items that may be found are names, dates, and places of birth, christening, confirmation, baptism, marriage, death, burial, and sometimes military service. Although most Bibles containing recorded information probably still remain in private hands, some of the information has been submitted for publication and some has been filed in libraries and archives throughout MA. You should inquire about such records at every possible library and archives in or near your ancestor's town, that is, all nearby LL. These repositories will be listed in Chapter 4 under the counties and towns/cities.

You should also seek Bible records in the larger archives and libraries in MA, starting with the NEHGS and the BPL, then all nearby RL. Also the indexes at FHC(FHL) should be consulted. In such repositories, there may be a special alphabetical Bible record file, or as is more often the case, data from Bibles may be listed in indexes or alphabetical files labelled something other than Bible records. The most likely labels are family records, genealogies, manuscripts, names, surnames. Also do not fail to look in the major card or computer index in each of these repositories for the names you are seeking. It is also important to use the locality and surname indexes at the nearest FHC.

There are some volumes listing and/or indexing MA Bible records which have been compiled. Among those that you should examine are the following:

_DAR OF MA, COLLECTION OF GENEALOGICAL RECORD VOLUMES, The Society, Various places in MA, Various dates, Numerous volumes, also on 43 reels of microfilm at FHL, available through FHC.

_E. M. Lewis, BIBLE RECORDS OF MA FAMILIES, The Author, Springfield,MA, 1960.

_E. K. Kirkham, AN INDEX TO SOME OF THE BIBLE AND FAMILY RECORDS OF THE US, National Society of the DAR, Everton Publishers, Logan, UT, 1984.

In addition, several agencies have published books, microfilms, and microforms of MA town vital records up to about 1849-50. Such materials are available for over 290 of the 351 MA towns/cities. Many of the 206 books contain not only official town governmental records, but also Bible, cemetery, and church records.

_VITAL RECORDS IN TOWNS OF MA TO THE YEAR 1849/50, published in book form by NEHGS, Topsfield Historical Society, Essex Institute, Wright and Potter, F. P. Rice, and other agencies.

Bible records also appear in genealogical periodical articles and in published family genealogies. These two record sources will be discussed in later sections of this chapter.

3. Biographies

There are several major national biographical works which contain sketches on nationally-prominent MA citizens of the past. If you suspect or know that your ancestor was that well known consult:

_NATIONAL CYCLOPEDIA OF AMERICAN BIOGRAPHY, White Co., New York, NY, 1893-present, over 54 volumes, cumulative index for volumes 1-51.

_DICTIONARY OF AMERICAN BIOGRAPHY, Scribners, New York, NY, 1928-37, 20 volumes, cumulative index.

_THE 20TH CENTURY BIOGRAPHICAL DICTIONARY OF NOTABLE AMERICANS, Gale Research Co., Detroit, MI, 1968, 10 volumes.

_AMERICAN BIOGRAPHY: A NEW CYCLOPEDIA, American Historical Society, New York, NY, 1916-33, 54 volumes, cumulative index for volumes 1-50.

_WHO WAS WHO IN AMERICA, 1607-1896, Who's Who, Chicago, IL, 1967.

Most of these works and over 500 more have been indexed in a large microfiche set containing over 6 million entries. This set is available in numerous large libraries, and is added to annually:

_BIOBASE, Gale Research, Detroit, MI, latest edition.

Several extensive biographical compilations for the Commonwealth of MA exist. These volumes list persons who have attained state-wide prominence in the fields of law, agriculture, business, politics, medicine, engineering, industry, science, military, manufacturing, teaching, government, public service, or philanthropy. Included among the better ones are:

_B. A. Ball, GOVERNMENT OF THE COMMONWEALTH OF MA, HISTORICAL, DESCRIPTIVE, AND BIOGRAPHICAL, Ticknor, Boston, MA, 1885.

_BIOGRAPHICAL ENCYCLOPEDIA OF MA OF THE 19TH CENTURY, Metropolitan Publishing Co., New York, NY, 1879-83, 2 volumes.

_BIOGRAPHICAL SKETCHES OF REPRESENTATIVE CITIZENS OF THE COMMONWEALTH OF MA, Graves and Steinbarger, Boston, MA, 1901.

_W. E. Boardman, BIOGRAPHIES OF THE FOUNDERS, EX-PRESIDENTS, PROMINENT EARLY MEMBERS, AND OTHERS OF THE MA DENTAL SOCIETY, The Society, Boston, MA, 1914.

_J. W. Carlevale, LEADING AMERICANS OF ITALIAN DESCENT IN MA, Memorial Press, Plymouth, MA, 1946.

_W. H. Clark and D. L. Marsh, THE STORY OF MA, American Historical Society, New York, NY, 1938, 4 volumes.

_W. J. Comley, COMLEY'S HISTORY OF MA, WITH PORTRAITS AND BIOGRAPHIES, Comley Brothers, Boston, MA, 1879.

_M. C. Crawford, FAMOUS FAMILIES OF MA, Little, Brown, Boston, MA, 1930, 2 volumes.

_W. R. Cutter and W. F. Adams, GENEALOGICAL AND PERSONAL MEMOIRS RELATING TO FAMILIES OF THE STATE OF MA, Lewis Historical Publishing Co., New York, NY, 1910, 4 volumes.

_W. R. Cutter, MEMORIAL ENCYCLOPEDIA OF THE STATE OF MA, American Historical Society, New York, NY, 1917, 3 volumes.

_W. T. Davis, BENCH AND BAR OF THE COMMONWEALTH OF MA, Boston History Co., Boston, MA, 1895, 2 volumes.

_H. M. and M. Dexter, THE ENGLAND AND HOLLAND OF THE PILGRIMS, Genealogical Publishing Co., Baltimore, MD, 1975.

_W. S. Downs, MEN OF NEW ENGLAND, New York, NY, 1941-65, 6 volumes.

_S. A. Eliot, BIOGRAPHICAL HISTORY OF MA, MA Biographical Society, Boston, MA, 1909-18, 10 volumes.

_J. Eliot, A BIOGRAPHICAL DICTIONARY OF THE FIRST SETTLERS IN NEW ENGLAND, Salem, MA, 1809.

_ENCYCLOPEDIA OF MA, BIOGRAPHICAL AND GENEALOGICAL, American Historical Society, New York, NY, 1916, 5 volumes.

_J. Farmer, A LIST OF THE GRADUATES AT ALL THE NEW ENGLAND COLLEGES TO ABOUT 1834, Genealogical Publishing Co., Baltimore, MD, 1971.

_A. Forbes and J. W. Greene, THE RICH MEN OF MA, Redding, Boston, MA, 1852.

_GENEALOGICAL AND BIOGRAPHICAL RECORDS OF AMERICAN FAMILIES, REPRESENTATIVE CITIZENS, MA, States Historical Society, Hartford, CT, 1930-, Vol. 1-, 26 volumes.

_A. B. Hart, COMMONWEALTH HISTORY OF MA, BIOGRAPHICAL VOLUME, Lewis Historical Publishing Co., New York, NY, 1936.

_R. Herndon, MEN OF PROGRESS, New England Magazine, Boston, MA, 1896.

_C. E. Hurd, GENEALOGY AND HISTORY OF REPRESENTATIVE CITIZENS OF THE COMMONWEALTH OF MA, New England Historical Publishing Co., Boston, MA, 1902.

_R. V. Jackson, MA HISTORICAL AND BIOGRAPHICAL INDEX, Accelerated Indexing Systems, Bountiful, UT, 1984.

_G. A. Marden, GOVERNMENT OF THE COMMONWEALTH OF MA, HISTORICAL, DESCRIPTIVE, AND BIOGRAPHICAL SKETCHES, Osgood, Boston, MA, 1880, 2 volumes.

_MEN OF MA, A COLLECTION OF PORTRAITS, Rockwell and Churchill, Boston, MA, 1903.

_S. E. Morison, BUILDERS OF THE BAY COLONY, Houghton Mifflin, Cambridge, MA, 1964.

_New England Historic Genealogical Society, MEMORIAL BIOGRAPHIES,

1845-97, The Society, Boston, MA, 1880-1908.

_THE PILGRIM FATHERS, OR THE LIVES OF SOME OF THE FIRST SETTLERS OF NEW ENGLAND, Shirley, Hyde, Portland, ME, 1830.

_C. H. Pope, THE PIONEERS OF MA, Boston, MA, 1900, with SUPPLEMENT, 1901.

_PUBLIC OFFICIALS OF MA, Boston Review, Boston, MA, 1906-44, 27 volumes.

_J. C. Rand, ONE OF A THOUSAND, BIOGRAPHICAL SKETCHES, First National Publishing Co., Boston, MA, 1890.

_REPRESENTATIVE MEN OF MA, MA Publishing, Everett, MA, 1898.

_O. A. Roberts, HISTORY OF THE MILITARY COMPANY OF MA, 1637-1888, The Company, Boston, MA, 1895-1901, 4 volumes.

_F. W. Russell, MOUNT AUBURN BIOGRAPHIES, DISTINGUISHED PERSONS INTERRED IN MOUNT AUBURN CEMETERY, CAMBRIDGE, MA, 1831-1952, Cambridge, MA, 1953.

_O. L. Stone, HISTORY OF MA INDUSTRIES, Clarke, Boston, MA, 1930, 4 volumes.

_D. P. Toomey and T. C. Quinn, MA OF TODAY, Columbia Publishing, Boston, 1892.

_WHO'S WHO IN MA, Larkin, Roosevelt, and Larkin, Boston, MA, 1940/2.

In addition to the state-wide biographical works, there are also a number of biographical collections for counties, sections, or regions of the state. Among the regional volumes with the largest number of names are:

_HISTORY OF THE CT VALLEY IN MA, L. H. Everts, Philadelphia, PA, 1879, 2 volumes. Franklin, Hampden, and Hampshire Counties.

_J. H. Lockwood, WESTERN MA, A HISTORY, 1636-1925, Lewis Historical Publishing Co., New York, NY, 1926, 4 volumes, last 2 biographical.

_REPRESENTATIVE MEN AND OLD FAMILIES OF SOUTHEASTERN MA, J. H. Beers, Chicago, IL, 1912, 3 volumes. Barnstable, Bristol, and Plymouth Counties.

_E. S. Thompson, HISTORY OF PLYMOUTH, NORFOLK, AND BARNSTABLE COUNTIES, Lewis Historical Publishing Co., New York, NY, 1928, 3 volumes, the 3rd being biographical.

_H. A. Wright, THE STORY OF WESTERN MA, Lewis Historical Publishing Co., New York, NY, 1949, 4 volumes.

County-wide biographical works of note include:

_(Barnstable) S. L. Deyo, HISTORY OF BARNSTABLE COUNTY, 1620-1890, H. W. Blake, New York, NY, 1890.

_(Berkshire) BIOGRAPHICAL REVIEW OF BERKSHIRE COUNTY, Biographical Review Publishing Co., Boston, MA, 1899.

_(Berkshire) R. H. Cooke, HISTORIC HOMES AND INSTITUTIONS AND GENEALOGICAL AND PERSONAL MEMOIRS OF BERKSHIRE COUNTY,

Lewis Historical Publishing Co., New York, NY, 1906, 2 volumes.

_(Bristol) D. H. Hurd, HISTORY OF BRISTOL COUNTY, Lewis, Philadelphia, PA, 1883.

_(Bristol) F. W. Hutt, A HISTORY OF BRISTOL COUNTY, Lewis Historical Publishing Co., New York, NY, 1924, 3 volumes.

_(Bristol) OUR COUNTY AND ITS PEOPLE, A DESCRIPTIVE AND BIOGRAPHICAL RECORD OF BRISTOL COUNTY, Boston History Co., Boston, MA, 1899.

_(Dukes) DUKES COUNTY TODAY, HISTORICAL, BIOGRAPHICAL, STATISTICAL, Vineyard Gazette, Edgartown, MA, 1915.

_(Essex) B. F. Arrington, MUNICIPAL HISTORY OF ESSEX COUNTY, Lewis HIstorical Publishing Co., New York, NY, 1922, 4 volumes, 3 and 4 biographical.

_(Essex) BIOGRAPHICAL REVIEW OF ESSEX COUNTY, Biographical Review Publishing Co., Boston, MA, 1898.

_(Essex) C. M. Fuess and S. H. Paradise, THE STORY OF ESSEX COUNTY, American Historical Society, New York, NY, 1935, 4 volumes, 3 and 4 biographical.

_(Essex) D. H. Hurd, HISTORY OF ESSEX COUNTY, Lewis, Philadelphia, PA, 1888, 2 volumes.

_(Essex) WHO'S WHO ALONG THE NORTH SHORE OF MA BAY, Salem Press, Salem, MA, 1907-10, 2 volumes.

_(Franklin) BIOGRAPHICAL REVIEW OF FRANKLIN COUNTY, Biographical Review Publishing Co., Boston, MA, 1895.

_(Hampden) BIOGRAPHICAL REVIEW OF HAMPDEN COUNTY, Biographical Review Publishing Co., Boston, MA, 1895.

_(Hampden) C. Johnson, HAMPDEN COUNTY, 1636-1936, American Historical Society, New York, NY, 1936, 3 volumes, 3rd biographical.

_(Hampshire) BIOGRAPHICAL REVIEW OF HAMPSHIRE COUNTY, Biographical Review PUblishing Co., Boston, MA, 1896.

_(Middlesex) BIOGRAPHICAL REVIEW OF MIDDLESEX COUNTY, Biographical Review Publishing Co., Boston, MA, 1898.

_(Middlesex) E. P. Conklin, MIDDLESEX COUNTY AND ITS PEOPLE, Lewis Historical Publishing Co., New York, NY, 1927, 4 volumes.

_(Middlesex) W. R. Cutter, HISTORIC HOMES AND PLACES AND GENEALOGICAL AND PERSONAL MEMOIRS OF MIDDLESEX COUNTY, Lewis Historical Publishing Co., New York, NY, 1908, 4 volumes.

_(Middlesex) L. S. Gould, ANCIENT MIDDLESEX WITH BRIEF BIOGRAPHICAL SKETCHES, Somerville Journal Print, Somerville, MA, 1905.

_(Middlesex) D. H. Hurd, HISTORY OF MIDDLESEX COUNTY, Lewis, Philadelphia, PA, 1890, 3 volumes.

_(Nantucket) E. Eleanor, AN ISLAND PATCHWORK, Houghton Mifflin, Boston, MA, 1941.

_(Norfolk) BIOGRAPHICAL REVIEW OF NORFOLK COUNTY, Biographical Review Publishing Co., Boston, MA, 1898.

_(Norfolk) L. A. Cook, HISTORY OF NORFOLK COUNTY, Clarke, Boston,

MA, 1918, 2 volumes, 2nd biographical.

__(Norfolk) D. H. Hurd, HISTORY OF NORFOLK COUNTY, Lewis, Philadelphia, PA, 1884.

__(Plymouth) BIOGRAPHICAL REVIEW OF PLYMOUTH COUNTY, Biographical Review Publishing Co., Boston, MA, 1897.

__(Plymouth) D. H. Hurd, HISTORY OF PLYMOUTH COUNTY, Lewis, Philadelphia, PA, 1884.

_(Worcester) BIOGRAPHICAL REVIEW OF WORCESTER COUNTY, Biographical Review Publishing Co., Boston, MA, 1899.

_(Worcester) E. B. Crane, HISTORIC HOMES AND INSTITUTIONS AND GENEALOGICAL AND PERSONAL MEMOIRS OF WORCESTER COUNTY, Lewis, Philadelphia, PA, 1907.

_(Worcester) E. B. Crane, HISTORY OF WORCESTER COUNTY, Lewis Historical Publishing Co., New York, NY, 1924.

_(Worcester) D. H. Hurd, HISTORY OF WORCESTER COUNTY, J. W. Lewis, Philadelphia, PA, 1889.

_(Worcester) J. Nelson, WORCESTER COUNTY, A NARRATIVE HISTORY, American Historical Society, New York, NY, 3 volumes.

Not only are there national, state, regional, and county biographical volumes for MA, there are also numerous local (town, city) biographical compilations. These works are very important since the local level is where you are most likely to find references to your ancestor. Local materials are listed in the following volumes:

_J. D. Haskell, Jr., MA, A BIBLIOGRAPHY OF ITS HISTORY, University Press of New England, Hanover, NH, 1976. Look under the town/city name.

_M. J. Kaminkow, US LOCAL HISTORIES IN THE LIBRARY OF CONGRESS, Magna Carta, Baltimore, MD, 1975, 5 volumes.

Biographical works at the local level will also be found listed in catalogs in the larger repositories in MA:

__CATALOGS (CARD, COMPUTER, PRINTED, TYPESCRIPT) IN NEHGS, BPL, SLM.

Practically all of the above biographical publications and most of the available local ones will be found in NEHGS, BPL, and SLM. Some of the state plus pertinent regional, county, and local publications are usually found in RL and LL. When you seek biographical compilations in a library, look under these headings in their catalogs: US-Biography, MA-Biography, [County name]-Biography, [City name]-Biography, [Town name]-Biography. In the larger cities you must not overlook the specialized biographical works which deal with persons in particular occupations (such as lawyers, sellers, engineers, pharmacists, merchants, sea captains, cabinet makers, military men, ministers, musicians, and police). All the categories mentioned in the preceding parentheses are available for Boston.

Biographical information is also sometimes found in ethnic publications, genealogical compilations, genealogical periodicals, manuscripts, military records, newspapers, published genealogies, regional records, and historical works (state, regional, county, town/city). All of these sources will be discussed in sections to follow.

4. Birth records

From the earliest times, the towns of MA were official keepers of birth records (as well as marriage and death records) of their inhabitants. At first the birth records were kept along with other town records (constable, early church, court, death, justice of peace, magistrate, marriage, proprietor, rate or tax, town meeting, selectmen) in one or a few books. Then, as the population grew, they came to be recorded in separate volumes dedicated especially to vital records. In 1841, in conformity to a new law, towns began reporting their births to the state, so that after that date, the records became available at both the town and state levels. Boston is an exception since it did not begin to comply until 1848. Original town records from the time of each town's origin to the present are available in the towns (town clerk, town archives, town library). From 1841-95 the official duplicates which were filed with the state are at the MSA and from 1896 forward, they are in the MA Registry of Vital Records and Statistics. Also available at the MSA is a state-wide birth record index for 1841-1971.

To obtain records for the period since 1895, you should write the following agency, enclosing the proper fee, the amount of which can be obtained by calling them:
_MA BIRTH RECORDS 1896-, MA State Registry of Vital Records and Statistics, Room B-3, 150 Tremont St., Boston, MA 02111. Telephone (617)-727-0110.
Records for the period 1841-95 are most readily accessed at the MSA or through the microfilm copies of them available at the NEHGS and at the FHL (and obtainable through their many branch FHC):
_MA BIRTH RECORDS 1841-95, and MA BIRTH RECORD INDEX 1841-1971, Office of the Secretary of State, MSA, Archives Division/Vital Records, 220 Morrissey Blvd., Boston, MA 02125. Telephone (617)-727-2816.
_MA BIRTH RECORDS, 1841-95, and MA BIRTH RECORD INDEX 1841-1971, on microfilm in FHL, can be borrowed through FHC. Also at NEHGS.

The birth records for the period before 1841 are available in several forms: originals in the towns, published volumes, copies on microfilm and microfiche, journal articles, typescript volumes, and manuscript copies. Of the 351 presently-existing MA towns, only about 10 of them do not have their birth records in some copied (published or manuscript) form. Among the more important are those on Plymouth and Boston.

_Boston Registry Department, RECORDS RELATING TO THE EARLY HISTORY OF BOSTON, The Record Commissioners, Boston, MA, 1876-1909, especially volumes 9, 24, 28, 30 for births.

_Boston Registry Department and W. S. Appleton, BOSTON BIRTHS, BAPTISMS, MARRIAGES, AND DEATHS, 1630-1800, Genealogical Publishing Co., Baltimore, MD, 1978. Births 1630-1800.

_Boston Registry Department and S. C. Gladden, INDEX TO 1630-99 BOSTON BIRTHS, BAPTISMS, MARRIAGES, AND DEATHS, Boulder Genealogical Society, Boulder, CO, 1969. Over 14000 records.

_EARLY BOSTON BIRTHS, FILMED FROM BOSTON VITAL RECORDS, 1630-1849, with INDEX, 1630-1799, Holbrook Research Institute, Oxford, MA, 1986, 25 microfiche.

_J. M. Holbrook, BOSTON BEGINNINGS, 1630-99, Holbrook Research Institute, Oxford, MA, 1980. Over 16000 names.

_N. B. Shurtleff and E. G. Bowman, PLYMOUTH COLONY, RECORDS OF BIRTHS, MARRIAGES, DEATHS, BURIALS, AND OTHER RECORDS, 1633-89, Genealogical Publishing Co., Baltimore, MD, 1979.

Some years ago, under the financial inducements of the state, various MA agencies began to publish town vital records (including births) for the time period up to 1850. The compilers of the many volumes which were printed drew not only upon official vital records, but they also often included court, Bible, church, and cemetery records. Later on, organizations, private companies, and individuals added volumes for other towns, published town vital records in genealogical journals, put town vital records on microfilm and microfiche, compiled typescript books, and made manuscript transcriptions. These materials include:

_PUBLISHED VOLUMES OF MA TOWN VITAL RECORDS UP TO 1850, for 227 towns, published by NEHGS, Essex Institute, Topsfield Historical Society, towns, private companies, and individuals.

_MA TOWN VITAL RECORDS PUBLISHED IN GENEALOGICAL JOURNALS, for 16 towns, chiefly published in New England Historical and Genealogical Register and The Mayflower Descendant.

_J. M. Holbrook, MA TOWN VITAL RECORDS UP TO 1890, over 120 towns on microfiche, Holbrook Research Institute, Oxford, MA.

_Daughters of the American Revolution for MA, COLLECTION OF GENEALOGICAL RECORD VOLUMES, The Society, various places in MA, various dates, numerous volumes, also on microfilm at FHL.

_MA TOWN RECORDS IN MANUSCRIPT FORM, for 52 towns, chiefly located in Corbin Collection and other collections at NEHGS and in Cooke Collection at Berkshire Athenaeum, Pittsfield, MA.

_MA TOWN RECORDS AND VITAL RECORDS, for many towns, on microfilm at FHL, available through FHC.

There is no overall index to this large number of compilations, but many of the births and marriages recorded in them are indexed in a microfiche set available at every FHC:

_INTERNATIONAL GENEALOGICAL INDEX, MICROFICHE FOR MA, at every FHC, look under surname.

In the fourth chapter, there are individual sections devoted to each town. In these sections, the birth-record publications, microfiche, microfilms, typescripts, and manuscripts pertaining to each town will be listed.

The basic guide to the original vital records (including births) which are in the MA towns is:

__C. D. Wright, REPORT ON THE CUSTODY AND CONDITION OF THE PUBLIC RECORDS OF PARISHES, TOWNS, AND COUNTIES, Wright and Potter, Boston, MA, 1889.

This volume is, of course, badly out of date, but it remains very valuable in that it indicates what records should be sought for each town, even though the record locations may differ today. Three other useful items along this line are:

_R. L. Bowen, MA RECORDS: A HANDBOOK FOR GENEALOGISTS, HISTORIANS, LAWYERS, AND OTHER RESEARCHERS, The Author, Rehoboth, MA, 1957.

_J. M. Holbrook, BIBLIOGRAPHY OF MA VITAL RECORDS, Holbrook Research Institute, Oxford, MA, 1986, 3 microfiche.

_Historical Records Survey, GUIDE TO PUBLIC VITAL STATISTICS RECORDS IN MA, The Survey, WPA, Boston, MA, 1942.

There are also some civil vital record collections available in the counties of MA. These will be listed in the county sections of Chapter 4, and they are also presented here.

_ESSEX COUNTY BIRTH RECORDS 1654-91, in Essex County at Salem.

_MIDDLESEX COUNTY BIRTH RECORDS 1632-1745, in Middlesex County at Cambridge.

_OLD NORFOLK COUNTY BIRTH RECORDS, 1641-71, in Essex County at Salem.

Similar volumes exist for several other counties, including Suffolk.

Excellent repositories for the books and microforms mentioned above are MSA, NEHGS, and BPL. In addition, the FHL(FHC) has much of the material on microfilm. LGL, especially those near MA, have some of the published works and some of the microforms, as do RL in MA.

Many other types of records often contain birthdate and birthplace information. Among the better ones are Bible, biography, cemetery, census, church, death, genealogical periodicals, manuscripts, marriage, military, mortuary, naturalization, newspaper, and published genealogies. All of these are treated in other sections of this chapter. When you are seeking birth data in archives and libraries, be certain to explore all the above mentioned sources, and do not fail to look under the county listings and the following heading in archive and library catalogs: Registers of births, etc.

5. Cemetery records

If you know or suspect that your ancestor was buried in a certain MA cemetery, the best thing to do is to write to the caretaker of the cemetery, enclose an SASE, and ask if records in the office and/or the tombstone inscriptions provide information about your forebear. Gravestones often display names, ages, dates of death and birth, and sometimes family names of wives. Tombstones of children often bear the names or initials of the parents. Office records at cemeteries, if available, usually give these same data plus more. In order to locate the caretaker or the present repository of the records, try writing the LL, the local historical society, the local genealogical society, or the town clerk. If you find that your ancestor is not buried there, then you should ask the above organizations about records for other cemeteries in the area. The addresses of these organizations will be given in Chapter 4. As you consider possible burial sites, please remember that most early cemeteries were in conjunction with churches. Therefore, if you know your progenitor's religious affiliation, this could be of help. Early on, this would most likely be Congregational.

Another important cemetery record source is provided by numerous collections of cemetery records which have been made by the DAR, by state, regional, county, and town genealogical, historical, and other-type societies, by towns, and by individuals. Some of these have been published in books, published in journals, put in typescript form, arranged in manuscript form, or incorporated in vital record compendia. Notable among them are:

_Cemetery records incorporated in PUBLISHED VOLUMES OF MA TOWN VITAL RECORDS UP TO 1850, for 227 towns, published by New England Historic Genealogical Society, Essex Institute, Systematic History Fund of Worcester, Topsfield Historical Society, towns, private companies, and individuals. Listed under death records.

_MA CEMETERY RECORDS PUBLISHED IN GENEALOGICAL JOURNALS AND SERIES, especially New England Historical and Genealogical Register, The Mayflower Descendant, and the Historical Collections of the Essex institute.

_MA CEMETERY RECORDS PUBLISHED IN DAR GENEALOGICAL RECORD VOLUMES, The DAR, various places in MA, various dates.

_MA CEMETERY RECORDS ON MICROFILM AT FHL, many of the above plus copies of numerous manuscript records available through FHC, all county and town listings in locality section of the catalog at each FHC.

_BOUND VOLUMES OF MA EPITAPHS, by towns, NEHGS, Boston, MA, 24 linear feet of volumes.

_MA CEMETERY RECORD MANUSCRIPTS in NEHGS, MSA, BPL, Berkshire Athenaeum in Pittsfield, RL, and LL in MA. See catalogs in these repositories for listings.

Many of the cemetery records published in genealogical journals, in DAR typescript volumes, and those available at FHL(FHC) are listed in

_J. D. and E. D. Stemmons, THE CEMETERY RECORD COMPENDIUM, Everton Publishers, Logan, UT, 1979.

Numerous articles describing cemeteries in MA, some of them listing early burials are referenced in

_J. D. Haskell, Jr., MA, A BIBLIOGRAPHY OF ITS HISTORY, University Press of New England, Hanover, NH, 1976.

There are also transcriptions of records of several leading cemeteries in Boston. These may be found in NEHGS and BPL. A card index to all known burials in Boston is available at that city's Mount Hope Cemetery.

In addition to the rich resources mentioned above there are several other compilations of note which are especially useful for MA cemetery records:

_B. Kingman, EPITAPHS FROM BURIAL HILL, PLYMOUTH, MA, 1657-1892, Genealogical Publishing Co., Baltimore, MD, 1977.

_C. D. Townsend, BORDER TOWN CEMETERIES OF MA, Chedwato Service, Middleboro, MA, 1953.

_H. Forbes, GRAVESTONES OF EARLY NEW ENGLAND AND THE MEN WHO MADE THEM, 1653-1800, Scribners, New York, NY, 1973.

_N. B. Shurtleff and E. G. Bowman, PLYMOUTH COLONY, RECORDS OF BIRTHS, MARRIAGES, DEATHS, BURIALS, AND OTHER RECORDS, 1633-89, Genealogical Publishing Co., Baltimore, MD, 1979.

All the above information indicates that the main sources of MA cemetery records (both gravemarker inscriptions and office records) are MSA, NEHGS, BPL, FHL(FHC), RL, and LL. The LL quite often have records in their own towns which are available nowhere else, and RL may also have similar materials. The major LL are listed in Chapter 4, and the principal RL are discussed in Chapter 3. In these libraries and in other repositories, cemetery records may be located by looking in their catalogs under the surname, county, city, and town, the church, the denomination, the ethnic group, and the cemetery name. Also look under the headings Epitaphs-MA and Cemeteries-MA. Further, you should not forget to inquire if there are any special cemetery record indexes, inventories, or files.

Several other important sources for cemetery records must not be overlooked, some of them already having been mentioned. These include Bible, biography, church, genealogical periodicals, manuscripts, and newspaper obituaries. The uses of all these are treated in other sections of this chapter.

6. Census records

Excellent ancestor information is available in eight types of census reports which have been accumulated for MA: some early census-like lists before 1800 (E), the regular federal censuses 1790-1910 (R), MA state censuses 1855/65 (S), agricultural censuses 1850-80 (A), industrial censuses 1820, 1850-80 (I), mortality censuses 1850-80 (M), the special 1840 Revolutionary War pensioner census (P), and the special 1890 Union Civil War veteran census (C).

For the colonial period and for the state period before 1800, there are some useful lists of MA inhabitants. Some of these early lists (E) are colony- or state-wide, most are local (county, city, town), but all are at least somewhat incomplete. They are of various types, the main categories being claimants, freemen, land grantees, landholders, militia members, persons taking an oath of allegiance, petitioners, residents, settlers, soldiers, and taxpayers. Many towns have tax lists on a frequent, sometimes annual basis. Among the most important published works of this type which contain large numbers of names are:

_L. R. Paige, LIST OF FREEMEN OF MA, 1630-91, with E. P. Bentley, INDEX, Genealogical Publishing Co., Baltimore, MD, 1980. 4500 names.

_Boston Registry Department, LISTS OF TAXPAYERS IN THE TOWN OF BOSTON, 1674-95, First Report of Record Commissioners, Appendix B, Boston, MA, 1881.

_Boston Registry Department, MISCELLANEOUS PAPERS, Tenth Report of the Commissioners, Boston, MA, 1886. 1707 census, some wills, deeds, taxes.

_J. H. Benton, EARLY CENSUS MAKING IN MA, 1643-1765, WITH THE LOST CENSUS OF 1765, The Compiler, Boston, MA, 1905.

_J. M. Holbrook, BOSTON BEGINNINGS, 1630-99, Holbrook Research Institute, Oxford, MA, 1980. Over 16000 names.

_B. H. Pruit, THE MA TAX VALUATION LIST OF 1771, Hall, Boston, MA, 1978.

_W. H. Dumont, A SHORT CENSUS OF MA, 1779, National Genealogical Society Quarterly, Volumes 49-51, 1961-3.

_M. H. Gorn, AN INDEX AND GUIDE TO THE MICROFILM EDITION OF THE MA AND ME DIRECT TAX CENSUS OF 1798, New England Historic Genealogical Society, Boston, MA, 1979, along with MICROFILM EDITION OF THE MA AND ME DIRECT TAX CENSUS OF 1798, The Society, Boston, MA. At NEHGS and FHL.

Numerous other special lists for the counties, cities, and towns of MA may be identified and located by looking the county, city, or town up in the following volumes:

_J. D. Stemmons, THE US CENSUS COMPENDIUM, Everton Publishers, Logan, UT, 1973. Also see the LOCALITY CATALOG at all FHC.

_New England Historic Genealogical Society, INDEX TO PERSONS AND PLACES IN VOLUMES 1-50 OF THE NEW ENGLAND HISTORICAL AND GENEALOGICAL REGISTER, Genealogical Publishing Co., Baltimore, MD, 1972.

_M. W. Parsons, INDEX TO VOLUMES 51-112 OF THE NEW ENGLAND HISTORICAL AND GENEALOGICAL REGISTER, The Author, Marlborough, MA, 1959.

Other compilations of names of inhabitants of MA during the early period will be referred to in other sections of this chapter, particularly those dealing with church records, colonial record compilations, court records, emigration and immigration, ethnic records, genealogical periodicals (including the New England Historical and Genealogical Register as mentioned above, but also The Mayflower Descendant, the Essex Antiquarian, the Essex Institute Historical Collections, and the Genealogical Advertiser), land records, military records (colonial and Revolutionary), naturalization records, and regional compilations.

Regular census records (R) taken by the federal government are available for MA in 1790, 1800, 1810, 1820, 1830, 1840, 1850, 1860, 1870, 1880, 1900, and 1910. The 1890 census for MA is not extant, though the Civil War veteran and widow schedule is a partial substitute. The 1840 federal census and all before it listed the head of the household and counted others in the household according to age and sex brackets. Beginning in 1850, the names of all persons were recorded along with age, sex, occupation, real estate, marital, and other information, including the state or country of birth. With the 1880 census, and thereafter, the birthplaces of the father and mother of each person are also shown. Starting in 1900 and thereafter, the year of immigration is shown for each foreign-born person. Chapter 4 lists the federal census records (R) available for each county.

Census data for 1790 are available in both a published transcript and two microfilms, the first and third items being indexed:

_US Bureau of the Census, HEADS OF FAMILIES AT THE FIRST CENSUS OF THE US TAKEN IN 1790 IN MA, Genealogical Publishing Co., Baltimore, MD, 1966. Indexed.

_US Bureau of the Census, FIRST CENSUS OF THE US, 1790, MA, The National Archives, Washington, DC, Microfilm M637, Roll 4. Unindexed.

_US Bureau of the Census, FIRST CENSUS OF THE US, 1790, MA, The National Archives, Washington, DC, Microfilm T498, Roll 1. Microfilm copy of the printed schedules, indexed.

Microfilms of the remaining original census records (1800-1910) are available as:

_US Bureau of the Census, SECOND CENSUS OF THE US, 1800, MA, The National Archives, Washington, DC, Microfilm M32, Rolls 13-19.

Part of Suffolk missing.

_US Bureau of the Census, THIRD CENSUS OF THE US, 1810, MA, The National Archives, Washington, DC, Microfilm M252, Rolls 17-22.

_US Bureau of the Census, FOURTH CENSUS OF THE US, 1820, MA, The National Archives, Washington, DC, Microfilm M33, Rolls 47-55.

_US Bureau of the Census, FIFTH CENSUS OF THE US, 1830, MA, The National Archives, Washington, DC, Microfilm M19, Rolls 59-68.

_US Bureau of the Census, SIXTH CENSUS OF THE US, 1840, MA, The National Archives, Washington, DC, Microfilm M704, Rolls 173-202.

_US Bureau of the Census, SEVENTH CENSUS OF THE US, 1850, MA, The National Archives, Washington, DC, Microfilm M432, Rolls 303-345.

_US Bureau of the Census, EIGHTH CENSUS OF THE US, 1860, MA, The National Archives, Washington, DC, Microfilm M653, Rolls 486-534.

_US Bureau of the Census, NINTH CENSUS OF THE US, 1870, MA, The National Archives, Washington, DC, Microfilm M593, Rolls 600-659.

_US Bureau of the Census, TENTH CENSUS OF THE US, 1880, MA, The National Archives, Washington, DC, Microfilm T9, Rolls 519-568.

_US Bureau of the Census, TWELFTH CENSUS OF THE US, 1900, MA, The National Archives, Washington, DC, Microfilm T623, Rolls 631-697.

_US Bureau of the Census, THIRTEENTH CENSUS OF THE US, 1910, MA, The National Archives, Washington, DC, Microfilm T624, Rolls 571-633.

The 1790 Census records are indexed in the published volume mentioned above and in the microfilm (T498) of the printed volume, and indexes have been published for the 1800, 1810, 1820, 1830, 1840, and 1850 census records. These are:

_E. P. Bentley, INDEX TO THE 1800 CENSUS OF MA, Genealogical Publishing Co., Baltimore, MD, 1978. Over 70,000 people. Boston and Chelsea (both of Suffolk County) missing. Hull and Cohasset incomplete.

_L. Welch, R. V. Jackson, and C. R. Teeples, MA 1800 CENSUS INDEX, Accelerated Indexing Systems, Provo, UT, 1973. Over 70,000 entries.

_R. V. Jackson, MA 1810 CENSUS INDEX, Accelerated Indexing systems, Bountiful, UT, 1976. Over 79,000 listings.

_R. V. Jackson, MA 1820 CENSUS INDEX, Accelerated Indexing Systems, Bountiful, UT, 1976. 91,000 entries.

_R. V. Jackson, MA 1830 CENSUS INDEX, Accelerated Indexing Systems, Bountiful, UT, 1976. Over 105,000 names.

_R. V. Jackson, MA 1840 CENSUS INDEX, Accelerated Indexing Systems, Bountiful, UT, 1978. Over 142,000 listings.

_R. V. Jackson, MA 1850 CENSUS INDEX, Accelerated Indexing Systems, Bountiful, UT, 1978. Over 369,000 names.

There are as yet no state-wide indexes to the 1860 and 1870 MA state censuses, even though a few county and town indexes are now available.

In addition to the above bound indexes, there is a microfilm index which contains only those families with a child under 10 in the 1880 census. There is also a microfilm index to the 1900 MA census, which indexes only the heads of households or residents with a different surname. These two census indexes are arranged according to a phonetic code called Soundex. Librarians and archivists can show you how to use it. These indexes are:

_US Bureau of the Census, INDEX (SOUNDEX) TO THE 1880 POPULATION SCHEDULES OF MA, The National Archives, Washington, DC, Microfilm T754, 70 rolls.

_US Bureau of the Census, INDEX (SOUNDEX) TO THE 1900 POPULATION SCHEDULES OF MA, The National Archives, Washington, DC, Microfilm T1051, 314 Rolls.

No index of the 1910 MA census schedules exists.

The indexes listed in the two previous paragraphs are exceptionally valuable as time-saving devices. However, few indexes of any sort are perfect, and therefore you need to exercise a little caution in using them. If you do not find your progenitor in them, do not conclude that she or he is not in the state; this may only mean that your forebear has been accidentally omitted or that the name has been misspelled, misread, or misprinted. Once you have located a name in the indexes, you can go directly to the reference in the census microfilms and read the entry. When indexes are not available (for all 1860, 1870, and 1910, and partially for 1880), it is necessary for you to go through the census listings entry-by-entry. This can be essentially prohibitive for the entire state, so it is necessary for you to know the county, or better the town, in order to limit your search. This information can often be obtained from the state-wide birth, death, and marriage records which are available for 1841-95/9 (see sections 4, 12, 23 of this chapter). Even though you may know or discover the town, if it turns out to be one of the larger cities of MA, you will still have a great number of listings to go through. To help, you can consult city directories for the pertinent census years (1860/70/80/1910). Addresses obtained from these directories can lead you to the proper sections of the census schedules. See section 8 of this chapter for a discussion of city directories. Both the census indexes and the census records are available in MSA, NEHGS, BPL, FHL (FHC), and NA (NAFB, NABB). They are also available in LGL, and some may be found in RL and LL, particularly records for their local areas. Also, the microfilmed census records and the microfilmed indexes may be borrowed by you or by your local library through AGLL (American Genealogical Lending Library, PO Box 244, Bountiful, UT 84010). There is a charge of a few dollars per roll.

MA state censuses (S) were taken a number of times after statehood, but some of them were only statistical in nature, and others have been partly or completely lost. The major surviving schedules which are useful and readily available to researchers are those of 1855 and 1865. The originals are in the MSA and microfilm copies are to be found in FHL.

_1855 AND 1865 MA STATE CENSUS RETURNS, MSA, Boston, MA, also on 31 and 37 reels, respectively, of microfilm at FHL(FHC).

These records list all persons with sex, country or state of birth, and occupation. The 1865 materials add marital status, whether voter, whether naturalized voter, and taxables. Sometimes the returns give the MA town of birth, but this was not mandatory. A number of works have recently appeared which present and index the 1855 and 1865 MA state censuses for many towns.

_A. S. Lainhart, MA STATE CENSUSES OF 1855 AND 1865 FOR VARIOUS TOWNS, The Compiler, Boston, MA, 1985-. Available for many towns.

Agricultural census records (A), also known as farm and ranch censuses are available for 1850, 1860, 1870, and 1880 for MA. These federally-generated records list the name of the owner, size of farm or ranch, value of the property, crops, livestock, and other details. If your ancestor was a farmer, it will be worthwhile to seek him in these records. No indexes are available, but you will probably know the county and town, so your entry-by-entry search should be fairly easy. The records for 1850/60/70 are in MSA, and the following microfilm of them may be found in the NA, the NABB and the FHL(FHC):

_US Bureau of the Census, FEDERAL NON-POPULATION CENSUS SCHEDULES, MA, 1850-80, The National Archives, Washington, DC, Microfilm T1204, 40 Rolls. Agricultural, industrial, mortality, and social statistics schedules.

Industrial census records (I), also known as manufactures censuses, were taken by the federal government in 1820, 1850, 1860, 1870, and 1880 for MA. The records list manufacturing businesses (in 1850/60/70/80 only those with over $500 of product), owner's name, product, machinery, number of employees, and other details. Indexes accompany the 1820 microfilmed records, but the others are unindexed. The records for 1850/60/70 are in the MSA, and the following microfilms may be found in the NA, the NABB and the FHL(FHC).

_US Bureau of the Census, RECORDS OF THE 1820 CENSUS OF MANUFACTURES, The National Archives, Washington, DC, Microfilm M279, 27 Rolls.

_US Bureau of the Census, FEDERAL NON-POPULATION CENSUS SCHEDULES, MA, 1850-80, The National Archives, Washington, DC, Microfilm T1204, 40 Rolls. Agricultural, industrial, mortality, and social statistics schedules.

There is also a printed work containing the 1820 records.

_National Archives, INDEXES TO MANUFACTURERS' CENSUS OF 1820, AN EDITED PRINTING OF THE ORIGINAL INDEXES AND INFORMATION, Bookmark, Knightstown, IN.

Mortality census records (M) are available for the one-year periods 01 June (1849/59/69/79) to 31 May (1850/60/70/80), respectively. The federal records give information on persons who died in the year preceding the 1st of June of each of the census years 1850/60/70/80. The data contained in the compilations include name, month of death, age, sex, occupation, place of birth, and other information. The records for 1850/60/70 are in the MSA, and there is a DAR typescript of the 1850 data in NEHGS. The NA, the NABB, and the FHL(FHC) all have the following microfilms.

_US Bureau of the Census, FEDERAL NON-POPULATION CENSUS SCHEDULES, MA, 1850-80, The National Archives, Washington, DC, Microfilm T1204, 40 Rolls. Agricultural, industrial, mortality, and social statistics schedules.

The records are not indexed, but with a little knowledge of the county and the town, you should not have too much difficulty locating entries. You may have noticed that in the above Microfilm T1204 there are social statistics schedules for 1850/60/70/80. These materials do not give names of people, but they can be of indirect help to searchers. They list and describe cemeteries, give information on societies and other organizations, and name churches then give short histories of them.

Revolutionary War pensioners (P) were included in the data collected in the 1840 regular federal census. An attempt was made to list all pension holders, however, there are some omissions and some false entries. The list has been copied out, indexed, and published:

_US Bureau of the Census, A CENSUS OF PENSIONERS FOR REVOLUTIONARY OR MILITARY SERVICES, with INDEX, Genealogical Publishing Co., Baltimore, MD, 1965/7.

These volumes are present in NEHGS, BPL, FHL(FHC), in most LGL, in many RL, and in some LL.

Civil War Union veterans (C) of MA were included in a special federal census taken in 1890, as were widows of the veterans. These records display the veteran's name, widow's name (if applicable), rank, company, regiment or ship, and other pertinent military data.

_US Veterans' Administration, SPECIAL SCHEDULES OF THE ELEVENTH CENSUS (1890) ENUMERATING UNION VETERANS AND WIDOWS OF UNION VETERANS OF THE CIVIL WAR, The National Archives, Washington, DC, Microfilm M123, rolls 11-16.

The above microfilms are available at NA, NABB, and the FHL(FHC).

The census records of all the above types (E, R, S, A, I, M, P, C) available for each of the MA counties will be shown in the county listings in Chapter 4. For a county for which all the above censuses are available (such as Essex), the listing will read: Pre-1800E, 1790R, 1800R, 1810R, 1820RI, 1830R, 1840RP, 1850RAIM, 1855S, 1860RAIM, 1865S, 1870RAIM, 1880RAIM, 1890C, 1900R, 1910R.

7. Church records

MA church records are very important genealogical sources because most of its churches have kept good to excellent records, and the large majority have survived. Church records can carry all sorts of pertinent information including names and dates of birth, baptism, christening, confirmation, intention to marry, marriage, admission, dismissal, removal, war service, death, funeral, and burial. During the colonial period and up into the 1800s, the Congregational Church (the church of the Puritans and the Pilgrims) remained predominant in MA. However, as time went on, and particularly after 1700 the link between the government and the denomination grew weaker and weaker. Other Protestant denominations established churches including Quakers, Episcopalians, and Baptists, and somewhat later Methodists and Lutherans. Jewish adherents also came. In the mid-1700s, a strong Unitarian movement began to develop within the MA Congregational churches. By 1815, it had resulted in many of the oldest Congregational churches becoming Unitarian, and some turning Universalist. The new Unitarian and Universalist congregations retained possession of the property and records of the Congregational bodies. As a result of these splits and later mergers, Congregational church records may now be found in churches belonging to the following three denominations: Congregational Christian Churches, Unitarian Universalist Association, and United Church of Christ (which came from a merger of the General Council of Congregational Churches and the Evangelical and Reformed Church). French and French Canadians dominated MA Catholicism until the 1840s when large numbers of Irish Catholics began coming into MA, followed by many other Catholics from Italy, Poland, Russia, and Portugal. By the turn of the 20th century, the religion of the majority of MA citizens had become Catholic.

There is a very important understanding that you must have concerning MA church records. In the earliest years of MA when the government and the church were effectively one, the church parish or church precinct records and the town records were generally kept together. That is, the records of towns during this early period were the church parish records. Then, as MA lost the very tight relation between the church and the government, the church parishes and the town governments separated and each kept its own records. Unfortunately, there is a very loose, indiscriminate use of the words church, parish, congregation, and religious society in the laws of MA and in the records of the religious communities. This further complicates the difficulty of finding out when and to what extent the religious and the town governmental record keeping were separated. This problem can be handled by remembering to carefully examine all town records and all church records during these early years.

Church records in MA are to be found in many forms and places: original records in the churches; original records in towns, LL, RL, NEHGS, and denominational archives; manuscripts in LL, RL, NEHGS, and denominational archives; typescript transcriptions in LL, RL, NEHGS, and denominational libraries and archives; microfilmed records in LL, RL, NEHGS, FHL(FHC), and denominational archives; records published as part of the material in the MA Town Vital Records volumes; and church records published as separate volumes. You can see from this array of possible sources that you need to search for church records on your ancestor in the churches, LL, RL, NEHGS, BPL, FHL(FHC), and denominational archives.

There are several types of very useful publications which will be of assistance to you in searching for your progenitor's church records. These include volumes which list churches, volumes and catalogs which list availabilities and locations of church records, and finally, volumes, microfilms, typescripts, and manuscripts which give the records, either in detail or in abstracted form. Volumes which list the churches of various denominations in MA towns are listed later in this section in paragraphs dedicated to the denominations. Volumes and catalogs which list availabilities and locations of church records include:

_H. F. Worthley, AN INVENTORY OF THE RECORDS OF THE PARTICULAR (CONGREGATIONAL) CHURCHES OF MA GATHERED (ORGANIZED) 1620-1805, Harvard University Press, Cambridge, MA, 1970. A listing by towns of Congregational Churches, the types and dates of records available for each, and the location of the records. Includes churches which later switched denominations. Also information on records which have been printed.

_C. D. Wright, REPORT ON THE CUSTODY AND CONDITION OF THE PUBLIC RECORDS OF MA PARISHES, TOWNS, AND COUNTIES, Wright and Potter, Boston, MA, 1889. Although out of date, still exceptionally valuable for indicating what is available, even though locations for some records have changed. Lists of current and extinct churches in MA towns along with the dates for which records exist for each as of 1885.

_Commissioner of MA Public Records, EXISTING CHURCHES BY TOWNS, EXISTING CHURCHES BY DENOMINATIONS, and EXTINCT CHURCHES BY TOWNS, in FIRST REPORT (1885) 9-132, TENTH REPORT (1897) 1-189, TWELFTH REPORT (1900) 10, FIFTEENTH REPORT (1902)

14-16. Remarks of previous listing apply.

_Historical Records Survey, INVENTORY OF CHURCH ARCHIVES OF MA: PROTESTANT EPISCOPAL, and INVENTORY OF CHURCH ARCHIVES OF MA: UNIVERSALIST, WPA, Boston, MA, 1942, 2 volumes.

_INVENTORIES OF DENOMINATIONAL ARCHIVES, see later listings in this section for Catholic and Episcopal archive inventories.

_J. D. Haskell, Jr., MA, A BIBLIOGRAPHY OF ITS HISTORY, University Press of New England, Hanover, NH, 1976. Lists some record volumes and many church history books and articles. Look in the index under Churches and under denominations.

_J. D. and E. D. Stemmons, THE VITAL RECORD COMPENDIUM, The Authors, Salt Lake City, UT, 1979.

_CARD, COMPUTER, AND MICROFORM CATALOGS in NEHGS, BPL, FHL(FHC), RL, Berkshire Athenaeum in Pittsfield, and LL. Look under town, county, denomination, and name of individual church.

Volumes, microfilms, typescripts, and manuscripts which give church records in detail or in abstracted form include:

_PUBLISHED VOLUMES OF MA TOWN VITAL RECORDS UP TO 1850, for 227 towns, published by New England Historic Genealogical Society, Essex Institute, Topfield Historical Society, towns, private companies, and individuals.

_MA CHURCH RECORDS PUBLISHED IN GENEALOGICAL JOURNALS, see indexes of New England Historical and Genealogical Register, Mayflower Descendant, Essex Antiquarian, Essex Genealogist, Essex Institute Historical Collections, Genealogical Advertiser, MA Magazine, and other journals and serials listed in section 18 of this chapter.

_MA CHURCH RECORDS IN MANUSCRIPT COLLECTIONS IN NEHGS, Berkshire Athenaeum in Pittsfield, on microfilm in FHL(FHC), RL, LL, and other repositories listed in section 22 of this chapter.

_Daughters of American Revolution for MA, COLLECTION OF GENEALOGICAL RECORD VOLUMES, The Society, various places in MA, various dates, numerous volumes, also on microfilm at FHL(FHC).

_CARD, COMPUTER, AND MICROFORM CATALOGS in NEHGS, BPL, FHL, (FHC), Berkshire Athenaeum in Pittsfield, RL, and LL. Look under town, county, denomination, and name of individual church.

_Boston Registry Department and W. S. Appleton, BOSTON BIRTHS, BAPTISMS, MARRIAGES, AND DEATHS, 1630-1800, Genealogical Publishing Co., Baltimore, MD, 1978, with S. C. Gladden, INDEX, The Indexer, Boulder, CO, 1969.

_PLYMOUTH CHURCH RECORDS, 1620-1859, Genealogical Publishing Co., Baltimore, MD, 1975. Over 50,000 indexed listings.

_R. D. Pierce, THE RECORDS OF THE FIRST CHURCH OF BOSTON, 1630-1868, Colonial Society of MA, Boston, MA, 1941, 3 volumes.

_R. D. Pierce, THE RECORDS OF THE FIRST CHURCH OF SALEM, 1629-1736, Essex Institute, Salem, MA, 1974.

_THE RECORDS OF TRINITY CHURCH IN BOSTON, 1728-1830,

Colonial Society of MA, Boston, MA, 1982.
_BOSTON CHURCH RECORD TRANSCRIPTS, Room 201, City Hall, Boston, MA. Include churches in towns which Boston annexed.

Should you know or strongly suspect your ancestor's church (probably Congregational if in the colonial era), you should first check the above references. Such an action is well advised because a high percentage of MA church records can be located and/or accessed by doing so. If you find nothing, or if you find the records are in the custody of the church, then write directly. Send an SASE, a check for $5, your progenitor's name, and the pertinent dates. Request a search of the records or information on the location of the records if the church no longer has them. If the church neither has them nor knows where the records are, dispatch inquiries to the NEHGS, the nearest RL, the LL, and the denominational archives, enclosing SASEs, and asking them if they know where the records are. The names and addresses of NEHGS and RL will be found in Chapter 3, those of LL in Chapter 4, and those for denominational archives in later paragraphs of this section.

If, as is often the case, you know your ancestor's town but not her/his church, you will need to dig a little deeper. First, you should examine all the compiled church records of the pertinent town and all neighboring towns. Many of the pertinent records can be located by using the materials in the paragraphs above. If you know or can guess the likely denomination(s), this can narrow your search, but do not too quickly rule out other denominations. Should you still not find what you are seeking, dispatch letters to LL, RL, and denominational repositories concerning churches in your forebear's area and the records of those churches.

Listed in this paragraph and in several to follow will be the major denominations of MA, their repositories, and pertinent genealogical and historical volumes (volumes which cover all or large parts of the state). <u>Baptist</u> repositories and publications include:
_(Archives) American Baptist Historical Society, 1106 S. Goodman St., Rochester, NY 14620.
_(Archives) Andover Newton Theological School, Trask Library, 169 Herrick Rd., Newton Centre, MA 02159. Records of 26 state and regional Baptist organizations and of 45 Baptist churches.
_W. G. McLaughlin, NEW ENGLAND DISSENT, 1630-1833, THE BAPTISTS AND SEPARATION OF CHURCH AND STATE, Harvard Univ. Press, Cambridge, MA, 1971.
_E. C. Starr, A BAPTIST BIBLIOGRAPHY, American Baptist Historical Society, Rochester, NY, 1947-.
_J. W. Brush, BAPTISTS IN MA, Judson Press, Valley Forge, PA, 1970.

For Catholic research, these archives and publications can be of assistance to you:

_(Archives) Archives of the Archdiocese of Boston, 2121 Commonwealth Ave., Brighton, MA 02135. Baptismal and marriage records of all 150 Catholic parishes in the archdiocese (Eastern MA) dated before 1910. These and other records described in volume listed next. Most Catholic records for Western MA remain in the parishes.

_J. M. O'Toole, GUIDE TO THE ARCHIVES OF THE ARCHDIOCESE OF BOSTON, Garland Publns., New York, NY, 1982.

_J. M. O'Toole, CATHOLIC CHURCH RECORDS, A GENEALOGICAL AND HISTORICAL RESOURCE, New England Historical and Genealogical Register, Volume 132, pages 251-63, 1978.

_OFFICIAL CATHOLIC DIRECTORY, Kenedy, Wilmette, IL, latest edition. Lists all active Catholic churches.

_STUDIES IN AMERICAN (CATHOLIC) CHURCH HISTORY, Catholic Univ. Press, Washington, DC, over 30 volumes.

The Congregational Church, as you will recall, was by far the most important religious community in MA until into the 1800s. Because of the Unitarian and Universalist take-overs of many congregations in the early 1800s, and denominational mergers of the 1900s, many former Congregational churches are now members of the Unitarian-Universalist Association or the United Church of Christ. These repositories will be discussed later, with the archives and some important volumes of the Congregational Church now being set out.

_(Archives) The Congregational Library, 14 Beacon St., Boston, MA 02108.

_H. F. Worthley, AN INVENTORY OF THE RECORDS OF THE PARTICULAR (CONGREGATIONAL) CHURCHES OF MA GATHERED (ORGANIZED) 1620-1805, Harvard University Press, Cambridge, MA, 1970.

_W. Willeston, THE HISTORY OF THE CONGREGATIONAL CHURCHES IN THE US, American Congregational Historical Society, New York, NY, 1894.

_J. S. Clark, A HISTORICAL SKETCH OF THE CONGREGATIONAL CHURCHES IN MA, 1620-1858, Congregational Board of Publication, Boston, MA, 1858.

The Episcopal Church archives and several publications that will serve you well as you search for church records and come to understand the religious background of an Episcopalian forebear are listed here:

_(Archives) The Diocesan Library and Archives, Episcopal Diocese of MA, 1 Joy St., Boston, MA 02108. Microfilm copies of pre-1805 parish registers of over 104 churches.

_THE EPISCOPAL CHURCH ANNUAL, New York, NY, latest edition.

_M. J. Duffy, GUIDE TO THE PAROCHIAL ARCHIVES OF THE EPISCOPAL CHURCH IN BOSTON, Episcopal Diocese of MA, Boston, MA, 1981.

_M. J. Duffy, THE EPISCOPAL DIOCESE OF MA, 1784–1984, The Diocese, Boston, MA, 1984.
_Historical Records Survey, INVENTORY OF CHURCH ARCHIVES OF MA: PROTESTANT EPISCOPAL CHURCH, WPA, Boston, MA, 1942.
_D. Tyng, MA EPISCOPALIANS, 1607–1957, Episcopal Diocese of MA, Boston, MA, 1960.

For MA Jewish progenitors, the following archives and volumes will be worthwhile to consult:
_(Archives) American Jewish Historical Society Library, 2 Thornton Road, Waltham, MA 02154. Hundreds of family histories, genealogies, and manuscripts; American Jewish Archives, 3101 Clifton Ave., Cincinnati, OH 45220.
_M. H. Stern, FIRST AMERICAN JEWISH FAMILIES, 600 GENEALOGIES, 1654–1977, American Jewish Archives, Cincinnati, OH, 1978.
_S. Broches, JEWS IN NEW ENGLAND, HISTORICAL STUDY OF JEWS IN MA, 1650–1750, Bloch Publishing, New York, NY, 1942.
_A. Ehrenfried, A CHRONICLE OF BOSTON JEWRY, FROM THE COLONIAL SETTLEMENT TO 1900, Boston, MA, 1963.

For Methodist research, the following archives and books may be consulted:
_(Archives) New England Methodist Historical Society Library, School of Theology, Boston University, 745 Commonwealth Ave., Boston, MA 02215. Have many records of defunct churches and some early records of existing churches.
_General Commission on Archives and History of the United Methodist Church, DIRECTORY OF COMMISSIONS ON ARCHIVES AND HISTORY, United Methodist Church, Madison, NJ, 1981.

Quaker archives and published works which are available include:
_(Archives) RI Historical Society Library, 121 Hope St., Providence, RI 02906. Quaker Meeting records for MA.
_R. P. Hallowell, THE QUAKER INVASION OF MA, Houghton Mifflin, Boston, MA, 1884.
_R. M. Jones, THE QUAKERS IN THE AMERICAN COLONIES, Russell and Russell, New York, NY, 1962.

The Unitarian–Universalist archives and several books which are valuable for researching members of these denominations are given below. Do not fail to remember that many Unitarian and Universalist churches were originally Congregationalist.
_(Archives) Andover–Harvard Theological Library, Harvard Divinity School, 45 Francis Ave., Cambridge, MA 02138. Records of many Universalist and Unitarian Churches.
_Unitarian–Universalist Association Archives Library, 25 Beacon St.,

Boston, MA 02108.

_R. E. Miller, THE LARGER HOPE, Boston, MA, 1979/85, 2 volumes.

_Historical Records Survey, AN INVENTORY OF UNIVERSALIST ARCHIVES IN MA, WPA, Boston, MA, 1942. OUtdated, but useful since it indicates what records were available.

_H. F. Worthley, AN INVENTORY OF THE RECORDS OF THE PARTICULAR (CONGREGATIONAL) CHURCHES OF MA GATHERED (ORGANIZED) 1620-1805, Harvard University Press, Cambridge, MA, 1970. Includes numerous churches which became Unitarian or Universalist.

For the United Church of Christ (which resulted from a merger of the General Council of Congregational Churches and the Evangelical and Reformed Church), the Congregational records should be sought in the Congregational Library (see Congregation section above) and the Andover-Harvard Theological Library (also listed above).

As you search for your progenitor's church records, please use first the materials referenced at the beginning of this section. In most cases, you will be led to the original, abstracted, transcribed, microfilmed, and/or published records. They will generally be located in the local church, LL, RL, or the NEHGS. If your search does not succeed, try the denominational archives listed above. When seeking church records in a library or archives catalog, you should look under the town name, the county name, the church name, and the denomination name. Church records are often found in several other sources, which are discussed in different sections of this chapter: cemetery, town and county histories, colonial, DAR, ethnic, genealogical indexes and compilations, genealogical periodicals, manuscripts, mortuary, newspaper, published genealogies, regional records, and WPA records.

8. City directories

Just before the turn to the 19th century, namely in 1789, Boston city directories began to be published, erratically at first (1789, 1796/8, 1800/3/5-10), then essentially annually (a few exceptions) afterward. In the early 19th century, such publications began to be issued for several other MA cities, and those for still other cities a little later. As in the case of Boston, the directories usually appeared irregularly at first, but then began to come out regularly (sometimes biannually at first, then annually) later on. They usually list heads of households and workers plus their home addresses and their occupations, and sometimes the names and addresses of their places of employment. Businesses, professions, institutions, churches, and organizations (sometimes with officers, rarely with all members) are also usually listed.

Notable among MA city directories are those of the following cities.

For each of these cities, the earliest directory is listed. Sometimes the first directory is followed by an annual or biannual series, sometimes erratic publication follows, and sometimes the town is annexed to a neighbor town and its listings then come under that town's directory: Boston (1789), Bradford (1853), Cambridge (1847), Charlestown (1831), Chelsea (1847), Clinton (1856), Dorchester (1848), East Boston (1848), Fall River (1844/5), Fitchburg (1846), Gloucester (1860), Haverhill (1853), Lawrence (1847), Lowell (1832), Lynn (1832), Medford (1849), Milford (1856), New Bedford (1836), Newburyport (1849), Pittsfield (1859), Plymouth (1846), Roxbury (1847), Salem (1837), Somerville (1849), South Boston (1852), Southbridge (1854), Springfield (1845), Taunton (1850), Worcester (1828). There are also MA state regional directories, which are largely commercially oriented (1835, 1849-59).

There is a large collection of city directories in the American Antiquarian Society (185 Salisbury St., Worcester, MA 01609-1634) and in the Library of Congress (Washington, DC). Hundreds of them have been put on microfilm by commercial agencies, for quite a number of cities through the 1901 volume. The microfilms and/or the original directories should be sought in the NEHGS, SLM, BPL, MSA, FHL(FHC), RL, and LL. Other MA cities and towns also issued directories, usually at starting dates later than the above ones, but you should not fail to look for them, especially in RL and LL in the pertinent places.

9. City, county, and town histories

Histories for MA counties, cities, and towns have been published. These volumes usually contain biographical data on leading citizens, details about early settlers, histories of organizations, businesses, trades, and churches, and often lists of clergymen, lawyers, physicians, teachers, governmental officials, farmers, military men, and other groups. Many early town histories contain detailed genealogy sections. Several works which list many of these histories are:

_J. D. Haskell, Jr., MA, A BIBLIOGRAPHY OF ITS HISTORY, University Press of New England, Hanover, NH, 1976.

_C. A. Flagg, A GUIDE TO MA LOCAL HISTORY, A BIBLIOGRAPHICAL INDEX TO THE LITERATURE OF TOWNS, CITIES, AND COUNTIES, Salem Press, Salem, MA, 1907.

_George Fingold Library, GENERAL INDEX OF, AND ARTICLES ON, MA PEOPLE AND PLACES, TO BE FOUND IN CERTAIN MA-IMPRINT PERIODICALS, The Library, Boston, MA, 1964.

_M. J. Kaminkow, US LOCAL HISTORIES IN THE LIBRARY OF CONGRESS, Magna Carta, Baltimore, MD, 1975, 4 volumes.

_P. W. Filby, BIBLIOGRAPHY OF COUNTY HISTORIES IN AMERICA, Genealogical Publishing Co., Baltimore, MD, 1985.

Most of the MA county, city, town, and community history volumes in these bibliographies can be found in NEHGS, SLM, BPL, and some are available in FHL(FHC). RL and LL are likely to have those relating to their particular areas. In Chapter 4, you will find listed under the counties, cities, and towns whether or not histories were published for each. This will facilitate your search and will make sure that you have seen the ones which are pertinent to your ancestor's area. In libraries, the easiest way to find local histories is to look in their catalogs under the names of the counties, cities, and towns. Communities are often listed under the towns. It is exceptionally important to read all local histories in your progenitor's region if you are going to understand the setting in which he/she lived, and thereby come to enter into his/her life more emphatically.

10. Colonial records

The colonial period of MA extended from 1620 to 1775. The period can be conveniently divided into the subperiods: Plymouth Colony (1620-92), MA Bay Colony (1630-92), and the Provincial Period (1692-1775). Many other sections in this chapter describe types of records relating to colonial MA, particularly the sections on census records (early census-like lists), church records, court records, DAR records, emigration and immigration records, land records, manuscripts, colonial and Revolutionary military records, newspaper records, town records, will and probate records, and vital records (births, marriages, deaths). This section presents the most important published colonial records, and is made up of five sub-sections: one dealing with general reference materials to all the colonies (including MA), a second which sets out published items on all of New England, a third treating volumes relating to Plymouth Colony (1620-92), a fourth having to do with books on MA Bay Colony (1630-92), and a fifth which gives colonial works applicable to all of MA (1620-1775).

Among the most important genealogical materials relating to all the colonies are the following. They should be consulted for your colonial MA ancestor. However, some of the volumes must be used with care since some of the information in them is not from original sources and is therefore often inaccurate.

_F. A. Virkus, THE ABRIDGED COMPENDIUM OF AMERICAN GENEALOGY, Genealogical Publishing Co., Baltimore, MD, 1968(1925-42), 7 volumes. [425,000 names of colonial people]

_G. M. MacKenzie and N. O. Rhoades, COLONIAL FAMILIES OF THE USA, Genealogical Publishing Co., Baltimore, MD, 1966(1907-20), 7 volumes. [125,000 names]

_H. Whittemore, GENEALOGICAL GUIDE TO THE EARLY SETTLERS OF AMERICA, Genealogical Publishing Co., Baltimore, MD, 1967(1898-

1906).

_T. P. Hughes and others, AMERICAN ANCESTRY, Genealogical Publishing Co., Baltimore, MD, 1968(1887-9), 12 volumes.

_BURKE'S DISTINGUISHED FAMILIES OF AMERICA, Burke's Peerage, London, England, 1948.

_C. E. Banks, PLANTERS OF THE COMMONWEALTH, Genealogical Publishing Co., Baltimore, MD, 1972.

_M. L. Call, INDEX TO THE COLONIAL AMERICAN GENEALOGY LIBRARY, Call, Salt Lake City, UT, 1982. Index to over 10,000 lineage charts in the NEHGS.

_G. R. Crowther, III, SURNAME INDEX TO 65 VOLUMES OF COLONIAL AND REVOLUTIONARY PEDIGREES, National Genealogical Society, Washington, DC, 1975.

_W. M. Clemens, AMERICAN MARRIAGE RECORDS BEFORE 1699, Genealogical Publishing Co., Baltimore, MD, 1926(1979). [10,000 entries]

_M. B. Colket, Jr., FOUNDERS OF EARLY AMERICAN FAMILIES, Order of Founders and Patriots of America, Cleveland, OH, 1985.

_H. K. Eilers, NSDAC BICENTENNIAL ANCESTOR INDEX, National Society Daughters of American Colonists, Ft. Worth, TX, 1976.

_National Society of Daughters of Founders and Patriots of America, FOUNDERS AND PATRIOTS OF AMERICA INDEX, The Society, Washington, DC, 1975.

_National Society of Colonial Dames of America, REGISTERS OF ANCESTORS, The Society, Richmond, VA, 1905/17/27/44/79.

_N. Currer-Briggs, COLONIAL SETTLERS AND ENGLISH ADVENTURERS, Genealogical Publishing Co., Baltimore, MD, 1971. [5000 names]

_N. Currer-Briggs, ENGLISH WILLS OF COLONIAL FAMILIES, Polyanthos, New Orleans, LA, 1972. [About 5000 names]

_P. W. Filby and M. K. Meyer, PASSENGER AND IMMIGRATION LISTS INDEX, Gale Research, Detroit, MI, 1981, 3 volumes, plus annual SUPPLEMENTS. [Over 1.6 million names]

_G. F. T. Sherwood, AMERICAN COLONISTS IN ENGLISH RECORDS, Sherwood, London, England, 1932, 2 volumes.

_P. W. Coldham, ENGLISH ESTATES OF AMERICAN COLONISTS, Genealogical Publishing Co., Baltimore, MD, 1980-1, 3 volumes.

_P. W. Coldham, ENGLISH ADVENTURERS AND EMIGRANTS, 1609-1773, Genealogical Publishing Co., Baltimore, MD, 1984/5.

_P. W. Coldham, THE COMPLETE BOOK OF EMIGRANTS, 1607-60, Genealogical Publishing Co., Baltimore, MD, 1987.

_P. W. Coldham, THE COMPLETE BOOK OF EMIGRANTS IN BONDAGE, 1614-1775, Genealogical Publishing Co., Baltimore, MD, 1988.

_P. W. Coldham, THE BRISTOL REGISTERS OF SERVANTS SENT TO FOREIGN PLANTATIONS, 1654-86, Genealogical Publishing Co., Baltimore, MD, 1988.

_G. Fothergill, EMIGRANTS FROM ENGLAND, 1773-6, Genealogical

Publishing Co., Baltimore, MD, 1964.

_E. French, LIST OF EMIGRANTS TO AMERICA FROM LIVERPOOL, 1697-1707, Genealogical Publishing Co., Baltimore, MD, 1962.

_M. Ghirelli, A LIST OF EMIGRANTS FROM ENGLAND TO AMERICA, 1682-92, Magna Carta, Baltimore, MD, 1968.

_J. and M. Kaminkow, A LIST OF EMIGRANTS FROM ENGLAND TO AMERICA, 1718-59, Magna Carta, Baltimore, MD, 1981.

_M. Tepper, PASSENGERS TO AMERICA, A CONSOLIDATION OF SHIP PASSENGER LISTS FROM THE NEW ENGLAND HISTORICAL AND GENEALOGICAL REGISTER, Genealogical Publishing Co., Baltimore, MD, 1977.

_J. Wareing, EMIGRANTS TO AMERICA, INDENTURED SERVANTS RECRUITED IN LONDON, 1718-33, Genealogical Publishing Co., Baltimore, MD, 1985.

_Daughters of the American Revolution, DAR PATRIOT INDEX, The Daughters, Washington, DC, 1966, 1979, 2 volumes.

_National Genealogical Society, INDEX OF REVOLUTIONARY WAR PENSION APPLICATIONS IN THE NATIONAL ARCHIVES, The Society, Washington, DC, 1976.

_F. Rider, THE AMERICAN GENEALOGICAL BIOGRAPHICAL INDEX, Godfrey Memorial Library, Middletown, CT, 1942-52, 48 volumes; THE AMERICAN GENEALOGICAL BIOGRAPHICAL INDEX, NEW SERIES, Godfrey Memorial Library, Middletown, CT, 1952-, in progress, over 140 volumes published.

_W. W. Spooner, HISTORIC FAMILIES OF AMERICA, The Author, New York, NY, 1907-8, 3 volumes. Be careful.

_H. D. Pittman, AMERICANS OF GENTLE BIRTH AND THEIR ANCESTORS, A GENEALOGICAL ENCYCLOPEDIA, Genealogical Publishing Co., Baltimore, MD, 1970.

_R. G. Thurtle and L. S. King, PEDIGREES OF DESCENDANTS OF THE COLONIAL CLERGY, Society of the Descendants of the Colonial Clergy, Lancaster, MA, 1976, with SUPPLEMENT, Mayo, Manchester, CT, 1978.

_Daughters of Colonial Wars, BICENTENNIAL ANCESTOR INDEX, The Daughters, Washington, DC, 1976.

_Daughters of Founders and Patriots of America, INDEX TO LINEAGE BOOKS, The Daughters, Somerville, MA, 1943, with recent SUPPLEMENTS.

_Daughters of American Colonists, BICENTENNIAL ANCESTOR INDEX, The Daughters, Washington, DC, 1976-84.

_National Society Colonial Dames 17th Century, 17TH CENTURY COLONIAL ANCESTORS, Genealogical Publishing Co., Baltimore, MD, 1976(1984).

_National Society of Colonial Daughters 17th Century, NEW LINEAGE BOOK, D. Baird, Rotan, TX, 1980.

_National Society Daughters of Colonial Wars, BICENTENNIAL ANCES-

TOR INDEX, R. Moncure, Clifton, VA, 1984.

_Order of Founders and Patriots of America, REGISTER, The Order, New York, NY, 1927, with SUPPLEMENTS, 1940, 1960, 1981.

_Society of Colonial Wars, INDEX TO ANCESTORS AND ROLL OF MEMBERS, The Society, New York, NY, 1921, with SUPPLEMENTS, 1941 and 1971.

_THE COLONIAL GENEALOGIST, incorporated later in THE AUGUSTAN, OMNIBUS VOLUMES, The Augustan Society, Harbor City, CA, 1970-.

_THE SECOND BOAT, SPECIALIZING IN COLONIAL GENEALOGY, Machias, ME, 1980-. Quarterly.

There are also important published record collections and published indexes relating to all of New England. Among the most useful of these for looking up your ancestor who came to MA before 1775 are the following volumes:

_J. Austin, ONE HUNDRED AND SIXTY ALLIED FAMILIES, Genealogical Publishing Co., Baltimore, MD, 1982.

_J. P. Baxter, THE PIONEERS OF NEW FRANCE IN NEW ENGLAND, 1720-5, Heritage Books, Bowie, MD, 1983.

_C. K. Bolton, THE REAL FOUNDERS OF NEW ENGLAND, 1602-28, Genealogical Publishing Co., Baltimore, MD, 1974. Pre-Mayflower settlers.

_E. S. Bolton, IMMIGRANTS TO NEW ENGLAND, 1700-75, Genealogical Publishing Co., Baltimore, MD, 1979.

_E. L. Coleman, NEW ENGLAND CAPTIVES CARRIED TO CANADA, 1677-1760, DURING THE FRENCH AND INDIAN WARS, Southworth Press, Portland, ME, 1925.

_S. G. Drake, A PARTICULAR HISTORY OF THE FIVE YEARS FRENCH AND INDIAN WAR IN NEW ENGLAND, Heritage Books, Bowie, MD, 1984. Participants in the war beginning in 1688.

_J. Farmer and S. G. Drake, A GENEALOGICAL REGISTER OF THE FIRST SETTLERS OF NEW ENGLAND, 1620-75, Genealogical Publishing Co., Baltimore, MD, 1983.

_E. W. Hanson, THE NON-ENGLISH NEW ENGLANDERS, A series beginning in the New England Historical and Genealogical Register, Volume 139.

_F. R. Holmes, DIRECTORY OF ANCESTRAL HEADS OF NEW ENGLAND FAMILIES, 1620-1700, Genealogical Publishing Co., Baltimore, MD, 1974.

_M. J. O'Brien, PIONEER IRISH IN NEW ENGLAND, Heritage Books, Bowie, MD, 1988.

_G. B. Roberts, ENGLISH ORIGINS OF NEW ENGLAND FAMILIES FROM THE NEW ENGLAND HISTORICAL AND GENEALOGICAL REGISTER, Genealogical Publishing Co., Baltimore, MD, 1984-5, 2 series, 3 volumes each. Over 1000 families.

_J. Savage, A GENEALOGICAL DICTIONARY OF THE FIRST SETTLERS OF NEW ENGLAND WHO CAME BEFORE 1692, Genealogical Publishing Co., Baltimore, MD, 1981, 4 volumes. Extremely important and useful, lists settlers who arrived in New England before 1692 and traces their descendants. Some errors.

_C. A. Torrey, NEW ENGLAND MARRIAGES PRIOR TO 1700, Genealogical Publishing Co., Baltimore, MD, 1985. Very important. Also available in manuscript and on microfilm. Microfilm and manuscript editions contain references to original sources.

_L. C. Towle, NEW ENGLAND ANNALS, HISTORY AND GENEALOGY, Heritage Books, Bowie, MD, 1980. Valuable sources with overall index.

_F. L. Weis, ANCESTRAL ROOTS OF 60 COLONISTS WHO CAME TO NEW ENGLAND BETWEEN 1623 and 1650, Genealogical Publishing Co., Baltimore, MD, 1976.

Now, let us turn to references to colonial MA. As indicated above, these will be treated under three headings: Plymouth Colony (1620-92), MA Bay Colony (1630-92), and all of MA (1620-1775). Published and some manuscript materials pertinent to the genealogy and history of Plymouth Colony (1620-92) include:

_A. A. Aspinwall, MANUSCRIPT COLLECTION ON PILGRIMS AND THEIR DESCENDANTS, New England Historic Genealogical Society, Boston, MA.

_C. E. Banks, THE ENGLISH ANCESTRY AND HOMES OF THE PILGRIM FATHERS WHO CAME TO PLYMOUTH IN 1620-1 and 1623, Genealogical Publishing Co., Baltimore, MD, 1979. [1250 names]

_G. E. Bowman, THE BOWMAN FILES, MA Society of Mayflower Descendants, Boston, MA, microfiche. Genealogies of Mayflower descendants. Also at NEHGS. Card index of names available at MA Society of Mayflower Descendants.

_G. E. Bowman, THE MAYFLOWER READER, Genealogical Publishing Co., Baltimore, MD, 1978. Articles from The Mayflower Descendant.

_W. T. Davis, GENEALOGICAL REGISTER OF PLYMOUTH FAMILIES, Genealogical Publishing Co., Baltimore, MD, 1977. Be careful.

_FAMILIES OF THE PILGRIMS, a set of pamphlets, MA Society of Mayflower Descendants, Boston, MA. [Mayflower passengers and three generations of descendants.]

_GENEALOGIES OF MAYFLOWER FAMILIES FROM THE NEW ENGLAND HISTORICAL AND GENEALOGICAL REGISTER, Genealogical Publishing Co., Baltimore, MD, 1985. Very important.

_A. A. Haxtun, SIGNERS OF THE MAYFLOWER COMPACT, Genealogical Publishing Co., Baltimore, MD, 1968. Signers and their families.

_L. C. Hills, HISTORY AND GENEALOGY OF THE MAYFLOWER PLANTERS AND FIRST COMERS TO YE OLDE COLONIE, Genealogical Publishing Co., Baltimore, MD, 1975. Be careful.

_L. M. Kellogg et al., MAYFLOWER FAMILIES THROUGH FIVE GENERATIONS, General Society of Mayflower Descendants, Plymouth, MA, 1975-, several volumes so far, more to come.

_D. T. Konig, PLYMOUTH COURT RECORDS, 1686-1859, Glazier, Wilmington, DE, 1978-81, 16 volumes. Very important. Only Plymouth County, not all of Plymouth Colony.

_J. T. Landis, MAYFLOWER DESCENDANTS AND THEIR MARRIAGES FOR TWO GENERATIONS AFTER THE LANDING, Genealogical Publishing Co., Baltimore, MD, 1981.

_THE MAYFLOWER DESCENDANT, MA Society of Mayflower Descendants, Boston, MA, 1899-1937, 1985-, with INDEX OF PERSONS, VOLUMES 1-34, MA Society of Mayflower Descendants, Boston, MA, 1959-62.

_THE MAYFLOWER QUARTERLY, General Society of Mayflower Descendants, Plymouth, MA, 1935-. Very important.

_W. A. McAuslan and L. E. Neff, MAYFLOWER INDEX, The General Society of Mayflower Descendants of DC, Washington, DC, 1960, with the DC REGISTER, The Society, Washington, DC, 1970.

_National Society of Sons and Daughters of the Pilgrims, LINEAGES OF MEMBERS, The Society, Philadelphia, PA, and Manchester, CT, 1929/53/81, 3 volumes.

_National Society of Old Plymouth Colony Descendants, LIST OF MEMBERS, The Society, Plymouth, MA, 1968.

_E. W. Peirce, PEIRCE'S COLONIAL LISTS OF PLYMOUTH AND RI COLONIES, Genealogical Publishing Co., Baltimore, MD, 1968.

_PILGRIM NOTES AND QUERIES, MA Society of Mayflower Descendants, Boston, MA, 1913-7, 5 volumes.

_PLYMOUTH CHURCH RECORDS, 1620-1859, Genealogical Publishing Co., Baltimore, MD, 1975. Very important.

_THE PLYMOUTH COLONY GENEALOGICAL HELPER and THE PLYMOUTH COLONY GENEALOGIST, The Augustan Society, Torrance, CA, 1974-.

_C. H. Pope, THE PLYMOUTH SCRAP BOOK, Goodspeed, Boston, MA, 1918.

_G. B. Roberts, MAYFLOWER SOURCE RECORDS FROM THE NEW ENGLAND HISTORICAL AND GENEALOGICAL REGISTER, Genealogical Publishing Co., Baltimore, MD, 1986. Very important.

_G. B. Roberts, MAYFLOWER SOURCE RECORDS, PRIMARY DATA CONCERNING SOUTHEASTERN MA, Genealogical Publishing Co., Baltimore, MD, 1986. Very important.

_H. K. Shaw, FAMILIES OF THE PILGRIMS, MA Society of Mayflower Descendants, Boston, MA, 1956.

_R. W. Sherman and R. S. Wakefield, PLYMOUTH COLONY PROBATE GUIDE, 1620-91, Plymouth Colony Research Group, Warwick, RI, 1983. Very useful.

_N. B. Shurtleff and E. G. Bowman, PLYMOUTH COLONY, RECORDS OF

BIRTHS, MARRIAGES, DEATHS, BURIALS, AND OTHER RECORDS, 1633-89, Genealogical Publishing Co., Baltimore, MD, 1979. Very important.

_N. B. Shurtleff and D. Pulsifer, RECORDS OF NEW PLYMOUTH COLONY, 1620-92, AMS Press, New York, NY, 1968, 6 volumes. Very important.

_F. R. Stoddard, THE TRUTH ABOUT THE PILGRIMS, Genealogical Publishing Co., Baltimore, MD, 1973. Exercise caution.

_E. A. Stratton, PLYMOUTH COLONY, ITS HISTORY AND PEOPLE, 1620-91, Ancestry, Salt Lake City, UT, 1986. Very important.

_M. E. Terry and A. B. Harding, MAYFLOWER ANCESTRAL INDEX, General Society of Mayflower Descendants, Plymouth, MA, 1981. Exercise caution.

_R. W. Wakefield, PLYMOUTH COLONY MARRIAGES TO 1650, Society of Mayflower Descendants of RI, Warwick, RI, 1980.

_R. W. Wakefield and numerous other compilers, MAYFLOWER FAMILIES IN PROGRESS, General Society of Mayflower Descendants, Plymouth, MA, 1980-, several volumes.

Published materials giving genealogical information on inhabitants of <u>MA Bay Colony</u> (1630-92) are numerous. Some of those carrying large numbers of names and/or important historical data are as follows:

_C. E. Banks, THE PLANTERS OF THE COMMONWEALTH, EMIGRATION IN COLONIAL TIMES, LISTS OF PASSENGERS TO BOSTON AND THE BAY COLONY, THE SHIPS THAT BROUGHT THEM, THEIR ENGLISH HOMES, AND WHERE THEY SETTLED IN MA, 1620-40, Genealogical Publishing Co., Baltimore, MD, 1979. [1250 names.]

_C. E. Banks, THE WINTHROP FLEET OF 1630, THE VESSELS, THE VOYAGE, THE PASSENGERS, AND THEIR ENGLISH HOMES, Genealogical Publishing Co., Baltimore, MD, 1980. Use with care; some English origins have been subject to correction.

_R. J. Crandall and R. J. Coffman, FROM EMIGRANTS TO RULERS, THE CHARLESTOWN OLIGARCHY IN THE GREAT MIGRATION, New England Historical and Genealogical Register, Volume 131, 1977. [Many names.]

_E. George, MA Probate Court, INDEX TO THE PROBATE RECORDS OF THE COUNTY OF SUFFOLK, 1636-1893, Rockwell and Churchill, Boston, MA, 1895, 3 volumes.

_S. F. Haven, RECORDS OF THE COMPANY OF MA BAY, 1628-41, Bolles and Houghton, Cambridge, MA, 1850.

_J. M. Holbrook, BOSTON BEGINNINGS, 1630-99, Holbrook Research Institute, Oxford, MA, 1980. [Over 16,000 names, many vital records.]

_M. P. Kuhns, THE MARY AND JOHN, A STORY OF THE FOUNDING OF DORCHESTER, MA, 1630, Tuttle, Rutland, VT, 1980.

_S. E. Morison, MA COUNTY COURT, SUFFOLK COUNTY, 1671-80,

The Colonial Society of MA, Boston, MA, 1933, 2 volumes.
_J. Noble and J. F. Cronin, RECORDS OF THE COURT OF ASSISTANTS OF THE COLONY OF MA BAY, 1630-92, Rockwell and Churchill, Boston, MA, 1901-28, 3 volumes.
_R. D. Peirce, RECORDS OF THE FIRST CHURCH OF BOSTON, 1630-1868, Colonial Society of MA, Boston, MA, 1941, 3 volumes.
_N. B. Shurtleff, RECORDS OF THE GOVERNOR AND COMPANY OF MA BAY IN NEW ENGLAND, 1628-86, AMS Press, New York, NY, 1971, 6 volumes. Very important.
_B. W. Spear, SEARCH FOR THE PASSENGERS OF THE MARY AND JOHN, 1630, The Mary and John Clearing House, Toledo, OH, 1985-7, 10 volumes, the last a master index.
_SUFFOLK DEEDS, 1629-97, Suffolk County, Boston, MA, 1880-1906, 14 volumes. Includes indexes by grantor, grantee, and other persons.
_A. Young, CHRONICLES OF THE FIRST PLANTERS OF THE COLONY OF MA BAY, 1623-36, Genealogical Publishing Co., Baltimore, MD, 1975.

There are also a sizable number of publications and some other items of genealogical data applying to <u>all of colonial MA</u>. Among the most valuable of these are:
_C. E. Banks and E. E. Brownell, TOPOGRAPHICAL DICTIONARY OF 2885 EMIGRANTS TO NEW ENGLAND, 1620-50, Genealogical Publishing Co., Baltimore, MD, 1974. Use with care.
_P. Belliveau, FRENCH NEUTRALS IN MA, ACADIANS ROUNDED UP BY SOLDIERS FROM MA AND THEIR CAPTIVITY IN THE BAY PROVINCE, 1755-66, Giffen, Boston, MA, 1972.
_J. H. Benton, EARLY CENSUS MAKING IN MA, 1643-1765, WITH THE LOST CENSUS OF 1765, The Compiler, Boston, MA, 1905.
_G. M. Bodge, SOLDIERS IN KING PHILIP'S WAR, Genealogical Publishing Co., Baltimore, MD, 1976. Soldiers, grantees, claimants, some heirs of deceased soldiers.
_C. K. Bolton, THE FOUNDERS, PERSONS WHO CAME TO THE COLONIES BEFORE 1701, WITH BIOGRAPHICAL OUTLINES, Genealogical Publishing Co., Baltimore, MD, 1976, 2 volumes.
_V. Q. Bond and C. W. Fuller, REGISTER OF ANCESTORS, THE NATIONAL SOCIETY OF COLONIAL DAMES OF AMERICA IN MA, The Society, Boston, MA, 1975.
_Boston Registry Department and W. S. Appleton, INDEX TO BOSTON BIRTHS, BAPTISMS, MARRIAGES, AND DEATHS, 1630-1800, Genealogical Publishing Co., Baltimore, MD, 1978. Births 1630-1800. Marriages and deaths 1630-99.
_Boston Registry Department and S. C. Gladden, INDEX TO 1630-99 BOSTON BIRTHS, BAPTISMS, MARRIAGES, AND DEATHS, The Indexer, Boulder, CO, 1969. Over 14,000 records.
_Boston Registry Department, RECORDS RELATING TO THE EARLY

HISTORY OF BOSTON, The Record Commissioners, Boston, MA, 1876-1909, 32 volumes. Thousands of names from births, marriages, deaths, land records, tax lists, wills, selectmen's records, and town meeting records.

_Boston Registry Department and W. H. Whitmore, PORT ARRIVALS AND IMMIGRANTS TO THE CITY OF BOSTON, 1715-6 and 1762-69, Genealogical Publishing Co., Baltimore, MD, 1973. Over 3000 names. Taken from above series.

_Boston Registry Department and E. W. McGleven, BOSTON MARRIAGES, 1700-1809, Genealogical Publishing Co., Baltimore, MD, 1977. 75,000 persons. Taken from the 32-volume series above.

_L. Brownson, G. Held, and D. Norton, MANUSCRIPT COLLECTION OF GENEALOGICAL NOTES OF CAPE COD FAMILIES, Sturgis Library, Barnstable, MA. Many southeastern MA families.

_CARD INDEX TO THE MA ARCHIVES, MSA, Boston, MA. Index to many volumes of MA documents 1629-1799.

_O. Codman, INDEX TO OBITUARIES IN BOSTON NEWSPAPERS, 1704-1800, Hall, Boston, MA, 1968, 3 volumes. Deaths in and out of Boston.

_M. R. Cowan, THE NATIONAL SOCIETY OF WOMEN DESCENDANTS OF THE ANCIENT AND HONORABLE ARTILLERY COMPANY, MEMBERS IN THE COLONIAL PERIOD, The Society, Washington, DC, 1958.

_M. E. Donahue, MA OFFICERS AND SOLDIERS, 1702-22, QUEEN ANNE'S WAR TO DUMMER'S WAR, Society of Colonial Wars in MA and the New England Historic Genealogical Society, Boston, MA, 1980. Over 3000 military men.

_C. Doreski, MA OFFICERS AND SOLDIERS IN THE 17TH CENTURY CONFLICTS, Society of Colonial Wars in the Commonwealth of MA and the New England Historic Genealogical Society, Boston, MA, 1982.

_E. George, MA Probate Court, INDEX TO THE PROBATE RECORDS OF THE COUNTY OF SUFFOLK, 1636-1893, Rockwell and Churchill, Boston, MA, 1895, 3 volumes.

_K. D. Goss and D. Zarowin, MA OFFICERS AND SOLDIERS IN THE FRENCH AND INDIAN WARS, 1755-6, New England Historic Genealogical Society, Boston, MA, 1985. Over 2300 listings with numerous places of birth.

_HISTORY AND LINEAGE BOOKS 1-7 OF THE NATIONAL SOCIETY OF WOMEN DESCENDANTS OF THE ANCIENT AND HONORABLE ARTILLERY COMPANY, The Society, Washington, DC, 1940-80.

_R. V. Jackson, EARLY MA, Accelerated Indexing Systems, Bountiful, UT, 1980. Many names from many sources.

_B. Kenyon, MA HERALDICA, AN ILLUSTRATED COMPILATION OF ARMS COMPRISING AN ALPHABETICAL LIST OF 103 ARMIGEROUS MEMBERS OF THE ANCIENT AND HONORABLE ARTILLERY COMPANY, 1637-1774, The National Society of Women Descendants of the Ancient and Honorable Artillery Company, Washington, DC, 1968.

_R. E. Mackay, MA SOLDIERS IN THE FRENCH AND INDIAN WARS, 1744-55, Society of Colonial Wars in MA and the New England Historic Genealogical Society, Boston, MA, 1978.
_E. W. McGleven, BOSTON MARRIAGES FROM 1700 TO 1809, Genealogical Publishing Co., Baltimore, MD, 1977.
_MA Colony, THE ACTS AND RESOLVES, PUBLIC AND PRIVATE, OF THE PROVINCE OF MA BAY, 1692-1780, Wright and Potter, Boston, MA, 1869-1922, 21 volumes.
_L. R. Paige, LIST OF FREEMEN OF MA, 1630-91, with E. P. Bentley, INDEX, Genealogical Publishing Co., Baltimore, MD, 1980. [4500 names] Very important.
_R. D. Peirce, THE RECORDS OF THE FIRST CHURCH OF BOSTON, 1630-1868, Colonial Society of MA, Boston, MA, 1941, 3 volumes.
_C. H. Pope, THE PIONEERS OF MA, Genealogical Publishing Co., Baltimore, MD, 1977. [About 5000 early settlers] Very important.
_B. H. Pruit, THE MA TAX VALUATION LIST OF 1771, Hall, Boston, MA, 1978.
_PUBLICATIONS OF THE COLONIAL SOCIETY OF MA, The Society, Boston, MA, Volumes 1-, 1895-, with INDEX TO VOLUMES 1-25.
_M O. Stachiw, MA OFFICERS AND SOLDIERS 1723-43, DUMMER'S WAR TO THE WAR OF JENKIN'S EAR, Society of Colonial Wars in the Commonwealth of MA and the New England Historic Genealogical Society, Boston, MA, 1979.
_N. E. Voye, MA OFFICERS IN THE FRENCH AND INDIAN WARS, 1748-63, Society of Colonial Wars in the Commonwealth of MA and the New England Historic Genealogical Society, Boston, MA, 1975. [Over 6500 officers.]
_H. F. Waters, GENEALOGICAL GLEANINGS IN ENGLAND, Genealogical Publishing Co., Baltimore, MD, 1969. [Early migrants to MA.]
_W. H. Whitmore, THE MA CIVIL LIST FOR THE COLONIAL AND PROVINCIAL PERIODS, 1630-1774, Genealogical Publishing Co., Baltimore, MD, 1969. [About 1000 names of civil officials.]

Most of the published works mentioned in the previous paragraphs are available in NEHGS and BPL, and many in MSA, SLM, and FHL(FHC), and some in LGL, RL, and larger LL. As was indicated at the beginning of this section, numerous other sections of this chapter give references to other colonial records. These should not be overlooked. Some of the above works will be listed again in sections to which they are very important so that you will not run any chance of overlooking them. The possibility of finding your colonial ancestor in the above volumes is fairly high provided you take the time and pains to carefully examine them all.

11. Court records

Down through the many years of the existence of the colony and the state (commonwealth) of MA, its laws have been administered by a wide variety of courts. These courts may be seen during all these years as operating at three levels: the upper level (courts operating at the colony or state level), the intermediate level (courts operating at the local or county level), and the lower level (courts operating chiefly in towns and cities). Each MA court, with some exceptions at the lower level, had a clerk or register or recorder who kept the records. Among the most important records generally kept by most of the courts were: (1) docket books listing cases in chronological order, (2) file papers or documents giving detailed accounts of the cases, (3) record books with case summaries and often with indexes. Since the early settlements in MA, the names of the various courts have undergone a number of changes, and so have the jurisdictions. These changes sometimes accompanied alterations in the overall governance of the colony or state. In the sections below the three levels of courts will be discussed historically and then the available records for each will be treated.

At the upper level, both Plymouth Colony and MA Bay Colony began with a legislature which was called the General Court. Early on they sat as a court, but very soon they both established a Court of Assistants which took over almost all judicial matters. These bodies consisted of the governor and his assistants. In 1686, when Plymouth and MA Bay Colonies were combined with others into the Dominion of New England, the courts were reorganized. The Dominion was given two upper courts, one called the Court of the President and the Council (1686) which was renamed the Court of the Governor and the Council (1686-9), and the other was known as the Superior Court of Judicature (1687-9). Then in 1689, when the Dominion was abandoned, the Court of Assistants was restored for a few years (1689-92). In 1691, MA Bay and Plymouth, along with some other territory, were combined into the Province of MA Bay, and the upper court took the name of Superior Court of Judicature (1692-1780). This court handled major cases, acted as an appeals court for intermediate and lower courts, and held sessions in each MA county. The court was renamed the Supreme Judicial Court when the state constitution was adopted in 1780. It has continued as such since then, except that it gradually became chiefly an appellate court. A subsidiary State Appeals Court to relieve the case load was set up in 1972. The development of these upper level courts is made clear by the chart in Figure 17.

Records of the series of MA upper-level courts are available as follows. Some important finding aids are also listed.

_MA GENERAL COURT [LEGISLATURE] COLONY RECORDS, 1629-1777, manuscript at MSA, Boston, MA, 35 volumes. Also on microfilm at FHL(FHC).

_N. B. Shurtleff and D. Pulsifer, RECORDS OF NEW PLYMOUTH COLO-

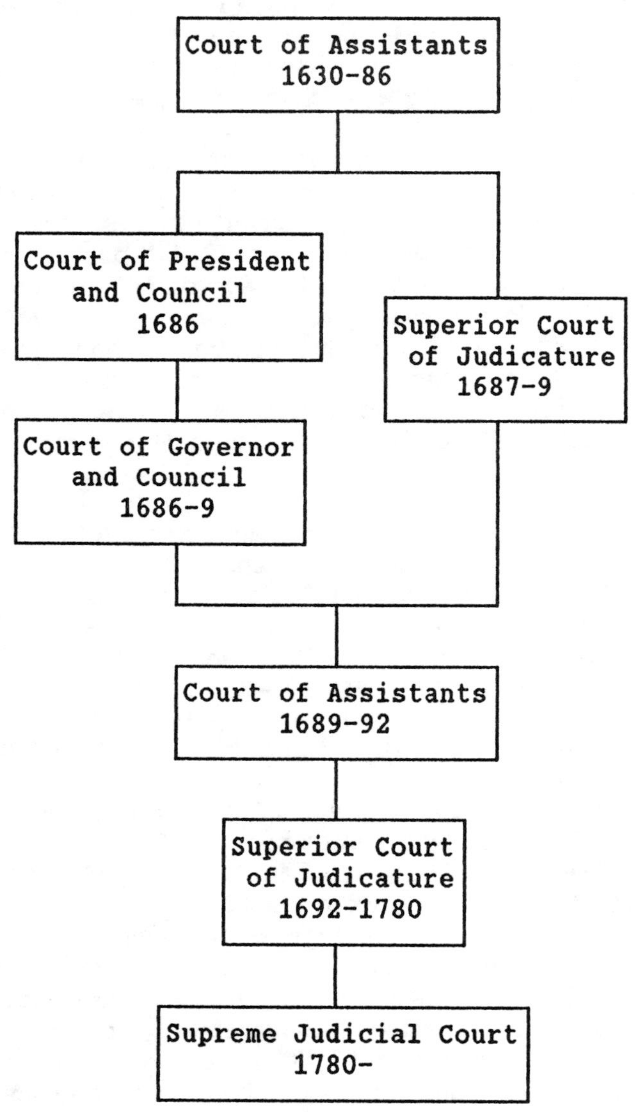

Figure 17. Upper Level Courts of MA

NY, 1620-92, AMS Press, New York, NY, 1968, 6 volumes.

_J. Noble and J. F. Cronin, RECORDS OF THE COURT OF ASSISTANTS OF THE COLONY OF MA BAY, 1630-92, Rockwell and Churchill, Boston, MA, 1901-28, 3 volumes.

_N. B. Shurtleff, RECORDS OF THE GOVERNOR AND COMPANY OF MA BAY IN NEW ENGLAND, 1628-86, AMS Press, New York, NY, 1972, 1971, 6 volumes.

_ORIGINAL COURT OF ASSISTANTS RECORDS OF PLYMOUTH COLONY, in Plymouth County Records, at Plymouth, MA. Microfilm copy in MSA.

_ORIGINAL COURT OF ASSISTANTS RECORDS OF MA BAY COLONY, in Suffolk Files Collection, Judicial Archives, MSA, Boston, MA. On microfilm at University of MA in Amherst and MA Historical Society at Boston. Also at FHL(FHC).

_ORIGINAL RECORDS OF THE SUPERIOR COURT OF JUDICATURE, 1692-1780, in Suffolk Files Collection, Judicial Archives, MSA, Boston, MA. On microfilm at University of MA in Amherst and MA Historical Society in Boston. Indexed. Also at FHL(FHC).

_J. Quincy, Jr., REPORTS OF CASES ARGUED AND ADJUDGED IN THE SUPERIOR COURT OF JUDICATURE OF THE PROVINCE OF MA BAY, 1761-72, Little, Brown, Boston, MA, 1865.

_ORIGINAL RECORDS OF THE SUPREME JUDICIAL COURT, 1780-, in each county in the Office of the Clerk of the Supreme Judicial Court or in MSA, with records of the full bench since 1859 in the Office of the Clerk of the Supreme Judicial Court of the Commonwealth. Some original records for Berkshire (1783-1862), Bristol (1796-1861), Franklin (1816-63), Hampden (1816-59), Hampshire (1797-1861), Middlesex (1797-1860), Norfolk (1801-62), Suffolk (1780-1860), and Worcester (1797-1861) Counties, and the Commonwealth (1859) transferred to Judicial Archives, MSA, Boston, MA; others being added. Microfilms of records 1780-1800 at University of MA in Amherst and MA Historical Society in Boston.

_CATALOGUE OF THE RECORDS AND FILES OF THE OFFICE OF THE CLERK, SUPREME JUDICIAL COURT, 1692-1797, Getchell, Boston, MA, 1897. Applies to entire colony/state.

_MA REPORTS OF CASES ARGUED BEFORE THE SUPREME JUDICIAL COURT OF MA, 1804-, Little and Brown and other publishers, Boston, MA, 1838-. Reports of all Supreme Judicial Court cases, with indexes.

_MA COLONIAL COURT RECORDS INDEX, 1664-1781, MSA, Boston, MA. A large name card file. Also on microfilm at FHL(FHC).

_D. T. Konig, PLYMOUTH COURT RECORDS, 1686-1859, Glazier, Wilmington, DE, 1978-81, 16 volumes. Unindexed.

_C. D. Wright, REPORT OF THE CUSTODY AND CONDITION OF THE PUBLIC RECORDS OF PARISHES, TOWNS, AND COUNTIES, Wright and Potter, Boston, MA, 1889, pages 305-64. Detailed listing of MA court records, including the Superior Court of Judicature and its successor the Supreme Judicial Court.

At the intermediate level in the MA court system, courts in regions of MA, generally called Inferior Quarter Courts (1636-43) began functioning, then became County Courts (1643-92) when MA Bay set up counties in 1643. Under the short-lived Dominion which came into place in 1686, these County Courts split into Courts of Common Pleas (1686-9) and Courts of Sessions (1686-9), which promptly reunited in 1689 to once again become County Courts (1689-92). When the Province of MA Bay was established in 1691, the courts were reorganized, three courts came into existence to replace each County Court: Inferior Courts of Common Pleas (1692-1782), Courts of General Sessions of the Peace (1692-1808), and Judges of Probate (1692-1783). The Judges of Probate were established in 1783 as Probate Courts (1783-) and have continued as such since. The Inferior Courts of Common Pleas (1692-1782) became the Courts of Common Pleas (1782-1811), then the Circuit Courts of Common Pleas (1811-21), then the Courts of Common Pleas of the Commonwealth (1821-59), then the Superior Courts (1859-present). All of those 1692-1859 are generally referred to as Courts of Common Pleas, but there were two specially designated ones during the time 1692-1859: the Boston Court of Common Pleas (1813-21) and the Superior Court for Suffolk County (1855-9). The Courts of General Sessions (1692-1808) became in 1808 Courts of Sessions (1808-27), but during the period 1808-27, they were coalesced with the Courts of Common Pleas, the exact dates differing for different counties. All of these changes can be more clearly seen in Figure 18 which shows the development of the intermediate courts.

Some of the records of some of the intermediate courts have been published, many have been microfilmed, some have to be sought in the counties, and some have been transferred to the MSA. Their availability is as follows. In general, the records will be referred to as those from the County Courts (1636-92), the Courts of Common Pleas (1692-1859), the Courts of General Sessions (1692-1827), and the Superior Courts (1855- for Suffolk, 1859- for other counties).

_ORIGINAL RECORDS OF COUNTY COURTS, 1636-92, located in each county and/or MSA, except Suffolk County records in Suffolk Files Collection, MSA, Boston, MA, and records of Old Norfolk County in Essex County records. Microfilm copies of Suffolk County records at University of MA in Amherst and MA Historical Society. Microfilm copies for many counties in FHL(FHC) and MSA. Original records for Middlesex (1649-99) transferred to MSA.

_S. E. Morison, RECORDS OF THE SUFFOLK COUNTY COURT, 1671-80, Colonial Society of MA, Boston, MA, 1933, 2 volumes.

_G. F. Dow, RECORDS AND FILES OF THE QUARTERLY COURTS OF

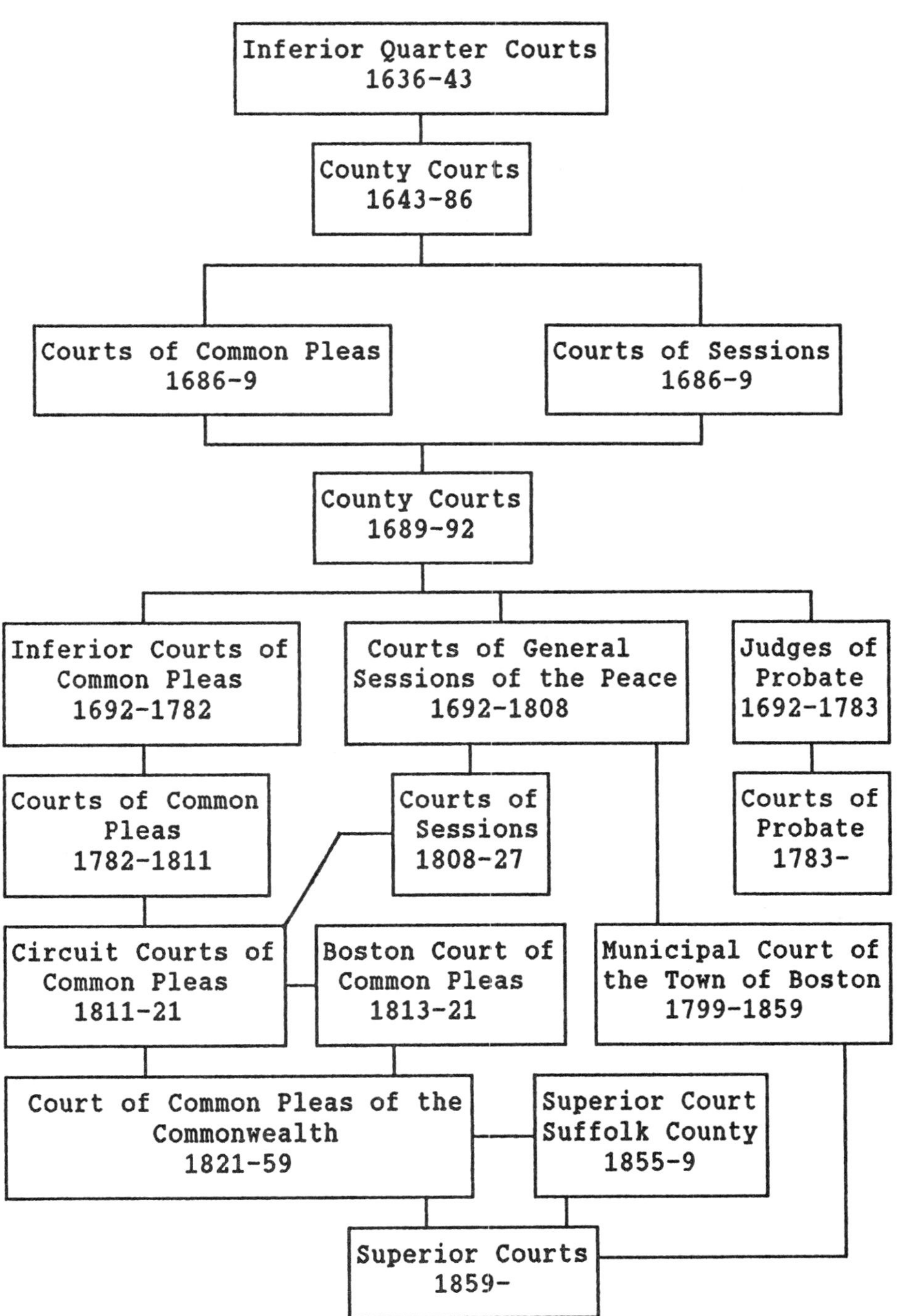

Figure 18. Intermediate Level Courts of MA

ESSEX COUNTY, MA, 1636-92, Essex Institute, Salem, MA, 1911-21, 8 volumes.

_N. B. Shurtleff and D. Pulsifer, RECORDS OF NEW PLYMOUTH COLONY, 1620-92, AMS Press, New York, NY, 1968, 6 volumes.

_SUFFOLK COUNTY AND OTHER COUNTY COURT FILES, 1629-1797, with indexes, MSA, Boston, MA. Also on microfilm at FHL(FHC).

_M. S. Hindus, A GUIDE TO THE COURT RECORDS OF EARLY MA, in D. R. Coquillette, R. J. Brink, and C. S. Menand, LAW IN COLONIAL MA, Boston, MA, 1985, pages 531-40, and C. S. Menand, RESEARCH GUIDE TO THE MA COURTS RECORDS, MSA, Boston, MA, 1987, p. 137 (microfiche appendix). The first is an inventory of court records available for MA counties. The second is a guide to the courts of MA and includes a listing of such records in the MSA as of 1987. There are many more now.

_ORIGINAL RECORDS OF COURTS OF GENERAL SESSIONS, 1692-1827, located in each county and/or in MSA, except Suffolk County Records in Suffolk Files Collection, MSA, Boston, MA. Microfilm of Suffolk records up to 1780 at University of MA in Amherst and at MA Historical Society in Boston. Microfilm copies for many counties in FHL(FHC) and MSA. Some original records for Berkshire (1762-1827), Bristol (1697-1830), Franklin (1812-28), Hampden (1783-1846), Hampshire (1721-1827), Middlesex (1737-1828), and Norfolk (1794-1856) Counties transferred to MSA, Boston, MA. Others being added.

_ORIGINAL RECORDS OF COURTS OF COMMON PLEAS, 1692-1859, located in each county and/or in MSA. Some of the records for Suffolk County are in Suffolk Files Collection, MSA, Boston, MA. These records are also on microfilm at the University of MA in Amherst and at the MA Historical Society in Boston. Microfilm copies for many counties in FHL(FHC) and MSA. Some original records for Berkshire (1761-1859), Bristol (1694-1859), Franklin (1812-59), Hampden (1812-59), Hampshire (1712-1859), Middlesex (1693-1859, Norfolk (1790-1859), and Worcester (1731-1859) Counties transferred to MSA, Boston, MA. Others being added.

_D. T. Konig, PLYMOUTH COURT RECORDS, 1686-1859, Glazier, Wilmington, DE, 1978-81, 16 volumes. Unindexed.

_ORIGINAL RECORDS OF SUPERIOR COURTS, 1859-, located in each county. Microfilm copies for some counties in FHL(FHC) and MSA.

_MA COLONIAL COURT RECORDS INDEX, 1664-1781, MSA, Boston, MA. A large name card file. Also on microfilm at FHL(FHC).

_Historical Records Survey, ABSTRACT AND INDEX OF THE RECORDS OF THE INFERIOR COURT OF PLEAS, SUFFOLK COUNTY COURT, 1680-98, WPA, Boston, MA, 1940.

At the beginning, the <u>lower</u> level of courts in MA was represented by magistrates courts (1631-86) which dealt with minor cases and usually functioned in each town. In 1686, these were redesignated as Justice of the Peace Courts (1686-) and have continued to the present. Much later, especially in centers where the population had grown quite large, lower courts with expanded jurisdiction were set up to assist the intermediate courts. In 1821 Police Courts (1821-1921) began to be established as needed. By 1859 there were 22 Police Courts in MA. The Boston Police Court (1821-66) became in 1866 the Boston Municipal Court (1866-), and shortly thereafter District Courts (1869-) began to replace the other Police Courts, these new courts encompassing several towns. The change from Police to District Courts was completed by 1921. The records are available as follows:

_ORIGINAL RECORDS OF MAGISTRATES AND JUSTICES OF THE PEACE, mostly as personal manuscripts in local repositories (libraries, historical societies), MA Historical Society, BPL, American Antiquarian Society, MSA, and others. Those in MSA include ones for Berkshire (1765-1831), Bristol (1726-1864), Franklin (1816-96), Hampshire (1787-1881), Middlesex (1789-1809), and Worcester (1777-1836) Counties. Others being added.

_ORIGINAL RECORDS OF POLICE COURTS AND DISTRICT COURTS (1821-), located in offices of the Clerks of the District Courts.

In addition to the above upper, intermediate, and lower-level courts, MA also had some special courts. The probate courts have already been mentioned, and their records will be discussed in detail in a later section on will and probate records. Various MA courts were involved in the naturalization process, and there is a later section which deals with which courts these were and with the records they generated. Admiralty (maritime) matters were handled by some of the early colony-wide courts and later by separate admiralty or maritime courts up until the ratification of the Federal Constitution (1788): Court of Assistants (1630-92), Admiralty Judges under direct jurisdiction of the British Crown (1692-1775), Maritime Courts (1775-88).

_RECORDS OF THE COURTS OF ADMIRALTY, 1714-72, MSA, Boston, MA.

You should also know about coroner's courts which look into suspicious deaths (inquests). Such records are to be found in the county court records up to 1692, then afterwards they appear in the records of the courts of general sessions and their successor courts until 1877. Following that date, reports are filed in the district courts. Excellent detailed treatments of MA courts and their records will be found in:

_C. S. Menand, RESEARCH GUIDE TO THE MA COURT RECORDS, MSA, Boston, MA, 1987.

_W. T. Davis, HISTORY OF THE JUDICIARY OF MA, Boston Book Co., Boston, MA, 1900.

In considering court records pertaining to MA, the federal circuit and district courts should not be overlooked. The entire state of MA was designated as a federal judicial district in 1789 and has remained so ever since. The records of the two courts and a printed source are:

_RECORDS OF THE US DISTRICT COURT FOR MA, 1789-1956, NABB, Waltham, MA.

_RECORDS OF THE US CIRCUIT COURT FOR MA, 1790-1911, NABB, Waltham, MA.

_M. M. Johnson and E. Everly, RECORDS OF THE US DISTRICT COURT FOR THE DISTRICTS OF ME, MA, AND NJ, National Archives and Records Service, Washington, DC, 1963.

There is an exceptionally useful set of volumes which indexes plaintiffs in MA appeal cases and in many cases of notable legal interest, including cases in some of the above-listed courts. No MA researcher should overlook this resource in an ancestor quest:

_1906 DECENNIAL EDITION OF THE AMERICAN DIGEST: A COMPLETE TABLE OF AMERICAN CASES FROM 1658 TO 1906, West Publishing Co., St. Paul, MN, 1911, Volumes 21-25. Alphabetical by surname. Subsequent volumes cover decade periods up to the present.

Included in this massive index are MA cases from the Supreme Judicial Court for the period from 1804 forward, plus appealed cases from Federal Courts operating in MA. Another volume which indexes MA cases from state and federal courts, the indexing being both by plaintiff and defendant, is:

_MA DIGEST ANNOTATED, 1761-1933, Little, Brown, and Co., Boston, MA, 1952, Volumes 20, 20A, 21.

Courts covered are the Superior Court of MA, the Supreme Judicial Court of MA, the Municipal Court of Boston, the US District Court, the US Circuit Court, the US Circuit Court of Appeals, the US Court of Appeals, and the US Supreme Court. You must under no circumstances fail to look up all your MA progenitors in these two very large indexes (1906 Decennial and MA Digest). They, along with the hundreds of volumes to which they refer, will be found in large law libraries. These can be most readily located in Colleges of Law at universities.

As you probably have noticed, some MA court records (Supreme Judicial Court, Court of General Sessions, Court of Common Pleas, Justice of Peace) for some counties have recently been transferred from the counties to the MSA. Others still remain in the counties. It is therefore important to search in both places when you are seeking these records. The following MA agency is supervising the transfer and preservation of these records. For detailed information on the location of these court records, you may contact:

_Commonwealth of MA, Supreme Judicial Court, Archives and Records Preservation, 1600 New Court House, Boston, MA 02108.

12. DAR records

The MA chapters of the Daughters of the American Revolution have done genealogists a helpful service by compiling and indexing a number of volumes (mostly typescript) of MA family history records. Included in these books are records of the following types: Bible, birth, cemetery, church, death, deed, landowner, marriage, military, newspaper, town, and will/ probate. These works will generally be found in the NEHGS, the BPL, pertinent RL and LL, and in the DAR Library in Washington, DC.

_DAR Chapters of MA, DAR COLLECTION FOR MA, numerous volumes, by different chapters, at several places in MA.

The following towns are represented in the collection. At least one type of record is included for each town. In Barnstable County [Barnstable, Brewster, Dennis, Falmouth, Provincetown, Truro, Yarmouth], in Berkshsire County [Alford, Egremont, Great Barrington, Homestead, New Marlboro, Otis, Peru, Sandisfield, Savoy, Sheffield, Stockbridge, Tyringham, Windsor], in Bristol County [Attleboro, Berkley, Dighton, Mansfield, New Bedford, Taunton], in Essex County [Andover, Haverhill, Lawrence, Marblehead, Merrimac, North Andover], in Franklin County [Bernardston, Conway, Heath, Montague, Northfield, Rowe], in Hampden County [Blandford, Chicopee, Granville, Longmeadow, Montgomery, Springfield, Wales, West Springfield, Westfield, Wilbraham], in Hampshire County [Chesterfield, Goshen, Granby, Northampton, Southampton, Ware, Westhampton], in Middlesex County [Arlington, Ashby, Ashland, Bedford, Billerica, Cambridge, Carlisle, Concord, Dracut, Dunstable, Holliston, Hopkinton, Lincoln, Lowell, Marlborough, Melrose, Natick, Newton, Pepperell, Somerville, Stoneham, Townsend, Wakefield, Watertown, Wilmington], in Norfolk County [Braintree, Needham, Quincy, Randolph, Stoughton], in Plymouth County [Abington, Marshfield, Rochester], in Suffolk County [Boston], and in Worcester County [Athol, Barre, Fitchburg, Gardner, Harvard, Holden, Lancaster, Leicester, Southborough, Sterling, Westminster]. In addition to these town records there are also materials on several counties: Barnstable County, Bristol County, Hampden County, Middlesex County, and Norfolk County.

In addition to the above transcripts, there are some large compilations put together by the National DAR listing Revolutionary War ancestors and detailing lineages from present-day DAR members back to them. These may be accessed by looking in the following volumes, the references of which will lead you to the pertinent ancestors and/or lineages.

_DAR, PATRIOT INDEX, The Daughters, Washington, DC, 1969-79, 2 volumes.

_DAR, INDEX TO THE ROLLS OF HONOR (ANCESTOR INDEX) IN THE LINEAGE BOOKS OF THE NATIONAL SOCIETY OF THE DAR, Genealogical Publishing Co., Baltimore, MD, 1916-40 (1980). Indexes 166 volumes of lineages 1890-1921.

The DAR does not vouch for the accuracy of the materials in these volumes, but they can be exceptionally valuable in leading you to the original records.

13. Death records

From the earliest times the towns of MA were official keepers of death records (as well as birth and marriage records) of their inhabitants. At first the death records were kept along with other town records (constable, birth, early church, court, justice of peace, magistrate, marriage, proprietor, rate or tax, town meeting, selectmen) in one or a few books. Then, as the population grew, they came to be recorded in separate volumes dedicated especially to vital records. In 1841, in conformity to a new law, towns began reporting their deaths to the state, so that after that date, the records became available at both the town and state levels. Boston is an exception since it did not begin to comply until 1848. Original town records from the time of each town's origin to the present are available in the towns (town clerk, town archives, town library). From 1841-99 the official duplicates which were filed with the state are at the MSA and from 1900 forward, they are in the MA Registry of Vital Records and Statistics. Also available at the MSA is a state-wide death record index for 1841-1971.

To obtain records for the period since 1899, you should write to the pertinent town or city or to the following agency, enclosing the proper fee, the amount of which can be obtained by calling them:

_MA DEATH RECORDS 1900-, MA State Registry of Vital Records and Statistics, Room B-3, 150 Tremont St., Boston, MA 02111. Telephone (617)-727-0110.

Records for the period 1841-99 are most readily accessed at the MSA or through the microfilm copies of them available at the NEHGS and at the FHL (and obtainable through their many branch FHC):

_MA DEATH RECORDS 1841-99, and MA DEATH RECORD INDEX 1841-1971, Office of the Secretary of State, Archives Division/Vital Records, 220 Morrissey Blvd., Boston MA 02125. Telephone (617)-727-2816.

_MA DEATH RECORDS 1841-99, and MA DEATH RECORD INDEX 1841-1971, on microfilm in FHL, can be borrowed through FHC. Also at NEHGS.

The death records for the period before 1841 are available in several forms: originals in the towns, published volumes, copies on microfilm and microfiche, journal articles, typescript volumes, and manuscript copies. Of the 351 presently-existing MA towns, only about 10 of them do not have their death records in some copied (published or manuscript) form. Among the more important of these publications are ones relating to Plymouth and Boston since these largely represent the earliest settlements.

_Boston Registry Department, RECORDS RELATING TO THE EARLY HISTORY OF BOSTON, The Record Commissioners, Boston, MA, 1876-1909, especially volumes 9, 24, 28, 30 for deaths.

_Boston Registry Department and W. S. Appleton, BOSTON BIRTHS, BAPTISMS, MARRIAGES, AND DEATHS, 1630-1800, Genealogical Publishing Co., Baltimore, MD, 1978. Deaths 1630-1800.

_Boston Registry Department and S. C. Gladden, INDEX TO 1630-99 BOSTON BIRTHS, BAPTISMS, MARRIAGES, AND DEATHS, Boulder Genealogical Society, Boulder, CO, 1969. Over 14000 records.

_J. M. Holbrook, BOSTON BEGINNINGS, 1630-99, Holbrook Research Institute, Oxford, MA, 1980. Over 16000 names.

_N. B. Shurtleff and E. G. Bowman, PLYMOUTH COLONY, RECORDS OF BIRTHS, MARRIAGES, DEATHS, BURIALS, AND OTHER RECORDS, 1633-89, Genealogical Publishing Co., Baltimore, MD, 1979.

Some years ago, under the financial inducements of the state, vital records (including deaths) of MA towns began to be published for the time period up to 1850. The compilers of the many volumes which were printed drew not only upon official vital records, but they also often included court, Bible, church, and cemetery records. Later on, organizations, private companies, and individuals added volumes for other towns, published town vital records in genealogical journals, put town vital records on microfilm and microfiche, compiled typescript books, and made manuscript transcriptions. These works include:

_PUBLISHED VOLUMES OF MA TOWN VITAL RECORDS UP TO 1850, for 227 towns, published by New England Historic Genealogical Society, Essex Institute, Topsfield Historical Society, towns, private companies, and individuals.

_MA TOWN VITAL RECORDS PUBLISHED IN GENEALOGICAL JOURNALS, for 16 towns, chiefly published in New England Historical and Genealogical Register and The Mayflower Descendant.

_J. M. Holbrook, MA TOWN VITAL RECORDS UP TO 1890, over 120 towns on microfiche, Holbrook Research Institute, Oxford, MA.

_Daughters of the American Revolution for MA, COLLECTION OF GENEALOGICAL RECORD VOLUMES, The Society, various places in MA, various dates, numerous volumes, also on microfilm at FHL.

_MA TOWN RECORDS IN MANUSCRIPT FORM, for 52 towns, chiefly located in Corbin Collection and other collections at NEHGS and in Cooke Collection at Berkshire Athenaeum, Pittsfield, MA.

_MA TOWN RECORDS AND VITAL RECORDS, for many towns, on microfilm at FHL, available through FHC.

There is no overall index to this large number of compiled pre-1850 death records, but many births and marriages in the same sources have been indexed in a microfilm set available at every FHC:

_INTERNATIONAL GENEALOGICAL INDEX, MICROFICHE FOR MA, at every FHL, look under surname.

This index will often permit you to locate your ancestor in a specific town, then you can examine the detailed records of that town to see if he or she may have died there. In the fourth chapter, there are individual sections devoted to each town. In these sections, the death-record publications, microfiche, microfilms, and manuscripts pertaining to each town will be listed.

The basic guide to the original vital records (including deaths) which are in the many MA towns is:

_C. D. Wright, REPORT ON THE CUSTODY AND CONDITION OF THE PUBLIC RECORDS OF PARISHES, TOWNS, AND COUNTIES, Wright and Potter, Boston, MA, 1889.

This volume is, of course, badly out of date, but it remains very valuable in that it indicates what records should be sought for each town, even though locations of records may now be different. Three other useful items along this line are:

_R. L. Bowen, MA RECORDS: A HANDBOOK FOR GENEALOGISTS, HISTORIANS, LAWYERS, AND OTHER RESEARCHERS, The Author, Rehoboth, MA, 1957.

_J. M. Holbrook, BIBLIOGRAPHY OF MA VITAL RECORDS, Holbrook Research Institute, Oxford, MA, 1986, 3 microfiche.

_Historical Records Survey, GUIDE TO PUBLIC VITAL STATISTICS RECORDS IN MA, The Survey, WPA, Boston, MA, 1942.

There are also some civil vital record collections available in the counties of MA. These will be listed in the county sections of Chapter 4, and they are also presented here.

_ESSEX COUNTY DEATH RECORDS 1654-91, in Essex County at Salem.

_MIDDLESEX COUNTY DEATH RECORDS 1632-1745, in Middlesex County at Cambridge.

_OLD NORFOLK COUNTY DEATH RECORDS, 1641-71, in Essex County at Salem.

Similar volumes exist for several other counties, including Suffolk.

Excellent repositories for the books and microforms mentioned above are MSA, NEHGS, and BPL. In addition, the FHL(FHC) has much of the material on microfilm. LGL, especially those near MA, have some of the published works and some of the microforms, as do RL in MA. Many other types of records often contain death date and death place information. Among the better ones are Bible, biography, cemetery, census, church, genealogical periodicals, manuscripts, military, mortuary, newspaper, published genealogies, and will and probate. All of these are treated in other sections of this chapter. When you are seeking death data in archives and libraries, be certain to explore all the above mentioned sources, and do not fail to look under the county listings and the following heading in archive and library catalogs: Registers of births, etc.

14. Divorce records

In the early years of MA, divorce was not a frequent occurrence. Prior to 1692, the Court of Assistants was the agency which handled divorce cases in MA Bay Colony, and in Plymouth Colony it was the General Court. In the pre-1692 period, fewer than 50 divorces were recorded. In 1692, jurisdiction passed into the hands of the Governor and the Council, who managed divorce actions until 1785. In that year Probate Courts and later the Superior Courts were given concurrent jurisdiction with the Supreme Judicial Court. This arrangement persisted until 1922, when sole jurisdiction was given over to the Probate Court. Divorce records should be sought in the records of these courts. In some counties, there are separate divorce record books or files and/or separate divorce record indexes. These are available in the counties, and some of them have been microfilmed and may be found in the FHL(FHC). Another useful source of divorce information is in local newspapers, which sometimes published notices of these actions. There is one state-wide listing of early divorce records which has data from various MA counties.

_MA DIVORCE RECORDS, 1760-86, various MA counties. On microfilm at FHL(FHC).

There are also early divorce records in the collection of 328 volumes of original MA records known as the MA Archives. Many volumes have individual indexes and there is a collective index which covers about 80 of the volumes.

_MA ARCHIVES ORIGINAL DOCUMENT COLLECTION, with partial INDEXES, MSA, Boston, MA.

15. Emigration and immigration records

Since MA was one of the earliest-established of the thirteen original colonies, many early settlers came in (immigrated), many others followed throughout the succeeding years, and many of these or their descendants moved out (emigrated) to establish and populate other New England colonies, then to the west (into NY and beyond). In 1850, MA-born persons represented the largest or second largest group among those living in some other state in CT, ME, NH, NY, RI, and VT. There are a number of good volumes available which list immigrants to the areas that became the US. You should consult these volumes because they include both people who came directly to MA and people who came to some other colony or state and then to MA. The first set of volumes is an index to thousands of ship passenger lists in over 1300 sources and contains well over 1.5 million listings. These references have been abstracted from many published lists. Each listing gives the full name of the immigrant, the names of accompanying relatives, ages, the date and port of arrival, and the source of the information. The books in this set are:

_P. W. Filby and M. K. Meyer, PASSENGER AND IMMIGRATION LISTS INDEX, Gale Research Co., Detroit, MI, 1981, with ANNUAL SUPPLEMENTS thereafter.

Do not fail to look for every possible immigrant ancestor of yours in this very large index. Also of importance for locating passengers or passenger lists are:

_P. W. Filby, PASSENGER AND IMMIGRATION LISTS BIBLIOGRAPHY, 1538-1900, BEING A GUIDE TO PUBLISHED LISTS OF ARRIVALS IN THE US AND CANADA, Gale Research Co., Detroit, MI, 1988.

There are several other valuable passenger lists and finding aids for locating passenger lists which give MA immigrants. These must not be overlooked. They include:

_US National Archives and Records Service, GUIDE TO GENEALOGICAL RESEARCH IN THE NATIONAL ARCHIVES, The Service, Washington, DC, 1982, pages 41-57.

_A. Eakle and J. Cerny, THE SOURCE, Ancestry Publishing Co., Salt Lake City, UT, 1984, pages 453-516.

_M. Tepper, AMERICAN PASSENGER ARRIVAL RECORDS, Genealogical Publishing Co., Baltimore, MD, 1988.

_US National Archives, IMMIGRANT AND PASSENGER ARRIVALS, A SELECT CATALOG OF NA MICROFILM PUBLICATIONS, National Archives, Washington, DC, 1983.

_C. W. Baird, HISTORY OF THE HUGUENOT EMIGRATION TO AMERICA, Genealogical Publishing Co., Baltimore, MD, 1973.

_V. R. Cameron, EMIGRANTS FROM SCOTLAND TO AMERICA, 1774-5, Genealogical Publishing Co., Baltimore, MD, 1959.

_P. W. Coldham, ENGLISH ESTATES OF AMERICAN COLONISTS, AMERICAN WILLS AND ADMINISTRATIONS IN THE PREROGATIVE COURT OF CANTERBURY, 1610-1858, Genealogical Publishing Co., Baltimore, MD, 1980-1.

_P. W. Coldham, PASSENGERS AND SHIPS TO AMERICA, 1618-88, National Genealogical Society Quarterly 71 (1983) 163-92, 284-94, 72 (1984) 132-45.

_P. W. Coldham, ENGLISH ADVENTURERS AND EMIGRANTS, ABSTRACTS OF EXAMINATIONS IN THE HIGH COURT OF ADMIRALTY WITH REFERENCE TO COLONIAL AMERICA, 1609-1773, Genealogical Publishing Co., Baltimore, MD, 1984-5.

_P. W. Coldham, THE COMPLETE BOOK OF IMMIGRANTS, 1607-60, COMPILED FROM ENGLISH PUBLIC RECORDS, THOSE WHO TOOK SHIP FOR AMERICA, THOSE WHO WERE DEPORTED, AND THOSE WHO WERE SOLD TO LABOR, Genealogical Publishing Co., Baltimore, MD, 1987.

_P. W. Coldham, THE COMPLETE BOOK OF EMIGRANTS IN BONDAGE,

1614-1775, Genealogical Publishing Co., Baltimore, MD, 1988.

__P. W. Coldham, THE BRISTOL REGISTERS OF SERVANTS SENT TO FOREIGN PLANTATIONS, 1654-86, Genealogical Publishing Co., Baltimore, MD, 1983.

__R. J. Dickson, ULSTER IMMIGRATION TO COLONIAL AMERICA, 1718-75, Ulster-Scot Historical Foundation, Belfast, Ireland, 1976.

__D. Dobson, DIRECTORY OF SCOTTISH SETTLERS IN NORTH AMERICA, Genealogical Publishing Co., Baltimore, MD, 1984-6, 6 volumes.

__A. B. Faust, G. M. Brumbaugh, and L. Schelbert, LISTS OF SWISS EMIGRANTS IN THE EIGHTEENTH CENTURY TO THE AMERICAN COLONIES, 1706-95, Genealogical Publishing Co., Baltimore, MD, 1976.

__G. Fothergill, EMIGRANTS FROM ENGLAND, 1773-6, Genealogical Publishing Co., Baltimore, MD, 1964.

__E. French, LIST OF EMIGRANTS TO AMERICA FROM LIVERPOOL, 1697-1707, Genealogical Publishing Co., Baltimore, MD, 1962.

__M. Ghirelli, A LIST OF EMIGRANTS FROM ENGLAND TO AMERICA, 1682-92, Magna Carta Book Co., Baltimore, MD, 1968.

__M. S. Giuseppi, NATURALIZATIONS OF FOREIGN PROTESTANTS IN THE AMERICAN AND WEST INDIAN COLONIES, Genealogical Publishing Co., Baltimore, MD, 1964.

__I. A. Glazier and P. W. Filby, GERMANS TO AMERICA, LISTS OF PASSENGERS ARRIVING AT US PORTS, 1850-5, Scholarly Resources, Wilmington, DE, 1988, further volumes to follow.

__D. A. Haury, INDEX TO MENNONITE IMMIGRANTS ON US PASSENGER LISTS, 1872-1904, Mennonite Library and Archives, North Newton, KS, 1986.

__J. and M. Kaminkow, A LIST OF EMIGRANTS FROM ENGLAND TO AMERICA, 1718-59, Magna Carta Book Co., Baltimore, MD, 1981.

__M. Kaminkow, PASSENGERS WHO ARRIVED IN THE US, September 1821-December 1823, Magna Carta Book Co., Baltimore, MD, 1969.

__D. L. Kent, BARBADOS AND AMERICA, The Author, Arlington, VA, 1980.

__B. Mitchell, IRISH PASSENGER LISTS, 1847-71, LISTS OF PASSENGERS SAILING FROM LONDONDERRY TO AMERICA ON SHIPS OF THE J. AND J. COOKE LINE AND THE McCORKELL LINE, Genealogical Publishing Co., Baltimore, MD, 1988.

__N. W. Olsson, SWEDISH PASSENGER ARRIVALS IN US PORTS 1820-50 EXCEPT NY, North Central Publishing Co., St. Paul, MN, 1979.

__G. E. Reaman, THE TRAIL OF THE HUGUENOTS IN EUROPE, THE US, SOUTH AFRICA, AND CANADA, Genealogical Publishing Co., Baltimore, MD, 1972.

__T. Schenk, R. Froelke, and I. Bork, THE WUERTTEMBERG EMIGRATION INDEX, Ancestry, Salt Lake City, UT, 1986-, in progress, 6 volumes so far.

__D. M. Schlegel, PASSENGERS FROM IRELAND ARRIVING AT AMERICAN PORTS, 1811-7, Genealogical Publishing Co., Baltimore, MD, 1980.

_R. P. Swierenga, DUTCH IMMIGRANTS IN US SHIP PASSENGER MANIFESTS, 1820-80, Scholarly Resources, Wilmington, DE, 1983.
_US Department of State, PASSENGER ARRIVALS, 1819-20, IN THE US, Genealogical Publishing Co., Baltimore, MD, 1967.
_F. A. Virkus, IMMIGRANTS TO THE COLONIES BEFORE 1750, Genealogical Publishing Co., Baltimore, MD, 1965.
_J. Wareing, EMIGRANTS TO AMERICA, INDENTURED SERVANTS RECRUITED IN LONDON, 1718-33, Genealogical Publishing Co., Baltimore, MD, 1985.
_H. F. Waters, GENEALOGICAL GLEANINGS IN ENGLAND, Genealogical Publishing Co., Baltimore, MD, 1969.

Having explored the above records, especially the books by Filby and Meyer, you can then look into some published volumes dealing particularly with immigration to MA.
_A. Ames, THE MAYFLOWER AND HER LOG, 1620-1, Houghton, Mifflin, Boston, MA, 1901.
_C. E. Banks and E. E. Brownell, TOPOGRAPHICAL DICTIONARY OF 2885 EMIGRANTS TO NEW ENGLAND, 1620-50, Genealogical Publishing Co., Baltimore, MD, 1974. Exercise caution.
_C. E. Banks, THE PLANTERS OF THE COMMONWEALTH, EMIGRATION IN COLONIAL TIMES, LISTS OF PASSENGERS TO BOSTON AND THE BAY COLONY, THE SHIPS THAT BROUGHT THEM, THEIR ENGLISH HOMES, AND WHERE THEY SETTLED IN MA, 1620-40, Genealogical Publishing Co., Baltimore, MD, 1979.
_C. E. Banks, THE WINTHROP FLEET OF 1630, THE VESSELS, THE VOYAGE, THE PASSENGERS, AND THEIR ENGLISH HOMES, Genealogical Publishing Co., Baltimore, MD, 1980.
_C. E. Banks, THE ENGLISH ANCESTRY AND HOMES OF THE PILGRIM FATHERS WHO CAME TO PLYMOUTH IN 1620-1 AND 1623, Genealogical Publishing Co., Baltimore, MD, 1980.
_E. S. Bolton, IMMIGRANTS TO NEW ENGLAND, 1700-75, Genealogical Publishing Co., Baltimore, MD, 1979.
_C. K. Bolton, THE REAL FOUNDERS OF NEW ENGLAND, 1602-28, Genealogical Publishing Co., Baltimore, MD, 1974. Pre-Mayflower settlers.
_Boston Registry Department and W. H. Whitmore, PORT ARRIVALS AND IMMIGRANTS TO THE CITY OF BOSTON, 1715-6 AND 1762-9, Genealogical Publishing Co., Baltimore, MD, 1973.
_C. Boyer, 3rd, SHIP PASSENGER LISTS, NATIONAL AND NEW ENGLAND, 1600-1825, The Author, Newhall, CA, 1977.
_M. B. Colket, Jr., FOUNDERS OF EARLY AMERICAN FAMILIES, EMIGRANTS FROM EUROPE, 1607-57, Order of the Founders and Patriots of America, Cleveland, OH, 1985.
_R. J. Crandall and R. J. Coffman, FROM EMIGRANTS TO RULERS, THE CHARLESTOWN OLIGARCHY IN THE GREAT MIGRATION, New England

Historical and Genealogical Register 131 (1977).

_N. Currer-Briggs, COLONIAL SETTLERS AND ENGLISH ADVENTURERS, Genealogical Publishing Co., Baltimore, MD, 1971.

_D. Douglas, THE HUGUENOTS, STORY OF HUGUENOT IMMIGRATION, PARTICULARLY TO NEW ENGLAND, The Author, New York, NY, 1954.

_A. Forbes and P. F. Cadman, THE BOSTON FRENCH, WELL KNOWN CITIZENS OF FRANCE WHO FOUND HOMES IN BOSTON AND NEW ENGLAND, Polyanthos, New Orleans, LA, 1971.

_P. A. Godbout, NOS ANCETRES AU XVIIe SIECLE, DICTIONNAIRE GENEALOGIQUE ET BIO-BIBLIOGRAPHIQUE DES FAMILLES CANADIENNES, Archiviste de la Province de Quebec, Canada, 1951-65.

_G. A. Hill, PASSENGER ARRIVALS AT SALEM AND BEVERLY, MA, 1798-1800, New England Historical and Genealogical Register 106 (1952) 203-9.

_Historical Records Survey, SHIPS REGISTERS, WPA, Boston, MA, 1938-42, 7 volumes. Covers Boston and Charlestown 1789-95, Barnstable 1814-1913, Plymouth 1789-1808, Dighton-Fall River 1789-1938, and New Bedford 1789-1939.

_THE IRISH IN NEW ENGLAND, The NEHGS, Boston, MA, 1985.

_J. B. Munroe, A LIST OF ALIEN PASSENGERS BONDED FROM 1847-51 FOR THE USE OF THE OVERSEERS OF THE POOR IN THE COMMONWEALTH [OF MA], MA Superintendent of Alien Passengers, Genealogical Publishing Co., Baltimore, MD, 1971.

_G. B. Roberts, ENGLISH ORIGINS OF NEW ENGLAND FAMILIES FROM THE NEW ENGLAND HISTORICAL AND GENEALOGICAL REGISTER, Genealogical Publishing Co., Baltimore, MD, 1985, 2 series of 3 volumes each.

_SHIP REGISTERS, DISTRICTS OF GLOUCESTER (1789-1875), NEWBURY (1789-1870), AND SALEM AND BEVERLY (1789-1900), Essex Institute Historical Collections 39-42, 70-73, 77-80.

_M. Tepper, PASSENGERS TO AMERICA, A CONSOLIDATION OF SHIP PASSENGER LISTS AND ASSOCIATED DATA FROM PERIODICAL LITERATURE, Genealogical Publishing Co., Baltimore, MD, 1979, 2 volumes.

The books mentioned just above are of a wide variety. Some give direct information on immigrants, others simply locate early settlers and thus indirectly indicate that immigration has taken place. Some of the volumes are indexed in Filby and Meyer's large compiled index, so you should use this index before going into the numerous volumes. Many of the works in the section on colonial records also carry direct or indirect immigration data, so they need to be considered also. The books indicated in this section will be found in NEHGS and BPL, many of them in SLM, FHL (FHC) and LGL, and some in RL and LL, especially the ones pertaining to their areas.

Other important sources of MA immigrant records are federal and state passenger lists. These lists and indexes to them are as follows:

_US Customs Service, PASSENGER LISTS OF VESSELS ARRIVING AT BOSTON, 1820-91, The National Archives, Washington, DC, Microfilm M277, 115 rolls.

_State of MA, INDEX TO PASSENGER LISTS OF VESSELS ARRIVING AT BOSTON, 1848-91, The National Archives, Washington, DC, Microfilm M265, 282 rolls.

_US Customs Service, COPIES OF LISTS OF PASSENGERS ARRIVING AT MISCELLANEOUS PORTS ON THE ATLANTIC AND GULF COASTS AND AT PORTS ON THE GREAT LAKES, 1820-73, The National Archives, Washington, DC, Microfilm M575, 16 rolls. Includes Barnstable (1820-6) on Roll 1, Dighton (1820-36) and Edgartown (1820-70) and Fall River (1837-65) on Roll 2, Gloucester (1820, 1832-9, 1867-8, 1870) and Hingham (1852) and Marblehead (1820-36, 1849) on Roll 4, Nantucket (1821-51, 1856-62) and New Bedford (1826-52) and Newburyport (1821-39) on Roll 5, Plymouth (1821-36, 1843) on Roll 8, and Salem (1865-6) on Roll 16.

_US Customs Service, A SUPPLEMENTAL INDEX TO PASSENGER LISTS OF VESSELS ARRIVING AT ATLANTIC AND GULF PORTS, EXCLUDING NEW YORK, 1820-74, The National Archives, Washington, DC, Microfilm M334, 188 rolls.

_Port of Boston, ALIEN PASSENGER ARRIVALS AT THE PORT OF BOSTON, 1848-91, with Historical Records Survey, SURNAME INDEX TO THE ALIEN PASSENGER ARRIVALS AT THE PORT OF BOSTON, 1848-91, WPA, Boston, MA, 1940. Both at MSA, index also at BPL.

There are also records of the US Immigration and Naturalization Service which include microfilmed passenger lists for dates later than those above. Among them are passenger lists, crew lists, and indexes for Boston (1889-1943), Gloucester (1918-43), and New Bedford (1902-54). Details on these federal microfilms may be had in:

_National Archives, IMMIGRANT AND PASSENGER ARRIVALS, A SELECT CATALOG OF NA MICROFILM PUBLICATIONS, NA Trust Fund Board, Washington, DC, 1983.

The federal microfilms listed above are available at NA, NAFB (including the Boston Branch), and BPL. Many of them can be borrowed through AGLL (American Genealogical Lending Library, PO Box 244, Bountiful, UT 84010) by individuals or on interlibrary loan through your LL. The NA also has a few original passenger lists and some transcripts which have not been microfilmed: Dighton (1819), New Bedford (1823-5, 1853-99), Provincetown (1887-9, 1893, 1895-6), and Salem and Beverly (1798, 1800, 1823). The 1798 and 1800 lists for Salem and Beverly have been published:

_CUSTOM LISTS OF ALIENS FOR THE PORTS OF SALEM AND BEVERLY, 1798, 1800, New England Historical and Genealogical Register 106 (1952) 203-9.

Not only did people immigrate to MA, they, of course, emigrated from it, many going into the other New England Colonies and states, many to areas further west. There are some volumes on this, and it is possible that they might help you in your search for a migratory MA progenitor.

_E. Cheney, MA PIONEERS, OH SERIES, MA Magazine 9-11.

_J. I. Coddington, MIGRATIONS FROM NEW ENGLAND TO NY AND NJ, World Conference and Genealogical Seminar, GSCJCLDS, Salt Lake City, UT, 1969.

_T. R. Cole, FAMILY, SETTLEMENT, AND MIGRATION IN SOUTHEASTERN MA, 1650-1805, New England Historical and Genealogical Register 132 (1978).

_H. W. Denio, MA LAND GRANTS IN THE STATE OF VT, Wilson and Son, Cambridge, MA, 1920.

_C. A. Flagg, AN INDEX OF PIONEERS FROM MA TO THE WEST, ESPECIALLY TO THE STATE OF MI, Genealogical Publishing Co., Baltimore, MD, 1980.

_F. M. Hawes, NEW ENGLANDERS IN THE FL CENSUS OF 1850, New England Historical and Genealogical Register 76 (1922).

_S. H. Holbrook, THE YANKEE EXODUS, AN ACCOUNT OF MIGRATION FROM NEW ENGLAND, University of WA Press, Seattle, WA, 1968.

_J. M. Holbrook, QUEBEC, CANADA 1825 CENSUS OF NEW ENGLAND IMMIGRANTS, Holbrook Research Institute, Oxford, MA, 1976, 2 volumes.

_L. K. M. Rosenberry, THE EXPANSION OF NEW ENGLAND, THE SPREAD OF NEW ENGLAND SETTLEMENTS AND INSTITUTIONS TO THE MS RIVER, 1620-85, Russell and Russell, New York, NY, 1962.

_US Bureau of the Census, A CENTURY OF POPULATION GROWTH, 1790-1900, The Bureau, Washington, DC, 1909. Tables showing numbers of people in each of the other states who were born in MA.

_E. Myers, MIGRATION PATTERNS AS SHOWN BY A STUDY OF THE FEDERAL CENSUS OF 1850, Central NY Genealogical Society, Syracuse, NY, 1977.

_J. D. B. DeBow, compiler, THE SEVENTH CENSUS OF THE US, 1850, EMBRACING A STATISTICAL VIEW OF EACH OF THE STATES AND TERRITORIES, US Bureau of the Census, Washington, DC, 1853. Information on MA natives who have moved to other states.

The last three references illustrate the value of census records, particularly those of 1850 and after, in tracing emigration patterns out of MA to other states. The same census records are equally valuable in discerning population movements into MA from other states and from overseas countries.

Numerous other immigration and emigration listings, especially ones published in periodicals, are referenced in the following works:

_O. K. Miller, MIGRATION, EMIGRATION, IMMIGRATION, Everton Publishers, Logan, UT, 1974, 1981, 2 volumes.

If you do not locate your immigrant ancestor in the references listed in the previous paragraphs, use these two volumes to locate several smaller sources. Also, do not forget to look into the catalogs of MSA, SLM, NEHGS, BPL, LL in port cities of MA and LGL under the heading MA-EMIGRATION AND IMMIGRATION. Also be sure and seek emigration and immigration materials at the county and town levels. In addition, sometimes naturalization records carry passenger arrival data, so do not overlook this possibility.

16. Ethnic records

The early settlement and colonial history of MA was dominated by one ethnic group, namely the English, to the exclusion of other groups except for small numbers. This remained the case until the 1840s, at which time, a flood of Irish immigrants began coming in. Following the Civil War (1861-5) other immigrants by the thousands poured in: Italians, Poles, Russians, French Canadians, Portuguese, and Eastern Europeans. Most of them, as the Irish, were Catholic. By 1907 70 percent of the MA population were either immigrants or children of one or both immigrant parents. Hence, ethnic groups of MA are of great importance in understanding the commonwealth, both historically and genealogically. For the most part, you can follow such ancestors through the conventional routes. But there are some specialized works which will give you an invaluable perspective.

First, we will mention some useful sources of detailed information on the ethnic groups of MA:

_J. D. Haskell, Jr., MA, A BIBLIOGRAPHY OF ITS HISTORY, University Press of New England, Hanover, NH, 1976. References to many books and journal articles on ethnic groups. Look up French, Germans, Indians, Irish, Italians, Jews, Lithuanians, Negroes, Poles, Russians, Scotch-Irish, and Scots in the index.

_O. Handlin, BOSTON'S IMMIGRANTS, A STUDY IN ACCULTURATION, 1790-1880, Harvard University Press, Cambridge, MA, 1959.

_F. A. Busbee, ETHNIC FACTORS IN THE POPULATION OF BOSTON, Macmillan, New York, NY, 1903.

_Historical Records Survey, GUIDE TO MANUSCRIPTS AND SOURCE MATERIALS RELATING TO THE NEGRO IN MA, WPA, Boston, MA, 1942.

The various ethnic groups tended to each be largely affiliated with a particular religious persuasion. The early English tended to be Congregational, later on Episcopalian, and many Congregationalists turned Unitarian, Universalist, or Baptist. Those who came in the 1800s were predominantly Catholic, although there were numerous Jews. Since there is such a tight tie between ethnic groups and their church affiliations, much pertinent data will be found in the church records, as was discussed earlier in this chapter.

Some special volumes and articles on European immigrants which you will find informative are:

__E. W. Hanson, THE NON-ENGLISH NEW ENGLANDERS, A series starting in New England Historical and Genealogical Register 139.

__M. K. Van Dyne, TRACE YOUR ROOTS, CATALOG OF ETHNIC RESOURCES IN MA, New England Institute of Pluralism, Boston, MA, 1980.

__W. Volkovich-Valkavicius, IMMIGRANTS AND YANKEES, St. James Book Account, Groton, MA, 1981. Story of Irish, Italians, Poles, French-Canadians, and Lithuanians who came to MA.

__(French) J. P. Baxter, THE PIONEERS OF NEW FRANCE IN NEW ENGLAND, 1720-5, Albany, NY, 1894.

__(French) P. Belliveau, FRENCH NEUTRALS IN MA, 1755-66, Giffen, Boston, MA, 1972.

__(French) A. Forbes and P. F. Cadman, THE BOSTON FRENCH, WELL KNOWN CITIZENS OF FRANCE WHO FOUND HOMES IN BOSTON AND NEW ENGLAND, Polyanthos, New Orleans, LA, 1971.

__(Irish) J. B. Cullen, THE STORY OF THE IRISH IN BOSTON, Plimpton, Boston, MA, 1893.

__(Irish) G. F. Donovan, THE PRE-REVOLUTIONARY IRISH IN MA, 1620-1775, Banta, Menasha, WI, 1932.

__(Irish) M. J. O'Brien, THE IRISH AT BUNKER HILL, Devin-Adair, New York, NY, 1968.

__(Irish) M. J. O'Brien, THE IRISH IN AMERICA, Genealogical Publishing Co., Baltimore, MD, 1974.

__(Irish) THE IRISH IN NEW ENGLAND, The New England Historic Genealogical Society, Boston, MA, 1985.

__(Italian) J. W. Carlevale, LEADING AMERICANS OF ITALIAN DESCENT IN MA, Memorial Press, Plymouth, MA, 1946.

__(Jews) J. Broches, JEWS IN NEW ENGLAND, PART 1, JEWS IN MA, 1650-1750, Bloch Publ. Co., New York, NY, 1942.

__(Jews) A. Ehrenfried, A CHRONICLE OF BOSTON JEWRY FROM THE COLONIAL SETTLEMENT TO 1900, Boston, MA, 1963.

__(Jews) L. M. Friedman, EARLY AMERICAN JEWS, JEWS OF MA, NY, AND OTHER AMERICAN LANDS, Cambridge, MA, 1943.

__(Jews) C. Huehner, THE JEWS OF NEW ENGLAND PRIOR TO 1800, Cornwall Press, Cornwall, CT, 1973.

__(Jews) J. R. Marcus, EARLY AMERICAN JEWRY, THE JEWS OF NY, NEW ENGLAND, AND CANADA, 1649-1794, Jewish Publication Society, Philadelphia, PA, 1951.

__(Jews) S. Schindler, ISRAELITES IN BOSTON, Berwick and Smith, Boston, MA, 1963.

__(Jews) A. A. Wiedner, THE EARLY JEWISH COMMUNITY OF BOSTON'S NORTH END, 1870-1900, Brandeis University, Waltham, MA, 1962.

_(Scots-Irish) C. K. Bolton, SCOTCH-IRISH PIONEERS IN ULSTER AND AMERICA, Genealogical Publishing Co., Baltimore, MD, 1981.

The black ethnic community of MA has a long history, this history being locked in tightly to the MA anti-slavery attitude and movements, which date quite far back. Special attention should be paid to the manuscript and source guide mentioned in the second paragraph of this section, and the numerous journal articles listed in the bibliography by Haskell which is referenced in the same place. There is also a very useful manuscript collection in MSA:

_Historical Records Survey, NEGRO CHURCHES, NEGRO MANUSCRIPTS, NEGRO FILES, AND NEGRO BIBLIOGRAPHY IN MA, WPA, Boston, MA, late 1930s and early 1940s, file material in MSA.

Another valuable resource is:

_J. Daniels, IN FREEDOM'S BIRTHPLACE, A STUDY OF BOSTON NEGROES, Houghton Mifflin, Boston, MA, 1914.

Special guidebooks and how-to research articles for investigating black genealogies should also be consulted:

_J. M. Rose and A. Eicholz, BLACK GENESIS, Gale Research, Detroit, MI, 1976.

_National Black Bibliographic and Research Center, BLACK SOLDIERS IN THE US, 1777-1977, AN EXTENSIVE BIBLIOGRAPHY, The Center, Newark, DE, 1978.

_C. L. Blockson, BLACK AMERICAN RECORDS AND RESEARCH, in J. C. Smith, ETHNIC GENEALOGY: A RESEARCH GUIDE, Greenwood Press, Westport, CT, 1983.

_A. Eakle and J. Cerny, THE SOURCE, A GUIDEBOOK OF AMERICAN GENEALOGY, Ancestry, Salt Lake City, UT, 1984, pages 578-95.

_C. L. Blockson and R. Fry, BLACK GENEALOGY, Prentice-Hall, Englewood Cliffs, NJ, 1977.

With reference to American Indian (native American) genealogy in MA, detailed works on the Indians will be found in the bibliography by Haskell. A set of three volumes can also be very instructive:

_L. Bonfanti, BIOGRAPHIES AND LEGENDS OF THE NEW ENGLAND INDIANS, Pride Publ., Wakefield, MA, 1970-2, 3 volumes.

Also important to research on the MA native Americans are MA histories, especially those written at the local levels (towns and countries).

17. Gazetteers, atlases, and maps

Detailed information regarding MA geography is exceptionally useful to the genealogical searcher, especially with regard to land records. These records usually mention locations in terms requiring an understanding of local geographical features. Several sorts of geographical aids are valuable in this regard: gazetteers, atlases, and maps. Gazetteers are volumes which list geographical features (towns, villages, crossroads, settlements, districts, rivers, streams, creeks, hills, mountains, valleys, coves, lakes, ponds), locate them, and sometimes give a few details concerning them. An atlas is a collection of maps in book form. Among the better gazetteer-type materials for MA are the following, listed in order of date:

_T. Greenleaf, GEOGRAPHICAL GAZETTEER OF THE TOWNS IN THE COMMONWEALTH OF MA, Greenleaf and Freeman, Boston, MA, 1784-5.

_J. Hayward, THE MA DIRECTORY, Boston, MA, 1835.

_J. Hayward, A GAZETTEER OF MA, ALL COUNTIES, TOWNS, AND DISTRICTS, Jewett, Boston, MA, 1849.

_J. Spofford, A HISTORICAL AND STATISTICAL GAZETTEER OF MA, Frothingham, Haverhill, MA, 1860.

_E. Nason, A GAZETTEER OF THE STATE OF MA, Russell, Boston, MA, 1874.

_H. Gannett, A GEOGRAPHIC DICTIONARY OF MA, Genealogical Publishing Co., Baltimore, MD, 1978 (1894).

_MA Geodetic Survey, MA LOCALITIES, A FINDING LIST OF MA CITIES, TOWNS, VILLAGES, LOCALITIES, RAILROAD STATIONS, AND POST OFFICES, The Survey, Boston, MA, 1938.

_US Writers Program, THE ORIGIN OF MA PLACE NAMES, WPA, Harian Publns., New York, NY, 1941.

_K. H. White, HISTORICAL DATA RELATING TO COUNTIES, CITIES, AND TOWNS IN MA, The Office of the Secretary of the Commonwealth of MA, Boston, MA, 1966.

_L. M. Merolla and F. M. Crowther, THE POST OFFICES OF MA, MA Postal Research Society, North Abingdon, MA, 1981.

_Richard B. Sealock, BIBLIOGRAPHY OF PLACE NAME LITERATURE, American Library Assn., Chicago, IL, 1982.

_M. J. Denis, MA TOWNS AND CITIES, Danbury House, Oakland, ME, 1984.

_MA GAZETTEER, American Historical Publications, Wilmington, DE, 1985.

_C. P. Davis, DIRECTORY OF MA PLACE NAMES CURRENT AND OBSOLETE, MA DAR, Lexington, MA, 1987.

Not only are there the above gazetteers for the state of MA, such volumes have been published for some MA counties. The above gazetteers and the county gazetteers may be found in SLM, NEHGS, the MA Historical Society Library, the University of MA at Amherst, and BPL; some are also available in other LGL and RL, and those pertaining to the counties are usually located in LL in those counties.

Atlases (collections of maps) published before 1906 (the time in which most researchers are interested) are available for the state of MA for every county, and for the major cities. Atlases containing maps for most MA towns are also in print. Some of the county and city atlases, and a few of the town map sections in atlases give the names of landowners. Listings of the numerous available atlases for MA are:

_C. E. LeGear, US ATLASES, Library of Congress, Washington, DC, 1950/3, 2 volumes.

Among the more important state atlases and other geographical works carrying MA maps are these volumes:

_H. F. Walling, MAPS OF THE COUNTIES OF MA, Walling, Cambridge, MA, 1870.

_H. F. Walling and O. W. Gray, OFFICIAL TOPOGRAPHICAL ATLAS OF MA, Stedman, Brown and Lyon, Philadelphia, PA, 1871.

_H. F. Walling, WALLING'S COUNTY MAPS OF MA, Walling, Cambridge, MA, 1875.

_MA Topographical Survey Commission, ATLAS OF MA FROM TOPOGRAPHICAL SURVEYS, 1884-8, The Commission, Boston, MA, 1890.

_O. W. Walker, ATLAS OF MA, Walker and Co., Boston, MA, numerous editions: 1891/4/1900/4/5/9.

_W. Thorndale and W. Dollarhide, MAP GUIDE TO THE US FEDERAL CENSUSES, 1790-1920, American Genealogical Lending Library, Bountiful, UT, 1986.

Atlases (with dates in parentheses) exist for the MA counties as follows: Barnstable (1880), Berkshire (1876), Bristol (1871, 1895), Essex (1872, 1884), Franklin (1871), Hampden (1870, 1894), Hampshire (1873), Middlesex (1875, 1889), Norfolk (1876, 1888), Plymouth (1870), Suffolk (1873-5), Worcester (1870, 1898). The atlases mentioned here and most of the others listed in the book by LeGear may be found in the same repositories referred to at the end of the previous paragraph.

Many maps are available for MA, for its counties, its cities, and its towns. There are several nation-wide books which either list MA maps and indicate sources of them or give descriptions of good map collections:

_National Archives and Records Service, GUIDE TO CARTOGRAPHIC RECORDS IN THE NATIONAL ARCHIVES, The Service, Washington, DC, 1971.

_National Archives and Records Service, GUIDE TO GENEALOGICAL RESEARCH IN THE NATIONAL ARCHIVES, The Service, Washington, DC, 1982, pages 255-62.

_American Geographic Society, INDEX TO MAPS IN BOOKS AND PERIODICALS, G. K. Hall, Boston, MA, 1968, 10 volumes, with SUPPLEMENTS.

_D. K. Carrington and R. W. Stephenson, MAP COLLECTIONS IN THE US AND CANADA, A DIRECTORY, Special Libraries Assn., New York, NY, 1978.

_J. C. Wheat, MAPS AND CHARTS PUBLISHED IN AMERICA BEFORE 1800, Yale Univ. Press, New Haven, CT, 1969.

_J. R. Hebert, PANORAMIC MAPS OF ANGLO-AMERICAN CITIES IN THE LIBRARY OF CONGRESS, The Library, Washington, DC, 1984. Beautiful pre-1900 maps available for MA cities and towns.

_R. W. Stephenson, LAND OWNERSHIP MAPS IN THE LIBRARY OF CONGRESS, The Library, Washington, DC, 1967. Pre-1900 county maps showing land owners, for MA counties.

_Library of Congress, FIRE INSURANCE MAPS IN THE LIBRARY OF CONGRESS The Library, Washington, DC, 1981, pages 401-53. Maps of cities and towns 1884-, much detail.

_M. H. Shelley, WARD MAPS OF US CITIES, Library of Congress, Washington, DC, 1975. Maps showing ward divisions to aid you in census searches.

Your attention needs to be drawn to several specialized types of maps which can assist you as you attempt to locate your progenitor's land holdings and as you look for streams, roads, bridges, churches, cemeteries, and villages in the vicinity. The first of these are highly detailed maps issued by the US Geological Survey which has mapped the entire state of MA and has produced a series of numerous maps, each covering a very small area. These maps are available at very reasonable cost. Write the following address and ask for the Catalog of and the Index to Topographic Maps of MA-RI-CT and a MA-RI-CT Map Order Form.

_Distribution Branch, US Geological Survey, Box 25286, Denver Federal Center, Denver, CO 80225.

A second type of map which is very useful are the landowner maps which show the names of persons who own each piece of property. These are available as separate maps and some of them are also often in atlases (see book by Stephenson above). A third type of map is represented by the city and town panorama maps which are careful depictions of cities as they would be viewed from a balloon flying overhead (see book by Hebert above). The fourth special type of maps are detailed city maps which were drawn for fire insurance purposes (see book by Library of Congress above). A fifth category of map is made up of those which have marked the ward boundaries of larger cities. These are useful when you want to search unindexed census records for city dwellers, especially when they are employed with city directories (which give street addresses, and also sometimes contain ward maps or give ward boundaries).

The best collections of genealogically-related maps and/or atlases of MA are in the MSA, SLM, NEHGS, BPL, MA Historical Society Library (1154 Boylston St., Boston, MA 02215), Boston Athenaeum (10 1/2 Beacon St., Boston, MA 02108), and the American Antiquarian Society Library (185 Salisbury St., Worcester, MA 01609). Other good collections are found in the NA and the Library of Congress, as well as in RL and LL in the areas where you are interested. When you seek gazetteers, atlases, and maps in these repositories, please be sure to look both in the main catalogs and the special map catalogs, indexes, listings, inventories, and collections. Most of the volumes mentioned in this section are available in SLM, NEHGS, BPL, MA Historical Society, American Antiquarian Society, and some will be found in FHL(FHC), LGL, RL, and LL.

18. Genealogical indexes and compilations

There are a number of indexes and compilations for the colonies and state of MA which list very large numbers of names. These are of considerable utility because they may save you going through many small volumes and detailed records, especially in the early stages of your search for MA ancestors. The nation-wide indexes and compilations of this sort include:

_SURNAME CATALOG and INTERNATIONAL GENEALOGICAL INDEX at FHL, Salt Lake City, UT, also available at every FHC. [See section on FHL and FHC in Chapter 3.] Over 135 million entries.

_FAMILY GROUP RECORDS COLLECTION, FHL, Salt Lake City, UT, access through FHC. [Be sure to search both the Patron and the Archives Sections of the Family Group Records Collection.] Over 9 million entries.

_National Archives, GENERAL INDEX TO COMPILED MILITARY SERVICE RECORDS OF REVOLUTIONARY WAR SOLDIERS, SAILORS, AND MEMBERS OF ARMY STAFF DEPARTMENTS, The Archives, Washington, DC, Microfilm M860, 58 rolls.

_F. Rider, AMERICAN GENEALOGICAL-BIOGRAPHICAL INDEX, Godfrey Memorial Library, Middletown, CT, 1942-, over 180 volumes. Over 12 million entries. Be sure to check both series.

_P. W. Filby and M. K. Meyer, PASSENGER AND IMMIGRATION LISTS INDEX, Gale Research Co., Detroit, MI, 1981-, 3 basic volumes plus annual supplements. Over a million entries.

_M. J. Kaminkow, GENEALOGIES IN THE LIBRARY OF CONGRESS, Magna Carta, Baltimore, MD, 1972-7, 3 volumes, plus A COMPLEMENT TO GENEALOGIES IN THE LIBRARY OF CONGRESS, Magna Carta, Baltimore, MD, 1981. Over 50,000 names.

_NYPL, DICTIONARY CATALOG OF THE LOCAL HISTORY AND GENEALOGY DIVISION, NYPL, G. K. Hall, Boston, MA, 1974.

_Library of Congress, NATIONAL UNION CATALOG OF MANUSCRIPT COLLECTIONS, The Library, Washington, DC, annual volumes since 1959, index in each volume.

_National Society of the DAR, LIBRARY CATALOG, VOLUME 1: FAMILY HISTORIES AND GENEALOGIES, The Society, Washington, DC, 1982.

_Newberry Library, GENEALOGICAL INDEX OF THE NEWBERRY LIBRARY, G. K. Hall, Boston, MA, 1960, 4 volumes.

_Everton Publishers, COMPUTERIZED ROOTS CELLAR and COMPUTERIZED FAMILY FILE, The Publishers, Logan, UT.

_J. Munsell's Sons, INDEX TO AMERICAN GENEALOGIES, 1711-1908, Genealogical Publishing Co., Baltimore, MD, 1967. 60,000 references.

In addition to the above nation-wide indexes and compilations, there are a sizable number of large indexes and compilations dealing exclusively with MA. Among the most notable of these are:

_INDEXES TO THE FEDERAL MA CENSUS SCHEDULES OF 1790, 1800/10/20/30/40/50, 1880, 1900. See census section in this chapter.

_CARD, COMPUTER, AND PRINTED CATALOGS, SPECIAL INDEXES, AND LISTS IN MSA, SLM, NEHGS, BPL, RL, and LL. See Chapter 3.

_National Archives, MICROFILM INDEXES OF COMPILED SERVICE RECORDS FOR MA SOLDIERS: (1) IN THE REVOLUTIONARY WAR, Microfilm Publication M860, 58 rolls, (2) IN THE WAR OF 1812, Microfilm Publicátion M602, 234 rolls, (3) IN THE CIVIL WAR, Microfilm Publication M544, 44 rolls, The Archives, Washington, DC.

_LARGE GENEALOGICAL COMPILATIONS: Adlow Collection in BPL, Bowman Files at MA Society of Mayflower Descendants, Brownson Genealogical Notes on Cape Cod Families on microfilm at NEHGS, Corbin Collection on microfilm at NEHGS, Judd Manuscripts at Forbes Library in Northampton, MA, Card Index to MA Archives Manuscript Collection at MSA, Shepard Genealogical Collection at Berkshire Athenaeum in Pittsfield, MA. All above also on microfilm at FHL (FHC).

_INDEXES TO MA BIRTHS, MARRIAGES, AND DEATHS, 1841-1971, MSA, Boston, MA. Also at NEHGS.

_US Customs Service, A SUPPLEMENTAL INDEX TO PASSENGER LISTS OF VESSELS ARRIVING AT ATLANTIC AND GULF PORTS, EXCLUDING NEW YORK, 1820-74, The National Archives, Washington, DC, Microfilm M334, 188 rolls.

_Historical Records Survey, SURNAME INDEX TO THE ALIEN PASSENGER ARRIVALS AT THE PORT OF BOSTON, 1848-91, WPA, Boston, MA, 1940.

_INDEX TO NEW ENGLAND NATURALIZATION PETITIONS, 1791-1906, National Archives Boston Branch, Waltham, MA.

_SUFFOLK COUNTY COURT RECORD INDEX, 1629-1797, SUFFOLK COUNTY COURT OF COMMON PLEAS INDEX, 1701-1855, MSA, Boston, MA.

_BIRTH, MARRIAGE, AND DEATH INDEXES FOR BOSTON AND ANNEXED TOWNS, 1630-1970, Boston City Registrar, Boston, MA.

_F. W. Bailey, EARLY MA MARRIAGES PRIOR TO 1800, Genealogical Publishing Co., Baltimore, MD, 1968.

_Boston City Registrars, RECORDS RELATING TO THE EARLY HISTORY OF BOSTON, Rockwell and Churchill and other publishers, Boston, MA, 1876-1909, 39 volumes.

_W. T. Davis, GENEALOGICAL REGISTER OF PLYMOUTH FAMILIES,

Genealogical Publishing Co., Baltimore, MD, 1975.

_INDEXES OF MARRIAGES AND OBITUARIES IN MA CENTINEL AND COLUMBIAN CENTINEL, 1794-1840, G. K. Hall, Boston, MA, 1961, 9 volumes.

_INDEXES OF OBITUARIES IN BOSTON NEWSPAPERS, 1704-1800, G. K. Hall, Boston, MA, 1968, 3 volumes.

_J. Farmer and S. G. Drake, A GENEALOGICAL REGISTER OF THE FIRST SETTLERS OF NEW ENGLAND, 1620-75, Genealogical Publishing Co., Baltimore, MD, 1983.

_W. P. Greenlaw, THE GREENLAW INDEX OF THE NEW ENGLAND HISTORIC GENEALOGICAL SOCIETY, The Society, Boston, MA, 1980, 2 volumes. Index to names in major works in the Society Library 1894-1945.

_J. M. Holbrook, BOSTON BEGINNINGS, 1630-99, Holbrook Research Institute, Oxford, MA, 1980.

_F. R. Holmes, DIRECTORY OF ANCESTRAL HEADS OF NEW ENGLAND FAMILIES, 1620-1700, Genealogical Publishing Co., Baltimore, MD, 1974.

_N. Ireland and M. Irving, A CONSOLIDATED INDEX OF CUTTER'S NINE GENEALOGY SERIES, Ireland Indexing Service, Fallbrook, CA, 1973.

_D. T. Konig, PLYMOUTH COURT RECORDS, 1686-1859, Glazier, Wilmington, DE, 1978-81, 16 volumes.

_INDEX OF PERSONS, PLACES, AND SUBJECTS IN VOLUMES 1-50 (1847-96) IN THE NEW ENGLAND HISTORICAL AND GENEALOGICAL REGISTER, Genealogical Publishing Co., Baltimore, MD, 1972.

_E. C. Lane, INDEX OF SURNAMES IN EARLY MA FROM PRINTED SOURCES, NEHGS, Boston, MA, 9 typescript volumes.

_PLYMOUTH CHURCH RECORDS, 1620-1859, Genealogical Publishing Co., Baltimore, MD, 1975, 2 volumes.

_C. H. Pope, THE PIONEERS OF MA, 1620-50, Genealogical Publishing Co., Baltimore, MD, 1977.

_G. B. Roberts, GENEALOGIES OF MAYFLOWER FAMILIES FROM THE NEW ENGLAND HISTORICAL AND GENEALOGICAL REGISTER, Genealogical Publishing Co., Baltimore, MD, 1985, 3 volumes.

_G. B. Roberts, MAYFLOWER SOURCE RECORDS, PRIMARY DATA CONCERNING SOUTHEASTERN MA, Genealogical Publishing Co., Baltimore, MD, 1986.

_G. B. Roberts, ENGLISH ORIGINS OF NEW ENGLAND FAMILIES FROM THE NEW ENGLAND HISTORICAL AND GENEALOGICAL REGISTER, Genealogical Publishing Co., Baltimore, MD, 1985, 2 series of 3 volumes each.

_J. Savage, A GENEALOGICAL DICTIONARY OF THE FIRST SETTLERS OF NEW ENGLAND WHO CAME BEFORE 1692, Genealogical Publishing Co., Baltimore, MD, 1981, 4 volumes.

_S. V. Talcott, GENEALOGICAL NOTES OF NY AND NEW ENGLAND, Genealogical Publishing Co., Baltimore, MD, 1973.

Most of the published works mentioned above are available in NEHGS and BPL, with many being found in FHL(FHC), LGL, and RL, and some in LL. The microfilms should be sought in MSA, NEHGS, BPL, FHL (FHC), NA, and NAFB. The above references are by no means all of the large indexes and compilations of genealogical materials for MA. They represent only a selection of some of the major ones. Numerous others are listed in other sections of this chapter.

19. Genealogical periodicals

Several genealogical periodicals and some historical periodicals carrying genealogical data or aids have been or are being published for MA. These journals, serial publications, and newsletters contain genealogies, local history data, genealogical records, family queries and answers, book reviews, research aids and methodology, and other pertinent information. If you have a MA progenitor, you will find it of great value to subscribe to one or more of the state-wide periodicals, as well as any periodicals published in the region, county, or city where he/she lived. Periodicals pertinent to MA research may be divided into two classes: (1) those that have state-wide coverage, and (2) those that have regional or local coverage.

Chief among the periodicals which have a state-wide coverage of MA are the following:

_THE AMERICAN GENEALOGIST, R. W. Sherman, co-editor, 128 Massasoit Drive, Warwick, RI, 1922-, volume 1-. Many MA data.

_BULLETIN BOARD OF THE AMERICAN-PORTUGUESE GENEALOGICAL SOCIETY, The Society, Taunton, MA.

_CAR-DEL SCRIBE, E. P. Bentley, editor, Ludlow, MA, 1963, volume 1-.

_CHEDWATO DISPATCH, Chedwato Publns., Westfield, MA.

_COLLECTIONS OF THE MA HISTORICAL SOCIETY, The Society, Boston, MA, 1846-1941. Irregular.

_THE GENEALOGICAL ADVERTISER, 1898-1901, L. H. Greenlaw, editor, 4 volumes. Reprinted by the Genealogical Publishing Co., Baltimore, MD, 1974.

_GENEALOGICAL MAGAZINE [known by several titles: SALEM PRESS HISTORICAL AND GENEALOGICAL RECORD, PUTNAM'S MONTHLY HISTORICAL MAGAZINE, and GENEALOGICAL QUARTERLY MAGAZINE], Salem, MA, 1890-1917.

_J. M. Glynn, Jr., NEW ENGLAND GENEALOGY, NEWSLETTER OF THE INSTITUTE OF FAMILY HISTORY AND GENEALOGY, The Institute, Newton, MA, 1980-, volume 1-.

_IRISH FAMILY HISTORY, The Irish Family History Society, Newton, MA.

_MA QUERIES, Pioneer Publications, Elk, WA.

_THE MA MAGAZINE, DEVOTED TO MA HISTORY, GENEALOGICAL BIOGRAPHY, Salem Press, Salem, MA, 1908-18, 11 volumes.
_MA VOLUNTEER CALENDAR, MA Genealogical Council, Boston, MA.
_MASSOG, PUBLICATION OF THE MA SOCIETY OF GENEALOGISTS, The Society, Dorchester Center, MA, 1979-.
_NEW ENGLAND HISTORICAL AND GENEALOGICAL REGISTER, NEHGS, Boston, MA, 1847-, volume 1-, with INDEX OF PERSONS, PLACES, AND SUBJECTS, VOLUMES 1-50, 1847-96, Genealogical Publishing Co., Baltimore, MD, 1972, and INDEX TO GENEALOGIES AND PEDIGREES, VOLUMES 1-50, 1847-96, The Society, Boston, MA, 1896, and M. W. Parsons, INDEX (ABRIDGED), VOLUMES 51-112, 1897-1958, The Compiler, Marlborough, MA, 1959, and SEPARATE INDEXES IN EACH VOLUME. The most important periodical for MA. Detailed, well documented, accurate.
_THE NY GENEALOGICAL AND BIOGRAPHICAL RECORD, NY Genealogical and Biographical Society, New York, NY, 1870-, volume 1-. With J. W. Worden, MASTER INDEX, 1870-1982, The Author, Franklin, OH, 1983, with F. E. Youngs, SUBJECT INDEX, Volumes 1-38, The Author, New York, NY, with G. A. Barber, SUBJECT INDEX, Volumes 39-94, The Author, New York, NY, and with G. A. Barber, NY GENEALOGICAL AND BIOGRAPHICAL RECORD SURNAME INDEX TO VOLUMES 1-40, The Author, New York, NY, 4 typescript volumes.
_NEWSLETTER OF THE IRISH ANCESTRAL RESEARCH ASSOCIATION, The Association, Sudbury, MA.
_NEXUS, newsletter, NEHGS, Boston, MA, 5 issues per year.
_PROCEEDINGS OF THE MA HISTORICAL SOCIETY, The Society, Boston, MA, 3 series, 1791-1957, with INDEX TO VOLUMES 1-60. Irregular.
_PUBLICATIONS OF THE COLONIAL SOCIETY OF MA, The Society, Boston, MA, 1895-, volume 1-. Irregular. Index to Volumes 1-25, 1932.
_H. C. Quimby, NEW ENGLAND FAMILY HISTORY, New York, NY, 1907-12, 4 volumes.
_THE SECOND BOAT, SPECIALIZING IN COLONIAL GENEALOGY, Machias, ME, 1980-.

Among the very useful regional, local, and special-area periodicals of MA are these listed below:
_AMERICAN ELMS, Western MA Genealogical Society, Springfield, MA.
_THE BERKSHIRE GENEALOGIST, Berkshire Family History Assn., Pittsfield, MA, 1982-.
_BULLETIN OF THE CAPE COD GENEALOGICAL SOCIETY, The Society, Harwich Center, MA.
_COLLECTIONS OF THE OLD COLONY HISTORICAL SOCIETY, The Society, Taunton, MA, 1879-1909. Irregular.
_DANVERS HISTORICAL SOCIETY COLLECTIONS, The Society, Danvers,

MA, 1916-67, 43 volumes. Material on Danvers and Salem.

_DEDHAM HISTORICAL REGISTER, The Dedham Historical Society, Dedham, MA, 1890-1903, 14 volumes. Also Norfolk County materials.

_THE ESSEX ANTIQUARIAN, Essex Antiquarian, Salem, MA, 1897-1909, 13 volumes.

_ESSEX GENEALOGIST, M. W. Wiswall, editor, Essex Society of Genealogists, Lynnfield Public Library, Lynnfield, MA.

_HISTORICAL COLLECTIONS OF THE TOPSFIELD HISTORICAL SOCIETY, The Society, Topsfield, MA, 1895-1951. Includes Essex County material.

_HISTORICAL COLLECTIONS OF THE ESSEX INSTITUTE, The Institute, Salem, MA, 1859-, volume 1-, with INDEX TO VOLUMES 1-105, 1859-1969. Chiefly Essex County.

_LIBRARY OF CAPE COD HISTORY AND GENEALOGY, C. W. Swift, Yarmouth, MA, 1912-24. Irregular.

_THE MAYFLOWER QUARTERLY, The General Society of Mayflower Descendants, Plymouth, MA, 1935-.

_THE MAYFLOWER DESCENDANT, The Mayflower Society, Boston, MA, 1899-1937, 34 volumes, with INDEX TO PERSONS, 1899-1937, MA Society of Mayflower Descendants, Boston, MA, 1956-62, 3 volumes, and INDEX, 1899-1937, Boston, MA, 1979, 2 volumes; restarted in 1985 with Volume 35, A. C. Williams, editor, 1985-, volume 35-.

_MEDFORD HISTORICAL REGISTER, Medford, MA, 1898-1940, 43 volumes.

_PILGRIM NOTES AND QUERIES, The MA Society of Mayflower Descendants, Boston, MA, 1913-7, 5 volumes.

_THE PILGRIM SOCIETY NEWSLETTER, The Pilgrim Society, Plymouth, MA.

_THE PLYMOUTH COLONY GENEALOGICAL HELPER, The Augustan Society, Torrence, CA, 1974-. Irregular.

_THE REGISTER OF THE LYNN HISTORICAL SOCIETY, The Society, Lynn, MA, 1898-1931.

Good collections of MA genealogically-oriented periodicals will be found in NEHGS and BPL, some of the above periodicals are in FHL(FHC) and LGL, and those relating to specific localities can be found in appropriate RL and LL. A useful index volume to many periodicals (not all the above) is:

_George Fingold Library of Boston, GENERAL INDEX OF AND ARTICLES ON MA PEOPLE AND PLACES TO BE FOUND IN CERTAIN MA IMPRINT PERIODICALS, The Library, Boston, MA, 1964.

Not only do articles pertaining to MA genealogy appear in the above publications, they are also printed in other genealogical journals. Fortunately, indexes to articles in major genealogical periodicals are available. However, most of these indexes do not include all names, so it is generally necessary to consult the more-detailed indexes usually carried in each volume of each periodical.

_For periodicals published 1858-1952, consult D. L. Jacobus and C. Boyer, 3rd, INDEX TO GENEALOGICAL PERIODICALS, 1858-1953, Boyer, Newhall, CA, 1983. Lists only major names.

_For periodicals published 1957-62, consult the annual volumes by I. Waldenmaier, ANNUAL INDEX TO GENEALOGICAL PERIODICALS AND FAMILY HISTORIES, The Author, Washington, DC, 1957-62.

_For periodicals published 1962-9 and 1974-89, consult the annual volumes by various editors, E. S. Rogers, G. E. Russell, L. C. Towle, and C. M. Mayhew, GENEALOGICAL PERIODICAL ANNUAL INDEX, various publishers, most recently Heritage Books, Bowie, MD, 1962-9, 1974-89.

_For periodicals published 1986 and after, consult THE PERIODICAL SOURCE INDEX, annually, Allen County Public Library Foundation, Fort Wayne, IN.

These index volumes should be sought in NEHGS, BPL, and FHL(FHC). Most LGL, some RL, and a few LL also have them. In these indexes, you ought to consult all general MA listings, then all listings under the counties and towns which concern you, as well as listings under family names, if such are included (only in the earlier index volumes, and then only partially).

20. Genealogical and historical societies

In the state of MA various societies for the study of genealogy, the discovery of hereditary lineages, the accumulation of ancestral data, and the publication of the materials have been organized. In addition to these genealogical societies, there are many historical societies which devote at least some time and effort to collection and publication of data which are useful to genealogists. Of course, there are some historical societies which have little or no genealogical interest. You should further recognize that some societies which once made notable genealogical and historical contributions no longer exist, and that smaller societies tend to come and go. The MA societies which have a genealogical focus are of two types: (1) state-wide or even wider, and (2) local societies (regional, county, city, town).

The major societies in MA which have a state-wide or wider coverage are as follows:

_American-Portuguese Genealogical Society, PO Box 644, Taunton, MA 02780.

_Irish Ancestral Research Association, PO Box 619, Sudbury, MA 01776.

_MA Society of Genealogists, PO Box 266, Dorchester Center, MA 02124. With numerous local chapters including ones in Bristol,

Franklin, Hampden, Hampshire, Middlesex, and Worcester Counties.

_MA Society, Sons of the American Revolution, 21 Milton Rd., Brookline, MA 02146.

_New England Historic Genealogical Society, 101 Newbury St., Boston, MA 02116.

_General Society of Mayflower Descendants, PO Box 3297, Plymouth, MA 02361.

_MA Society of Mayflower Descendants, 101 Newbury St., Boston, MA 02116.

In addition to the above genealogical organizations which have state-wide (or wider) coverage, there are some important local societies. Among them are these:

_Berkshire Family History Association, PO Box 1437, Pittsfield, MA 02101.

_Bristol County Chapter, MA Society of Genealogists, 459 Madison St., Fall River, MA 02720.

_Cape Cod Genealogical Society, Brooks Library, Harwich Center, MA 02645.

_Concord Genealogical Roundtable, Concord Public Library, Concord, MA 01742.

_Essex Society of Genealogists, Lynnfield Public Library, 18 Summer St., Lynnfield, MA 01940.

_Franklin County Chapter, MA Society of Genealogists, c/o Wallace Trumper, Anderson Rd., Shelburne, MA 01370.

_Hampden County Chapter, MA Society of Genealogists, 25 Edison Dr., Ludlow, MA 01056.

_Hampshire County Chapter, MA Society of Genealogists, c/o W. B. Cook, Rt. 1, Matthews Rd., Conway, MA 01341.

_Jewish Genealogical Study Group of Boston, PO Box 620, Belmont, MA 02178.

_Middlesex County Chapter, MA Society of Genealogists, 75 Hemingway St., Apt. 203, Winchester, MA 01890.

_Middlesex North Chapter, MA Society of Genealogists, 117 Offut Rd., Bedford, MA 01731.

_Middlesex South Chapter, MA Society of Genealogists, 33 Bigelow Rd., Waltham, MA 02154.

_Norfolk County Chapter, MA Society of Genealogists, PO Box 55, Walpole, MA 02181.

_North Shore Jewish Genealogical Society, 31 Exchange St., Lynn, MA 01901.

_Plymouth Colony Genealogists, 26 Rochester Rd., Carver, MA 02330.

_Western MA Genealogical Society, PO Box 206, Forest Park Station, Springfield, MA 01108.

_Worcester County Chapter, MA Society of Genealogists, c/o D. Beal, 11 Thayer Pond Dr., #1, North Oxford, MA 01537.

It may be that the addresses of some of the above local societies will be in error since their addresses sometimes change when new officers are elected. If you fail to contact a society using the addresses above, inquire at the county library. They usually know of the organizations and can often give you the current address. County libraries are named with their addresses in Chapter 4. It may also be that some of the above societies have become inactive. Again, the county libraries usually know. They also can tell you if new societies have been started up in their areas. Resident members of genealogical societies, particularly local ones, can often be of immense help to you. They are ordinarily very knowledgeable about the background, the early families, and the available records of their local areas. By consulting them, you can often save valuable time as they guide you in your work. The local societies also can often tell you if anyone else is working on or has worked on your family line.

In addition to the genealogical societies in MA, there are also many MA historical societies which may often be of help to you in your progenitor hunt. However, you must recognize, as was stated before, that not all these societies are interested in genealogy. Nonetheless, it often pays to contact them. These numerous societies are listed in:

_American Association of State and Local History, DIRECTORY OF HISTORICAL AGENCIES IN THE US AND CANADA, The Association, Nashville, TN, latest edition.

_DIRECTORY OF HISTORICAL AGENCIES IN MA, Bay State Historical League, Boston, MA, latest issue.

21. Land records

In the very early years of MA when the first lands of Plymouth Colony and MA Bay Colony were being settled (1620, 1630), the land was distributed by the local governments of the two small settlements. However, as more people came to both places, the lands beyond them were granted to special settlement-minded groups (called proprietors) in tracts of proper size to establish towns (usually about 6 by 6 miles). The proprietors then parcelled the land out to various settlers. Records of these grants to the first individual owners were recorded in books called Proprietors Records, although sometimes they appear in town records. Subsequent transfers of the land generally appeared in town records, although proprietors sometimes dominated such affairs and sometimes turned them over to town government in lesser or greater degrees. When counties came to be organized (1643 in MA Bay Colony and 1685 in Plymouth Colony), deed registration was put on a county level and has remained so since. Later on some proprietors who received town grants were largely land speculators who never settled in the granted tract themselves. In other words, to be sure that all land records are located, you need to look at all available proprietors records, all towns records (since there is often record overlap with the records of both the proprietors and the county), all County Records from the beginnings of the counties in which the town was located, and, if pertinent, the colony records of early pre-county Plymouth Colony and/or MA Bay Colony. Be cautious here because many towns existed first in one county then later in another county when county division occurred.

Following are some notes on the locations of the county deed records for the various counties of MA. This can be a little complicated because of formations of new counties, accompanying changes in the shiretowns (county seats), the shifting of towns between counties, and the establishing of more than one deed registry in more highly populated counties.

_Barnstable County (established 1685 from Plymouth Colony): records before 1685 at Plymouth, records since then recorded at Barnstable, fire in 1827 destroyed most previous records, those for 1804-8 and 1827- available at Barnstable, plus some rerecorded deeds for the period before 1827 [FHL has microfilms of records 1804-8, 1827-66, and index 1703-1868, also in MSA.]

_Berkshire County (established 1761 from Hampshire County which was established in 1662 from Middlesex County which was established 1643 from MA Bay Colony): records before 1761 at Springfield, records 1761-88 at Pittsfield, records of Northern District 1788- at Adams, records of Middle District 1788 at Pittsfield, records of Southern District 1788- at Great Barrington [FHL has microfilms of records 1761-1871, also in MSA.]

_Bristol County (established 1685 from Plymouth Colony): records before 1685 at Plymouth, records 1685-1837 at Taunton, records of Northern District 1837-92 at Taunton, records of Southern District 1837-92 at New Bedford, records of Northern District 1892- at Taunton, records of Fall River District 1892- at Fall River, records of Southern District 1892- at New Bedford [FHL has microfilms of records 1686-1956, also in MSA.]

_Dukes County (established as a MA county 1695 from a NY county which was established 1683 from NY territory): records 1641- at Edgartown [FHL has microfilms of records 1641-1859 with index, also proprietors records 1641-1717, also in MSA.]

_Essex County (established 1643 from MA Bay Colony): records before 1643 at Boston, records 1639-1869 at Salem, Ipswich records (for towns of Ipswich, Newbury, Rowley) 1640-94 at Salem, records for Southern District 1869- at Salem, records for Northern District 1869- at Lawrence [FHL has microfilms of Essex County records 1639-1866 with index 1640-1879 and Ipswich records 1640-94 with index, also in MSA.]

_Franklin County (established 1811 from Hampshire County which was established 1662 from Middlesex County which was established 1643 from MA Bay Colony): records before 1787 at Springfield, deed abstracts 1663-1786 and records 1787- at Greenfield [FHL has microfilms of records 1787-1867 with index 1787-1889, also in MSA.]

_Hampden County (established 1812 from Hampshire County which was established 1662 from Middlesex County which was established 1643 from MA Bay Colony): records 1636- at Springfield [FHL has microfilms of records 1636-1867 with index 1636-1869, also in MSA.]

_Hampshire County (established 1662 from Middlesex County which was established 1643 from MA Bay Colony): records 1636-1787 at Springfield, records of Northampton District 1787-1812 at Northampton, records of Northern District 1787-1811 at Greenfield, records of Southern District at Springfield 1787-1812, records 1812- at Northampton [FHL has microfilms of records 1636-1865 with index, also in MSA.]

_MA Bay Colony (1630-92): early deeds in SUFFOLK DEEDS, 1629-97, Rockwell and Churchill, Boston, MA, 1880-1906, 14 volumes, early grants in N. B. Shurtleff, RECORDS OF THE GOVERNOR AND COMPANY OF MA BAY IN NEW ENGLAND, 1628-86, AMS Press, New York, NY, 1971, 6 volumes, S. F. Haven, RECORDS OF THE COMPANY OF MA BAY, 1628-41, Bolles and Houghton, Cambridge, MA, 1850, also see Suffolk County.

_Middlesex County (established 1643 from MA Bay Colony): records 1649-1855 at Cambridge, records of Southern District 1855- at Cambridge, records of Northern District 1855- at Lowell [FHL has microfilms of records 1649-1900 with index 1649-1950, also in MSA.] See above listing for 1629-49.

_Nantucket County (established 1695 from NY territory Dukes County): records 1659- at Nantucket [FHL has microfilms of records 1659-1875 with index, also in MSA.]

_Norfolk County (established 1793 from Suffolk County which was established 1643 from MA Bay Colony): records before 1793 at Boston, records 1793- at Dedham [FHL has microfilms of records 1793-1890 with index, also in MSA.]

_Old Norfolk County (established 1643 from MA Bay Colony, disestablished in 1679, towns of Haverhill, Amesbury, and Salisbury annexed to Essex County, others went to NH): records 1647-1714 at Salem, note that some records were kept long after the county was officially dissolved [FHL has microfilms of records 1647-1714 cataloged under Essex County, also in MSA.]

_Plymouth Colony (1620-92): early land grants and deeds in N. B. Shurtleff and D. Pulsifer, RECORDS OF THE COLONY OF NEW PLYMOUTH IN THE NEW ENGLAND, 1620-92, AMS Press, New York, NY, 1968, 6 volumes, also C. H. Pope, THE PLYMOUTH SCRAPBOOK, THE OLDEST ORIGINAL DOCUMENTS EXTANT IN PLYMOUTH

ARCHIVES PRINTED VERBATIM, Goodspeed, Boston, MA, 1918, original records 1620-99 at Plymouth [FHL has microfilms of records 1620-99, also in MSA], also see Plymouth County.

_Plymouth County (established 1685 from Plymouth Colony): records 1620- at Plymouth [FHL has microfilms of records 1620-1900 with index 1620-1914, also in MSA], also see Plymouth Colony.

_Suffolk County (established 1643 from MA Bay Colony): records 1629- in Boston, see SUFFOLK COUNTY DEEDS, 1629-97, Rockwell and Churchill, Boston, MA, 1880-1906 [FHL has microfilms of records 1639-1885 with index 1639-1920, also in MSA], also see Boston Registry Department, RECORDS RELATING TO THE EARLY HISTORY OF BOSTON, The Record Commissioners, Boston, MA, 1876-1909, 22 volumes. Also see MA Bay Colony above.

_Worcester County (established in 1731 from Suffolk and Middlesex Counties, both of which were established 1643 from MA Bay Colony): records before 1731 at Cambridge, Boston, and Springfield, records 1731-1884 at Worcester, records for Southern District 1884- at Worcester, records for Northern District 1884- at Fitchburg [FHL has microfilms of records 1721-1866 with index 1731-1889, also in MSA.]

Please recall that the above listings refer chiefly to the county deed records, although some data on the pre-county colony period are included. For the majority of land grant records and for pre-county and often post-county deed records, you must thoroughly search the proprietors records and the town records which are kept in the towns. Many of them are also available on microfilm at the FHL(FHC). Much more detail on the county and town land records will be given in Chapter 4 where there is a section devoted to each county and a sub-section to each town. Included in the county sections will be the towns which are in each deed registration district in the cases of counties which have more than one such district. A very useful history of land records in MA is:

_J. Sullivan, HISTORY OF LAND TITLES IN MA, Arno Press, New York, NY, 1972.

And a listing of proprietor's records available as of 1885 is given in:

_C. D. Wright, REPORT ON THE CUSTODY AND CONDITION OF THE PUBLIC RECORDS OF THE PARISHES, TOWNS, AND COUNTIES OF MA, Wright and Potter, Boston, MA, 1889, pages 5-8.

Though out of date, this is an exceedingly useful listing because it alerts you regarding proprietors' records which should be sought. However, if records are not listed here, you must not draw the conclusion that they do not exist. Seek them out carefully, because they may have been discovered after the above publication came out.

22. Manuscripts

One of the most useful and yet one of the most unused sources of genealogical data are the various manuscript collections relating to MA. These collections will be found in state, regional, county, town, and private libraries, archives, museums, societies, and repositories in numerous places in MA, including universities, colleges, and church agencies. Manuscript collections consist of all sorts of records of religious, educational, patriotic, business, social, civil, professional, governmental, and political organizations; documents, letters, memoirs, notes, and papers of early settlers, ministers, politicians, business men, educators, physicians, dentists, lawyers, judges, land speculators, and farmers; records of churches, cemeteries, mortuaries, schools, corporations, and industries; works of artists, musicians, writers, sculptors, photographers, architects, and historians; and records, papers, letters, and reminiscences of participants in various wars, as well as records of military organizations and campaigns.

The major MA repositories for manuscripts of genealogical importance are:

_In Amherst, University of MA/Amherst Library, 01003.

_In Boston, Memorial Shrine of the GAR, Room 27, State House, 02133. (Civil War)

_In Boston, Boston Athenaeum, 10 1/2 Beacon St., 02108. (History, genealogy, biography)

_In Boston, BPL, Copley Sq., 02117. (History, genealogy, biography, personal papers)

_In Boston, Congregational Library, 14 Beacon St., 02108.

_In Boston, Episcopal Diocese of MA Library and Archives, 1 Joy St., 02108.

_In Boston, Baker Library, Harvard University, 02163. (Business, commercial, shipping, trade records)

_In Boston, Countway Library of Medicine, Harvard University, 02115. (Medical history)

_In Boston, MA Historical Society, 1154 Boylston St., 02215. (MA and New England history and biography, family and personal papers)

_In Boston, MSA, 220 Morrisey Blvd., 02125. (Public records of colony, province, and state of MA, including the 328-volumed MA Archives, colonial and Revolutionary records of many types with partial indexes. No genealogist working on MA progenitors should miss it.)

_In Boston, MA Society of Mayflower Descendants, 101 Newbury St., 02116.

_In Boston, NEHGS, 101 Newbury St., Boston, MA 02116. (Largest genealogical manuscript collection in MA, but not limited to MA.)

_In Boston, New England Methodist Historical Society, 745 Commonwealth Ave., 02215.

_In Boston, Roman Catholic Archdiocese of Boston, 2121 Commonwealth, 02135.
_In Boston, Social Law Library, 1200 Court House, 02108. (Court records including Suffolk County Inferior Court of Common Pleas records 1692-1820)
_In Boston, Society for the Preservation of New England Antiquities, 141 Cambridge St., 02114. (Commerce, photographs, family manuscripts)
_In Boston, Unitarian-Universalist Association, 25 Beacon St., 02108.
_In Cambridge, Harvard University Libraries, 02138. (Especially Houghton Library, Manuscript Division)
_In Cambridge, Andover-Harvard Theological Library, Harvard University, 45 Francis Ave., 02138. (Unitarian and Universalist records)
_In Cambridge, Schlesinger Library, Radcliffe College, 10 Garden St., 02138. (Women)
_In Medford, Universalist Historical Society, Tufts University Library, 02155.
_In Methuen, United Methodist Church, NH Conference, Lowell and Pelham Sts., 01844.
_In Newton Center, Andover-Newton Theological School Library, 169 Herrick Rd., 02159. (Baptist)
_In Northampton, Forbes Library, 20 West St., 01060. (Western MA, CT Valley)
_In Northampton, Smith College Library, 01063. (Women)
_In Pittsfield, Berkshire Athenaeum, 1 Wendell Ave., 01201. (The Berkshire region of MA)
_In Plymouth, The Pilgrim Society, 75 Court St., 02360-3891.
_In Salem, Essex Institute, 132 Essex St., 01970. (Eastern MA)
_In Waltham, American Jewish Historical Society, 2 Thornton Rd., 02154.
_In Waltham, NABB, 380 Trapelo Rd., 12154. (Federal records for CT, ME, MA, RI, VT.)
_In Worcester, American Antiquarian Society, 185 Salisbury St., 01609. (Early histories, directories, newspapers, manuscripts.)

Among the larger genealogical manuscript collections for the state are the Adlow Collection (BPL), the Banks Collection (Library of Congress in Washington, DC), the Bowman Collection (MA Society of Mayflower Descendants and NEHGS), the Brownson Collection (Sturgis Library in Barnstable), the Corbin Collection (NEHGS), the Judd Collection (Forbes Library in Northampton), MA Archives Manuscript Collection (MSA), and the Shepard Collection (Berkshire Athenaeum). Microfilm copies of all of these are available at FHL and through its branch FHC. The Adlow Collection has Boston coroner records, the Banks Collection has records on the English origins of MA settlers, the Bowman Collection deals with Mayflower families, the Corbin Collection has town records, so does the Judd Collection, the MA Archives Manuscript Collection is a huge group of colonial and early state government records, and the Shepard Collection is made up of genealogical data for western MA families.

In addition to the major repositories listed above, there are a sizable number of smaller institutions which have notable collections, most of them being local in character. That is, they have materials from one or a few towns or in some instances somewhat larger areas. Included are:

_Abingdon (Dyer Memorial Library), Amesbury (Amesbury Public Library), Amherst (Jones Library), Andover (Andover Historical Society and Memorial Hall Library), Arlington (Arlington Historical Society), Ashland (Ashland Historical Society), Attleboro (Attleboro Public Library), Barnstable (Sturgis Library), Barre (Barre Historical Society), Bedford (Bedford Historical Society),

_Belchertown (Belchertown Historical Association), Beverly (Beverly Historical Society), Bolton (Bolton Historical Society), Boston (Bostonian Society), Boylston (Boylston Public Library), Brewster (Brewster Ladies Library), Brookline (Public Library of Brookline), Centerville (Centerville Historical Society), Chelmsford (Chelmsford Historical Society), Chesterfield (Chesterfield Historical Society),

_Clinton (Clinton Historical Society), Concord (Concord Free Public Library), Danvers (Danvers Archival Center), Dedham (Dedham Historical Society), Deerfield (Memorial Libraries), Dennis (Dennis Historical Society), Dighton (Dighton Historical Society), Dorchester (Dorchester Historical Society), Duxbury (Duxbury Rural and Historical Society), Eastham (Eastham Historical Society),

_Edgartown (Dukes County Historical Society), Essex (Essex Historical Society), Fall River (Fall River Historical Society), Falmouth (Falmouth Historical Society), Fitchburg (Fitchburg Historical Society), Foxboro (Foxboro Historical Commission), Framingham (Framingham Public Library, Framingham Historical and Natural History Society), Gloucester (Annisquam Historical Society),

_Haverhill (Haverhill Public Library), Hingham (Hingham Public Library), Holliston (Holliston Historical Society), Hopedale (Bancroft Memorial Library), Hull (Means Library), Hyde Park (Hyde Park Historical Society), Ipswich (Ipswich Historical Society, Ipswich Public Library), Lancaster (Lancaster Historical Commission, Lancaster Town Library),

_Lawrence (Immigrant City Archives), Lexington (Lexington Historical Society), Lincoln (Lincoln Public Library), Longmeadow (Storrs Library), Lowell (University of Lowell Libraries), Lynn (Lynn Historical Society), Manchester (Manchester Historical Society), Marblehead (Marblehead Historical Society), Marlborough (Marlborough Public Library), Medford (Medford Historical Society),

_Mendon (Mendon Historical Society), Middleboro (Middleboro Historical Association), Nantucket (Nantucket Historical Association), Natick (Morse Association), Needham (Needham Free Public Library, Needham Historical Society), New Bedford (New Bedford Free Public Library, Old Dartmouth Historical Society), Newton (Jackson Homestead, Newton Free Library),

_North Andover (Museum of American Textile History, North Andover

Historical Society, Stevens Memorial Library), Northampton (Forbes Library, and Northampton Historical Society), Northborough (Northborough Historical Society), Oxford (Oxford Free Public Library), Peabody (Peabody Historical Society), Petersham (Petersham Historical Society), Quincy (Quincy Historical Society), Reading (Reading Antiquarian Society),

_Rehoboth (Annawan Historical Society), Revere (Revere Public Library), Royalston (Royalston Historical Society), Salem (Phillips Library), Sandwich (Sandwich Archives and Historical Center, Sandwich Historical Society), Sharon (Kendall Whaling Museum), Shirley (Hazen Memorial Library, Shirley Historical Society), Shrewsbury (Shrewsbury Historical Society), South Hadley (Mount Holyoke College Library and Museum),

_South Natick (Natural History and Library Society of South Natick), South Sudbury (Goodnow Public Library), Southbridge (Edwards Library), Springfield (CT Valley Historical Museum), Stockbridge (Stockbridge Library Association), Stoughton (Stoughton Historical Society), Sturbridge (Old Sturbridge Village), Swansea (Swansea Historical Society), Taunton (Old Colony Historical Society),

_Templeton (Narragansett Historical Society), Topsfield (Topsfield Historical Society), Wakefield (Wakefield Historical Society), Waltham (Waltham Historical Society, Waltham Public Library), Wayland (Wayland Free Public Library), Wellfleet (Wellfleet Historical Society), Wenham (Wenham Historical Association), West Barnstable (Cape Cod Community College Library),

_West Boxford (Ingalls Memorial Library Association), West Boylston (Beaman Memorial Public Library), West Brookfield (Quabeag Historical Society), Westborough (Westborough Historical Society), Westfield (Westfield State College Library), Westford (Fletcher Library), Westwood (Westwood Public Library), Weymouth (Weymouth Public Libraries),

_Winchendon (Winchendon Historical Society), Winchester (Winchester Archival Center), Winthrop (Winthrop Public Library), Woburn (Woburn Public Library), Worcester (Worcester Historical Museum).

You will have noticed above that the main places which house manuscripts of importance to ancestral research are usually local public libraries and local historical societies. This should tip you off to look into all such institutions in the regions of your ancestors.

The holdings of many manuscript depositories in MA have been briefly or broadly described in special publications. Among the more valuable of these are the following:

_US National Historical Publications and Records Commission, DIRECTORY OF ARCHIVES AND MANUSCRIPT REPOSITORIES IN THE US, The Commission, Oryx Press, New York, NY, 1988.

_P. M. Hamer, A GUIDE TO ARCHIVES AND MANUSCRIPTS IN THE US, Yale University Press, New Haven, CT, 1961.

_Historical Records Survey, GUIDE TO DEPOSITORIES OF MANUSCRIPT COLLECTIONS IN MA, WPA, Boston, MA, 1939.
_Historical Records Survey, GUIDE TO MANUSCRIPT MATERIALS IN THE BOSTONIAN SOCIETY, WPA, Boston, MA, 1939. Typescript in MSA.
_Historical Records Survey, GUIDE TO MANUSCRIPT COLLECTIONS IN MA, WPA, Boston, MA, 1939, 9 volumes. Typescript in MSA.
_Historical Records Survey, NEGRO CHURCHES, NEGRO MANUSCRIPTS, NEGRO FILES, AND NEGRO BIBLIOGRAPHY IN MA, WPA, Boston, MA, 1930s. Large volume of file material in MSA.
_CATALOG OF BOOKS AND MANUSCRIPTS IN THE HARVARD COLLEGE LIBRARY, Belknap Press of Harvard University Press, Cambridge, MA, 1964-.
_CATALOG OF MANUSCRIPTS IN THE HOUGHTON LIBRARY, HARVARD UNIVERSITY, Chadwyck-Healey, Cambridge, MA, 1986, 8 volumes.
_CATALOG OF MANUSCRIPTS IN THE MA HISTORICAL SOCIETY, The Society, Boston, MA, 1969, with SUPPLEMENTS, The Society, Boston, MA, 1980-.
_CATALOGUE OF THE MANUSCRIPT COLLECTION OF THE AMERICAN ANTIQUARIAN SOCIETY, G. K. Hall, Boston, MA, 1974, 4 volumes.
_DESCRIPTION OF THE MANUSCRIPT COLLECTIONS IN THE MA DIOCESAN (EPISCOPAL) LIBRARY, The Library, Boston, MA, 1939.
_M. J. Duffy, GUIDE TO THE PAROCHIAL ARCHIVES OF THE EPISCOPAL CHURCH IN BOSTON, Episcopal Diocese of MA, Boston, MA, 1981.
_C. A. Elliott, A DESCRIPTIVE GUIDE TO THE HARVARD UNIVERSITY ARCHIVES, Harvard University Press, Cambridge, MA, 1975.
_H. Forbes, NEW ENGLAND DIARIES, 1602-1800, A DESCRIPTIVE CATALOG OF DIARIES, ORDERLY BOOKS, AND SEA JOURNALS, Russell and Russell, New York, NY, 1967.
_MANUSCRIPT, SUBJECT, AND AUTHOR CATALOGS OF THE SMITH COLLECTION, WOMEN'S HISTORY ARCHIVE, SMITH COLLEGE, NORTHAMPTON, MA, G. K. Hall, Boston, MA, 1975.
_W. Matthews and others, AMERICAN DIARIES WRITTEN PRIOR TO 1861, Canner, Boston, MA, 1959.
_W. Matthews, AMERICAN DIARIES IN MANUSCRIPT, 1580-1954, University of GA Press, Athens, GA, 1974.
_J. M. O'Toole and M. M. McGuinness, GUIDE TO THE ARCHIVES OF THE (CATHOLIC) ARCHDIOCESE OF BOSTON, Garland Publications, New York, NY, 1982.
_C. S. Price, A GUIDE TO THE MANUSCRIPTS OF THE PILGRIM SOCIETY, The Society, Plymouth, MA, 1976.

Finally, we need to call to your attention an indispensable series of volumes which you must not fail to look into. These books were published by the Library of Congress in order to put into print the manuscript holdings of archives and repositories all over the US. There is an annual volume from 1959 to the present. And best of all, this tremendous finding aid is thoroughly indexed:

_US Library of Congress, THE NATIONAL UNION CATALOG OF MANUSCRIPT COLLECTIONS, The Library, Washington, DC, issued annually 1959-. Cumulative indexes 1959-62, 1963-6, 1967-9, 1970-4, 1975-9, 1980-4. Volumes indexed separately thereafter.

There is also an overall index covering the volumes for 1959-84:

_E. Altham and others, INDEX TO PERSONAL NAMES IN THE NATIONAL UNION CATALOG OF MANUSCRIPT COLLECTIONS, 1959-84, Chadwyck-Healey, Arlington, VA, 1988, 2 volumes.

Be certain to look in all of these indexes for your family surnames, then under counties of interest to you, then under pertinent cities and towns, then under MA, then under various subjects (for example, cavalry, churches, Civil War, Colonial period, coroners, courts, customs, estates, family papers, French and Indian War, genealogy, history, immigration, Indian Wars, infantry, Jews, juries, justices of the peace, land, leases, licenses, local history, magistrates, maps, military affairs, militia, mortgages, newspapers, pardon, parole, personal accounts, pioneer life, ports of entry, prisons, Revolutionary War, slavery, surveys, tax records, travel, trials, vital records, War of 1812, wills). Do not overlook the many listings under the general heading genealogy, and don't forget to look under Boston. These efforts will introduce you quickly and easily to the vast world of MA manuscript materials. Most of the reference books mentioned in the two previous paragraphs are available in NEHGS, BPL, and in MA university and college libraries. Many of them may be found at FHL (FHC), LGL, and RL. If you find in these volumes materials which you suspect relate to your progenitor, write to the appropriate repository asking for details. Don't forget to send a long SASE and to request names of researchers if you cannot go in person. In MSA, NEHGS, BPL, and most other MA manuscript repositories, there are special indexes, catalogs, inventories, and other finding aids to facilitate your search. In some cases, there are several of these, so you need to be careful to examine all.

23. Marriage records

From the earliest times the towns of MA were official keepers of marriage records (as well as birth and death records) of their inhabitants. At first the marriage records were kept along with other town records (constable, early church, court, birth, death, justice of the peace, magistrate, proprietor, rate or tax, town meeting, selectmen) in one or a few books. Then, as the population grew, they came to be recorded in separate volumes dedicated especially to vital records. In 1841, in conformity to a new law, towns began reporting their marriages to the state, so that after that date, the records became available at both the town and state levels. Boston is an exception since it did not begin to comply until 1848. Original town records from the time of each town's origin to the present are available in the towns (town clerk, town archives, town library). From 1841-95 the official duplicates which were filed with the state are at the MSA, and from 1896 forward, they are in the MA Registry of Vital Records and Statistics. Also available at the MSA is a statewide marriage record index for 1841-1971.

To obtain records for the period since 1895, you should write the following agency, enclosing the proper fee, the amount of which can be obtained by calling them:

_MA MARRIAGE RECORDS 1896-, MA State Registry of Vital Records and Statistics, Room B-3, 150 Tremont St., Boston, MA 02111. Telephone (617)-727-0110.

Records for the period 1841-95 are most readily accessed at the MSA or through the microfilm copies of them available at NEHGS and at the FHL (and obtainable through their many branch FHC):

_MA MARRIAGE RECORDS 1841-95, and MA MARRIAGE RECORD INDEX 1841-1971, Office of the Secretary of State, Archives Division/ Vital Records, 220 Morrissey Blvd., Boston, MA 02125. Telephone (617)-727-2816.

_MA MARRIAGE RECORDS 1841-95, and MA MARRIAGE RECORD INDEX 1841-1971, on microfilm in FHL, can be borrowed through FHC. Also at NEHGS.

The marriage records for the period before 1841 are available in several forms: originals in the towns, published volumes, copies on microfilm and microfiche, journal articles, typescript volumes, and manuscript copies. Of the 351 presently existing MA towns, only about 10 of them do not have their marriage records in some copied (published or manuscript) form. For early Boston and Plymouth, these are:

_Boston Registry Department, RECORDS RELATING TO THE EARLY HISTORY OF BOSTON, The Record Commissioners, Boston, MA, 1876-1909, especially volumes 9, 24, 28, 30 for marriages.

_Boston Registry Department and W. S. Appleton, BOSTON BIRTHS, BAPTISMS, MARRIAGES, AND DEATHS, 1630-1800, Genealogical Publishing Co., Baltimore, MD, 1978. Marriages 1630-99.

_Boston Registry Department and S. C. Gladden, INDEX TO 1630-99 BOSTON BIRTHS, BAPTISMS, MARRIAGES, AND DEATHS, The Indexer, Boulder, CO, 1969. Over 14000 records.

_Boston Registry Department and W. E. McGlenen, BOSTON MARRIAGES FROM 1700-1809, Genealogical Publishing Co., Baltimore, MD, 1977. 75000 persons.

_J. M. Holbrook, BOSTON BEGINNINGS, 1630-99, Holbrook Research Institute, Oxford, MA, 1980. Over 16000 names.

_N. B. Shurtleff and E. G. Bowman, PLYMOUTH COLONY, RECORDS OF BIRTHS, MARRIAGES, DEATHS, BURIALS, AND OTHER RECORDS,

1633-89, Genealogical Publishing Co., Baltimore, MD, 1979.

Some years ago, under the financial inducements of the state, various agencies began to publish MA town vital records (including marriages) for the time period up to 1850. The compilers of the many volumes which were printed drew not only upon official vital records, but they also often included court, Bible, church, and cemetery records. Later on, organizations, private companies, and individuals added volumes for other towns, published town vital records in genealogical journals, put town vital records on microfilm and microfiche, compiled typescript books, and made manuscript transcriptions. These works include:

_PUBLISHED VOLUMES OF MA TOWN VITAL RECORDS UP TO 1850, for 227 towns, published by New England Historic Genealogical Society, Essex Institute, Topsfield Historical Society, towns, private companies, and individuals.

_MA TOWN VITAL RECORDS PUBLISHED IN GENEALOGICAL JOURNALS, for 16 towns, chiefly published in New England Historical and Genealogical Register and The Mayflower Descendant.

_J. M. Holbrook, MA TOWN VITAL RECORDS UP TO 1890, over 120 towns on microfiche, Holbrook Research Institute, Oxford, MA.

_Daughters of the American Revolution for MA, COLLECTION OF GENEALOGICAL RECORD VOLUMES, The Society, various places in MA, various dates, numerous volumes, also on microfilm at FHL.

_MA TOWN RECORDS IN MANUSCRIPT FORM, for 52 towns, chiefly located in Corbin Collection and other collections at NEHGS and in Cooke Collection at Berkshire Athenaeum, Pittsfield, MA.

_MA TOWN RECORDS AND VITAL RECORDS, for many towns, on microfilm at FHL, available through FHC.

There is no overall index to this large number of compilations, but many of the marriages and births recorded in them are indexed in a microfiche set available at every FHC:

_INTERNATIONAL GENEALOGICAL INDEX, MICROFICHE FOR MA, at FHL and every FHC, look under surname. This index also includes many indirect references to marriages. All the data in the IGI must be checked in original sources.

In the fourth chapter, there are individual sections devoted to each town. In these sections, the marriage-record publications, microfiche, microfilms, typescripts, and manuscripts pertaining to each town will be listed.

In addition to the above marriage record compilations, there are three further published works which are of special value since they cover early marriages throughout all or some of MA.

_C. A. Torrey, NEW ENGLAND MARRIAGES PRIOR TO 1700, Genealogical Publishing Co., Baltimore, MD, 1985. 37000 entries. Detailed references to the data should be sought in the manuscript edition at NEHGS.

_F. W. Bailey, EARLY MA MARRIAGES PRIOR TO 1800, WITH PLYMOUTH COUNTY MARRIAGES 1692-1746, Genealogical Publishing Co., Baltimore, MD, 1979. 21000 entries for Berkshire, Bristol, Hampshire, Middlesex, Plymouth, and Worcester Counties.

_R. S. Wakefield, PLYMOUTH COLONY MARRIAGES TO 1650, Society of Mayflower Descendants in the State of RI, Warwick, RI, 1978.

The basic guide to the original vital records (including marriages) which are in the many MA towns is:

_C. D. Wright, REPORT ON THE CUSTODY AND CONDITION OF THE PUBLIC RECORDS OF PARISHES, TOWNS, AND COUNTIES, Wright and Potter, Boston, MA, 1889.

This volume is, of course, badly out of date, but it remains very valuable in that it indicates what records should be sought for each town, even though record locations may have changed. Three other useful items along this line are:

_R. L. Bowen, MA RECORDS: A HANDBOOK FOR GENEALOGISTS, HISTORIANS, LAWYERS, AND OTHER RESEARCHERS, The Author, Rehoboth, MA, 1957.

_J. M. Holbrook, BIBLIOGRAPHY OF MA VITAL RECORDS, Holbrook Research Institute, Oxford, MA, 1986, 3 microfiche.

_Historical Records Survey, GUIDE TO PUBLIC VITAL STATISTICS RECORDS IN MA, The Survey, WPA, Boston, MA, 1942.

There are also some civil vital record collections available in the counties of MA. These will be listed in the county sections of Chapter 4, and they are also presented here:

_BERKSHIRE COUNTY MARRIAGE RECORDS 1788-95, in Berkshire County at Pittsfield.

_BRISTOL COUNTY MARRIAGE RECORDS 1783-95, in Bristol County at Taunton.

_DUKES COUNTY MARRIAGE RECORDS 1761-8, 1773-95, in Dukes County at Edgartown.

_ESSEX COUNTY MARRIAGE RECORDS 1654-1795, in Essex County at Salem.

_HAMPSHIRE COUNTY MARRIAGE RECORDS 1786-90 in Hampshire County at Northampton.

_MIDDLESEX COUNTY MARRIAGE RECORDS 1632-1793, in Middlesex County at Cambridge.

_NANTUCKET COUNTY MARRIAGE RECORDS 1766-90, in Nantucket County at Nantucket.

_NORFOLK COUNTY MARRIAGE RECORDS 1793-5, in Norfolk County at Dedham.

_OLD NORFOLK COUNTY MARRIAGE RECORDS 1641-71 in Essex County at Salem.

_PLYMOUTH COUNTY MARRIAGE RECORDS 1724-88 in Plymouth County at Plymouth.

The dates above do not mean to imply that every individual year is represented.

Excellent repositories for the books and microforms mentioned above are MSA, NEHGS, and BPL. In addition, the FHL(FHC) has much of the material on microfilm. LGL, especially those near MA, have some of the published works and some of the microforms, as do RL in MA. Many other types of records often contain marriage date and place information or indirectly indicate a marriage. Among the better ones are Bible, biography, birth, cemetery, census, church, death, divorce, genealogical periodicals, manuscripts, land, military, mortuary, newspaper, published genealogies, and will/probate. All of these are treated in other sections of this chapter. When you are seeking marriage data in archives and libraries, be certain to explore all the above mentioned sources, and do not fail to look under county listings and the following heading in archive and library catalogs: Registers of births, etc.

24. Military records: colonial

Before going into detail on sources of military records (sections 24–27), you need to understand the types of records which are available and what they contain. There are five basic types which are of value to genealogists: (a) service, (b) pension, (c) bounty land, (d) claims, and (e) military unit history. Service records contain a number of the following: name, rank, military unit, personal description, plus dates and places of enlistment, mustering in, payrolls, wounding, capture, death, imprisonment, hospital stay, release, oath of allegiance, desertion, promotion, battles, heroic action, re-enlistment, leave of absence, mustering out, and discharge. Pension records (applications and payment documents) contain a number of the following: name, age, rank, military unit, personal description, name of wife, names and ages of children, residences during pension period, plus dates and places of enlistment, service, wartime experiences, birth, marriage, pension payments, and death. Bounty land records (applications and awards of land) contain a number of the following: name. age, rank, military unit, plus dates and places of enlistment, service, wartime experience, and birth. Claims of military participants for back pay and of civilians for supplies or service contain some of the following: name, details of the claim, date of the claim, witnesses to the claim, documents supporting the claim, action on the claim, amount awarded. Military unit history records trace the detailed events of the experiences of a given military unit throughout a war, often referring to officers, enlisted men, battles, campaigns, and deaths, plus dates and places of organization, mustering in, reorganization, mustering out, and other pertinent events. Now with this background, you are ready to learn where these records may be found.

Colonial MA maintained a militia for defense and for other emergencies. The major wars during colonial times centered around conflicts with Indians and the struggle between Great Britain and France for control of North America. The chief conflicts were known as The Pequot Indian War (1637), King Phillip's Indian War (1675-8), King William's War (1689-97), Queen Anne's War (1701-13), the War of Jenkins' Ear (1739), King George's War (1744-8), and the French and Indian War (1756-63). After many years of French attacks on the expanding British frontier and many counterattacks by the British and the colonists, with Indians fighting on both sides, the French and Indian War ended in a British victory. The French and their Spanish allies ceded to Britain all of Canada and essentially all lands resting east of the MS River including FL.

MA military men participated in these wars, and a sizable number of records exist, but they are seldom very detailed. The records related to these wars which contain names of participants and describe the MA activities include:

_C. Doreski, MA OFFICERS AND SOLDIERS IN THE 17TH CENTURY CONFLICTS, Society of Colonial Wars in the Commonwealth of MA and the New England Historic Genealogical Society, Boston, MA, 1982.

_G. M. Bodge, SOLDIERS IN KING PHILIP'S WAR, Genealogical Publishing Co., Baltimore, MD, 1976. Lists of soldiers, grantees, and claimants.

_E. L. Coleman, NEW ENGLAND CAPTIVES CARRIED TO CANADA, 1677-1760, DURING THE FRENCH AND INDIAN WARS, Southworth Press, Portland, ME, 1925.

_S. G. Drake, A PARTICULAR HISTORY OF THE FIVE YEARS FRENCH AND INDIAN WARS IN NEW ENGLAND, Heritage Books, Bowie, MD, 1985. Many names of participants in the war beginning in 1688.

_M. E. Donahue, MA OFFICERS AND SOLDIERS, 1702-22, QUEEN ANNE'S WAR TO DUMMER'S WAR, Society of Colonial Wars in the Commonwealth of MA and the New England Historic Genealogical Society, Boston, MA, 1980. Over 3000 military men.

_M. O. Stachiw, MA OFFICERS AND SOLDIERS, 1723-43, DUMMER'S WAR TO THE WAR OF JENKINS' EAR, Society of Colonial Wars in the Commonwealth of MA and the New England Historic Genealogical Society, Boston, MA, 1979.

_R. E. MacKay, MA SOLDIERS IN THE FRENCH AND INDIAN WARS, 1744-55, Society of Colonial Wars in the Commonwealth of MA and the New England Historic Genealogical Society, Boston, MA, 1978.

_N. E. Voye, MA OFFICERS IN THE FRENCH AND INDIAN WARS, 1748-63, Society of Colonial Wars in the Commonwealth of MA and the New England Historic Genealogical Society, Boston, MA, 1975. Over 6500 officers.

_K. D. Goss and D. Zarowin, MA OFFICERS AND SOLDIERS IN THE FRENCH AND INDIAN WARS, 1755-6, New England Historic Genealogical Society, Boston, MA, 1985. Over 2300 listings with numerous places of birth.

_P. Belliveau, FRENCH NEUTRALS IN MA, ACADIANS ROUNDED UP BY SOLDIERS FROM MA AND THEIR CAPTIVITY IN THE BAY PROVINCE, 1755-6, Giffen, Boston, MA, 1972.

_MA ARCHIVES SUPPLEMENTARY CARD CATALOG INDEX TO COLONIAL MILITARY RECORDS, Volumes 67-80, MSA, Boston, MA, and MA ARCHIVES SUPPLEMENTARY CARD CATALOG INDEX TO MUSTER ROLLS, Volumes 91-99, 268-269, MSA, Boston, MA, also MA ARCHIVES MAIN CARD CATALOG, MSA, Boston, MA.

_M. E. Baker and R. E. MacKay, BIBLIOGRAPHY OF LISTS OF NEW ENGLAND SOLDIERS, New England Historic Genealogical Society, Boston, MA, 1977.

_National Society of Women Descendants of the Ancient and Honorable Artillery Company, HISTORY AND LINEAGE BOOKS 1-7, The Society, Washington, DC, 1940-80.

_M. R. Cowan, NATIONAL SOCIETY OF WOMEN DESCENDANTS OF THE ANCIENT AND HONORABLE ARTILLERY COMPANY, MEMBERS IN THE COLONIAL PERIOD, The Society, Washington, DC, 1958.

_B. Kenyon, MA HERALDICA, AN ILLUSTRATED COMPILATION OF ARMS COMPRISING AN ALPHABETICAL INDEX OF 103 ARMIGEROUS MEMBERS OF THE ANCIENT AND HONORABLE ARTILLERY COMPANY, 1637-1774, The National Society of Women Descendants of the Ancient and Honorable Artillery Company, Washington, DC, 1968.

_O. A. Roberts, HISTORY OF THE MILITARY COMPANY OF MA NOW CALLED THE ANCIENT AND HONORABLE ARTILLERY OF MA, 1637-1888, Boston, MA, 4 volumes, with biographies.

25. Military records: Revolutionary War

Although the first actions of the Revolutionary War occurred in MA, the arenas of conflict soon shifted to the other colonies. As you will recall from Chapter 1, the fortification of Dorchester Heights in March 1776 forced the British to leave Boston, which essentially ended the land war in MA. However, out of Salem, which was one of only a few ports remaining uncontrolled by the British, over 200 privateers were based and supplied. MA fielded the largest number of troops of any colony: almost 68,000 in the Continental Army and over 15,000 in the militia. Those in the Continental Army served under Washington and the Continental Congress. The militia were under state supervision. MA had participants in practically every major northern campaign or area; Seige of Boston, Defense of Canada, Lake Champlain, Trenton-Princeton, Saratoga, Defense of Philadelphia, Philadelphia-Monmouth, Rhode Island, New York City, New Jersey, Northern NJ, Mohawk Valley, and the Iroquois Conflicts.

The first step you should take in searching for your MA ancestor who may have served in this war or supported it is to employ the following large indexes and look for him in them:

_MA Secretary of the Commonwealth, MA SOLDIERS AND SAILORS OF THE REVOLUTIONARY WAR, Wright and Potter, Boston, MA, 1896-1908, 17 volumes, plus microfilm supplement. Alphabetical listings with summarized service records. Supplement must not be overlooked.

_The National Archives, GENERAL INDEX TO COMPILED SERVICE RECORDS OF REVOLUTIONARY WAR SOLDIERS, SAILORS, ARMY STAFF, The Archives, Washington, DC, Microfilm Publication M860, 58 rolls. [Mostly Continental forces plus militia who supported them. Copies in NA, NAFB, NA-Boston Branch, FHL(FHC), may be borrowed through your LL or directly from AGLL, PO Box 244, Bountiful, UT 84010.]

_The National Archives, INDEX TO COMPILED SERVICE RECORDS OF NAVAL PERSONNEL DURING THE REVOLUTIONARY WAR, The Archives, Washington, DC, Microfilm Publication M879, 1 roll. [Includes Marines. Sources same as above.]

_The National Genealogical Society, INDEX TO REVOLUTIONARY WAR PENSION [AND SOME BOUNTY LAND] APPLICATIONS IN THE NATIONAL ARCHIVES, The Society, Washington, DC, 1976.

_F. Rider, AMERICAN GENEALOGICAL INDEX, Godfrey Memorial Library, Middletown, CT, 1942-52, 48 volumes, and F. Rider, AMERICAN GENEALOGICAL-BIOGRAPHICAL INDEX, Godfrey Memorial Library, Middletown, CT, 1952-89, over 170 volumes, more to come. [Continental, state, and militia service.]

_US Pay Department, War Department, REGISTERS OF CERTIFICATES ISSUED BY JOHN PIERCE TO OFFICERS AND SOLDIERS OF THE CONTINENTAL ARMY, Genealogical Publishing Co., Baltimore, MD, 1983.

_National Society of the DAR, DAR PATRIOT INDEX, The Society, Washington, DC, 1966/79, 2 volumes. [Continental, state, militia, public service, military aid.] DAR no longer accepts this index as authoritative. New applications must be based on original source material.

_National Society of the DAR, INDEX TO THE ROLLS OF HONOR [Ancestor Index], Genealogical Publishing Co., Baltimore, MD, 1972, and LINEAGE BOOKS, The Society, Washington, DC, 1890-1921, 166 volumes.

The five reference works just mentioned (not the microfilms) will be found in NEHGS, BPL, FHL(FHC) and in many LGL. Some of them are available in MSA, SLM, and some LL.

If you discover from these sources that your ancestor served in the Continental forces or units which aided them, you may proceed to obtain his service records from the NA or read them from these microfilms:

_The National Archives, COMPILED SERVICE RECORDS OF SOLDIERS WHO SERVED IN THE AMERICAN ARMY DURING THE REVOLUTION-

ARY WAR, The Archives, Washington, DC, Microfilm Publication M881, 1097 rolls.

_The National Archives, COMPILED SERVICE RECORDS OF AMERICAN NAVAL, QUARTERMASTER, AND COMMISSARY PERSONNEL WHO SERVED DURING THE REVOLUTIONARY WAR, The Archives, Washington, DC, Microfilm Publication M880, 4 rolls.

_The National Archives, REVOLUTIONARY WAR ROLLS, 1775-83, The Archives, Washington, DC, Microfilm Publication M246, 138 rolls.

And the federal pension and bounty land records are found in:

_The National Archives, REVOLUTIONARY WAR PENSION AND BOUNTY LAND WARRANT APPLICATION FILES, The Archives, Washington, DC, Microfilm Publication M804, 2670 rolls.

These microfilm sets are available at NA, NAFB, FHL(FHC), and some can be borrowed from your LL, or AGLL, PO Box 244, Bountiful, UT 84010, or CMRF, PO Box 2940, Hyattsville, MD 20784. Alternately, you can write the NA (8th and PA Ave., Washington, DC 20408) for 3 copies of NATF-80 which you can use to request service, pension, and bounty land records by mail. A third alternative is to hire a searcher in Washington, DC to go to the NA for you. Lists of such searchers will be found in:

_J. N. Chambers, editor, THE GENEALOGICAL HELPER, Everton Publishers, Logan, UT, latest September/October issue.

The second step you should take is to look into further state sources. Foremost among these are:

_REVOLUTIONARY WAR ROLLS FROM MA ARCHIVES, 77 volumes, 13 on microfilm, REVOLUTIONARY WAR SERVICE APPENDIX, microfilm, indexed, REVOLUTIONARY WAR AND WAR OF 1812 PENSIONERS, microfilm, alphabetized by county, MA CONTINENTAL ARMY BOOKS, 21 volumes, MILITARY PAYROLLS FOR THE REVOLUTIONARY WAR, MA Treasury Records, all these sets available at MSA, Boston, MA.

_G. W. Allen, MA PRIVATEERS OF THE REVOLUTION, MA Historical Society, Boston, MA, 1927.

_Mrs. B. Draper, HONOR ROLL OF MA PATRIOTS WHO LOANED MONEY TO THE FEDERAL GOVERNMENT DURING THE YEARS, 1777-9, MA Chapters of the DAR, Boston, MA, 1899.

_GRAVE LOCATIONS OF MA MEN WHO SERVED IN THE REVOLUTIONARY WAR, 1775-83, WITH SERVICE RECORDS, DAR, alphabetical card file, NEHGS, Boston, MA.

_C. E. Hambrick-Stowe and D. D. Smerlas, MA MILITIA COMPANIES AND OFFICERS IN THE LEXINGTON ALARM, Society of Colonial Wars in the Commonwealth of MA and the NEHGS, Boston, MA, 1976.

_Mrs. L. Irwin for the DAR of MA, MA STATE DIRECTORY OF [DAR] MEMBERS AND ANCESTORS, The Editor, Newton, MA, 1974.

_J. W. Lynn, MA LINEAGES OF REVOLUTIONARY WAR REGIMENTS, Lynn Research, Grand Junction, CO, 1986. Brief regimental histories.

_L. K. McGhee, MA PENSION ABSTRACTS OF THE REVOLUTIONARY

WAR, WAR OF 1812, AND INDIAN WARS, The Compiler, Washington, DC, 1966.

_W. Pencak, THE REVOLT AGAINST GERONTOCRACY, GENEALOGY, AND THE MA REVOLUTION, National Genealogical Society Quarterly, Volume 66, December 1978. Revolutionary leaders, Loyalists, early participants. Numerous names with vital data.

_ROLL OF MEMBERSHIP WITH ANCESTRAL RECORDS OF THE SONS OF THE REVOLUTION OF MA, also YEARBOOKS and REGISTERS, The Society, Boston, MA, 1893-1936, numerous volumes.

_C. C. Tucker, A LIST OF PENSIONERS IN THE STATE OF MA UNDER THE ACTS OF CONGRESS PASSED 1818, 1828, AND 1832, Washington, DC, 1854. About 3800 pensioners.

_B. A. Whittemore, MEMORIALS OF THE MA SOCIETY OF THE CINCINNATI, The Society, Boston, MA, 1964. MA Revolutionary officers and their descendants. Also see previous volumes of MEMORIALS published in 1873, 1890, and 1931.

_LIST OF REVOLUTIONARY SOLDIERS AND/OR WIDOWS RECEIVING STATE PENSIONS OR LAND GRANT BOUNTIES, Main Desk, MSA, Boston, MA. MA gave bounty land grants only to those who did not receive federal bounty land grants.

All the above volumes, (not the microfilms, files, and the list) are in NEHGS, most in BPL, and some in FHL(FHC), LGL, RL, and LL.

The Loyalists in MA, their activities, and the actions against them gave rise to many records, both within and outside the state. Chief among them are the following which may be sought in NEHGS, BPL, and the MA Historical Society:

_E. A. Jones, THE LOYALISTS OF MA, Genealogical Publishing Co., Baltimore, MD, 1969. 501 Loyalists from claim lists in the Public Record Office in London.

_D. E. Maas, DIVIDED HEARTS, MA LOYALISTS, 1765-90, A BIOGRAPHICAL DIRECTORY, Society of Colonial Wars in the Commonwealth of MA and the NEHGS, Boston, MA, 1980. Numerous listings.

_J. Noble, SOME MA TORIES, Publications of the Colonial Society of MA, Volume 5, Transactions, 1897/8, pages 257-97.

_W. H. Siebert, THE COLONY OF MA LOYALISTS AT BRISTOL, ENGLAND, Proceedings of the MA Historical Society, Boston, MA, January, 1912, and W. H. Siebert, LOYALIST TROOPS OF NEW ENGLAND, New England Quarterly, Volume 4, January, 1931, pages 108-47.

_J. H. Stark, THE LOYALISTS OF MA AND THE OTHER SIDE OF THE AMERICAN REVOLUTION, Kelley, Clifton, NJ, 1972. Over 100 Loyalist biographies.

Also of help are:

_ROYALIST (LOYALIST) RECORDS in the MA ARCHIVES, MSA, Boston, MA.

_UNITED EMPIRE LOYALISTS COLLECTION, American Antiquarian

Society, Worcester, MA.
_AMERICAN LOYALIST CLAIMS, microfilm, BPL, Boston, MA.
_DISPOSITION OF LOYALIST ESTATES, MA Treasury Records, MSA, Boston, MA.
_LOYALIST MATERIALS, Manuscript Collections, NEHGS, Boston, MA.
And further Loyalist records and chronicles can be located by using:
_G. Palmer, BIBLIOGRAPHY OF LOYALIST SOURCE MATERIAL IN THE US, CANADA, AND GREAT BRITAIN, Mecker, Westport, CT, 1982.
_R. M. Gephart, REVOLUTIONARY AMERICA, 1763-89, A BIBLIOGRAPHY, Library of Congress, Washington, DC, 1984, 2 volumes.

For considerably more detail about genealogical data which can be gleaned from Revolutionary War records, you may consult a book especially dedicated to this:
_Geo. K. Schweitzer, REVOLUTIONARY WAR GENEALOGY, available from the author at the address shown on the title page of this volume.
This volume goes into detail on local, state, and national records, discusses both militia and Continental Army service, deals in detail with service, pension, bounty land, and claims records, and treats the subject of regimental histories, battle accounts, medical records, courts-martial, foreign participants, Loyalist data, maps, museums, historic sites, patriotic organizations, and many other related topics. Two other very useful detailed source books listing Revolutionary War records are:
_J. C. and L. L. Neagles, LOCATING YOUR REVOLUTIONARY WAR ANCESTOR, Everton Publishers, Logan, UT, 1983.
_M. Deputy and others, REGISTER OF FEDERAL US MILITARY RECORDS, VOLUME 1, 1775-1860, Heritage Books, Bowie, MD, 1986, pages 1-137.

26. Military records: War of 1812

During the period between the Revolutionary War and the Civil War (1784-1861), the US was involved in two major foreign wars: The War of 1812 (1812-5) and the Mexican War (1846-8).

A number of MA men were involved in the War of 1812. They served both in national and state organizations, and therefore several types of national records (service, bounty land, pension), as well as state records need to be sought. Only relatively few national pensions were given before 1871, by which time not too many veterans were still living. To obtain national records (only for men who served in national units) you may write the NA and request copies of NATF-80, which may be used to order military service, bounty land, and pension information. Or you may choose to visit the NA or to employ a searcher in Washington to do the work for you. Alternately, some of the indexes and records are available on loan from AGLL, PO Box 244, Bountiful, UT 84010, and also through your local library. Among the microfilm indexes and alphabetical files which you need to search or have searched for you are:

_The National Archives, INDEX TO COMPILED SERVICE RECORDS OF VOLUNTEER SOLDIERS WHO SERVED DURING THE WAR OF 1812, The Archives, Washington, DC, Microfilm Publication M602, 234 rolls. [Leads to service records, which are available at the NA.]

_The National Archives, INDEX TO WAR OF 1812 PENSION (AND SOME BOUNTY LAND) APPLICATIONS, The Archives, Washington, DC, Microfilm Publication M313, 102 rolls. [Leads to applications, which are available at the NA.]

_The National Archives, WAR OF 1812 MILITARY BOUNTY LAND WARRANTS, 1815-58, The Archives, Microfilm Publication M848, 14 rolls, 4 indexes in first roll. [Leads to bounty land warrant applications, which are alphabetically filed in NA.]

_The National Archives, POST-REVOLUTIONARY WAR BOUNTY LAND WARRANT APPLICATION FILE, The Archives, Washington, DC, arranged alphabetically.

Copies of the three microfilm publications mentioned above are available at NA, some NAFB, some LGL, and at FHL (and through FHC). Microfilm publications M602, M313, and M848 are available on interlibrary loan from AGLL (address above). Among published national sources for War of 1812 data are:

_F. I. Ordway, Jr., REGISTER OF THE GENERAL SOCIETY OF THE WAR OF 1812, The Society, Washington, DC, 1972.

_E. S. Galvin, 1812 ANCESTOR INDEX, National Society of the US Daughters of 1812, Washington, DC, 1970.

_C. S. Peterson, KNOWN MILITARY DEAD DURING THE WAR OF 1812, The Author, Baltimore, MD, 1955.

Among the state source volumes, records, and reference works which you should search for MA War of 1812 military service records are:

_J. Baker, RECORDS OF MA VOLUNTEER MILITIA CALLED OUT BY THE GOVERNOR OF MA TO SUPPRESS A THREATENED INVASION DURING THE WAR OF 1812-4, MA Adjutant General's Office, Boston, MA, 1913.

_L. K. McGhee, MA PENSION ABSTRACTS OF THE REVOLUTIONARY WAR, WAR OF 1812, AND INDIAN WARS, The Compiler, Washington, DC, 1966.

_M. E. Baker and R. MacKay, BIBLIOGRAPHY OF LISTS OF NEW ENGLAND SOLDIERS, NEHGS, Boston, MA, 1977.

_MA BOARD OF WAR COMMISARY AND QUARTERMASTER RECORDS FOR THE REVOLUTION AND WAR OF 1812, mainly supplies, WAR OF 1812 RECORDS IN GOVERNOR AND EXECUTIVE COUNCIL RECORDS, letters, petitions, rosters, commissions, officers, RECORDS OF MA MILITIA IN THE WAR OF 1812, 9 volumes of photostatic copies of payrolls, muster rolls, inspection rolls, company rolls, indexed by regiment, all these in MSA, Boston.

_RECORDS OF EARLY MA MILITIA (1776-1820), MA MILITIA PERIOD (1820-40), AND MA MILITIA PRE-CIVIL WAR PERIOD (1840-60), MA Adjutant General's Office, Military Records Division, Natick, MA.

This last reference points you to MA militia records before, during, and after the War of 1812.

The Mexican War was fought 1846-8. As before, NATF-80 should be obtained and used, or you should visit the NA, or you should hire a researcher as indicated in previously-given instructions (see Revolutionary War section). Again, military service, pension, and bounty land records should all be asked for. The NA indexes which lead to the records and some alphabetical national records include:

_The National Archives, INDEX TO THE COMPILED SERVICE RECORDS OF VOLUNTEER SOLDIERS DURING THE MEXICAN WAR, The Archives, Washington, DC, Microfilm Publication M616, 41 rolls.

_The National Archives, INDEX TO MEXICAN WAR PENSION FILES, The Archives, Washington, DC, Microfilm Publication T317, 14 rolls.

_The National Archives, POST-REVOLUTIONARY WAR BOUNTY LAND APPLICATION FILE, The Archives, Washington, DC, arranged alphabetically.

Three useful publications, one a complete roster of officers in the Mexican War, another a list of the dead, a third an index to pension applications, are:

_W. H. Roberts, MEXICAN WAR (OFFICER) VETERANS, 1846-8, Washington, DC, 1887.

_C. S. Peterson, KNOWN MILITARY DEAD DURING THE MEXICAN WAR, The Author, Baltimore, MD, 1957.

_B. S. Wolfe, INDEX TO MEXICAN WAR PENSION APPLICATIONS, Ye Olde Genealogie Shoppe, Indianapolis, IN.

27. Military records: Civil War

Over 152,000 MA men participated in the Civil War. Records which are available for these participants (1861-5) include national service records for soldiers, sailors, and marines, national pension records for the same participants, national claims records, numerous state records (service, bounty, muster rolls, descriptive rolls, substitutes, recruits), and some town records. No bounty land awards were made for service in this war. A major index lists MA military service records which are in the NA:

_The National Archives, INDEX TO COMPILED SERVICE RECORDS OF VOLUNTEER UNION SOLDIERS WHO SERVED IN ORGANIZATIONS FROM THE STATE OF MA, The Archives, Washington, DC, Microfilm Publication M544, 44 rolls.

This index leads to the compiled service records which are in files in the NA. The index to Union veteran national pension applications is:

_The National Archives, GENERAL INDEX TO PENSION FILES, 1861-1934, The Archives, Washington, DC, Microfilm Publication T288, 544 rolls.

The pension file index points to pension records which are filed in the NA. The first index may be consulted in BPL, NA, NAFB, and FHL(FHC). The second is available at NA, NAFB, and FHL(FHC), and can also be borrowed by your local library or by you from AGLL. Or you may choose to have the indexes examined and to obtain the service and pension records on your MA Civil War veteran by employing NATF-80 in a mail request, or by going to the NA personally, or by hiring a researcher to do the work at NA for you. Instructions for these three possibilities were given in the Revolutionary War section. Details of many other Civil War records which are in the NA will be found in:

_National Archives Staff, GUIDE TO GENEALOGICAL RESEARCH IN THE NATIONAL ARCHIVES, The Archives, Washington, DC, 1982, Chapters 4-10, 16.

The most important published materials on Civil War personnel of MA are:

_MA SOLDIERS, SAILORS, AND MARINES IN THE CIVIL WAR, MA Adjutant General's Office, Boston, MA, 1931-35, 8 volumes, with INDEX TO ARMY RECORDS, MA Adjutant General's Office, Boston, MA, 1937. The records for the Navy and Marines appear alphabetically in volumes 7-8.

_RECORD OF THE MA VOLUNTEERS, 1861-5, Wright and Potter, Boston, MA, 1868-70.

_J. L. Bowen, MA IN THE WAR, 1861-5, Bowen and Son, Springfield, MA, 1889. General officers, pages 875-1010.

_T. W. Higginson, MA IN THE ARMY AND NAVY DURING THE WAR OF 1861-5, Wright and Potter, Boston, MA, 1895-6.

_CENSUS INDEX OF 1890 MA VETERANS, Index Publications, Salt Lake City, UT, 1984.

_Military Order of the Loyal Legion of the US, REGISTER OF THE COMMANDERY OF THE STATE OF MA, Rockwell and Churchill, Boston, MA, 1891.

_G. W. Nason, HISTORY AND COMPLETE ROSTER OF MA REGIMENTS, 1861, Smith and McCance, Boston, MA, 1904.

Not to be overlooked if you want to go further in investigating your ancestor's Civil War acticities are many manuscript sources:

_RECORDS FOR THE CIVIL WAR, muster rolls, issue books, clothing lists, descriptive rolls, substitutes, recruits, MSA, Boston, MA.

_CIVIL WAR RECORDS (1861-5) AND RECONSTRUCTION ERA RECORDS (1866-97) OF MA MILITIA, MA Adjutant General's Office, Military Records Division, Natick, MA. Very important for a wealth of detail on soldiers. Much correspondence between Adjutant General's Office, soldiers' families, and soldiers.

_RECORDS OF SOLDIERS IN THE REBELLION, 1861-5, in Town Records of 56 MA towns. See Chapter 4 for listings.

For a detailed in-depth discussion of Civil War records as sources of genealogical information, consult:

_Geo. K. Schweitzer, CIVIL WAR GENEALOGY, order from the author at the address given on the title page of this book.

This book treats local, state, and national records, service and pension records, regimental and naval histories, enlistment rosters, hospital records, court-martial reports, burial registers, national cemeteries, gravestone allotments, amnesties, pardons, state militias, discharge papers, officer biographies, prisons, prisoners, battle sites, maps, relics, weapons, museums, monuments, memorials, deserters, black soldiers, Indian soldiers, and many other topics.

There is in the NA an index to service records of the Spanish-American War (1898-9) which has been microfilmed:

_The National Archives, GENERAL INDEX TO COMPILED SERVICE RECORDS OF VOLUNTEER SOLDIERS WHO SERVED DURING THE WAR WITH SPAIN, The Archives, Washington, DC, Microfilm Publication M871, 126 rolls, leads to service records in the NA.

The pension records for this war are indexed in:

_The National Archives, GENERAL INDEX TO PENSION FILES, 1861-1934, The Archives, Washington, DC, Microfilm Publication T288, 544 rolls, leads to pension records in the NA.

Both these indexes should be sought in NA, NAFB, FHL(FHC), and from AGLL. Again properly submitted NATF-80s (see section 26 for instructions) will bring you both military service and pension records (there were no bounty land records). Or you may choose to hire a searcher or go to the NA yourself. State of MA sources which you may find of value include:

_CLAIMS FOR STATE PAY BY VETERANS OF THE SPANISH-AMERICAN WAR, 1898-1901, correspondence, MSA, Boston, MA.

_SPANISH-AMERICAN WAR, MA MILITIA RECORDS, MA Adjutant General's Office, Military Records Division, Natick, MA.

Some national records for World War I and subsequent wars may be obtained from the following address. However, many documents were destroyed by an extensive fire in 1972. Write for Form 160:

_National Personnel Records Center (MPR), 9700 Page Blvd., St. Louis, MO 63132.

Draft records for World War I are in Record Group 163 (Records of the Selective Service System of World War I) at:

_The National Archives, Atlanta Branch, 1557 St. Joseph Ave., East Point, GA 30344.

There are also useful MA sources of some data on World War I military activity in the state:

_MILITARY RECORDS OF MA DURING THE WORLD WAR I PERIOD (1917-9), MA Adjutant General's Office, Military Records Division, Natick, MA.

28. Mortuary records

Very few MA mortuary records have been transcribed or microfilmed, even though a few are to be found in manuscript form in archives. This means that you must write directly to the mortuaries which you know or suspect were involved in burying your ancestor. Sometimes a death account will name the mortuary; sometimes it is the only one nearby; sometimes you will have to write several to ascertain which one might have done the funeral arrangements. And you need to realize that before there were mortuaries, the furniture or general merchandise store in some communities handled burials, especially in the supplying of coffins. You may discover that the mortuary that was involved is now out of business, and so you will have to try to discover which of the existing ones may have inherited the records. Mortuaries for MA with their addresses are listed in the following volumes:

_C. O. Kates, editor, THE AMERICAN BLUE BOOK OF FUNERAL DIRECTORS, Kates-Boyleston Publications, New York, NY, latest issue.

_NATIONAL DIRECTORY OF MORTICIANS, The Directory, Youngstown, OH, latest issue.

One or both of these reference books will usually be found in the offices of most mortuaries. In general, the older mortuaries should be the more likely sources of records on your progenitor. Please don't forget that contemporary mortuaries are listed in city directories. In all correspondence with mortuaries be sure to enclose an SASE and make your letters very brief and to the point.

29. Naturalization records

In the colonial period, many of the immigrants to the territory that later became the US were from the British Isles and since the colonies were British, they were citizens. When immigrants of other nationalities began to arrive, they found that English traditions, customs, governmental structures, and language generally prevailed. The immigrant aliens were supposed to take oaths of allegiance and abjuration and/or to become naturalized by presenting themselves in court. In a few cases, naturalizations were by special acts of the colonial assemblies. In 1740, the English Parliament passed a law setting requirements for naturalization: 7 years residence in one colony plus an oath of allegiance to the Crown.

In 1776-7, all those who supported the Revolution were automatically considered to be citizens. During the period 1777-91, immigrants were obligated to take an oath of allegiance. In the year 1781, the Articles of Confederation of the newly established US made all citizens of states citizens of the new nation. The US Congress in 1790 enacted a national naturalization act which required one year's state residence, two year's US residence, and a loyalty oath taken in court. In 1795, a five year's residence came to be required along with a declaration of intent three years before the oath. Then in 1798, these times became 14 and 5 years respectively. Revised statutes of 1802 reverted to the 5 and 3 years of 1795. The declaration and oath could be carried out in any court which kept records (US, MA, county, city). Wives and children of naturalized males became citizens automatically. And persons who gave military service to the US and received an honorable discharge also received citizenship.

In 1906, the Bureau of Immigration and Naturalization was set up, and this agency has kept records on all naturalizations since then. Thus, if you suspect your ancestor was naturalized after September 1906, write to the following address for a Form 6641 which you can use to request records:

_Immigration and Naturalization Service, 425 I Street, Washington, DC, 20536.

For naturalization records before October 1906, you need to realize that the process could have taken place in any of several courts, in fact, any court which kept records could have been used.

An important book and an article containing pre-1790 naturalization records for MA are:

_M. S. Giuseppe, NATURALIZATIONS OF FOREIGN PROTESTANTS IN THE AMERICAN COLONIES PURSUANT TO STATUTE 13 GEORGE II, Huguenot Society of London, London, England, Volume 24. Naturalizations 1743-72.

_NATURALIZATION IN AMERICAN COLONIES, WITH MORE PARTICULAR REFERENCE TO MA, Proceedings of the MA Historical Society, Volume 4, pages 337-64. Includes naturalizations 1782-94 also.

During the post-1790 period, naturalizations will be found in federal, state, county, and city courts. The MA courts which could handle the actions and the dates during which they were authorized to do so are as follows: Supreme Judicial Court (1790-present), Court of Common Pleas (1790-1860), Superior Court (1860-present), Police Courts (1790-1855), Superior Court of Suffolk County (1855-60), Municipal Court of Boston (1858-60), District, Police, and Municipal Courts (1855-1906). In addition, the US District and Circuit Courts could function in this capacity. Early on, the naturalization records were kept in the regular court record books, but later counties tended to set up separate volumes for them. For example, separate volumes for the following counties begin on the dates indicated: Berkshire (1856-), Essex (1867-), Hampden (1853-), Middlesex (1842-), Worcester (1837-). Working through all these court records to find a progenitor's naturalization records would be a time-consuming task. However, researchers are spared that by virtue of an index to and copies of naturalization records from all federal, state, county, and city courts in MA. These utterly invaluable sources are:

_DEXIGRAPH COPIES OF NATURALIZATION RECORDS FROM FEDERAL, STATE, COUNTY, AND MUNICIPAL COURTS IN ME, MA, NH, VT, AND RI, 1791-1906, copied by the WPA in the 1930s, located at NABB, Waltham, MA. Petitions and naturalizations only. Declarations of intent may sometimes be in different courts.

_CARD INDEX TO DEXIGRAPH COPIES OF NATURALIZATION RECORDS FROM FEDERAL, STATE, COUNTY, AND MUNICIPAL COURTS IN ME, MA, NH, VT, AND RI, 1791-1906, in NABB, Waltham, MA.

_National Archives, MICROFILM INDEX TO DEXIGRAPH COPIES OF NATURALIZATION RECORDS FROM FEDERAL, STATE, COUNTY, AND MUNICIPAL COURTS IN ME, MA, NH, VT, AND RI, 1791-1906, The Archives, Washington, DC, Microfilm Publication M1299, 117 reels, copy in NABB, Waltham, MA, another copy in FHL.

The index will allow you to locate a forebear, then you can look at the Dexigraph copies of the records and also the originals in the appropriate court records to which you will be referred in the index. MA naturalization records often give data on age, birthplace, date of arrival in US, and other useful information. The National Archives Boston Branch (NABB) also has:

_NATURALIZATION RECORDS OF THE US DISTRICT AND CIRCUIT COURTS FOR MA, 1790-1950, NABB, Waltham, MA. Also see separate series of records of Declarations of Intent.

There is a separate index available for these records:

_INDEX TO US DISTRICT AND CIRCUIT COURT NATURALIZATIONS IN MA, 1790-1926, US District Court, Boston, MA, and on microfilm at FHL.

30. Newspapers

The first newspaper published in the American Colonies, the Publick Occurrences Both Foreign and Domestick, was issued in Boston in 1690. Four days later it was suspended by the Governor. Fourteen years later in 1704 another attempt was made to establish a continuously-published newspaper in Boston, this try being called the Boston Newsletter. The effort was successful and the paper, having Tory or Loyalist sentiments, endured until the British left Boston early in the Revolution. In 1719 the Boston Gazette was started and entered upon a long, influential period of publication, enduring until 1798. In 1721, the New England Courant was set up, giving Boston four of the first five newspapers established in the colonies. During the Revolution, the Boston Gazette and the MA Spy (founded 1770) were very effective political instruments of the Patriots. The colonial papers were not intended to comprehensively cover local news and much was disregarded, including the majority of detailed data which genealogists are interested in. Colonial newspapers were published on a monthly, biweekly, or weekly basis, with daily papers coming in only after the Revolution. Also after the Revolution, many newspapers were set up, both in Boston, and in the other population centers of MA. As time went on, and as newspapers turned toward better coverage of local events, they became more valuable as genealogical sources. There is an increase in their treatment of marriages, anniversaries, deaths (obituaries), court actions, and town and county government activities.

The best repositories for original and microfilm copies of MA newspapers are the American Antiquarian Society (in Worcester), the BPL, the MA Historical Society, and the Boston Athenaeum, the latter being especially good for Boston, although it also has many MA papers also. In addition, LL and historical societies, as well as some of the larger MA universities, have newspaper holdings. To locate them, consult first these three national listings and finding aids which will point the way to many (not all) MA newspapers:

_C. S. Brigham, HISTORY AND BIBLIOGRAPHY OF AMERICAN NEWSPAPERS, 1690-1820, American Antiquarian Society, Worcester, MA, 1961, 2 volumes.

_W. Gregory, AMERICAN NEWSPAPERS, 1821-1936, H. W. Wilson, New York, NY, 1937.

_Library of Congress, NEWSPAPERS IN MICROFORM, The Library, Washington, DC, 1973, plus SUPPLEMENTS, to date.

Then you need to pursue some published specialized MA lists of papers (with locations in some cases):

_M. F. Ayer, CHECK LIST OF BOSTON NEWSPAPERS, 1704-80, Colonial Society of MA, Boston, MA, 1907. Outdated, but useful.

_E. C. Latham, CHRONOLOGICAL TABLES OF AMERICAN NEWSPAPERS, 1690-1820 [HELD BY THE AMERICAN ANTIQUARIAN SOCIETY], The Society, Worcester, MA, 1961.

_BPL, A LIST OF PERIODICALS AND NEWSPAPERS IN PRINCIPAL LIBRARIES OF BOSTON AND VICINITY, Trustees of the Library, Boston, MA, 1897. Outdated, but useful.

_BPL, US NEWSPAPERS ON MICROFORM AT THE BPL, The Library, Boston, MA, 1987, pages 11-118 for MA.

_BPL, NEWSPAPER INDEXES IN THE BPL, The Library, Boston, MA, typescript.

In the major newspaper repositories (American Antiquarian Society, BPL, MA Historical Society, Boston Athenaeum), you will discover finding aids and catalogs which will lead you to newspapers which they hold for your progenitor's county. Also be sure to inquire about newspaper holdings of RL and LL, local archives, local historical and genealogical societies, museums, and newspaper offices. Some older still-existing MA newspaper publishers have files of previous issues, and a few have indexed some or all of their holdings. Unfortunately, not too many newspapers are indexed, so you will need to go through them one-by-one during the times pertinent for your ancestor. This means you can avoid arduous searching only if you have a good idea of the approximate dates of the events you are seeking (marriage, anniversary, death, court action). Some useful indexes have been published, and they can be very valuable, but exercise caution, because some of them are incomplete and/or selective:

_American Antiquarian Society, INDEX TO MARRIAGES IN THE MA CENTINEL AND THE COLUMBIAN CENTINEL, 1784-1840, Hall, Boston, MA, 1961, 5 volumes. Over 87,000 names.

_American Antiquarian Society, INDEX TO OBITUARIES IN THE MA CENTINEL AND THE COLUMBIAN CENTINEL, 1784-1840, Hall, Boston, MA, 1961, 5 volumes. Over 102,000 names.

_O. Codman, INDEX OF OBITUARIES IN BOSTON NEWSPAPERS, 1704-1800, Hall, Boston, MA, 1968, 3 volumes. Deaths both in and outside of Boston.

_Historical Records Survey, INDEX TO LOCAL NEWS IN THE HAMPSHIRE GAZETTE, 1787-1937, WPA, Boston, MA, 1939, 3 volumes. Northampton, Hampshire, and Franklin Counties.

_M. Pugh, LEADS TO ANCESTORS, MARRIAGE NOTICES AND DEATH NOTICES, 1852-3, FROM NOTICES AT BOSTON, The Author, Boston, MA, 1976.

_F. Rider, AMERICAN GENEALOGICAL INDEX, Godfrey Memorial Library, Middletown, CT, 1942-52, 48 volumes, and AMERICAN GENEALOGICAL-BIOGRAPHICAL INDEX, Godfrey Memorial Library, Middletown, CT, 1952-, Volume 1-. Over 160 volumes so far. Indexes, among many other items, the genealogical columns of the Boston Transcript, 1896-41.

In addition to the above published newspaper indexes, there are also a number of unpublished typescript and manuscript indexes available. Many of these are listed in:

_New England Library Association, A GUIDE TO NEWSPAPER INDEXES IN NEW ENGLAND, The Association, Holden, MA, 1978, pages 19-41, 61-70.

Included in this listing are details on indexes for pre-1900 MA newspapers in the following cities/towns: Arlington (1871-), Ashland (1869-1914), Athol (1866-1935), Boston (1704-), Brookline (1874-1922), Cambridge (1876, 1881-), Dedham (1870-1928), Fairhaven (1879-), Gloucester (1827-76), Greenfield (1792-1830), Haverhill (1792-1936),

Hingham (1832-), Lexington (1871-1912), Lynn (1880-), Malden (1852-), Medford (1880-), Natick (1881-1935), Needham (1875-85), New Bedford (1843-), Newton (1866-84, 1892-1913), North Adams (1844-74), Northampton (1786-), Pittsfield (1800-1905), Plymouth (1822-), Quincy (1837-), Somerville (1876-), Springfield (1800-49), Waltham (1863-), Wellesley (1883-8, 1898-), Winchester (1881-), Worcester (1783-1848). Please don't forget that local newspapers often cover surrounding towns and sometimes an entire county.

31. Published indexes for the US

There are many published indexes, microfilm indexes, and card indexes which list exceptionally large numbers of published genealogies or lots of genealogical data at the national level. The most important indexes dealing exclusively with MA have been listed in a previous section, the one entitled genealogical indexes. This section sets out further indexes to genealogies all over the US (and overseas in some instances). These indexes contain many references to genealogies of MA people and therefore you must not fail to look into them. Among the larger ones are:

_INTERNATIONAL GENEALOGICAL INDEX, FHL and FHC, microfiche. [over 120 million entries] Search under MA for name(s).

_FAMILY GROUP RECORDS COLLECTION and TEMPLE INDEX BUREAU, at FHL, applications to have them searched at FHC. [over 40 million entries]

_AIS INTEGRATED CENSUS INDEXES, 1790/1800/10, 1820, 1830, 1840, 1850NE, 1850S, 1850MW&W, FHL and FHC. [19 million entries]

_F. Rider, AMERICAN GENEALOGICAL (AND BIOGRAPHICAL) INDEX, Godfrey Memorial Library, Middletown, CT, Series 1(1942-52), 48 volumes, Series 2(1952-), over 170 volumes, more to come. [13 million entries so far]

_P. W. Filby and M. K. Meyer, PASSENGER AND IMMIGRATION LISTS INDEX, Gale Research Co., Detroit, MI, 1981-, 9 volumes, SUPPLEMENT volumes being published. [1.5 million entries so far]

_The Newberry Library, THE GENEALOGICAL INDEX OF THE NEWBERRY LIBRARY, G. K. Hall, Boston, MA, 1960, 4 volumes. [512 thousand entries]

_1906 DECENNIAL EDITION OF THE AMERICAN DIGEST: A COMPLETE TABLE OF AMERICAN CASES, 1658-1906, West Publishing Co., St. Paul, MN, 1911, volumes 21-25. [500 thousand entries] Subsequent volumes bring the index up to date.

_COMPUTERIZED GENEALOGICAL LIBRARY, 1864 S. State, Salt Lake City, UT 84115. [400 thousand entries]

_COMPUTERIZED ROOTS CELLAR, COMPUTERIZED FAMILY FILE, and COMPUTERIZED 4-GENERATION PEDIGREE CHART DATA BANK, Genealogical Helper, PO Box 368, Logan, UT 84321. [400 thousand entries in each of the first two, 250 thousand in the third]

_NY Public Library, DICTIONARY CARD CATALOG OF THE LOCAL HISTORY AND GENEALOGY DIVISION OF THE NY PUBLIC LIBRARY, G. K. Hall, Boston, MA, 1974, 20 volumes. [318 thousand entries]

_Library of Congress, LIBRARY OF CONGRESS INDEX TO BIOGRAPHIES, The Library, Washington, DC, 40 rolls of microfilm. [170 thousand entries]

_National Society of the DAR, DAR PATRIOT INDEX, The Society, Washington, DC, 1966/79, 2 volumes. [115 thousand entries]

_FHL LIBRARY CATALOG, SURNAME SECTION, original at FHL, microfilm copies at each FHC. [70 thousand entries]

_J. Munsell's Sons, INDEX TO AMERICAN GENEALOGIES, 1711-1908, Genealogical Publishing Co., Baltimore, MD, 1967. [60 thousand entries]

_M. J. Kaminkow, GENEALOGIES IN THE LIBRARY OF CONGRESS, Magna Carta, Baltimore, MD, 1981,and COMPLEMENT TO GENEALOGIES IN THE LIBRARY OF CONGRESS, Magna Carta, Baltimore, MD, 1981. [Over 50 thousand entries]

The books listed above are generally available at NEHGS, BPL, and FHL(FHC), as well as most LGL, some RL, and a few LL. The FHL materials are at FHC or access to them can be had through FHC. And the computerized data materials may be accessed through the places named.

32. Regional publications

In addition to national, state, and local publications, there are also some regional publications which should not be overlooked by any MA researcher. For the most part, these are volumes which are basically historical in character, but carry much genealogical information. They vary greatly in accuracy and coverage, so it is well to treat the data cautiously. In general, they cover specific regions which are usually made up of a few MA counties. In deciding which ones of these books to search for your forebears, you will need to make good use of the state and county maps of Chapter 1.

The following works are ones which should prove useful to you if one or more are from areas of concern to you:

_W. R. Cutter, GENEALOGICAL AND PERSONAL MEMOIRS RELATING TO BOSTON AND EASTERN MA, Lewis Historical Publishing Co., New York, NY, 1908, 4 volumes.

_J. H. Lockwood, WESTERN MA, A HISTORY, Lewis Publishing Co., New York, NY, 1926, 4 volumes, volumes 3-4 biographical.

_REPRESENTATIVE MEN AND OLD FAMILIES OF SOUTHEASTERN MA, Beers, Chicago, IL, 1912, 3 volumes.

_L. H. Smith, Jr., VITAL RECORDS OF SOUTHEASTERN MA, The Author,

Clearwater, FL, 1980-1, 3 volumes. Vital records of Eastham, Orleans, Sandwich, Middleborough, Barnstable, Wareham.

_H. A. Wright, THE STORY OF WESTERN MA, Boston, MA, 1949, 4 volumes, volumes 3-4 biographical and genealogical.

The listings of works dealing with the two original colonies of MA (Plymouth, MA Bay) in section 10 which treats colonial records are distinctly regional and must not be overlooked. Further, histories of counties, cities, and towns are important regional publications. These have been discussed in section 9 of this Chapter, and are indicated in detail under the counties, cities, and towns in Chapter 4.

33. Tax records

During the history of MA, there have been various direct taxes levied on its inhabitants. These have included taxes on individuals (the poll or head tax), on land (the real property tax), on personal belongings (the personal property tax), and on income (the income tax). In addition there have been indirect taxes: tariffs, duties, licenses, and permits. The assessment and collection of these taxes in MA has usually been assigned to the town government. Assessments in MA are often referred to or are included in lists called valuation lists, and taxes are often called rates. In early times, tax records sometimes were included in the town meeting or proceedings records, but more generally the assessment lists were written out on separate sheets. The listings were ordinarily in geographical order in which property was situated. The lists were given to the constable or other collector, who collected the taxes, then returned the lists to the Town Clerk or the Town Treasurer, or the Town Selectmen, or Town Assessors. They were then usually folded and tied in bundles, or bound in volumes, or transcribed in volumes, and then filed by the receiving officer. Males were obligated to begin paying individual tax (poll or head tax) at age 21, although the age may have gone as low as 16 in some special instances.

The tax records of MA towns and cities generally give names, type of tax, amount of property and/or possessions, location of property, and amount of tax. By following tax records for consecutive years, you can sometimes tell when young men come of age, when individuals purchase and sell land, when people enter or leave an area, when people move within a town, and when persons die and leave their land to heirs. Most MA towns have preserved their tax records and they are in the office of the Town Clerk, the Office of the Town Treasurer, and/or in some local repository (library, historical society, archives). The FHL in Salt Lake City, UT, has microfilmed some of these and they are available in FHC.

_TOWN ASSESSORS RECORDS, MA Town and City Offices or Repositories, some also on microfilm at FHL(FHC).

There are also some compiled tax valuation records which warrant your attention. These are in several forms: books, microfilms, and manuscripts, and are available in different places, as noted below.

_MA ARCHIVES, TAX RECORDS, 1738-86, Volumes 130-4, 161-3, 322-4, originals and microfilm copy in MSA, some indexed in MA ARCHIVES MAIN CARD CATALOG at MSA, others in volumes, some not indexed, MSA, Boston, MA, FHL(FHC) has microfilm copy of the MA ARCHIVES MAIN CARD CATALOG, available through FHC.

_R. Crandall, TAX AND EVALUATION LISTS OF MA BEFORE 1776, The Compiler, Cambridge, MA, 1971, microfilm, MSL, Boston, MA. Among these records are ones for Beverly (1739-79), Boxford (1760-75), Chelmsford (1727-36, 1740-79), Danvers (1752-74), Dedham (1636-1801), Lunenburg (1761-70), Marblehead (1757, 1767-76), Medford (1675-1781), Middleton (1728-99, 1862-3), Milton (1668-1792), Needham (1711-31), Reading (1663-1705, 1773-93, 1815-52), Salem (1689-1831), Stoughton (1727-76), Topsfield (1744-79), Walpole (1724-77), Waltham (1738-1820), Wenham (1731-77), Westford (1745-83), Woburn (1673-1776), Wrentham (1736-76), plus numerous other miscellaneous dates.

_MA State Archives, MA PROPERTY VALUATIONS AND TAXES, 1760-71, 1780-92, 1810-11, in MSA, Boston, MA. Incomplete records for some towns. Also on microfilm at FHL(FHC).

_MA State Library, MA TAX VALUATION LISTS, 1780/83/84/91/92/93/1800/01/10/11, MSL, Boston, MA.

_B. H. Pruitt, THE MA TAX VALUATION LIST OF 1771, G. K. Hall, Boston, MA, 1978.

_Boston Registry Department, MISCELLANEOUS PAPERS, Tenth Report of the Commissioners, Boston, MA, 1886. Census of 1707, some wills, deeds, and tax records.

_Boston Registry Department, RECORDS RELATING TO THE EARLY HISTORY OF BOSTON, The Record Commissioners, Boston, MA, 1876-1909, 32 volumes. Thousands of names from births, marriages, deaths, land records, tax lists, and wills. Includes the 1798 direct tax records.

_BOSTON TAX ASSESSOR RECORDS, 1789-, BPL, Boston, MA.

_L. B. Rohrbach, BOSTON TAXPAYERS IN 1821, NEHGS, Boston, MA, 1988.

In 1798, the first federal direct tax, a tax on dwelling houses, tried to list the owner or tenant of every house. The records are very important because they list tenants, that is, non-property owners, for whom there tend to be fewer data. The MA records of this taxation are in the NEHGS along with an exceptionally useful guide to their use:

_US Department of the Treasury, US DIRECT TAX OF 1798, TAX LISTS FOR MA AND ME, NEHGS, Boston, MA, both originals and microfilm copy. Partially indexed, arranged by county, then town; parts of

Norfolk and Suffolk Counties missing. Also on microfilm at FHL(FHC).

_M. H. Gorn, AN INDEX AND GUIDE TO THE MICROFILM EDITION OF THE MA AND ME DIRECT TAX CENSUS OF 1798, NEHGS, Boston, MA, 1979. The tax records were also published in one volume of the 32-volumed Boston Record Commissioners series mentioned above.

34. Town records

The MA towns were the original record-keeping jurisdictions, and as far as genealogical research is concerned, are the major source of original data. The town government is the most likely institution to have recorded detailed information on any individual because of its close contact with its people. The records kept by towns include those of alderman, assessors (tax, rate), births, council, deaths, marriage intentions, marriages, miscellaneous, parish, proprietors, selectmen, selectmen and assessors (combined), soldiers in the Rebellion (Civil War), town proceedings (minutes), vital records (combined births, marriages, deaths). As you will recall from previous discussion, grants of land were made to groups called proprietors for the establishment of towns. These officials assigned land to the settlers and thereby initiated the town. For this reason proprietors records usually antedate the other types. In early years, most records were kept in a single volume (town minutes or proceedings or records), but later on, as expansion occurred and the need arose, separate volumes began to be used for the different categories of records.

The holdings of the various MA towns were surveyed in 1885 by a commission, and the results are listed in the following volume:

_C. C. Wright, REPORT ON THE CUSTODY AND CONDITION OF THE PUBLIC RECORDS OF PARISHES, TOWNS, AND COUNTIES, Wright and Potter, Boston, MA, 1889.

As you can see from the title, the book also reports on church and county records. The material is exceptionally valuable because it informs you in general about the town records which existed in 1885. But caution needs to be exercised, since the details are sometimes not correct compared with what is known today. This is because some of the 1885 reportage was incomplete, some was in error, some records have since been lost, and some records have since been found. In fact, in the years following 1889 (when the book was published), Wright added many additional data to his personal copy of the work and corrected a number of entries. Copies of his annotated volume are available at NEHGS and may also be purchased from them. In spite of its limitations, the book is very useful, because it alerts you with regard to which records may be sought in each town, even though you may find more or less when you actually investigate. The Historical Records Survey of the WPA also surveyed town records in the late 1930s, but their findings remain largely in typescript and manuscript form in the MSA:

_Historical Records Survey, SURVEYS OF MA COUNTY, CITY, AND TOWN RECORDS, WPA, Boston, MA, late 1930s, 132 bundles of typescript and manuscript material in MSA. Data on over 310 cities and towns. Data on all counties except Essex and Middlesex. Information includes governmental record listings, town history material, and church record listings.

As mentioned in sections 4 (birth records), 12 (death records), and 23 (marriage records) in this Chapter, vital records from about 340 MA towns/cities have been put in published, microfilm, microfiche, typescript, and/or manuscript form. These include:

_PUBLISHED VOLUMES OF MA TOWN VITAL RECORDS UP TO 1850, for 227 towns, published by New England Historic Genealogical Society, Essex Institute, Topsfield Historical Society, towns, private companies, and individuals.

_MA TOWN VITAL RECORDS PUBLISHED IN GENEALOGICAL JOURNALS, for 16 towns, chiefly published in New England Historical and Genealogical Register and The Mayflower Descendant.

_J. M. Holbrook, MA TOWN VITAL RECORDS UP TO 1890, over 120 towns on microfiche, Holbrook Research Institute, Oxford, MA.

_Daughters of the American Revolution for MA, COLLECTION OF GENEALOGICAL RECORD VOLUMES, The Society, various places in MA, various dates, numerous volumes, also on microfilm at FHL.

_MA TOWN RECORDS IN MANUSCRIPT FORM, for 52 towns, chiefly located in Corbin Collection and other collections at NEHGS and in Cooke Collection at Berkshire Athenaeum, Pittsfield, MA.

Further, the FHL has microfilmed many town records of most MA towns/cities.

_MA TOWN RECORDS AND VITAL RECORDS, for many towns, on microfilm at FHL, available through FHC.

Please remember that original and/or copied town records may be at one or more locations in the town: Town Clerk, town archives, library, historical society.

35. Will and intestate records

When a person died leaving property (an estate), it was necessary for MA governmental authorities to see that it was properly distributed according to the law. If a will had been written, it was presented for authentication (probate) to the proper officials. When the process had been carried through, the executor(s) named in the will did the actual work of distributing the estate, usually under the supervision of the officials. If no will had been written, this being called an intestate situation, the authorities appointed an administrator who carried out the distribution of the estate. Estate records therefore may consist of wills, administrator appointments, bonds, appraisals, inventories, reports, bills of sale, petitions, annual accounts, partitions, and distributions. The MA probate officials also had jurisdiction over minor children left after a death, and thus kept guardianship records (appointments, accounts, reports). Later on, probate officials exercised authority over adoptions (1851-) and name changes (1854-). The will and probate records were kept in books and various papers involved in the settlement of the estate were gathered together in case files or in probate packets. These files or packets can be extraordinarily rich genealogical sources and should be sought out in all instances. Sometimes they are no longer available.

Will and probate records have been kept in MA since its beginnings. Until the establishment of counties, the records were kept by the Inferior Quarter Courts (1635-43) in MA Bay Colony and by the General Court and Court of Assistants (1620-85) in Plymouth Colony. Jurisdiction was then transferred to the County Courts (1643-92, or 1685-92). During the Andros administration of the Dominion of New England (1686-9) all estates valued over 50 pounds had to be probated at Boston in Suffolk County. In 1692, Judges of Probate (1692-1783) were appointed in each county for the handling of probate matters. Then after independence, in 1783, Probate Courts were established in each county. They have continued to the present. The records are generally to be found in the counties in the offices of the Probate Court. In populous counties, you will usually need to use the probate index to lead you to the probate docket books which will then refer you to the record volumes. In less populous counties, the record volumes usually have indexes in them. Don't forget to seek the case files or probate packets. Caution must be exercised in thinking that if a probate record is not found in the Probate Courts then no record exists. This is not necessarily so because the Superior Court of Judicature and the Supreme Judicial Court had some degree of concurrent jurisdiction over probate during some times, so their records may need to be searched.

In the following lines, some notes regarding the records in each of the MA counties will be made. This will point out to you what is available, the dates being given in parentheses. When a date is followed by only a dash, this means the records continue to the present.

_Barnstable County (1686-, before 1686 in Plymouth Colony). Case files for 1686-1827 lost in fire of 1827. Numerous records abstracted in various issues of the Mayflower Descendant. Early record transcripts in Hinckley Collection in NEHGS. Records 1686-1894 on microfilm in FHL(FHC) and MSA.

_Berkshire County (1761-, before 1761 in Hampshire County). Records 1761-1865 on microfilm at Berkshire Athenaeum in Pittsfield, at FHL(FHC), and at MSA.

_Bristol County (1687-, before 1687 in Plymouth Colony). Record abstracts published in H. L. P. Rounds, ABSTRACTS OF BRISTOL COUNTY, MA, PROBATE RECORDS, 1687-1762, Boston, MA, 1987-8, 2 volumes. Records 1686-1926 on microfilm at FHL(FHC) and MSA.

_Dukes County (1696-). Records 1696-1938 on microfilm at FHL(FHC) and MSA.

_Essex County (1635-). Records published in F. G. Dow, THE PROBATE RECORDS OF ESSEX COUNTY, MA, 1635-81, Salem, MA, 1916-20, 3 volumes. See also M. L. Sanborn, ESSEX COUNTY PROBATE INDEX, 1638-1840, The Author, Boston, MA, 1987. Records 1635-1881 at FHL(FHC) and MSA.

_Franklin County (1812-, before 1812 in Hampshire County). Records 1812-1971 at FHL(FHC) and MSA.

_Hampden County (1812-, before 1812 in Hampshire County). Records 1812-1919 at FHL(FHC) and MSA.

_Hampshire County (1660-, before 1660 in Middlesex County). Some of the records 1660-1820 on microfilm at BPL. Records 1660- on microfilm at FHL(FHC), and at MSA.

_Middlesex County (1648-). Index published in S. H. Folsom and W. E. Rogers, INDEX TO THE PROBATE RECORDS OF THE COUNTY OF MIDDLESEX, 1648-1871, Cambridge, MA, 1914. Previous records in Suffolk County. In early years of Middlesex County, some estates were settled in Suffolk County. Records 1648-1871 on microfilm at BPL. Records 1648- on microfilm at FHL(FHC) and MSA.

_Nantucket County (1706-). Records 1706- at FHL(FHC) and MSA.

_Norfolk County (1793-, before 1793 in Suffolk County). Records 1793- at FHL(FHC) and MSA.

_Old Norfolk County (1637-1714, located in Essex County). Records 1637-1714 at FHL(FHC) and MSA.

_Plymouth County (1685-, before 1685 in Plymouth Colony). See R. W. Sherman and R. S. Wakefield, PLYMOUTH COLONY PROBATE GUIDE, WHERE TO FIND WILLS FOR 800 PEOPLE OF PLYMOUTH COLONY, 1620-91, Plymouth Colony Research Group, Warwick, RI, 1983. Also N. B. Shurtleff, RECORDS OF THE COLONY OF NEW PLYMOUTH IN NEW ENGLAND, 1633-89, Genealogical Publishing Co., Baltimore, MD, 1979. And R. Van Wood, Jr., PLYMOUTH COUNTY, MA, PROBATE INDEX, 1686-1881, NEHGS, Boston, MA, 1988. And D. T. Konig, PLYMOUTH COURT RECORDS, 1686-1859, Glazier, Wilmington, DE, 1978-81, 16 volumes. Plymouth Colony records in transcript and on microfilm at MSA. Records 1633- at FHL(FHC) and MSA.

_Suffolk County (1636-). See E. George, INDEX TO THE PROBATE RECORDS OF THE COUNTY OF SUFFOLK, 1636-1894, Boston, MA, 1895, 3 volumes. Also SUFFOLK COUNTY WILLS, ABSTRACTS OF THE EARLIEST WILLS UPON RECORD IN THE COUNTY OF SUFFOLK, MA, Genealogical Publishing Co., Baltimore, MD, 1984. And Boston Registry Department, RECORDS RELATING TO THE EARLY HISTORY

OF BOSTON, The Record Commissioners, Boston, MA, 1876-1909, 32 volumes. Also Boston Registry Department, MISCELLANEOUS PAPERS [SOME WILLS], Tenth Report of the Commissioners, Boston, MA, 1886. Microfilm of records 1636-1852 in BPL. Records 1636- on microfilm at FHL(FHC) and MSA.

_Worcester County (1731-, before 1731 in Middlesex, Suffolk, and Hampshire Counties). See G. H. Harlow, INDEX TO THE PROBATE RECORDS OF THE COUNTY OF WORCESTER, MA, 1731-1881, O. B. Wood, Worcester, MA, 1898, 2 volumes. Records 1731- at FHL(FHC) and MSA.

Other materials that must not be passed over, especially the first two items, are:

_MA ARCHIVES, Volumes 9A, 15B-19B, 38B-46, 81-86, 140, 164-179, 281-2, MSA, Boston, MA. Early probate records. Most of these are indexed either in the Main Card Catalog to the MA Archives or in the individual volumes, both at MSA.

_INDEX TO MA PROBATE RECORDS, 1686-9, American Genealogist <u>12</u>, 175, 222, <u>13</u>, 98, <u>14</u>, 34. Probates during the period of the Dominion of New England.

_Daughters of the American Revolution [of MA], COLLECTION OF GENEALOGICAL RECORD VOLUMES, The Society, Various places in MA, Various dates, Numerous volumes, also on microfilm at FHL. Volumes include probate material.

_N. Currer-Briggs, ENGLISH WILLS OF COLONIAL FAMILIES, Polyanthos, New Orleans, LA, 1972. About 5000 names.

_H. F. G. Waters, GENEALOGICAL GLEANINGS IN ENGLAND [RELATING TO AMERICANS], Genealogical Publishing Co., Baltimore, MD, 1969, 2 volumes. Mainly wills.

When you locate probate records on your family, recall that this invokes the possibility of other death-related groups: Bible, cemetery, census (mortality), church, military (pension), mortuary, newspaper, and town (vital records). These should all be looked into.

36. <u>WPA records</u>

During the late 1930s and early 1940s, the Historical Records Survey of the Works Progress Administration (WPA) did a very large amount of work in surveying and inventorying many MA records. The typescript volumes which they produced are valuable for indicating what records existed and where they were about 50 years ago. They also produced a sizable volume of manuscript materials largely meant to be employed to produce books, but which never reached that state. All these items can serve as guides to records which you might want to use in your progenitor search. You need, of course, to bear in mind that they are out of date, and thus some of the records have been lost and others are no longer in the places indicated. Among the various typescripts and manuscripts for MA are the following. Many of these have been mentioned previously in other sections to which they especially apply.

_Historical Records Survey, GUIDE TO MANUSCRIPT COLLECTIONS IN MA, WPA, Boston, MA, 1939, 9 volumes. Typescript in MSA and other repositories.

_Historical Records Survey, GUIDE TO MANUSCRIPT MATERIALS IN THE BOSTONIAN SOCIETY, WPA, Boston, MA, 1939. Typescript in MSA and other repositories.

_Historical Records Survey, GUIDE TO MANUSCRIPT REPOSITORIES IN MA, WPA, Boston, MA, 1939. Typescript in MSA and other repositories.

_Historical Records Survey, GUIDE TO MANUSCRIPTS AND SOURCE MATERIALS RELATING TO THE NEGRO IN MA, WPA, Boston, MA, 1942. Typescript in MSA and other repositories.

_Historical Records Survey, GUIDE TO PUBLIC VITAL STATISTICS RECORDS IN MA, WPA, Boston, MA, 1942. Typescript in MSA and other repositories.

_Historical Records Survey, INDEX TO LOCAL NEWS IN THE HAMPSHIRE GAZETTE, 1787-1937, WPA, Boston, MA, 1939, 3 volumes. Typescript in MSA and other repositories. Northampton, Hampshire, and Franklin Counties.

_Historical Records Survey, INVENTORY OF THE CHURCH ARCHIVES OF MA: PROTESTANT EPISCOPAL, WPA, Boston, MA, 1942. Typescript in MSA and other repositories.

_Historical Records Survey, INVENTORY OF THE CHURCH ARCHIVES OF MA: UNIVERSALIST, WPA, Boston, MA, 1942. Typescript in MSA and other repositories.

_Historical Records Survey, INVENTORY OF COUNTY ARCHIVES OF MA, NO. 5, ESSEX COUNTY, WPA, Boston, MA, 1937. Typescript in MSA and other repositories.

_Historical Records Survey, NEGRO CHURCHES, MANUSCRIPTS, FILES, AND BIBLIOGRAPHY IN MA, WPA, Boston, MA, late 1930s and early 1940s. Manuscript materials in the MSA.

_Historical Records Survey, SHIPS REGISTERS, WPA, Boston, MA, 1938-42, 7 volumes. Typescript in MSA and other repositories. Covers Boston (1789-95), Charlestown (1789-95), Barnstable (1814-1913), Plymouth (1789-1808), Dighton-Fall River (1789-1939), New Bedford (1789-1939).

_Historical Records Survey, SURNAME INDEX TO THE ALIEN PASSENGER ARRIVALS AT THE PORT OF BOSTON, 1848-91, WPA, Boston, MA, 1940.

_Historical Records Survey, SURVEYS OF CHURCH RECORDS IN MA, RESEARCH NOTES, WPA, Boston, MA, late 1930s and early 1940s. Typescript and manuscript research notes on Baptist, Congregational,

Episcopal, Jewish, Methodist, Roman Catholic, and Unitarian Churches. In MSA.

__Historical Records Survey, SURVEYS OF MA COUNTY, CITY, AND TOWN RECORDS, WPA, late 1930s and early 1940s. 132 bundles of typescript and manuscript material in MSA. Data on over 310 cities and towns. Data on all county records except Essex and Middlesex. Information includes governmental record listings, town history material, church record listings.

Key to Abbreviations

A	=	Agricultural census records
AGLL	=	American Genealogical Lending Library
BPL	=	Boston Public Library
C	=	Civil War Union veterans census
DAR	=	Daughters of the American Revolution
E	=	Early census-like lists
FHC	=	Family History Center(s)
FHL	=	Family History Library
FHLC	=	Family History Library Catalog
I	=	Industrial census records
IGI	=	International Genealogical Index
LGL	=	Large genealogical libraries
LL	=	Local library(ies) in MA
M	=	Mortality census records
MD	=	Mayflower Descendant
MHS	=	MA Historical Society
MSA	=	MA State Archives
NA	=	National Archives
NABB	=	National Archives, Boston Branch
NAFB	=	National Archives, Field Branch(es)
NEHGS	=	New England Historic Genealogical Society
P	=	Revolutionary War pensioner census
R	=	Regular census records
RL	=	Regional library(ies) in MA
S	=	MA state census records
SASE	=	Long, self-addressed, stamped envelope
SLM	=	State Library of MA

Chapter 3

RECORD LOCATIONS

1. Introduction

The purpose of this chapter is to describe for you the major genealogical record repositories for MA records. These repositories are of two major types, libraries and archives. In general, libraries hold materials which have been published in printed, typescript, photocopied, and microfilm (microcard, microfiche) forms. Archives, on the other hand, are repositories for original records, largely in manuscript (hand-written) form, but also often as microfilm copies. Usually, libraries will have some original materials, and archives will have some published materials, but the predominant character of each is as indicated. When visiting and making use of the materials of repositories, there are several rules which almost all of them have. (1) You are required to check all overcoats, brief cases, and packages. (2) You are required to present some identification and to sign a register or fill out a form. (3) There is to be no smoking, no eating, no loud talk, and the use of pencils only. (4) All materials are to be handled with extreme care, with no injury to or defacing of any of them. (5) Materials are usually not to be returned to the stacks or drawers from which they came, but are to be returned to designated carts, tables, or shelves. (6) Upon leaving you should submit all materials for inspection and/or pass through security devices.

As mentioned at the beginning of Chapter 2, the major repositories for MA genealogical materials are the New England Historic Genealogical Society (NEHGS), the MA State Archives (MSA), and the Boston Public Library (BPL), all three in Boston, the Genealogical Society of Utah Family History Library (FHL) in Salt Lake City and its numerous Family History Center branches (FHC) all over the world, the National Archives (NA) in Washington and its Field Branches (NAFB) in several cities, regional libraries (RL) in various MA cities and towns, local libraries (LL) in many MA cities and towns, and county court houses, city halls, town halls, and other local repositories (LR) in MA cities and towns. Please note that the abbreviation LR refers to county court houses, city halls, town halls, and other local repositories in cities and towns of MA. These other local repositories can include historical societies, genealogical societies, record archives and institutes, and museums.

Libraries and archives have finding aids to facilitate locating the records which they hold. These aids are usually alphabetically arranged lists or indexes according to names or locations or subjects or authors or titles, or combinations of these, or they may be by dates. They consist of computer catalogs, card catalogs, microform catalogs, printed catalogs, typed catalogs and lists, various indexes, inventories, calendars, and tables of contents. In using these aids, especially computer, card, and microform catalogs, they must be searched in as many ways as possible to ensure that you extract everything from them. These ways are by name, by location, by subject, by author, by title, and sometimes by date. Sometimes certain catalogs are arranged by only one or two of these categories, but otherwise be sure and search them for all that are applicable. To help you to recall these categories, remember the word SLANT, with S standing for subject, L for location, A for author, N for name, and T for title. This is not, however, the order in which they should be searched for the maximum efficiency. They should be searched N-L-S-A-T. First, search the catalog for N(name), that is, for the surnames of all your MA forebears. Second, search the catalog for L(location), that is, look under all places where your ancestor lived (MA Plymouth colony, MA Bay Colony, MA Province, MA state, region, county, town, village), but especially the county, city, and town. Examine every entry in order to make sure you miss nothing. Third, look under appropriate S(subject) headings, such as the titles related to the sections in Chapter 1 [Bible, biography, birth, cemetery, census, church denomination, church name, court, Daughters of the American Revolution, death, divorce, emigration, ethnic group name (such as Germans, Huguenots, Irish), genealogy, historical records, immigration, marriage, US-history-Revolutionary War, US-history-War of 1812, US-history-Civil War, naturalization, newspaper, MA (colony), pensions, tax, will], but never neglecting these [biography, deeds, epitaphs, family records, genealogy, registers of births etc., wills]. Then finally, look under A(author) or T(title) for books mentioned in the sections of Chapter 2 which you need to examine.

When you locate references in finding aids to materials you need to examine, you will usually find that a numbered or alphabetized or combined code accompanies the listing. This is the access code which you should copy down, since it tells you where the material is located. For books it will usually be a code which refers to shelf positions. For microfilms, it usually refers to drawers and reel numbers. For manuscripts, it usually refers to folders, files, or boxes. In some repositories, the materials will be out on shelves or in cabinets to which you have access. In other repositories you will need to give the librarian or archivist a call slip on which you have written the title and code for the material so that it can be retrieved for you. In the microfilm areas of repositories you will find microform readers which attendants can help you with, if necessary.

Never leave a library or archives without discussing your research with a librarian or archivist. These people are trained specialists who know their collections and the ways for getting into them. And they can often suggest innovative approaches to locating data relating to your progenitors. They also can usually guide you to other finding aids. When you do discuss your work with librarians and archivists, please remember that they are busy people with considerable demand on their time. So be brief, get to the point, and don't bore them with irrelevant detail. They will appreciate this, and you and others will get more and better service from them.

In general, you cannot expect to do much of your genealogy by corresponding with libraries and archives. The reason is that the hard-working professionals who run these repositories have little time to give to answering mail. This is because of the heavy demands of serving the institutions which employ them, of maintaining the collection, and of taking care of patrons who visit them. Some simply cannot reply to mail requests. Others will answer one brief question which can be quickly looked up in a finding aid, but none of them can do even brief research for you. If you do write them, make your letter very brief, get right to the point, enclose an SASE, and be prepared to wait. Repositories will generally not recommend researchers you can hire, but they will sometimes provide you with a list of researchers. Such a list will bear no warranty from the repository, and they in no way have any responsibility toward either you or the researcher, because they are not in the business of certifying searchers.

2. The New England Historic Genealogical Society (NEHGS)

The New England Historic Genealogical Society (NEHGS) maintains the oldest genealogical library in the US and one of the largest. In actuality the NEHGS is a combined library and archives which has huge collections of both published (printed, typescript, microfilmed, microfiche) and manuscript materials. The Society, which has functioned since 1845, has its library at 101 Newbury St., Boston, MA 02116-3087. The times of opening are 9-5 Tuesday, 9-9 Wednesday, 9-9 Thursday, 9-5 Friday, 9-5 Saturday, closed Sunday, closed Monday, closed Holidays. (Times change, so be sure to call ahead.) The telephone number is 1-(617)-536-5740. All facilities are free for the use of members and they cordially invite you to join, especially if you have New England ancestors. The major finding aids and published materials are available to non-members for a $10 daily fee. The NEHGS has a Book Loan Service for its members. This service consists of a genealogical lending library of about 20,000 volumes which may be borrowed for two weeks by payment of a small postage and handling fee. Every person with MA ancestors should join this very important society so as to support its excellent collection and its exceptionally valuable periodical, THE NEW ENGLAND HISTORICAL AND GENEALOGICAL REGISTER.

There are a number of good hotels within walking distance of the NEHGS. These include the Boston Park Plaza Hotel [50 Park Plaza at Arlington St., Boston, MA 02117, Telephone 1-(800)-225-2008], the Copley Plaza Hotel [138 St. James Ave., Boston, MA 02116, Telephone 1-(800)-225-7653], the Copley Square Hotel [47 Huntington Ave., Boston, MA 02116, Telephone 1-(800)-225-7062], the Lenox Hotel [710 Boylston St., Boston, MA 02116, Telephone 1-(800)-225-7676], and the Westin Hotel [10 Huntington Ave., Boston, MA 02116, Telephone 1-(800)-228-3000]. There are numerous other hotels within a short subway (MBTA) ride from the NEHGS. The nearest stop of the MA Bay Transit Authority (MBTA), the subway which is called the T, is the Copley Stop on the Green Line. It is not a good idea to drive into downtown Boston because of the congestion, the narrow winding one-way streets, and the high cost of parking. Leave your car at your hotel and ride the subway to the NEHGS. Some of the hotels listed above have special senior citizen rates and/or special packages for several-day stays. You should inquire about these worthwhile discounts. A detailed listing of hotels in and around Boston may be obtained by writing

_Greater Boston Convention and Visitors Bureau, Inc., PO Box 490, Boston, MA 02199.

When you arrive at the NEHGS, ring the buzzer, and the receptionist will admit you. Show some identification, pay the daily fee if you are not a member, sign in, then take the elevator to the 6th floor. Get off the elevator, go left down the hall, and hang your coat on the rack located there. Take notice of the rest rooms. Now retrace your steps and enter the door just across the hall from the elevator. You will find yourself in the Reading Room. The service desk sits immediately to your left, the walls are filled with major reference works, and to your far left you will see a door into the stacks. Flanking the door are several large card catalogs. Find yourself a seat and carefully review the general rules for conduct in a library/archive as given in section 1 of this Chapter. Also reread the procedures for searching catalogs given in that same section.

The NEHGS holds practically everything genealogical that has been published on MA, numerous important microfilms and microfiche, and has very large genealogically-oriented manuscript holdings. The keys to these resources are in seven card catalogs. In addition, there are some other notable finding aids which will get you in touch rapidly with materials of concern to you. The seven card catalogs (located to the sides of the door to the stacks) are:

_(CC-1) LIBRARY OF CONGRESS CATALOG [of books since 1975 and some reclassified pre-1975 books], white labels on 126 drawers, NEHGS, Boston, MA. Search by name, location (colony, state, county, city, town), subject, author, title.

_(CC-2) OLD GENEALOGIES CATALOG [of pre-1975 family genealogies], pink labels on 52 drawers, NEHGS, Boston, MA. Search by name and author.

_(CC-3) OLD LOCAL HISTORIES CATALOG [of pre-1975 local histories and records], blue labels on 30 drawers, NEHGS, Boston, MA. Search by location by looking under MA, then county, city, and town.

_(CC-4) OLD GENERAL CATALOG [of pre-1975 publications], white labels on 21 drawers, NEHGS, Boston, MA. Search by location, colony, state, county, city, town), subject, and author.

_(CC-5) OLD MANUSCRIPT CATALOG [of manuscripts mostly before 1975], green labels on 16 drawers, NEHGS, Boston, MA. Search by name, location (colony, state, county, city, town), subject, author, title.

_(CC-6) NEW MANUSCRIPT CATALOG [of manuscripts mostly after 1975], orange labels on 18 drawers, NEHGS, Boston, MA. Search by name, location (colony, state, county, city, town), subject, author, title.

_(CC-7) RARE BOOKS CATALOG [of books and other items published before 1840], light blue labels on 26 drawers, NEHGS, Boston, MA. Search by name, location (colony, state, county, city, town), subject, author, title.

In addition to the above seven card catalogs, there are some other major finding aids in the NEHGS. These are large indexes which lead, as do the seven card catalogs, to original documents containing data on ancestors. They function to save you time since they often give you rapid results.

_(FA-8) THE INTERNATIONAL GENEALOGICAL INDEX, FHL, Salt Lake City, the numerous FHC all over the world, and the NEHGS, Boston, MA. A microfiche index which lists many births and marriages for MA, mostly pre-1850. Look under name.

_(FA-9) THE AMERICAN GENEALOGICAL-BIOGRAPHICAL INDEX, Godfrey Memorial Library, Middletown, CT, 1st series, 48 volumes, 1942-52; 2nd series, over 170 volumes, in progress, 1952-. References to over 12 million items from books, biographies, genealogies, articles. Look under name.

_(FA-10) W. P. Greenlaw, THE GREENLAW INDEX OF THE NEW ENGLAND HISTORIC GENEALOGICAL SOCIETY, G. K. Hall, Boston, MA, 1979, 2 volumes. Over 35,000 entries taken from many periodicals, histories, biographies, and genealogies, chiefly in New England. Search by name. See manuscript copy in NEHGS for references.

_(FA-11) E. C. Lane, INDEX OF SURNAMES IN EARLY MA FROM PRINTED SOURCES, NEHGS, Boston, MA, 9 typescript volumes. State-wide surname index to birth, marriage, death, cemetery, church, and other records contained in about 220 published volumes of MA town pre-1850 vital records. Search by name.

_(FA-12) C. A. Torrey, NEW ENGLAND MARRIAGES PRIOR TO 1700, Genealogical Publishing Co., Baltimore, MD, 1985. Over 37,000 names. Search by name.

_(FA-13) J. Savage, A GENEALOGICAL DICTIONARY OF THE FIRST SETTLERS OF NEW ENGLAND, Genealogical Publishing Co., Baltimore, MD, 1981, 4 volumes. Very valuable, but some errors, so use it as a finding aid to the original records. Search by name.

_(FA-14) H. Whittemore, GENEALOGICAL GUIDE TO THE EARLY SETTLERS OF AMERICA, Genealogical Publishing Co., Baltimore, MD, 1967. Some errors, so use cautiously. Verify all data from original records. Search by name.

_(FA-14) M. B. Colket, FOUNDERS OF EARLY AMERICAN FAMILIES, Founders and Patriots of America, Cleveland, OH, 1985. Excellent references to basic sources. Search by name.

_(FA-16) INDEXES TO THE 1790, 1800, 1810, 1820, 1830, 1840, 1850, AND 1880 FEDERAL CENSUSES FOR MA, Genealogical Publishing Co., Baltimore, MD, 1966/78, Accelerated Indexing Systems, Bountiful, UT, 1973-8, and National Archives, Washington, DC. See section 6, Chapter 2. Over 1.4 million entries. Search by name.

_(FA-17) MA STATEWIDE BIRTH, MARRIAGE, AND DEATH INDEXES, 1841-1895, NEHGS, Boston, MA. Microfilm indexes. Search by name.

_(FA-18) MA CITY DIRECTORY CARD CATALOG, labelled DIRECTORIES, NEHGS, Boston, MA. Search under city, town, county.

_(FA-19) INDEXES TO NEW ENGLAND HISTORICAL AND GENEALOGICAL REGISTER, including INDEX OF PERSONS, PLACES, AND SUBJECTS, VOLUMES 1-50, 1847-96, Genealogical Publishing Co., Baltimore, MD, 1972, and INDEX TO GENEALOGIES AND PEDIGREES, VOLUMES 1-50, 1847-96, The Society, Boston, MA, 1896, and M. W. Parsons, INDEX (ABRIDGED), VOLUMES 51-112, 1897-1958, The Compiler, Marlborough, MA, 1959. Also see Indexes in G. B. Roberts' books: GENEALOGIES OF MAYFLOWER FAMILIES FROM THE NEW ENGLAND HISTORICAL AND GENEALOGICAL REGISTER, MAYFLOWER SOURCE RECORDS: PRIMARY DATA CONCERNING SOUTHEASTERN MA, ENGLISH ORIGINS OF NEW ENGLAND FAMILIES FROM THE NEW ENGLAND HISTORICAL AND GENEALOGICAL REGISTER, all published by the Genealogical Publishing Co., Baltimore, MD, 1985-6. Search under name, location, subject, author, title.

_(FA-20) CATALOG OF MANUSCRIPTS IN THE MA HISTORICAL SOCIETY, G. K. Hall, Boston, MA, 1969, 7 volumes. Search under name, location (colony, state, county, city, town), subject.

_(FA-21) CATALOGUE OF THE MANUSCRIPT COLLECTION OF THE AMERICAN ANTIQUARIAN SOCIETY, G. K. Hall, Boston, MA, 1974, 4 volumes. Search under name, location (colony, state, county, city, town), subject.

_(FA-22) MAP CARD CATALOG, NEHGS, Boston, MA. Search by state, then by town under the state.

_(FA-23) DAR CARD INDEX TO MA REVOLUTIONARY WAR VETERANS' GRAVES, NEHGS, Boston, MA. Search by name.

_(FA-24) DAR PATRIOT INDEX, Daughters of the American Revolution, Washington, DC, 1966/79, 2 volumes. Search by name.

All the above catalogs and finding aids will be found in the Reading room, except FA-8 and FA-17 which are on the lower floor of the stack area, and FA-12, FA-13, FA-14, FA-15, FA-16, and FA-24 which are on the upper floor (6th) of the stack area in the Reference Section.

Now that you have seen 24 major catalogs (CC) and finding aids (FA) in the NEHGS, we can recommend to you the best order in which to use them the first time you visit (or have a hired searcher visit). Practically all of the printed and typescript materials, many of the microform materials, and some of the manuscript materials mentioned in Chapter 2 are in NEHGS and can be located by using these catalogs and finding aids. First, search the following items for all MA surnames of interest to you: CC-1, 3, 5, 6, 7, FA-8, 9, 10, 11, 12, 13, 14, 15, 16, 17, 18, 19, 20, 21, 23, 24. When you find references that could refer to your ancestor(s), copy down the information, then proceed to the records to which the indexes refer. These records will include books in the reading room and the stacks, typescripts in the same places, manuscripts which can be brought from the storage area, microforms on the lower stack floor, rare books in a special area. Some of these will be transcripts of original records and some will be photocopied (microfilmed) original records. You should be well aware that transcribed records have the possibility of error, so it is necessary for good solid genealogy that you get back to the originals or photocopies of them. The transcriptions will generally tell you where they are (or were). By the time you have completed this first step, you will probably know the colony, county, city, and/or town of your ancestor. This will put you in position to take the second step.

Second, you should now proceed to examine the pertinent catalogs and finding aids for the place(s) where your ancestor(s) lived in MA. Under these places, you will find listings of many sorts of records which are available for your further searching. These should be examined for the locations (MA-Plymouth Colony, MA-MA Bay Colony, MA-Colony, MA-Province, the pertinent region, county, city, town) where your progenitor(s) lived. Examine every card or listing under each of the location topics. Write down from the cards and listings the finding information on all promising materials, then find and search them for ancestor data. The catalogs and finding aids for this second endeavor are CC-1, 3, 4, 5, 6, 7, FA-18, 19, 20, 21, 22. Third, you should check the appropriate items for special subjects in which you are interested. The headings of the sections of Chapter 2 will suggest some of the better possibilities, and others were suggested to you in section 1 of this chapter. Fourth, look carefully at the large number of books and other items listed in the many sections of Chapter 2. If you have not checked these out for records on your ancestor, locate those NEHGS holds by author or title in these catalogs: CC-1, 2, 4, 7.

A final note regarding the exceptionally large manuscript holdings of NEHGS is in order. Since this collection is the largest genealogical manuscript collection in the US (over a million items), the manuscript catalogs (CC-5, 6) often do not give great detail, especially on some of the larger and more valuable holdings. This situation is partly alleviated by a series of white ring binders which sit on top of the manuscript catalogs.

_MANUSCRIPT INVENTORIES, 8 white notebooks, NEHGS, Boston, MA. Arranged alphabetically by collection name.

The manuscript inventories in these notebooks go into detail (sometimes great detail, sometimes not) about the contents of the collections. Usually, the manuscript catalogs will lead you to the inventories, which you should go through carefully to see if family data might be in them. Some manuscript collections deal with specific locales (Andover, Barnstable, Barnstable County, Berkshire County, Braintree, Dukes County, Martha's Vineyard, Pittsfield, Scituate, Worcester County, for example), specific families (Andrews, Barbour, Davis, Dudley, Endicott, Freeman, Goodrich, Gorham, Hamlin, Hartshorn, Mixer, Moriarty, Mowbray, Nickerson, Palmer, Pillsbury, Scott, Standish, Woolson, for example), and specific groups (Loyalists, MA Direct Tax of 1798, Mayflower descendants, for example). The Corbin Collection represents the largest compilation of MA material produced for a region of the state. Many types of data for 97 MA towns are included in the 60 linear feet of material. As is the case with some other very valuable NEHGS manuscript collections, this one has been microfilmed and it occupies 55 reels.

3. The MA State Archives

The MA State Archives (MSA) is the official repository for non-current governmental records of the Commonwealth of MA (colony, province, state, and much county material). Its holdings are of utterly inestimable value to genealogists who are researching MA ancestors. They include records dating from the earliest settlement and from every branch of the government [legislative, judicial (courts), and executive (governor, council, secretary, treasurer, adjutant general)]. The major types of records of genealogical value which they have are census, county, land, manuscript, map, military, naturalization, passenger list, tax, town, and vital. The MSA, officially known as the MA Archives at Columbia Point, is located at 220 Morrissey Boulevard, Boston, MA 02125. The telephone number is 1-(617)-727-2816. They are open 9-5 Monday, 9-5 Tuesday, 9-5 Wednesday, 9-5 Thursday, 9-5 Friday, 10-3 Saturday, closed Sunday. These times are subject to change, so telephone ahead. Since the MSA is out of central Boston, there is ample free parking. If you are staying in town near the NEHGS (as is recommended), getting to the MSA is quite straightforward. Take the Green Line of the T (the subway) to the Park Street stop. Transfer to the Red Line and take an Ashmont-bound train to the JFK U Mass stop. Just outside the subway entrance board the JFK/Archives shuttle bus, which leaves on the hour and on the half hour from 9:00 am to 4:30 pm. The shuttle bus returns from the Archives at 15 minutes and 45 minutes past the hour from 9:15 am to 5:15 pm.

Upon entering the MSA, check in at the desk, give them some identification, read and sign the rules sheet given you, lock your coat, briefcase and/or handbag in the locker provided you. Take note of the rest rooms just beyond the locker room. Return to the desk and enter the semi-circular glassed-in reading room just opposite it. Now take a look around you to get your bearings with regard to the contents of the room and its adjacent areas. Directly ahead you will see four sets of shelves containing these items:

__(SH-1) 1790, 1800/10/20/30/40/50 US FEDERAL CENSUS INDEXES FOR MA, 7 books, various authors and publishers.

__(SH-2) 1855/65 MA STATE CENSUS INDEX BOOKS, compiled by A. S. Lainhart, available for many towns.

__(SH-3) MA TAX EVALUATION LIST FOR 1771, one volume, by B. H. Pruitt, alphabetically arranged.

__1850/60/70 US FEDERAL CENSUS SCHEDULES, originals.

__(SH-4) MA SOLDIERS AND SAILORS OF THE REVOLUTIONARY WAR, 17 volumes, indexed. Leads to further records in MSA (payrolls).

__(SH-5) MA SOLDIERS, SAILORS, AND MARINES IN THE CIVIL WAR, 9 volumes, indexed. Leads to further records in MSA (muster rolls, issue books, clothing rolls, descriptive rolls, substitutes, recruits).

__(SH-6) VOLUMES ON MA OFFICERS AND SOLDIERS, 1701-22, and 1723-43, and 1744-55, and 1748-63, and 1755-6. All indexed.

__(SH-7) RECORDS OF THE COLONY OF NEW PLYMOUTH IN NEW ENGLAND, 1633-92, 12 volumes, indexed.

__(SH-8) RECORDS OF THE MA MILITIA CALLED OUT TO SUPPRESS A THREATENED INVASION DURING THE WAR OF 1812-4, one volume, indexed. Leads to further records (Governor and Executive Council records, letters, petitions, rosters, commissions, officers; also payrolls, muster rolls, inspection rolls, company rolls).

__LAWS AND RESOLVES AND ACTS OF MA, 1780-, numerous volumes, legislative records, index in each volume.

__(SH-9) PUBLISHED MA TOWN VITAL RECORDS (MOST UP TO 1850), over 210 volumes, alphabetically arranged by town, indexes in each volume.

__(SH-10) MA BIRTH, MARRIAGE, AND DEATH RECORD INDEXES, 1841-95, originals, many volumes.

_(SH-11) BOSTON CITY DIRECTORIES, 1866-, annual volumes, originals.

Flanking these shelves on both sides you will see film and microfiche readers. Out in the open space of the room are research tables with chairs.

Now glance to your left and you will see four rows of tan microfilm/ microfiche cabinets. In the first row will be found:

_(MF-12) HOLBROOK TOWN VITAL RECORDS (OFTEN UP TO 1890), over 120 towns on microfiche, index in each.

_MF-13) BOSTON CITY DIRECTORIES, 1789-1860/1, on microfiche, each year is alphabetically arranged by name.

_(MF-14) OTHER CITY DIRECTORIES: FALL RIVER 1861-1901, LOWELL 1861-1901, WORCESTER 1861-1901, on microfilm, each year is alphabetically arranged by name.

_(MF-15) SUFFOLK COUNTY SUPREME JUDICIAL COURT, CALENDAR INDEX 1629-1799, and COUNTY INDEX 1687-1799, both on microfilm.

_SUFFOLK COUNTY SUPREME JUDICIAL COURT DOCKET BOOKS 1702-97, arranged under Suffolk County, then under the other MA counties, on microfilm.

_MIDDLESEX COUNTY FOLIO COLLECTION, FOLIOS, 27 reels of microfilm.

_MIDDLESEX COUNTY COURT OF COMMON PLEAS RECORD BOOKS 1807-11, 1823-45, on microfilm.

In the second row of cabinets will be found:

_1855/65 MA STATE CENSUS RECORDS, on microfilm.

_MA MAPS AND PLANS FROM 1794, 1830, AND OTHER DATES, on microfilm.

_PASSENGER LISTS, 1865-88, on microfilm.

_REVOLUTIONARY WAR ROLLS (from MA ARCHIVES), on microfilm.

_(MF-16) REVOLUTIONARY WAR SERVICE APPENDIX, 17 rolls of microfilm, indexed. Supplements SH-4.

_(MF-17) REVOLUTIONARY WAR AND WAR OF 1812 PENSIONERS, on microfilm, alphabetical by county.

_(MF-18) FRENCH AND INDIAN WAR INDEX, 32 rolls of microfilm.

_MA ARCHIVES COURT RECORDS, 1642-1832, on microfilm.

_MA ARCHIVES COUNCIL RECORDS, 1650-1899, on microfilm.

_MA FEDERAL CENSUSES 1800/10/20/30/40/50/80/90/1900, on microfilm.

_MA INDUSTRIAL, MORTALITY, AGRICULTURAL, AND SOCIAL STATISTICS SCHEDULES, 1850/60/70/80, on microfilm.

_(MF-19) MA ARCHIVES PARTIAL INDEX, 1622-1801, On microfilm. Also in card index form. See later.

_MA ARCHIVES, microfilms of 328 volumes of original records. See description later.

In the third row of microfilm/microfiche cabinets will be found:
_FHL MICROFILMS, a large majority of the microfilms available at FHL and through FHC. Include state, county (deeds, land, courts), city and town (vital, assessors, proprietors, town meeting, selectmen) records. Detailed listings in Chapter 4.
The exceptionally large number of FHL microfilmed records continue over into the fourth cabinet, which also contains:
_(MF-20) MA STATE BIRTH, MARRIAGE, AND DEATH REGISTRATION INDEXES, 1841-95, on microfilm.
_MA STATE BIRTH, MARRIAGE, AND DEATH REGISTRATIONS, 1841-95, on microfilm.

Situated to the left of the microform cabinets you will see a set of ten card catalog cabinets. Two of them face the microform cabinets and the other eight are arranged in the shape of a flat U just beyond the first two. Those card catalog cabinets facing the microform cabinets have the following:
_(CC-21) MAPS AND PLANS CARD CATALOG, by town, city, or county.
_(CC-22) FHL MICROFILM CARD LIST, by state, by county, by city, by town.
_(CC-23) CARD NAME INDEX TO MIDDLESEX COUNTY FOLIO COLLECTIONS, by name.
_(CC-24) ALPHABETICAL CARD NAME INDEX TO PASSENGER LISTS, 1841-91, by name.

Now we come to the remaining eight card catalog cabinets. They house card indexes to the vast collection of 17th and 18th century documents of the colony, province, and state of MA known as the MA ARCHIVES. The 328 volumes in this exceptionally large and rich collection deal approximately with the following subjects: Volume 1 (agricultural)#*, 2-6 (colonial)#*, 7 (commercial)#*, 8 (depositions)#*, 9 (domestic relations)#*, 10-14 (ecclesiastical)#*, 15A (emigrants)#*, 15B-19B (estates)#*, 20-22 (foreign relations)#*, 23-24 (French neutrals)#*, 25-28 (Hutchinson's letters, history of MA)#*, 29-33 (Indians)#*, 35-37 (inter-charter)#*, 38A (journals)#*, 38B-44 (judicial)#*, 45-46 (lands)#*-,47 (laws)#*, 48-50 (legislature)#*, 51-55 (letters)#*, 56-57 (letters)*, 58 (literacy)*, 59 (manufactures)*, 60-61 (maritime)#, 62-66 (maritime)*, 67-80 (military)#*, 81-86 (council)#, 87-88 (miscellaneous)*, 89-90 (military)#, 91-99 (muster rolls)#, 100-104 (pecuniary), 105 (petitions)*, 106 (political)*, 107 (Revolution)*, 108-110 (speeches), 111 (taverns)*, 112-118 (towns), 119-120 (trade), 121 (travel), 122-125 (treasury)*, 126-129 (usurpation)*, 130-134 (valuations of towns)#, 135 (witchcraft)*, 136 (miscellaneous), 137 (reports), 138-146 (Revolutionary miscellaneous), 147 (Indian)*, 148-151 (Board of War), 152 (Board of War)*, 153 (Board of War), 154-155 (Revolutionary Royalists), 156 (Revolutionary Provincial Congress), 157 (maritime miscellaneous), 158

(Revolutionary messages), 159 (Revolutionary prize cases), 160 (Revolutionary constitution), 161-163 (valuations of towns), 164 (Revolutionary Council papers)#, 165-172 (council papers), 172-188 (Revolutionary papers and petitions), 189-90 (Shay's rebellion), 191-192 (Shay's rebellion)#, 193-205 (Revolutionary letters)#*, 206-239 (Revolutionary resolves) some*, 240-242 (Hutchinson papers)*, 243 (ancient plans and grants)#*, 244-245 (accounts)#, 246-67 (accounts) some*, 268-9 (billeting accounts)#*, 270-272 (Board of War), 273 (bonds, deeds, wills)*, 274-275 (certificates), 276-278 (Constitutional Convention), 279 (Council), 280 (absentees)*, 281 (estates of absentees)*, 282 (judicial), 283-286 (legislature), 287-290 (letters)*, 291 (maritime)*, 292 (maritime), 293-294 (military), 295 (miscellaneous), 296-302 (orders), 303 (petitions)*, 304-311 (receipts), 311-317 (petitions), 318-319 (Shay's rebellion)#*, 320-321 (treasury), 322 (valuations and taxes)#, 323-324 (valuations and taxes), 325-326 (warrants), 327-328 (Hutchinson papers). The volumes marked with an asterisk * have indexes within the individual volumes. Those volumes marked with a cross-hatch # are indexed or partially indexed in MA ARCHIVES indexes which will now be described.

The other eight card catalog cabinets contain name indexes to portions of the 328 volumes of the MA ARCHIVES. These are:

_(CC-25) MA ARCHIVES MAIN CARD CATALOG, index to the majority of the volumes marked with cross-hatch # above, search by name, location, subject.

_(CC-26) MA ARCHIVES SUPPLEMENTARY CARD CATALOG, INDEX TO LEGISLATURE RECORDS, Volumes 49-51, search by name, subject.

_(CC-27) MA ARCHIVES SUPPLEMENTARY CARD CATALOG INDEX TO COLONIAL MILITARY RECORDS, Volumes 67-80, search by name, subject.

_(CC-28) MA ARCHIVES SUPPLEMENTARY CARD CATALOG INDEX TO MUSTER ROLLS, Volumes 91-99, 268-269, search by name, subject.

_(CC-29) MA ARCHIVES SUPPLEMENTARY CARD CATALOG INDEX TO REVOLUTIONARY COUNCIL PAPERS, Volume 164, search by name, subject.

_(CC-30) MA ARCHIVES SUPPLEMENTARY CARD CATALOG INDEX TO SHAY'S REBELLION, Volume 318, search by name, subject.

_(CC-31) MA ARCHIVES SUPPLEMENTARY CARD CATALOG INDEX TO SHAY'S REBELLION, Volume 319, search by name, subject.

Please note that the MA ARCHIVES Indexes are also available on microfilm (MF-18), and that the MA ARCHIVES volumes are available in both microfilm and original form. The MSA asks you to use the microfilms of the MA ARCHIVES to save wear on the originals.

In addition to the many records mentioned above, there are a large number of other records stored on the balcony above the search room and in other special areas. These records are accessed by several finding aids available at the main desk. Included among the most genealogically important of these finding aids are:

_(MD-32) INVENTORY OF WPA HISTORICAL RECORDS SURVEY MATERIALS, Main Desk. Leads to numerous typescript and manuscript guides to and surveys of records in manuscript repositories, towns, cities, churches, and black institutions. See notice of some important ones later.

_(MD-33) MA ARCHIVES FINDING AIDS, Main Desk. List general information about the 328 volumes. Notebook also gives tables of contents and indexes for some volumes which lack such tables of contents and indexes.

_(MD-34) KNIGHT'S GUIDE TO 1860/70 CENSUS RECORDS OF BOSTON, Main Desk. Permits you to look ancestors up in 1860/70 Boston City Directory where address will be found, then KNIGHT'S GUIDE tells you where to find that street address in the 1860/70 census records. Saves time since no census index is available.

_(MD-35) LIST OF REVOLUTIONARY SOLDIERS AND/OR WIDOWS RECEIVING STATE PENSIONS OR LAND GRANT BOUNTIES, Main Desk.

_(MD-36) NOTEBOOK LISTING OF MA COURT RECORDS TRANSFERRED TO MSA BY THE COUNTIES, listed by county, then by court, then by type of record (record books, docket books, file papers), then by dates. Many pre-1860 records for most counties, including all for Suffolk County. Includes the very important SUFFOLK FILES COLLECTION, approximately 1618-1800, 1284 volumes, with indexes.

Among the useful materials to which finding aid MD-32 will lead you are:

_Historical Records Survey, GUIDE TO MANUSCRIPT MATERIALS IN THE BOSTONIAN SOCIETY, WPA, Boston, MA, 1939. Typescript in MSA.

_Historical Records Survey, GUIDE TO MANUSCRIPT COLLECTIONS IN MA, WPA, Boston, MA, 1939, 9 volumes. Typescript in MSA.

_Historical Records Survey, SURVEYS OF MA COUNTY, CITY, AND TOWN RECORDS, WPA, Boston, MA, 1930s. 132 bundles of typescript and manuscript material in MSA. Data on over 310 cities and towns. Data on all counties except Essex and Middlesex. Information includes governmental record listings, town history material, church record listings.

_Historical Records Survey, SURVEYS OF CHURCH RECORDS IN MA, RESEARCH NOTES, WPA, Boston, MA, 1930s. Typescript research notes on Baptist, Congregational, Episcopal, Jewish, Methodist, Roman Catholic, and Unitarian Churches.

_Historical Records Survey, NEGRO CHURCHES, NEGRO MANUSCRIPTS, NEGRO RECORD FILES, AND NEGRO BIBLIOGRAPHY IN MA, WPA, Boston, MA, 1930s. File material in MSA.

You can now see the large extent of the record holdings of the

MSA, but you must not be daunted by its volume for a very simple reason. There is an easy way to approach the holdings and to assure yourself that you have found everything they have to offer on your ancestor. Practically all of the genealogically-oriented holdings are accessed through the 36 major finding aids listed above: the shelf items (SH-1 through SH-11), the microfilm/microfiche items (MF-12 through MF-20), the card catalogs (CC-21 through CC-31), and the finding aids at the main desk (MD-32 through MD-36). Please recognize that most of these finding aids are essentially indexes which lead to more detailed records, but a few of them are records themselves listed alphabetically.

Here is how you should proceed to make your search. First, examine the following finding aids for your ancestor's name: SH-1/2/3/4/5/6/7/8/9/10/11, MF-12/13/14/15/16/17/18/20, CC-23/24/25/26/27/28/29/30/31, MD-34/35. You may, of course, omit those that are not pertinent because of date or location. When you find references which you believe to be to your ancestor, consult the materials that are indicated. Second, examine the following aids for the location (county., city, and/or town) of your ancestor: CC-21/22/25/26/27/28/29/30/31, MD-32/36. When you locate references to materials relating to your ancestor's locality, seek out the materials and examine them carefully for information on your forebears. It is important to pay careful attention to the MA ARCHIVES card catalog indexes (CC-25 through CC-31) because the references to locations will sometimes lead you to lists of people which have not been indexed by name. Also consider every microfilm listed under your ancestor's locality (including state, county, city, town) in CC-22. These FHL microfilmed records are of immense value and not a single one should be lightly by-passed. Third, if there are important subjects that are related to your progenitor, do not fail to look them up in CC-25/26/27/28/29/30/31, MD-33. Now, fourth, scan back through all the records and finding aids listed in this section to make sure you have looked into all relevant ones. Finally, do not forget to consult the archivist if you have difficulties or special problems.

4. The State Library of MA (SLM)

The State Library of MA (SLM) is an official governmental research library set up to serve the legislative and executive branches of the MA state government. In keeping with this, the SLM has extensive holdings in the areas of MA governmental publications, law, public affairs, government, federal documents relating to MA, state and local history, MA maps and atlases, MA tax valuations, MA newspapers (late 18th and early 19th centuries), and MA manuscripts. The address of the SLM is room 341, State House, Beacon St., Boston, MA 02133. The telephone number is 1-(617)-727-2591. The nearest MBTA stop is Park Street which is on both the Green and Red Lines. The hours are 9-5 Monday through

Friday, but times change, so be sure to call ahead.

Among the materials serving the special mission of the SLM are many which have genealogical relevance. Of these, the most important are:

_MA town, city, county, and state histories. Largest collection.
_MA town, city, county, and state maps and atlases.
_MA town, city, and county directories, 1789-.
_MA town and city vital record compilations, published volumes with records up to 1850, microfiche with records often up to 1890.
_MA manuscripts (General Court, biographies, civic and fraternal organizations).
_MA family histories.
_MA newspapers, late 18th and early 19th centuries.
_US Census non-population schedules for MA: 1820 Manufactures, 1850/60/70/80 Agriculture, 1850/60/70/80 Manufactures, 1850/60/70/80 Social Statistics, Mortality 1850/60/70/80 [1880 Mortality withdrawn from localities that kept official records].
_MA tax valuation returns: state (1780/83/84/91/92/93/1800/01/10/11), Beverly (1735-79), Boxford (1760-75), Chelmsford (1727-78), Danvers (1752-73), Dedham (1648-1750), Lunenburg (1761-70), Marblehead (1734-76), Medford (1684-1735), Middleton (1729-98), Milton (1674-1792), Needham (1712-32), Reading (1664-1703, 1756-76), Stoughton (1727/52/53/1771-6), Topsfield (1744-79), Walpole (1726-51), Waltham (1738-1820), Wenham (1731-77), Westford (1728-77), Woburn (1673-1779), Wrentham (1736-76).

The means for finding all the above items plus other materials that the SLM has on persons, towns, cities, counties, and the state of MA are two sizable card catalogs plus a few other finding aids.

_OLD CARD CATALOG (before July 1975), Dewey system catalog, SLM, Boston, MA. Search by name, location (state, county, city, town), subject, author, title, governmental agency. Also do not fail to look under Registers of births, etc.
_NEW CARD CATALOG (after June 1975), Library of Congress system catalog, SLM, Boston, MA. Catalog is in two sections. Search first section by author and title. Search second section by name, location (state, county, city, town), and subject. Also do not fail to look under Registers of births, etc.
_ZIMMER INDEX TO SEVERAL MAJOR MA NEWSPAPERS, 1878-1937, SLM, Boston, MA. Search by name.
_ALPHABETICAL CARD CATALOG TO MA GENERAL COURT AND STATE CONSTITUTIONAL CONVENTION MEMBERS, SLM, Boston, MA. Gives details of birth, residence, occupation, service, and death. Search by name.
_NEWSPAPER TITLE CARD FILE, behind desk, SLM, Boston, MA. Look

under title.
_NOTEBOOK LIST OF CITY DIRECTORIES IN SLM, behind desk, SLM, Boston, MA. Look under city or town.
For many of the items which you will locate in the card catalogs, the librarians will send you down to Room 55 in the State House. The Special Collections Department, which is located there, has newspapers, maps, atlases, histories, early publications, scrapbooks, manuscripts, photographs, pictures, and prints.

5. The Boston Public Library (BPL)

The Boston Public Library (BPL) is an exceptionally large institution with many of the published and many of the microform materials referred to in Chapter 2. The library is located at Copley Square, Boston, MA 02117. The hours are 9-9 Monday, 9-9 Tuesday, 9-9 Wednesday, 9-9 Thursday, 9-5 Friday, 9-5 Saturday, and 2-6 Sunday. These hours are subject to change so be sure and call ahead. The telephone number is 1-(617)-536-5400. The nearest MBTA (subway) stop is Copley on the Green Line, which means that the BPL is very close to the NEHGS. There are three areas of principal interest to genealogists in the BPL: (1) The Social Sciences Department in the northeastern corner of the 2nd floor of the Research Library, (2) the Catalog Rooms adjacent to the Social Sciences Department, and (3) the Microtext Department in the Southeastern corner of the 1st floor of the Research Library. The numerous genealogically-oriented books and journals in the library are located in the Social Sciences Department and in the closed stack areas. The genealogically-oriented microforms are in the Microtext Department. All these materials can be located by using the card catalogs in the Catalog Rooms and some finding aids in the Microtext Department.

When you enter the BPL, go first to the Social Sciences Department. Then survey the genealogical reference works which you will find on the open shelves there. Among the items will be:
_Histories of MA, MA counties, Boston, other MA cities, and MA towns.
_Published MA town vital records.
_Published MA church histories.
_Major MA genealogical reference works such as Savage, Torrey, military volumes (Revolution, War of 1812, Civil War), records of Plymouth Colony and MA Bay Colony, and the Greenlaw Index, collections of records taken from the New England Historical and Genealogical Register.
_The New England Historical and Genealogical Register, with Indexes.
These volumes represent only a small portion of the collection of genealogical books in the BPL. Many more are in the closed stacks. Before leaving the room, locate the catalog of family genealogies and look in it for the names of interest to you. If you find references which are

possibly to your progenitors, request the materials at the desk.

_CATALOG OF FAMILY GENEALOGIES, Social Sciences Department, BPL, Boston, MA. BPL attempts to collect all published family genealogies relating to MA families.

Next, proceed to the Microtext Department. The major holdings of this department are microforms (microfilms, microfiche), but they also have some reference books and index books. Notice the microform readers, then glance at the volumes on the wall shelves, and take note of the service desk and card catalog cabinet near the door. The most important materials available in this area include (most on microfilm, microfiche, or microcards):

_Microform Copies of the Printed MA Town Vital Records (210 towns) in the Genealogy and Local History Collection, and the Holbrook Microfiche MA Town Records (over 120 towns).
_US Federal Censuses for MA, 1790-1910, with all available Indexes.
_City Directories for Boston and numerous other MA Cities, 1789-1910.
_British Colonial Record Office records for MA.
_Records of the American Colonization Society.
_Passenger Arrivals at Boston, 1820-1918, with Indexes for 1848-91 and 1899-1916.
_Passenger Arrivals at Miscellaneous Gulf and Atlantic Ports 1820-74, with Index.
_Over 2000 Family Genealogies in the Genealogy and Local History Collection. Many are of MA families.
_Microfilm Publications of the MA Historical Society. Largely papers of prominent persons, many of MA.
_American Loyalist Claims Abstracted from the Public Record Office of London.
_Compiled Civil War Service Records of MA Volunteers, 1861-5, with Index.
_Microfilmed Newspapers from 1704.
_Indexes to Obituaries in Some Boston Newspapers, 1704-1840, 1875-1941.
_Boston Transcript Genealogy Columns, 1901-35, with Index. References to thousands of MA persons.
_Tax and Valuation Lists for MA Towns in the Colonial and Revolutionary Periods.
_Boston Town and City Records and Documents, 1634-1914.
_Middlesex County Town Records Collection. Many towns represented.
_Middlesex County Probate Records through 1871, with Index through 1909.
_Suffolk County Probate Records through 1852, with Index through 1909.

Now that you have some idea of the richness of the records in the

BPL, and have surveyed the two major areas where these records may be obtained, you need to know about the finding aids which will lead you to the records pertinent to your ancestor. The major ones of these aids are in the Catalog Rooms on the 2nd Floor. Return there and you will discover two main card catalogs:

_PRE-1981 CARD CATALOG, Catalog Rooms, Research Library, BPL, Boston, MA.

_POST-1980 MICROFICHE CATALOG, Catalog Rooms, Research Library, BPL, Boston, MA.

In accordance with the search procedure described in section 1 of this chapter, use both of these catalogs. In each catalog, search first for all names of interest to you, then look carefully at all locations (state, county, city, town) which are pertinent, then at applicable subjects, then authors and titles of volumes which were referenced in Chapter 2. When you find materials which you believe might relate to your forebear(s), copy down the reference numbers, then obtain the materials from the shelves in the Social Sciences Department, from the desk in the Social Sciences Department, from the shelves in the Microtext Department, or from the desk in the Microtext Department. The reference numbers will indicate to you where the materials are to be accessed. In addition to the above major finding aids (and the Catalog of Family Genealogies in the Social Sciences Department), there are some noteworthy finding aids in the Microtext Department:

_CARD CATALOG OF MICROFORM SETS, Microtext Department, BPL, Boston, MA.

_US NEWSPAPERS ON MICROFORM AT THE BPL, The Library, Boston, MA, 1987, pages 11-118 for MA newspapers. Available at the desk.

_NEWSPAPER INDEXES IN THE BPL, The Library, Boston, MA, typescript. Available at the desk.

These should all be used to make certain that you have found all items which might assist your ancestor search.

In addition to the two above-mentioned institutions, there are two others that are specialized repositories, one ethnic, the other for early published materials. They serve not just MA, but the entire US. The first of these is

_The American Jewish Historical Society Library, 2 Thornton Road, Waltham, MA 02154, Tel. 1-(617)-891-8110.

They have numerous family histories, family papers, histories of Jewish institutions, indexes to many articles, a large number of manuscript collections, and Jewish passenger lists. If you are seeking information on a Jewish MA ancestor, by no means neglect this repository. The other is

_The American Antiquarian Society Library, 185 Salisbury Street, Worcester, MA 01601 -1634, Tel. 1-(617)-891-8110.

This library holds millions of books, pamphlets, journals, maps, directories, newspapers, manuscripts, prints, and other materials, most dating before 1877. It has more printed source material dating from 1600-1850 and relating to the area that became the US than any other repository. Items of special value to genealogists include the largest collection of early newspapers in the US, the sizable city directory holdings, and the many local and family histories.

6. Other MA repositories

In the Boston area, where the previously-discussed repositories (NEHGS, MSA, SLM, BPL) are, there are some other repositories, mostly of a subsidiary nature as concerns genealogy. However, for those researchers who wish to go into depth regarding the cultural, religious, political, historical, economic, and geographical contexts of their forebears' lives, they can be very valuable. These institutions are (1) the MA Historical Society Library in Boston, and (2) the MA Adjutant General's Office, Military Records Section in nearby Natick.

When you have gathered considerable basic genealogical information on a MA ancestor (birth, marriage, death, census, immigration, land, military, probate), and if you care to go into depth on the period in which he/she lived, then a visit to the MA Historical Society Library (MHS) is in order. The society is the oldest historical society in the US (1791), and its holdings of original historical materials are exceedingly large and equally valuable. The address is 1154 Boylston Street, Boston, MA 02215, its telephone number is 1-(617)-536-1609. The hours are 9-4:45 Monday through Friday. The nearest MBTA (subway) stop is Auditorium on the Green Line (just one stop west of Copley). When you emerge from the subway, walk two blocks west on Boylston Street. Enter the library, present identification, store all coats, briefcases, handbags, books and notebooks in the locker assigned to you, read the rules, sign the register and the statement that you will abide by the rules, then take only blank note paper and pencils into the reading room. Then, it is mandatory that you consult a library staff member, to whom you should tell where you are in your research, and from whom you should seek advice on further help the library might have for you.

The keys to the massive collections of the MA Historical Society Library (MHL) are in its several card catalogs which are located in the main reading room and an adjacent room:

_MANUSCRIPT CARD CATALOG, MHS, Boston, MA. Very large catalog. Search by name, location, subject.

_PUBLICATIONS CARD CATALOG, MHS, Boston, MA. Very large catalog. Search by name, location, subject.

_CARD CATALOG OF ENGRAVINGS, PORTRAITS, DRAWINGS, PAINTINGS, PHOTOGRAPHS, PRINTS, AND WOODCUTS, MHS, Boston, MA. Search by name and location.

_MAP CARD CATALOG, MHS, Boston, MA. Search by location (county, city, town).
_MAP CARD CATALOG, CHRONOLOGICAL, MHS, Boston, MA. Search by date.
_MEDICAL HISTORY CARD CATALOG, MHS, Boston, MA. Search by name, subject.
_MICROFILM CARD CATALOG, MHS, Boston, MA. Search by name, location, subject.
_NUCMC CARD CATALOG (Some of the Major Holdings of the MHS), MHS, Boston, MA. Search by name, location, subject.
_NEW ENGLAND PRINTERS CARD CATALOG, MHS, Boston, MA. Search by name, subject.
_NEWSPAPER CARD CATALOG, MHS, Boston, MA. Look under MA, then under city and/or town, then under title.
_REFERENCE WORKS CARD CATALOG [sources, bibliographies, catalogs, lists, collections], MHS, Boston, MA. Look under location, subject.
_Several CARD CATALOGS OF Specific Large Collections, MHS, Boston, MA. Search by name, location, subject.
_THWING COLLECTION CARD CATALOG OF PRE-1800 BOSTON INHABITANTS, MHS, Boston, MA. Very large catalog, 107 drawers of cards. Search by name.
_BIOGRAPHY CARD CATALOG, MHS, Boston, MA. Search by name.
All of these catalogs are potential sources of information on where in the MHS records you might find progenitor data.

In addition to the above finding aids, there are numerous guides to manuscript collections in the MHS and guides to individual manuscript collections.
_CATALOG OF MANUSCRIPTS IN THE MHS, The Society, Boston, MA, 1969, with SUPPLEMENTS, The Society, Boston, MA, 1980-.
_NOTEBOOK GUIDES TO MANUSCRIPT COLLECTIONS, MHS, Boston, MA.
Remember the utterly essential need to consult with the very knowledgeable staff in the MHS.

The MA Adjutant General's Office, Military Records Section (MRS) is located at Building 1, 143 Speen Street, Natick, MA 01760-5766. The telephone number is 1-(617)-651-5766. All visits to the facility are by appointment only, during the hours of 9-4 Monday through Friday. As mentioned above, you should look into the records of the Military Records Section only after you have thoroughly examined the federal and MA military records available in the previously-mentioned repositories (NEHGS, MSA, SLM, BPL) and in some yet to be detailed (FHL-FHC, NA-NAFB, NABB). When you have done this, and you think you want further military information in the period after 1776, you may investigate the

Military Records Section holdings. The collection is quite extensive and relates to the following periods of time:

_Early Militia Records, 1776-1820, including War of 1812.
_MA Militia Records, 1820-40.
_Pre-Civil War Records, 1840-60, including the Mexican War.
_Civil War Records, 1861-5.
_Reconstruction Period Records, 1866-97.
_Spanish American War and Philippine Insurrection Records, 1898-1917.
_Later Records, 1916-73.

The Military Records Section has several useful finding aids which they will introduce to you if you decide to do this detailed advanced work on the military aspect of your progenitor's life.

7. Family History Library (FHL) and Its Branches (FHC)

The largest genealogical library in the world is the Family History Library of the Church of Jesus Christ of Latter-Day Saints (FHC), often referred to as Mormon Library or the LDS Library. This repository holds well over 1.7 million rolls of microfilm plus more than 175,000 books, all genealogical material. It is located at 35 North West Temple, Salt Lake City, UT 84150. The library opens every day except Sunday and holidays at 7:30 am. It closes at 5 pm Saturday, 6 pm Monday, and 10 pm Tuesday through Friday. The general telephone number is 1-(801)-521-0130. The basic key to the library is a massive index called the Family History Library Catalog (FHLC), a set of microfiche (with five sections: surname, locality, subject, author-title, foreign-language-locality). In addition to the main library, the Church maintains a large number of branches called Family History Centers (FHC) all over the world. Each of these has microfiche copies of the Family History Library Catalog (FHLC), plus several other major indexes, plus forms for borrowing microfilm copies of the records at FHL. This means that the astonishingly large holdings of the FHL are available on loan through each of its numerous FHC (Family History Centers or Branch Libraries of the FHL).

There are four Family History Centers (FHC) in the state of MA:

_Family History Center, Boston Stake, Church of Jesus Christ of Latter-Day Saints, 150 Brown Street, Weston, MA 02193. Telephone 1-(617)-235-9892.
_Family History Center, Hingham Stake, Church of Jesus Christ of Latterday Saints, 76 Main, Foxboro, MA 02035. Telephone 1-(617)-543-5284.
_Family History Center, Church of Jesus Christ of Latterday Saints, 67 Chester Street, Worcester, MA.
_Family History Center, Church of Jesus Christ of Latterday Saints, 400 Essex Street, Lynnfield, MA 01940.

When you get ready to visit these FHC or any of the hundreds of others we will soon mention, call them or write them (including an SASE) inquiring about open hours and exact locations.

Other FHC are to be found in the cities listed below. They may be located by looking in the local telephone directories under the listing CHURCH OF JESUS CHRIST OF LATTER DAY SAINTS or in the yellow pages under CHURCHES-LATTER-DAY SAINTS.

_In AL: Birmingham, Huntsville, in AK: Anchorage, Fairbanks, in AZ: Campe Verde(Cottonwood), Flagstaff, Globe, Holbrook, Mesa, Page, Phoenix, Prescott, St. David, Safford, St. Johns, Show Low, Snowflake, Tucson, Winslow, Yuma, in AR: Little Rock,

_In CA: Anaheim, Bakersfield, Barstow, Blythe(Needles), Camarillo, Cerritos(Santa Fe Springs, Lakewood), Covina (West Covina), Cypress-(Buena Park), El Centro, Escondido, Eureka, Fairfield, Fresno, Garden Grove, Glendale, Gridley, Hacienda Heights, Hemet, La Crescenta(La Canada), Lancaster, Long Beach, Los Angeles(Alhambra, Canyon Country), Menlo Park, Mission Viejo, Modesto, Monterey(Seaside), Napa, Newbury Park, Oakland, Orange, Palmdale, Palm Springs(Cathedral City), Pasadena(East Pasadena), Redding, Ridgecrest, Riverside, Sacramento(Carmichael), San Bernardino, San Diego, San Jose, San Luis Obispo, Santa Barbara(Goleta), Santa Clara, Santa Maria, Santa Rosa, Simi Valley, Southern CA(Los Angeles), Stockton, Upland, Ventura, Whittier,

_In CO: Arvada, Boulder, CO Springs, Columbine(Littleton), Cortez, Denver(Northglenn), Durango, Ft. Collins, Grand Junction, LaJara, Littleton, Meeker(Glenwood Springs), Montrose, Pueblo, in CT: Hartford, in DE: Wilmington(Newark), in FL: Cocoa, Gainesville(Alachua), Hialeah/Ft. Lauderdale, Jacksonville(Orange Park), Lakeland, Marianna, Miami, Orlando(Fern Park), Pensacola, St. Petersburg, Tallahassee, Tampa, West Palm Beach(Boca Raton), in GA: Macon, Marietta-(Powder Spring), Sandy Springs(Dunwoody), in HI: Hilo, Honolulu, Kaneohe, Kona(Kailua), Laie,

_In ID: Bear Lake(Montpelier), Blackfoot(Moreland), Boise, Burley, Caldwell, Driggs, Firth, ID Falls, Iona, Lewiston, Malad, Meridian(Boise), Moore(Arco), Nampa, Pocatello, Post Falls, Salmon, Shelley, Twin Falls, Upper Snake River(Rexburg), in IL: Champaign, Chicago Heights(Lossmoor), Naperville(Downers Grove), Rockford, Wilmette, in IN: Fort Wayne, Indianapolis(Greenwood), in IA: Cedar Rapids, Davenport, Des Moines, in KS: Topeka, Wichita, in KY: Hopkinsville(Benton), Lexington, Louisville, in LA: Baton Rouge, Shreveport,

_In ME: Augusta(Hallowell), in MD: Silver Spring, in MA: See above, in MI: Bloomfield Hills, Grand Blanc, Grand Rapids, Lansing(East Lansing), Midland, Westland, in MN: Minneapolis(Richfield), St. Paul, in MS: Hattiesburg, in MO: Columbia, Kansas City(Shawnee Mission), Liberty, Springfield, St. Louis(Berkeley), in MT: Billings, Bozeman,

Butte, Great Falls, Helena, Kalispell, Missoula, in NE: Omaha,

_In NV: Elko, Ely, Fallon, Las Vegas, Logandale, Reno, Sparks, in NJ: East Brunswick, Morristown(Chatham), in NH: Nashua, in NM: Albuquerque(Los Alamos), Farmington, Gallup, Grants, Los Cruces, Roswell, Santa Fe, in NY: Albany(Loudonville), Buffalo(Williamsville), Ithaca (Vestal), New York City, Plainview(Massapequa), Rochester(Webster), Syracuse, Yorktown(New Canaan, CT), in NC: Asheville(Arden), Charlotte, Fayetteville, Hickory, Kinston, Raleigh(Bailey Road), Wilmington(Hampstead), in OH: Cincinnati, Cleveland(North Olmstead), Columbus(Reynoldsburg), Dayton(Jettering), Kirtland, Toledo(Maumee), in OK: Norman, Oklahoma City, Tulsa,

_In OR: Beaverton, Bend, Coos Bay, Corvallis, Eugene, Grants Pass, Gresham(Fairview), Klamath Falls, LaGrande, Lake Oswego(West Linn), Medford, Nyssa(Ontario), Oregon City, Portland, Prineville, Roseburg, Salem, The Dallas, in PA: Philadelphia(Broomall), Pittsburgh, Reading, State College, York, in SC: Charleston(Hanahan), Columbia(Hopkins), Greenville, in TN: Chattanooga, Kingsport, Knoxville(Bearden), Memphis, Nashville(Madison), in TX: Austin(Georgetown), Beaumont(Nederland), Corpus Christi, Dallas, El Paso, Hurst, Friendswood, Houston-(Bellaire), Longview, Lubbock, Odessa, Plano(Richardson), San Antonio,

_In UT: Beaver, Blanding, Bountiful, Brigham City, Cache(Logan), Castledale(Orangeville), Cedar City, Delta, Duchesne, Fillmore, Heber City, Hurricane, Kanab, Lehi(Salt Lake City), Loa, Moroni, Mount Pleasant, Nephi, Ogden, Parowan, Price, Richfield, Roosevelt, Rose Park(Salt Lake City), Sandy, Santaquin, South Jordan(Riverton), St. George, Springville, Tremonton, UT Valley(Provo), Uintah(Vernal), in VA: Annandale, Charlottesville, Fairfax(Springfield), Norfolk(VA Beach), Oakton, Richmond, Roanoke,

_In WA: Bellevue, Bellingham(Ferndale), Bremerton, Ephrata(Quincy), Everett, Kennewick, Longview, Moses Lake, Mount Vernon, Olympia, Pasco, Pullman, Puyallup(Sumner), Richland, Seattle, Spokane, Tacoma, Vancouver, Walla Walla, Wenatchee(East Wenatchee), Yakima, in WI: Appleton, Beloit(Belvidere), Milwaukee, in WY: Afton, Casper, Cody, Evanston, Gillette(Sheridan), Green River, Kemmerer, Lovell, Rock Springs, Worland, Wyoming(Cheyenne).

The FHL is constantly adding new branches, so this list will probably be out-of-date by the time you read it. An SASE and a $2 fee to the FHL (address in the 1st paragraph above) will bring you the most-recent listing of FHC.

When you go to a FHC, you need to first look up the MA surnames of interest to you in the following indexes:

_The MA Section of the INTERNATIONAL GENEALOGICAL INDEX (IGI).

_The Surname Portion of the FAMILY HISTORY LIBRARY CATALOG (FHLC).

_THE FAMILY REGISTER.

_The AIS INTEGRATED CENSUS INDEXES for 1790/1800/10, for 1820, for 1830, for 1840, and for the 1850 Eastern States.
_The Subject Portion of the FAMILY HISTORY LIBRARY CATALOG (FHLC), under the heading Family Group Records.

The second set of index investigations you should make is to look at all entries under MA, then all entries under the MA counties of interest to you, and then all entries under the MA towns which concern you in:
_The Locality Portion of the FAMILY HISTORY LIBRARY CATALOG (FHLC).
You will find extensive listings of these types of records: administrative, business, census, church, county/town histories, court, family histories, genealogical collections, land, military, newspaper, probate, tax, town, vital record (birth, marriage, death), and will. The only other place that some of these records are available is the county or town itself (or the MSA), so this is an exceptionally useful source. When you find entries which you think are applicable to your progenitor(s), copy down the reference numbers and names of the records. These data will permit the FHC librarian to borrow for you the microfilm(s) containing the detailed information from the FHL. The cost is only a few dollars per roll, and when your microfilms arrive (usually 3-6 weeks), you will be notified so that you can return and examine them. A third action you should take is to ask the FHC librarian for a form (Temple Ordinance Indexes Request) to request from the FHL an examination of the Temple Index Bureau Records and the Family Group Records Archive. The above three actions will lead you to many of the materials mentioned in Chapter 2 and many of the records listed under the counties and towns in Chapter 4.

In case you happen to visit the FHL in Salt Lake City, UT, you should proceed by examining all the above indexes plus the Computer-Assisted Catalog(s) looking under both surnames and localities. Pertinent records can be requested or found on the open shelves. The main and the second floors of the building are where most of the MA records can be found.

We cannot leave this section without reminding you that the MSA has most of the MA microfilms held by the FHL, a truly large number of rolls with an exceptional volume of records. The microfilms in the MSA are listed under the counties and towns in a card catalog at the MSA, which will give you easy access to them. Further, the NEHGS has the Family History Library Catalog (FHLC) and the International Genealogical Index (IGI), but not the large collection of microfilms (only at FHL and MSA).

8. The National Archives (NA) and Its Branches (NAFB)

The National Archives and Records Service (NA), located at Pennsylvania Avenue and 8th Street, Washington, DC 20408, is the central national repository for federal records, many being of importance to genealogical research. The NA does not concern itself with colonial records (pre-1776), state, county, city, or town records. Among the most important NA records which pertain to MA are the following:
_Census records: Federal census records for MA, 1790-1910
_Immigration records: Passenger lists for Boston, 1820-91, and for some other MA ports, 1820-73
_Military records: Service, bounty land, pension, claims records, and indexes for the Revolution, War of 1812, Mexican War, Civil War, Spanish-American War
_Naturalization records: New England (including MA) naturalization documents, 1790-1906 (in Boston Field Branch)
Details on all of these have been given in the pertinent sections of Chapter 2. Further detail on them may be obtained in:
_NA Staff, GENEALOGICAL RESEARCH IN THE NATIONAL ARCHIVES, NA, Washington, DC, 1982.

The numerous records of the NA may be examined in Washington in person or by a hired researcher. Microfilm copies of many of the major records and/or their indexes may also be seen in Field Branches of the National Archives (NAFB) which are located in or near Atlanta (1557 St. Joseph Ave., East Point, GA 30344), Boston (380 Trapelo Rd., Waltham, MA 02154), Chicago (7358 S. Pulaski Rd., Chicago, IL 60629), Denver (Bldg. 48, Federal Center, Denver, CO 80225), Fort Worth (501 West Felix St., Ft. Worth, TX 76115), Kansas City (2312 E. Bannister Rd., Kansas City, MO 64131), Los Angeles (24000 Avila Rd., Laguna Niguel, CA 92677), New York (Bldg. 22-MOT, Bayonne, NJ 07002), Philadelphia (9th and Market Sts., Philadelphia, PA 19107), San Francisco (1000 Commodore Dr., San Bruno, CA 94066), and Seattle (6125 Sand Point Way, NE, Seattle, WA 98115). Take special note of the Boston Branch in Waltham, MA. They hold all MA census records, Revolutionary War service, pension, and bounty land records, records of US District Courts, US Courts, and the US Court of Appeals for MA, privateer records during the War of 1812, many maritime records (vessel registers, registers of seamen, crew lists, trading ships, whaling, naval shipyards, coast guard), passenger lists for Boston, 1891-1920, passenger lists for some other MA ports, 1820-73, service records for the War of 1812, and the special non-population census records (agriculture 1850/60/70/80, manufactures 1820/50/ 60/70/80, social statistics 1850/60/70/80). They also hold the following very valuable naturalization materials:
_New England Naturalization Petitions [over 5000 federal, state, county, and local courts, including MA], 1790-1906, with Index.

Many of the NA records pertaining to MA, as was noted in detail in Chapters 2 and 3, are also available at BPL and the FHL(FHC), and some are available at LGL and RL. In addition, practically any local library in the US can borrow NA microfilms for you from AGLL (American Genealogical Lending Library, PO Box 244, Bountiful, UT 84010). Or you may borrow from them directly. Included are NA census records (1790-1910), military records (Revolutionary War, War of 1812, Mexican War, Civil War), and passenger lists (1820-91).

9. Regional libraries (RL)

In the commonwealth of MA there are a number of regional libraries (RL) and larger county and city libraries which have good genealogical collections. Their holdings are larger than most local libraries (LL), but are smaller than the holdings of NEHGS and BPL. As might be expected, the materials in each RL are best for the immediate and surrounding counties or towns. Among the better of these RL for genealogical research are the following (listed in order of the cities where they are found):

_(Amherst) Jones Library, 43 Amity Street, 01002-2285, Tel 1-(413)-256-0246. Local history, genealogy, newspapers, censuses, church records, manuscripts (Boltwood).

_(Amherst) University of MA at Amherst, University Library, 01003, Tel 1-(413)-545-0284. MA history, censuses, newspapers, Hampshire and Suffolk County records, MA city directories, some town records, land ownership maps, atlases, local histories.

_(Barnstable) Sturgis Library, Main Street, 02630, Tel 1-(617)-362-6636. Local history, genealogy, Cape Cod deeds, maritime history.

_(Brockton) Brockton Public Library, 304 Main Street, 02401-5390, Tel 1-(617)-587-2515. Local history, genealogy, city directories, tax books, newspapers, MA town histories and vital records.

_(Cambridge) Cambridge Public Library, 449 Broadway, 02138, Tel 1-(617)-498-9080. Local history, genealogy, newspapers, tax lists, city directories, MA genealogy and local history.

_(Deerfield) Memorial Libraries, Memorial Street, 01342-0053, Tel 1-(413)-774-5581. Franklin County, Western MA, and CT River Valley family papers, manuscripts, diaries, town records, censuses, cemetery readings, genealogies, and local histories.

_(Haverhill) Haverhill Public Library, 99 Main Street, 01830-5092, Tel 1-(617)-373-1588. MA town vital records, local histories, family genealogies, military history, Essex County and Merrimack Valley genealogy and local history, maps.

_(Lynn) Lynn Public Library, 5 North Common Street, 01902, Tel 1-(617)-595-0567. Local genealogy and history, newspapers, MA town vital records.

_(Lynnfield) Lynnfield Public Library, 18 Summer Street, 01940, Tel 1-

(617)-334-5411. Local history and genealogy, MA town histories, family histories, town vital records, Essex County censuses and city directories.

_(New Bedford) New Bedford Free Public Library, 613 Pleasant Street, 0274-6203, Tel 1-(617)-999-6291. Regional genealogy, whaling history, town histories and vital records, customs records, newspapers, censuses, immigration lists, southeastern MA families.

_(Newburyport) Newburyport Public Library, 94 State Street, 01950, Tel 1-(617)-462-4031. Local history, genealogy, town records, tax lists, city directories, censuses, MA town vital records.

_(Northampton) Forbes Library, 20 West Street, 01060, Tel 1-(413)-584-8399. Hampshire County history, genealogy, manuscripts, town records, probate records.

_(Pittsfield) Berkshire Athenaeum, 1 Wendell Avenue, 01201-6385, Tel 1-(413)-499-9480. Berkshire County and Western MA local history, genealogies, newspapers, town records, vital records, manuscripts.

_(Salem) Essex Institute Library, 132 Essex Street, 01970, Tel 1-(617)-744-3390. Essex County local history, genealogy, vital records, town records, county records, newspapers, manuscripts.

_(Springfield) Springfield City Library, 200 State Street, 01103, Tel 1-(413)-739-3871. MA vital records, censuses, genealogies, Hampden County cemetery records, town records, settlement records, local city directories, maps, atlases, history, manuscripts, newspapers, French-Canadian genealogy, Irish genealogy.

When a visit is made to any of these libraries, your first endeavor is to search the card catalog. You can remember what to look for with the acronym SLANT (standing for Subject, Locality, Author, Name, and Title) and by searching the categories out in the order: name-locality-subject-author-title. This procedure should give you very good coverage of the library holdings which are indexed in the card catalog. The second endeavor at any of these libraries is to ask about any special indexes, catalogs, collections, lists, finding aids, or materials which might be pertinent to your search. You should make it your aim particularly to inquire about Bible, cemetery, church, map, manuscript, military, mortuary, and newspaper materials. In some cases, microform (microfilm, microfiche, microcard) records are not included in the regular card catalog but are separately indexed. It is important that you be alert to this possibility.

10. Large genealogical libraries (LGL)

Spread around the US there are a number of large genealogical libraries (LGL) which have at least some major MA genealogical source materials. In general, those of these LGL which are nearest to MA are the ones which have the better MA collections. The fourteen libraries which are probably those which have the largest genealogical collections in the US are:

_Family History Library of the Genealogical Society of UT, 35 North West Temple St., Salt Lake City, UT 84150.
_Public Library of Fort Wayne and Allen County, 301 West Wayne St., Fort Wayne, IN 46802.
_New England Historic Genealogical Society Library, 101 Newbury St., Boston, MA 02116.
_NY Public Library, 5th Avenue and 42nd St., New York, NY 10022-1939.
_Library of Congress, First and Second Sts. at East Capitol St. and Independence Ave., Washington, DC 20540.
_NY Genealogical and Biographical Society Library, 122-126 East 58th St., New York, NY 10022.
_Library of the National Society of the Daughters of the American Revolution, 1776 D St., Washington, DC 20006-5392.
_Western Reserve Historical Society Library, 10825 East Blvd., Cleveland, OH 44106.
_Detroit Public Library, 5201 Woodward Ave., Detroit, MI 48202.
_Newberry Library, 60 West Walton St., Chicago, IL 60610.
_State Historical Society of WI Library, 816 State St., Madison, WI 53703.
_Dallas Public Library, 1515 Young St., Dallas, TX 75201.
_Los Angeles Public Library, 630 West 5th St., Los Angeles, CA 90071.
_Public Library of Cincinnati and Hamilton County, 800 Vine Street, Library Square, Cincinnati, OH 45202-2071.

Among other large libraries which have good genealogical collections are the following:

_In AL: Birmingham Public Library, Davis Library at Samford University in Birmingham, in AZ: Mesa FHC, AZ State Library in Phoenix, Phoenix Public Library, in AR: Central AR Library in Little Rock, AR State Library in Little Rock, in CA: see above, San Diego Public Library, CA Genealogical Society in San Francisco, CA State Library (Sutro) in San Francisco, San Francisco Public Library, in CO: Denver Public Library,
_In CT: CT Historical Society in Hartford, CT State Library in Hartford, Godfrey Memorial Library in Middletown, in DC: see above, in FL: Miami-Dade Public Library, Orange County Library in Orlando, FL State Archives in Tallahassee, Tampa-Hillsborough County Public Library, in GA: Atlanta-Fulton Public Library, GA Department of Archives in Atlanta, Washington Memorial Library in Macon, in HI: HI State Library in Honolulu,
_In ID: ID State Historical Society Library in Boise, Ricks College Library in Rexburg, in IL: see above, IL State Historical Society in Springfield, in IN: see above, IN State Library in Indianapolis, Valparaiso Public Library, in IA: IA State Historical Society in IA City, in KS: KS State

Historical Society Library in Topeka, Wichita Public Library, in KY: KY Historical Library in Frankfort, Filson Club Library in Louisville,

__In LA: LA State Library in Baton Rouge, New Orleans Public Library, in ME: ME State Library in Augusta, ME Historical Society in Portland, in MD: MD Historical Society in Baltimore, in MA: see above, Boston Public Library, in MI: see above, Library of MI in Lansing, in MN: Minneapolis Public Library, MN Historical Society Library in St. Paul, in MS: MS Department of Archives and History in Jackson, in MO: Mid-Continent Public Library in Independence, Kansas City Public Library, St. Louis County Library,

__In MT: MT Historical Society in Helena, in NE: NE State Historical Society in Lincoln, in NV: Las Vegas FHC, NV Historical Society Library in Reno, in NH: NH Historical Society in Concord, NH State Library in Concord, Manchester City Library, in NJ: Joint Free Public Library and Morristown and Morris Township, NJ Historical Society in Newark, NJ State Library in Trenton, in NM: Albuquerque Public Library,

__In NY: see above, NY State Library in Albany, Buffalo and Erie County Public Library, Rochester Public Library, Onondaga County Public Library in Syracuse, in NC: Public Library of Charlotte, NC State Library in Raleigh, in ND: Red River Valley Genealogy Society in West Fargo, in OH: see above, State Library of OH in Columbus, in OK: OK Metropolitan Library in Oklahoma City, Oklahoma Historical Society in Oklahoma City,

__In OR: Genealogical Forum of OR in Portland, Multnomah County Library in Portland, in PA: State Library of PA in Harrisburg, Historical and Genealogical Society of PA in Philadelphia, Carnegie Library of Pittsburgh, in RI: Westerly Public Library, in SC: South Caroliniana Library in Columbia, Greenville County Library in Greenville, in SD: SD State Archives in Pierre, in TN: Knox County Public Library in Knoxville, Memphis and Shelby County Public Library, TN State Library and Archives in Nashville,

__In TX: see above, TX State Library in Austin, Fort Worth Public Library, Clayton Library of the Houston Public Library, in UT: see above, Brigham Young University Library in Provo, in VT: Genealogy Library of the Bennington Museum, in VA: National Genealogical Society Library in Arlington, VA State Library and Archives in Richmond, in WA: Seattle Public Library, Spokane Public Library, Tacoma Public Library, in WV: WV Archives and History Library in Charleston, in WI: see above, Milwaukee Public Library, in WY: Laramie County Library in Cheyenne.

11. Local libraries (LL) and local repositories

Listed under the MA counties and towns in Chapter 4 are the most important local libraries (LL) in the state. These are libraries which have indicated in published compilations (such as the American Library Association Directory, Directory of American Libraries with Genealogical or Local

History Collections) that they have genealogical holdings. There are several types of local libraries in MA: system libraries (serving several towns), county libraries, city libraries, town libraries, village libraries, local historical society libraries, college and university libraries, county historical center libraries, county archives, town historical center libraries, local genealogical society libraries, local museum libraries, historical park libraries, and private libraries. As you might imagine, these institutions are of a wide variety, some having sizeable genealogical materials, some having practically none. Many of the LL (particularly the town and village ones) are affiliates of a nearby larger library which has much greater holdings. What is of importance, however, is that you not overlook any LL in your ancestor's region, county, city, town, or village. Sometimes they will have local records or collections available nowhere else. This is particularly true for Bible, cemetery, church, manuscript, and newspaper records. It is also sometimes the case that counties, cities, towns, and villages have turned older records over to LL, especially the county or town historical societies. You will almost inevitably find local librarians to be very knowledgeable concerning genealogical sources in their areas. Further, they are also usually acquainted with the people in the town (city, county, village) who are experts in the region's history and genealogy. Thus, both local libraries and local librarians can be of inestimable value to you.

When you visit a LL, the general procedure described previously should be followed. First, search the card catalog or catalogs. Look under the headings summarized by SLANT: Subject, Location, Author, Name, Title, doing them in the order N-L-S-A-T. Then, second, inquire about special indexes, catalogs, collections, materials, manuscripts, finding aids, and microforms. Third, ask about any other local sources of data such as cemetery records, church records, maps and atlases, genealogical and historical societies, museums, mortuary records, and old newspapers, plus indexes to all of these. Every local area in MA has many other local repositories which must not be missed. These are the appropriate offices related to the records just mentioned: offices of cemeteries, churches, societies (DAR, Masonic Lodge, GAR, etc.) mortuaries, and newspapers.

If you choose to write to a LL, please remember that librarians are very busy people. Always send them an SASE and confine your questioning to one brief straight-forward item. Librarians are usually glad to help you if they can employ readily-available indexes to answer your question, but you must not expect them to do research for you. In case research is required, they can often provide you with a list of researchers which you may hire, but which they do not guarantee.

Chapter 4

RESEARCH PROCEDURE AND COUNTY/TOWN/CITY LISTINGS

1. Introduction

Now that you have read Chapters 1–3, you should have a good idea of MA history, its genealogical records, and the locations and availabilities of these records. The emphasis in the first three chapters was on records at levels higher than the county. Detailed information on national, state-wide, and regional records was given, but county records were treated only in general. We now will turn our focus upon the county records, and those of lower levels, namely, city and town records. We will also emphasize non-governmental records available at or below the county level (Bible, biography, cemetery, directories, histories, DAR, ethnic, maps, periodicals, genealogies, manuscripts, mortuary, newspaper). The reason for all this attention to county, town, and city records is that these records are likely to contain more information on your ancestors than any other type. Such records were generally recorded by people who knew your forebears, and they relate to the personal details of his/her life.

In the state of MA, many of the original governmental records of the counties, cities, and towns remain within the counties, but quite a sizable number, especially court records, have been transferred to the MSA. Many of these original governmental records and some non-governmental records have been microfilmed by the FHL, and the microfilms are available at FHL, by interlibrary loan through the many FHC throughout the US, and in the MSA. Some of these original governmental records and numerous non-governmental records have been published either in printed volumes or as typescripts. Most of these publications are available in BPL, FHC, NEHGS, and SLM. Some are available in LGL, and those pertinent to their regions are available in RL and LL.

Chapter 4 will deal with county, city, and town records in detail. We will first discuss procedures for finding the county and city or town in which your MA progenitor(s) lived. This is important because knowing that your ancestors were simply from MA is not enough to permit genealogical research. You need to know the county and city or town since many genealogically-applicable records were kept on a local basis, and since you will often find more than one person in MA state bearing the name of your forebear. In such a case, the county/city-town location will often let you tell them apart. After discussing ways to find the county, we will second suggest approaches for doing genealogy in MA, recommending the order in which the various repositories should be used.

2. Locating the town or city and the county

As you will recall from Chapter 1. MA record keeping began in the two original colonies. Plymouth Colony in 1620, and MA Bay Colony in 1630. Essentially from the beginnings, each colony was subdivided into towns which also kept important records. This dual (colony-town) record-keeping system was expanded in 1643 in MA Bay Colony and in 1685 in Plymouth Colony when towns were gathered into counties. Three levels of record-keeping then came to exist: colony-county-town. The development of this record-keeping system followed the same trend in the islands off the south MA coast when their towns were transferred from NY in 1691. and when counties were superimposed in 1695. If you happen to know your ancestor's town or city and county, you may skip the remainder of this section. If not, your first priority must be a search for the town or city and county.

The most efficient method for discovering the town or city and the county depends on the time period in which your progenitor lived in MA. We will discuss town/city-county finding techniques for four basic periods in MA history: (a) 1620-1700. (b) 1700-90. (c) 1790-1850. and (d) 1850-1971. A point of special note is that experts in NEHGS estimate that upwards of 90% of MA ancestors can be located and partially documented by using published source materials.

If your forebear's time period was 1620-1700, you should look in the following major sources for your progenitor's name:

_(1)INTERNATIONAL GENEALOGICAL INDEX. MA SECTION. microfiche publication of the FHL. Salt Lake City. UT. available at FHL, all FHC, and NEHGS.

_(2)E. C. Lane. INDEX OF SURNAMES IN EARLY MA FROM PRINTED MA TOWN VITAL RECORDS. NEHGS. Boston. MA. 9 typescript volumes.

_(3)J. Savage. A GENEALOGICAL DICTIONARY OF THE FIRST SETTLERS OF NEW ENGLAND. Genealogical Publishing Co., Baltimore. MD, 1965.

_(4)M. B. Colket. FOUNDERS OF EARLY AMERICAN FAMILIES. Founders and Patriots of America. Cleveland. OH. 1985.

_(5)C. A. Torrey. NEW ENGLAND MARRIAGES PRIOR TO 1700. Genealogical Publishing Co.. Baltimore. MD. 1985.

_(6)W. P. Greenlaw. THE GREENLAW INDEX OF THE NEW ENGLAND HISTORIC GENEALOGICAL SOCIETY. G. K. Hall. Boston. MA. 1979. 2 volumes.

_(7)F. Rider. the AMERICAN GENEALOGICAL-BIOGRAPHICAL INDEX. Godfrey Memorial Library. Middletown. CT. 1st series. 48 volumes, 1942-52; 2nd series. over 160 volumes. in progress. 1952-.

_(8)INDEXES TO THE NEW ENGLAND HISTORICAL AND GENEALOGICAL REGISTER: INDEX OF PERSONS. PLACES, AND SUBJECTS, VOL-

UMES 1-50, 1847-96, Genealogical Publishing Co., Baltimore, MD, 1972, and INDEX TO GENEALOGIES AND PEDIGREES, VOLUMES 1-50, 1847-96, NEHGS, Boston, MA, 1896; also indexes in G. B. Roberts' books: GENEALOGIES OF MAYFLOWER FAMILIES FROM THE NEW ENGLAND HISTORICAL AND GENEALOGICAL REGISTER, MAYFLOWER SOURCE RECORDS, ENGLISH ORIGINS OF NEW ENGLAND FAMILIES FROM THE NEW ENGLAND HISTORICAL AND GENEALOGICAL RECORD, all published by Genealogical Publishing Co., Baltimore, MD, 1985-6.

_(9)CARD CATALOGS, NEHGS, Boston, MA. Especially CC-1/2/5/6/7 as described in Section 2, Chapter 3.

For the time period 1700-90, items (1), (2), (6), (7), (8), and (9) are the most important to consult. In addition, the following should be looked at:

_National Archives, GENERAL INDEX TO COMPILED SERVICE RECORDS OF REVOLUTIONARY WAR SOLDIERS, SAILORS, AND ARMY STAFF, The Archives, Washington, DC, Microfilm Publication M860, 58 rolls, and the records to which this index leads; see Chapter 2, Section 25.

_B. H. Pruitt, THE MA TAX VALUATION LIST OF 1771, G. K. Hall, Boston, MA, 1978.

If your ancestor was somewhere in the state of MA during 1790-1850, the major finding aids include items (1), (2), (6), (7), (8), and (9), plus these indexes:

_US Bureau of the Census, E. P. Bentley, L. Welch, R. V. Jackson, and C. R. Teeples, INDEXES TO THE 1790, 1800, 1810, 1820, 1830, 1840, AND 1850 MA CENSUSES, Genealogical Publishing Co., Baltimore, MD; The National Archives, Washington, DC, and Accelerated Indexing Systems, Bountiful, UT, 1966-78.

_M. H. Gorn, AN INDEX AND GUIDE TO THE MICROFILM EDITION OF THE MA AND ME DIRECT TAX CENSUS OF 1798, NEHGS, Boston, MA, 1979. Original records at NEHGS. Microfilm copies at NEHGS and FHL.

For progenitors who lived in MA during the years 1841-1971, sources (1), (6), (8), and (9) may be employed in addition to these very useful items:

_MA BIRTH, MARRIAGE, AND DEATH INDEXES, 1841-1971, Office of the Secretary of State, MSA, Boston, MA. Also at FHL.

_R. V. Jackson, MA 1850 CENSUS INDEX, Accelerated Indexing Systems, Bountiful, UT, 1978.

_US Bureau of the Census, INDEXES (SOUNDEX) TO THE 1880 AND 1900 POPULATION SCHEDULES OF MA, The National Archives, Washington, DC, Microfilms T754 and T1051, 70 and 314 rolls, respectively.

_The National Archives, INDEX TO COMPILED SERVICE RECORDS OF VOLUNTEER UNION SOLDIERS WHO SERVED IN ORGANIZATIONS FROM THE STATE OF MA, The Archives, Washington, DC, Microfilm Publication M544, 44 rolls.

The work of locating your MA ancestor can generally be done from where you live or nearby. This is because the key items are either indexes or indexed records which means that they can be scanned rapidly. Also many are in published form which means that they are in numerous LGL outside of MA as well as being available through FHC. Some can be borrowed from AGLL. Therefore, you should not have to travel too far to find many of the indexes that you need. If however, it is more convenient, you may hire a researcher in Boston to delve into the records at NEHGS, MSA, and BPL to locate your progenitor. This should not cost too much because you can instruct your searcher to look into the indexes which are noted above in this section.

3. Research approaches

Having identified the town/city and county of your forebear's residence, you are in position to ferret out the details. This means that you need to identify what non-governmental, federal, state(colonial), county, and city/town records are available, then to locate them, and finally to examine them in detail. The most useful non-governmental records have been discussed in Chapter 2 (sections 2-3, 5, 7-9, 12, 16-19, 22, 28, 30-32, 36). The federal records which are most important for consideration also have been treated in Chapter 2 (sections 6, 15, 25-27, 29). State records of the greatest utility for genealogical research are examined in certain sections of Chapter 2 (4, 6, 11, 13-14, 21, 23, 25-27, 29, 33). Colonial governmental records were listed principally in section 10 of Chapter 2, but other sections also deal with them (6, 11, 15, 21, 24, 35). The types of records which were generated by MA counties and towns/cities are listed in Chapter 1 (section 9) and Chapter 2 (section 1), and they are discussed in various sections of Chapter 2 (4, 11, 13-14, 21, 23, 27, 29, 33-35). County and city/town records which have been microfilmed are in FHL (available through FHC and MSA), and county and city/town records which have been published (printed and typescript) are in NEHGS, BPL, and SLM. Some of these published materials are also located in LGL, RL, and LL. Both the major microfilmed records and the major published records are listed in detail in later sections of this chapter.

The general approach for doing an utterly thorough job of researching a MA ancestor is to follow this pattern:
_1st, check all family sources (oral, records, mementos, Bible)
_2nd, locate your forebear's city/town and county (section 2, this

chapter)
_3rd, use the nearest LGL (indexes, publications, microfilms)
_4th, use the nearest FHC or the FHL (IGI, FHL surname and locality indexes, integrated census indexes, borrow microfilmed records)
_5th, borrow any major federal records you haven't seen from AGLL (census, military, passenger lists)
_6th, use the NEHGS (original, microfilmed, and published federal, state, colony, and non-governmental records; published, manuscript, and microfiche county, city, and town records)
_7th, use the MSA (manuscripts, original state documents, FHL microfilms)
_8th, use the BPL, SLM, MHS, and NABB (published and microfilmed federal, state, colony, and non-governmental records; published county and city/ town records; manuscripts)
_9th, use LL (indexes, manuscripts, local records), visit offices of cemeteries, churches, mortuaries, newspapers, organizations, use RL (if LL directs you there)
_10th, use court houses and offices of city/town record keepers (for local records not seen)
_11th, use NAFB and NA (further federal, military, census, passenger list, naturalization, and court materials)
_12th, use Church Archives (if church records still not found)

The precise way in which you use this scheme is chiefly determined by how far you are from Boston, MA where NEHGS, MSA, SLM, BPL, MHS, and NABB are located. It is in these six repositories that the best total collection of MA genealogical materials in the whole world exists (even though they do not have copies of all county and city/town records). This county and city/town record shortfall means that visits to the county and the city or town are also essential. Therefore, the major idea that you must recognize is that eventually you will have to go to Boston, the county, and the city/town, or hire a researcher to go for you. In short, research in these repositories is an absolute necessity if your ancestor quest is to be complete.

If you live very far from Boston, you should follow the research procedure essentially as it is. In the 3rd, 4th, and 5th steps (LGL, FHC, FHL, AGLL), just as many items as possible should be examined, since this will reduce what remains to be done at the rest of the repositories (6th through 12th), but especially at the county, and city or town offices. It is preferable to visit FHL rather than FHC, so you should elect that option if you are near enough to Salt Lake City, UT (where FHL is). You then need to hire a researcher to go to NEHGS, MSA, SLM, BPL, MHS, and NABB, or go there yourself. Be sure and explain to your hired researcher exactly what records you have seen so that your money will not be wasted on duplicated work. Once the 6th, 7th, and 8th steps have been done, a hired researcher or a personal visit will again be involved for the 9th and 10th steps (LL and county, city, town, and village offices). The 11th step can be done at the NAFB in your region, and the 12th can be conducted by mail.

If you live within range of MA, the 12-step pattern can be modified substantially. By "within range" is meant that you deem a personal visit to Boston workable within the near future. In such a case, you can skip the 3rd and 4th steps, then do the 5th by mail, then the 6th through the 10th by personal visit, and finally the 11th at NABB or at some other NAFB (or the NA) and the 12th by mail.

In selecting a research approach, whether it be one of the above or a modified one which you design, you need to think about three items. The first is expense. You need to balance the cost of a hired researcher over against the cost of personal visits (to Boston, the city/town, and the county): travel, lodging, meals. Also do not forget the costs of borrowing microfilms from your nearest FHC (a few dollars per roll). Of course, your desire to look at the records for yourself (rather than have a researcher do it) may be an important consideration.

The second item is a reminder about interlibrary loans. With the exceptions of books from NEHGS, the microfilms of FHL (available through FHC) and those of AGLL (available personally or through your local library), very few libraries and practically no archives will lend out genealogical materials. The third item is also a reminder. Correspondence with librarians, governmental officials, and archivists is of very limited use. The reason is that these helpful and hard-working state, local, and private employees do not have time to do any detailed work for you because of the demanding duties of their offices. In some cases, these people will have time to look up one specific item for you (a land grant, a deed record, a will, a military pension) if an overall index is available. Please don't ask them for detailed data, and please don't write them a long letter. If you do write them, enclose a long SASE, a check for $5 with the payee line left blank, and a brief request (no more than one-third page) for one specific item in an index or catalog. Ask them to use the check if there is a charge for their services or for copying, and if they do not have the time to look themselves, that they hand the check and your letter to a researcher who can do the work.

4. Format of county-town-city listings

In the next 15 sections (5 through 19), you will find listings of major records in MA counties, towns, and cities. Most of the records are governmental, but a number of important private records are given. In addition, libraries in the towns and cities are shown because they are valuable sources of information.

Under the sections labelled with numbers only (5, 6, 7, etc.), the counties are treated. First, the name of the county is given, then the date on which it was established (or first listed in MA laws), and the parent from which it came. This is followed by the name and zip code of the present county seat. After this, if needed, you will find some notes regarding the county and its records, especially data on record location and/or loss. Second, there is a category labelled Records to be sought. This is a listing gathered from numerous inventories of county records (Wright in 1885, Bowen in 1957, Hindus in 1977 and 1984, Menand in 1987, FHL Catalog in 1988). These inventories sometimes disagree because of the different times they were taken, the possibility of different record identifications, the finding and loss of records, the fact that some records of one type were labelled as another type, and the situation that types of records are often mixed (both in record books and files). Hence, a judgment has been made regarding what records you are likely to find if you search the county, the MSA, and the holdings of the FHL (FHC). The entries are not precise; they are approximations, which means they are to be used as a guide for your search. If you find after careful investigation that the dates are slightly off or find that some dates are missing, don't worry that you are overlooking something. All courts whose names contain the word session are treated under the topic courts of sessions (courts of sessions, courts of general sessions of the peace). In a similar fashion, all courts whose names contain the words common pleas are treated under the topic courts of common pleas (courts of common pleas, inferior courts of common pleas, Boston court of common pleas, court of common pleas of the commonwealth). Third, the census records available for the counties are set out. Remember what the alphabetical symbols stand for: E (early lists), R (regular federal censuses), I (industrial or manufacturing censuses), P (Revolutionary War pensioners), A (agricultural censuses), M (mortality censuses), S (MA state censuses), and C (Civil War veterans).

The fourth category under the counties is one shown as Books. Listed here are the dates when biographical and historical books were published for the county. Also presented are volumes of published county records and the dates these records cover. Published records for Plymouth Colony and MA Bay Colony are included under Plymouth and Suffolk Counties respectively. Not all pertinent books are listed, but some of the essential ones are set forth. You must not treat the list as exhaustive, which means you still need to make a thorough search of card and computer catalogs (under the county) in pertinent libraries and archives. The fifth topical listing is one headed FHL microfilms (MSA). Under this, you will find the records which the FHL has microfilmed, and which are available in the FHL and its many FHC branches. These microfilms are also available in the MSA. Sometimes the FHL microfilm dates will differ somewhat from those given in the section of records to be sought. There are various reasons for this including loss of records, misreadings of dates, failures to recognize that certain record books contain data from several courts, the fact that certain records apply to the area before it was designated as the present county, and the fact that FHL often has not microfilmed more recent material. Finally, there is a section which tells where the deed records may be found.

Under the subsections labelled with a number and a letter (5a, 5b, 5c, etc.), the towns and cities are treated. First, the name of the town or city is given, then the date of establishment and the parent town or land, then any towns split off from it. Second, records which should be looked for are listed. These listings are abstracted from numerous inventories of town/city records (see 2 paragraphs back), and since they were taken at different times, there were often discrepancies. Hence a judgment has been made regarding what records you are likely to find when you search the town/city, MSA, and FHL (FHC). The listings are approximate, and you must not expect to find all the records for every town/city. The listings are simply a setting out of items you should try to locate. Third, there is an indication of whether the vital records (usually up to at least 1850) have been copied (most have) and in what form they are found (book, microfiche, journal, manuscript). If manuscript, the location is given.

Fourth, the earliest church records in the town/city are indicated. If the earliest ones are after 1850, there may be no listing. Listings which show Unitarian or Universalist churches holding records before 1800 are almost always churches which were originally Congregational. Fifth, any books which deal with the history and/or genealogy of the town/city are noted to alert you to look for them in card catalogs. Sixth, the major record listings found in the FHL locality catalog are presented. As you will recall, these are microfilm items which can be ordered from FHL through its branch FHCs. They are also to be found in MSA. Seventh, the name, address, and telephone number of the local library is set down. And some notes regarding its collections are often presented. When there are several libraries in the town/city, the one or ones of greater genealogical interest are listed. Finally, for towns/cities in some counties, there is a capital letter (N, M, S, F) indicating the deed registration district.

5. Barnstable County

Barnstable County established 1685 from Plymouth Colony. County seat Barnstable (02630). Fires in 1701 and 1827, many records lost in 1827. Records to be sought: courts of common pleas (1783-1859), courts of sessions (1783-91, 1805-27), deed (1703-) incomplete 1703-1827, naturalization (1889-), probate (1686-), superior court

(1859–), superior court of judicature (1693–1780), supreme judicial court (1780–). Census: Pre–1800E, 1790R, 1800R, 1810R, 1820RI, 1830R, 1840RP, 1850RAIM, 1855S, 1860RAIM, 1865S, 1870RAIM, 1880RAIM, 1890C, 1900R, 1910R. Books: biography (1890), history (1844/58–62/69/90, 1928/58/65), FHL microfilms (MSA): biography (1890), cemetery, deeds (1703–) incomplete 1703–1827, deeds (1804–8) left after fire, deeds recopied (1783–1870), genealogical collection, history (1869/90, 1928/58/65), Library of Cape Cod History and Genealogy (107 issues), probate (1637–1894), town, vital. Deed repository: At Barnstable.

5a. Town of Barnstable. Recognized in 1638. Records to be sought: assessors (1831–), miscellaneous, proprietors (1703–95), soldiers, town (1640–), vital (1640–). Copied vital records: MD, book. Earliest church records: Baptist (1772–), Congregational (1716–), Methodist (1812–), Unitarian (1725–). Books: town records (1649–1779), proprietors records (1703–95), history. FHL microfilms (MSA): accounts (1792–1825), birth (1641–1784), cemetery, Congregational (1668–1807), genealogical collection, land (1703–95), town (1640–1855), vital (1752–1898). Library: Sturgis Library, Main St. (02630), 1-617-362-6636. Good genealogy collection.

5b. Town of Bourne. Established 1884 from part of Sandwich. Records to be sought: selectmen and assessors (1884–), town (1884–), vital (1884–). Copied vital records: see Sandwich. Earliest church records: Baptist (1838–), Methodist (1828–). Book: history. FHL microfilms (MSA): history, town (in Library of Cape Cod History and Genealogy, No. 104). Library: Jonathan Bourne Public Library, 19 Sandwich Rd. (02532), 1–617–759–3172. Genealogy collection.

5c. Town of Brewster. Established 1803 from part of Harwich. Records to be sought: assessors, town (1803–), vital (1803–). Copied vital records: book. Earliest church records: Baptist (1824–), Unitarian (1747–), Universalist (1824–). Book: history. FHL microfilms (MSA): assessors (1838–49), birth (early–1850), cemetery, history, school (1834–69), town (1803–71), treasury (1811–29), vital (1753–1871). Library: Brewster Ladies' Library (02631), 1–617–896–3913. History collection.

5d. Town of Chatham. Established 1712 from tract called Manamoit. Records to be sought: assessors, parish (1824–69), town (1693–) including records of Manamoit. Copied vital records: MD. Earliest church records: Baptist (1834–), Congregational (1824–), Methodist (1821–), Universalist (1820–). Book: history. FHL microfilms (MSA): birth (1696–1795), early settlers (1690–1711), history, selectmen (1804–54), town (1854–74). Library: Eldridge Public Library, 564 Main St. (12633), 1–

617-945-0274. Genealogy collection.

5e. Town of Dennis. Established 1793 from part of Yarmouth. Records to be sought: assessors, miscellaneous, town (1794-), vital (1794-). Copied vital records: book, MD, microfiche. Earliest church records: Congregational (1817-). Book: history. FHL microfilms (MSA): assessor (1794-1836), birth (1712-1819), cemetery, church (1728-1925), deed (1836-52), history, town (1722-1865), vital (1710-1860). Library: Dennis Memorial Library Association, 1020 Old Bass River Rd. (02638), 1-617-385-2255.

5f. Town of Eastham. Established 1646 as the Town of Nawsett, name changed 1651 to Eastham. Split off Wellfleet 1763, Orleans 1797. Records to be sought (some in Eastham, some in Orleans): assessors, miscellaneous (1654-), proprietors, selectmen, town (1646-), vital (1654-). Copied vital records: book, MD. Earliest church records: Methodist (1819-). Books: biography, early settlers, history. FHL microfilms (MSA): biography, birth (1654-1826), early settlers, history, marriage (1700-1905), proprietors (1654-1855), roads (1828-1956), town (1643-1865), vital (1649-1839). Library: Eastham Public Library, Samoset Rd. (02648), 1-617-255-3070.

5g. Town of Falmouth. Recognized in 1694. Records to be sought: assessors, proprietors (1661-1805), town (1681-), vital (1681-). Copied vital records: book. Earliest church records: Congregational (1731-), Quaker (1709-), Methodist (1811-). Books: histories. FHL microfilms (MSA): birth (1659-1838), church, manuscript guide to Falmouth Historical Society, proprietor (1661-1891), town (1668-1878), vital (1780-). Library: Falmouth Historical Society, Genealogy Archives Library, Palmer Ave. at the Village Green (12541), 1-617-548-4857.

5h. Town of Harwich. Established 1694 from tract called Satuckett. Split off Brewster 1803. Records to be sought: proprietors, selectmen (1815-), town (1703-), vital (1703-). Copied vital records: book, MD. Earliest church records: Baptist (1773-), Congregational (1747-). Books: histories. FHL microfilms (MSA): birth (1694-1850), genealogical collection, history, vital (1703-1850). Library: Brooks Free Library, 739 Main St. (02645), 1-617-432-1799.

5i. Town of Mashpee. Established 1763 as the District of Mashpee, called Marshpee in 1788, then called Plantation of Marshpee, incorporated 1870 as the Town of Mashpee. Records to be sought: assessors (1834-), miscellaneous (1834-), proprietors (1834-), town (1834-), vital (1834-). Copied vital records: None. Earliest church records: Baptist (1832-). Book: history. FHL microfilms (MSA): history, town (1830-80), vital (1834-70).

5j. Town of Orleans. Established 1797 from part of Eastham. Records to be sought: assessor, miscellaneous (1797–), selectmen, town (1797–), vital (1797–). Copied vital records: book, MD. Earliest church records: Congregational (1648–), Methodist (1837–), Universalist (1835–). Books: histories. FHL microfilms (MSA): birth (1760–1839), histories, proprietors (1798–1845), town (1643–1865), vital (1649–1905). Library: Snow Library, Main St. (02653), 1-617-255-3848. History collection.

5k. Town of Provincetown. Established 1714 as Precinct of Cape Cod, established 1727 as Town of Provincetown. Records to be sought: miscellaneous (1853–), selectmen and assessors, town (1724–), vital (1696–). Copied vital records: MD, microfiche. Earliest church records: Congregational (1769–), Methodist (1839–), Universalist (1829–). Books: biography, histories. FHL microfilms (MSA): birth (1696–1843), cemetery, church, histories, vital (1843–66). Library: Provincetown Public Library, 330 Commercial St. (02657), 1-617-487-0850.

5ℓ. Town of Sandwich. Recognized in 1638. Split off Bourne 1884. Records to be sought: miscellaneous (1650–), proprietors (1685–1768), selectmen and assessors, soldiers, town (1650–), vital (1638–). Copied vital records: book, MD, microfiche. Earliest church records: Congregational (1639–), Quakers (1672–), Methodist (1796–), Catholic (1843–), Unitarian (1695–). Books: histories. FHL microfilms (MSA): assessors (1791–1829), cemetery, church, histories, militia (1839–83), proprietor (1665–1770), road (1839–1930), town (1640–1886), treasurer (1780–1829), vital (1640–1886). Library: Sandwich Public Library, 142 Old Main St. (02563), 1-617-888-0625.

5m. Town of Truro. Established 1709 from tract called Pawmett. Records to be sought: miscellaneous (1871–), proprietors (1699–1800), selectmen and assessors, town (1710–), vital (1844–), vital records (1710–1844) are in town records. Copied vital records: book, microfiche. Earliest church records: Congregational (1709–), Methodist (1794–). Books: histories. FHL microfilms (MSA): birth (to 1850), church, death (1786–1826), genealogical collection, histories, marriage (1850–99), proprietors (1696–1800), town (1709–1870), vital (to 1849).

5n. Town of Wellfleet. Established 1763 as District of Wellfleet from part of Eastham, established 1775 as Town of Wellfleet. Records to be sought: miscellaneous, selectmen and assessors, soldiers, town (1723–), vital (1763–). Copied vital records: manuscript in NEHGS, microfiche. Earliest church records: Congregational (1723–), Methodist (1818–), Universalist (1840–). Books: histories. FHL microfilms (MSA): history, town (1763–1858), vital (1734–1875). Library: Wellfleet Public Library, Main St. (02667), 1-617-349-6009. History collection.

5o. Town of Yarmouth. Recognized 1639 as having been set up from land called Mattacheeset. Split off Dennis 1793. Records to be sought: assessors, proprietors (1669-1733), town (1677-), vital (1698-). Copied vital records: book, microfiche. Earliest church records: Baptist (1844-), Congregational (1679-), Quaker (1709-), Methodist (1840-), New Jerusalem (1838-), Universalist (1836-). Books: histories. FHL microfilms (MSA): birth (1641-1850), cemetery, histories, proprietors (1710-87), town (1677-1887), vital (to 1860). Library: Yarmouth Library Association, 297 Main St. (02675), 1-617-362-3717.

6. Berkshire County

Berkshire County established 1761 from Hampshire County. County seat Pittsfield (01201). Since 1788 deeds also registered at Adams and Great Barrington. Records to be sought: courts of common pleas (1761-1859), courts of sessions (1761-1827), deed (1761-), justice of peace (1765-1868), marriage (1788-95), naturalization (1823-), probate (1761-), superior court (1859-), superior court of judicature (1763-80), supreme judicial court (1783-), vital records (1787-95). Census: Pre-1800E, 1790R, 1800R, 1810R, 1820RI, 1830R, 1840RP, 1850RAIM, 1855S, 1860RAIM, 1865S, 1870RAIM, 1880RAIM, 1890C, 1900R, 1910R. Books: biography (1885/9, 1906/42), history (1829/55/85)90, 1912/61). FHL microfilms (MSA): biography (1885, 1906/42), cemetery, Congregational (1743-1945), courts of common pleas (1761-1859), deed (1761-1871), divorce (1847-1916), gazetteer (1885), history (1829/55/85, 1912/61), naturalization (1843-1941), probate (1761-1865), proprietors, superior court (1859-1916), supreme judicial court (1877-87). Deed repositories: Records 1761-88 at Pittsfield, records 1788- for Northern District at Adams, for Middle District at Pittsfield, for Southern District at Great Barrington. In the town/city listings which follow, the pertinent districts are indicted with capital letters (N for Northern, M for Middle, S for Southern) placed at the ends of the listings.

6a. Town of Adams. Established 1778 from a plantation called East Hoosuck. Early records at North Adams. Records to be sought: assessors, miscellaneous (1878-), proprietors, selectmen (1878-), town (1778-), vital (1786-). Copied vital records: manuscript at Berkshire Athenaeum in Pittsfield. Earliest church records: Baptist (1826-), Congregational (1840-). FHL microfilms (MSA): birth (1766-1847-), marriage (1766-1850), Quaker (1713-1880), town (1778-1855). Library: Adams Free Library, Library Park (01220), 1-413-743-0540. N

6b. Town of Alford. Established 1773 as the District of Alford from a part of Great Barrington and some other land, made a town 1775.

Records to be sought: assessors (1861-), selectmen (1822-), town (1774-), vital (1765-). Copied vital records: book. Earliest church records: Congregational (1846-). FHL microfilms (MSA): assessors (1815-7), cemetery, town (1773-1875), vital (to 1850). Library: Alford Town Library, RD3, Great Barrington (01230), 1-413-528-2190. S

6c. Town of Becket. Established 1765 from a plantation called Number Four. Land split off to form part of new Town of Middlefield 1783. Records to be sought: proprietors (1737-65), selectmen and assessors (1765-), town (1765-), vital (1765-). Copied vital records: book. Earliest church records: Congregational (1758-). Books: history. FHL microfilms (MSA): Congregational (1755-1873), vital (to 1850). Library: Becket Athenaeum, Inc. Library, Main St., (01223), 1-413-613-8740.

6d. Town of Cheshire. Established 1793 from parts of Adams, Lanesborough, Windsor, and some of the district of New Ashford. Records to be sought: assessors, soldiers, town (1793-). Copied vital records: microfiche. Earliest church records: Baptist (1834-), Methodist (1850-), Universalist (1849-). Books: history. FHL microfilms (MSA): Baptist (1769-1808, 1821-), history. Library: Cheshire Public Library, Depot St. (01225), 1-413-743-1690. N

6e. Town of Clarksburg. Established 1798 from land north of Adams. Records to be sought: assessors (1860-), selectmen (1836-), town (1855-), vital (1846-). Copied vital records: none. Books: history. FHL microfilms (MSA): cemetery. Library: North Adams Public Library, W. Cross Rd., North Adams (01247), 1-413-662-2545. N

6f. Town of Dalton. Established 1784 from land called Ashuelet Equivalent. Land split off to form part of Hinsdale 1803. Records to be sought: selectmen and assessors (1784-), town (1784-), vital (1784-). Copied vital records: book. Earliest church records: Congregational (1809). Books: history. FHL microfilms (MSA): Congregational (1772-1856), vital (to 1850). Library: Dalton Free Public Library, Main St. (01226), 1-413-684-0049. M

6g. Town of Egremont. Established 1760 as the District of Egremont from land west of Sheffield, made a town 1775. Records to be sought: assessors, miscellaneous (1845-), proprietors (1756-1862), selectmen, town (1840-), vital (1842-). Copied vital records: none. Earliest church records: Baptist (1789-), Congregational (1833-). FHL microfilms (MSA): cemetery, church (1766-1950), Congregational (1770-1876), history. S

6h. Town of Florida. Established 1805 from lands called Barnardstones Grant and part of Bullocks Grant. Records to be sought: miscellaneous (1805–), selectmen and assessors (1805–), town (1805–), vital (1805–). Copied vital records: none. Earliest church records: Baptist (1810–). Library: Florida Free Public Library, RD 2, North County Rd., North Adams (01247), 1-413-664-6023. N

6i. Town of Great Barrington. Established 1761 from part of Sheffield. Land split off to form part of Alford 1773, land split off to form part of Lee 1777. Records to be sought: assessors, miscellaneous (1878–), town (1742–), vital (1742–). Copied vital records: book. Earliest church records: Congregational (1753–), Methodist (1842–), Episcopal (1821–). Books: history. FHL microfilms (MSA): cemetery, church and vital statistics (1666–1870), Congregational (1743–1945), histories, land (1726–64), vital (to 1850). Library: Mason Library, 231 Main St. (01230), 1-413-528-2403. S

6j. Town of Hancock. Established 1776 from a plantation called Jericho. Records to be sought: assessors, miscellaneous (1833–), town (1776–), vital (1765–). Copied vital records: manuscript in NEHGS. Earliest church records: Baptist (1830–), Shakers (1790–). FHL microfilms (MSA): Baptist. Library: Taylor Memorial Library, Main St. (01237), 1-413-738-5970. N

6k. Town of Hinsdale. Established 1804 from parts of Partridgefield (later Peru) and Dalton. Records to be sought: selectmen and assessors, town (1795–), vital (1795–). Copied vital records: book. Earliest church records: Baptist (1792–), Congregational (1795–). FHL microfilms (MSA): Congregational (1795–1896), vital (to 1850). Library: Hinsdale Public Library, Maple St. (01235), 1-413-655-8186. M

6ℓ. Town of Lanesborough. Established 1765 from a plantation called New Framingham. Land split off to form part of Cheshire 1793. Records to be sought: assessors, proprietors (1742–66), selectmen, town (1765–), vital (1765–) with early data in town records. Copied vital records: book, microfiche. Earliest church records: Baptist (1833–), Congregational (1785–), Episcopal (1767–). Books: histories. FHL microfilms (MSA): cemetery, Episcopal (1767–1900), history. Library: Lanesborough Public Library, 83 N. Main St. (01237), 1-413-442-0222. N

6m. Town of Lee. Established 1777 from parts of Great Barrington and Washington and two grants called Glassworks Grant and Williams Grant. Records to be sought: assessors, selectmen (1777–), town (1777–), vital (1777–). Copied vital records: book. Earliest church records: Baptist (1850–), Congregational (1780–), Methodist (1839–),

Episcopal (1856–), Union (1827–). Books: histories, town records (to 1801). FHL microfilms (MSA): cemetery, Church of Christ (1780–1849), vital (to 1850). Library: Lee Library Association, 100 Main St. (01238), 1-413-243-0385. M

6n. Town of Lenox. Established 1767 as District of Lenox from part of Richmont (later Richmond). Records to be sought: assessors, miscellaneous (1800–), proprietors (1764–9), town (1767–), vital (1767–) with early data in town records. Copied vital records: microfiche. Earliest church records: Congregational (1769–), Methodist (1834–), Episcopal (1794–). Books: histories. FHL microfilms (MSA): cemetery, Congregational (1771–1952), history, vital (1750–1849). Library: Lenox Library Association, Main St. (01240), 1-413-637-0197. Historical collection. M

6o. Town of Monterey. Established 1847 from part of Tyringham. Records to be sought: assessors, proprietors (1737–62), selectmen (1847–), town (1847–), vital (1847–). Copied vital records: see Tyringham. Earliest church records: Congregational (1769–). Books: histories. FHL microfilms (MSA): cemetery, church (1741–1809). Library: Monterey Library, Main Rd. (01245), 1-413-528-3795. Historical collection. S

6p. Town of Mount Washington. Established 1779 from a plantation called Tauconnuck Mountain. Records to be sought: assessors, miscellaneous (1835–), proprietors (1750–), selectmen (1863–), town (1796–), vital (1860–). Copied vital records: none. Earliest church records: Congregational (1874–). Books: history. FHL microfilms (MSA): cemetery. Library: Mount Washington Public Library (01258), 1-413-528-1294. S

6q. Town of New Ashford. Established 1781 as the District of New Ashford from land called New Ashford, made a town 1835. Land split off to form part of Cheshire 1793. Records to be sought: assessors, town (1775–), vital (1775–) with early data in town records. Copied vital records: book. Earliest church records: Methodist (1825–). FHL microfilms (MSA): vital (to 1850). N

6r. Town of New Marlborough. Established 1759 as the District of New Marlborough from a plantation called New Marlborough, made a town 1775. Records to be sought: proprietors (1737–1801), selectmen and assessors (1840–), town (1797–), vital (1734–). Copied vital records: microfiche. Earliest church records: Baptist (1847–), Congregational (1790–). Books: history. FHL microfilms (MSA): vital (1730–1870). S

6s. City of NORTH ADAMS. Established 1878 from part of Adams, made a city 1895. Records to be sought: assessors (1876–), town

(1778–) with early records being those of Adams, vital (1878–). Copied vital records: see Adams. Earliest church records: Baptist (1808–), Congregational (1827–), Methodist (1792–). Books: histories. FHL microfilms (MSA): Baptist, cemetery, history, vital (1775–1845). Library: North Adams Public Library, Houghton Memorial Bldg., Church St. (01247), 1-413-662-2545. Historical collection. N

6t. Town of Otis. Established 1773 as the Town of Loudon from land called Tyringham Equivalent, name changed 1810 to Otis. Records to be sought: selectmen and assessors, soldiers, town (1776–), vital (1765–). Copied vital records: book. Earliest church records: Congregational (1812–), Episcopal (1828–). Books: history. FHL microfilms (MSA): cemetery, Congregational (1775–1900), history, vital (to 1850). M

6u. Town of Peru. Established 1771 as the Town of Partridgefield from a plantation called Number Two, name changed 1806 to Peru. Records to be sought: assessors (1775–), miscellaneous (1775–), town (1775–), vital (1775–). Copied vital records: book. Earliest church records: Congregational (1820–). FHL microfilms (MSA): Congregational (1790–1870), vital (to 1850). M

6v. City of PITTSFIELD. Established 1761 as a town from a plantation called Pontoosuck, made a city 1889. Records to be sought: assessors, parish (1753–1845), town (1753–), vital (1753–). Copied vital records: microfiche. Earliest church records: Baptist (1800–), Congregational (1764–), Methodist (1831–), Episcopal (1832–), Catholic (1844–). Books: histories. FHL microfilms (MSA): church, histories, newspaper, vital (1753–1890). Library: Berkshire Athenaeum, One Wendell Ave. (01201), 1-413-499-9480. Excellent genealogical collection. M

6w. Town of Richmond. Established 1765 as Town of Richmont from a plantation called Yokun Town and Mount Ephraim, name changed 1785 to Richmond. Records to be sought: miscellaneous (1827–67), proprietors (1764–9), selectmen and assessors, soldiers, town (1776–), vital (1765–) with a few early data in town records. Copied vital records: book. Earliest church records: Congregational (1784–). Books: histories. FHL microfilms (MSA): church (1769–1959), Congregational (1784–1949), history, school (1828–66), town (1791–1959), treasurer (1828–65), vital (to 1850). Library: Richmond Free Public Library, State Rd. (01254), 1-413-698-3834. M

6x. Town of Sandisfield. Established 1762 from a plantation called Number Three. Records to be sought: assessors, miscellaneous (1708–), proprietors (1735–1862), selectmen, town (1762–), vital (1756–).

Copied vital records: book. Earliest church records: Baptist (1779-98), Congregational (1756-). Books: histories. FHL microfilms (MSA): Baptist (1779-98), cemetery, Congregational (1756-1905), history, vital (to 1850). Library: Sandisfield Free Public Library, Rt. 57 (01255), 1-413-258-4966. S

6y. Town of Savoy. Established 1797 from a plantation called Number Six. Records to be sought: assessors, proprietors (1771-1801), town (1797-), vital (1797-). Copied vital records: microfiche. Earliest church records: Baptist (1786-). Books: history. FHL microfilms (MSA): cemetery, marriage (1795-1865), town (1771-1801). Library: Savoy Public Library, Loop Rd. (01256), 1-413-743-2681. N

6z. Town of Sheffield. Established 1733 from lands of a plantation called Houssatunnock. Split off Great Barrington 1761. Records to be sought: assessors (1769-), miscellaneous (1772-), proprietors, town (1733-), vital (1725-). Copied vital records: manuscript in NEHGS and in Berkshire Athenaeum at Pittsfield. Earliest church records: Congregational (1791-), Methodist (1848-). Books: histories. FHL microfilms (MSA): birth (1733-1870), cemetery, Congregational (1791-1870), history, town (1730-1843), vital (1733-1850). Library: Bushnell-Sage Memorial Library (01257), 1-413-229-7788. S

6aa. Town of Stockbridge. Established 1739 from a plantation called Indian Town. Records to be sought: assessors, proprietors (1739-1825), selectmen, town (1739-), vital (1739-). Copied vital records: microfiche. Earliest church records: Congregational (1759-), Methodist (1835-), Episcopal (1839-). Books: histories. FHL microfilms (MSA): cemetery, Congregational (1759-1850), histories, town (1735-1832), vital (1737-1844). Library: Stockbridge Library Association, Main St. (01262), 1-413-298-5501. M

6bb. Town of Tyringham. Established 1762 from a plantation called Number One. Split off Monterey 1847. Records to be sought: assessors, miscellaneous (1834-), selectmen (1834-), soldiers, town (1834-), vital (1756-). Copied vital records: book. Earliest church records: Methodist (1852-). Books: histories. FHL microfilms (MSA): cemetery, town (1737-1840), vital (to 1850). Library: Tyringham Free Public Library, Main Rd. (01264), 1-413-243-1225. M

6cc. Town of Washington. Established 1777 from a plantation called Hartwood and several bordering grants. Land split off to form part of Middlefield 1783. Records to be sought: assessors, miscellaneous, town, vital. Copied vital records: book. Earliest church records: Methodist (1843-). FHL microfilms (MSA): cemetery, Congregational (1774-1900), vital (to 1850). M

6dd. Town of West Stockbridge. Established 1774 as the District of West Stockbridge from part of Stockbridge, made a town 1775. Records to be sought: assessors (1861-), miscellaneous, soldiers, town, vital (1779-). Copied vital records: book. Earliest church records: Congregational (1829-), Methodist (1838-). Books: history. FHL microfilms (MSA): cemetery, town (1736-1850), vital (to 1850). S

6ee. Town of Williamstown. Established 1765 from a plantation called West Hoosuck. Records to be sought: assessors, proprietors, town (1804-), vital (1765-1843, 1861-). Copied vital records: book. Earliest church records: Congregational (1833-). Books: histories. FHL microfilms (MSA): biography, histories, school, town (1753-1882), vital (to 1850). Library: Williamstown Public Library, 762 Main St. (01267), 1-413-458-5369. N

6ff. Town of Windsor. Established 1771 as Town of Gageborough from a new plantation called Number Four, name changed 1778 to Windsor. Land split off to form part of Cheshire 1793. Records to be sought: assessors, selectmen, town (1772-), vital (1768-). Copied vital records: book. Earliest church records: Congregational (1773-). Books: history. FHL microfilms (MSA): cemetery, Congregational (1773-1870), vital (to 1850). N

7. Bristol County

Bristol County established 1685 from Plymouth Colony. County seat Taunton (02780) since 1746, before that Bristol (now in RI). Since 1837 deeds also registered at New Bedford and since 1892 also at Fall River, some proprietor (land) records also at Fall River, RI. Records to be sought: county court (1685-92), courts of common pleas (1696-1859), courts of sessions (1697-1830), deed (1686-), justice of peace (1726-1864), marriage (1699-1805), naturalization (1852-68), notary (1832-82), probate (1687-), superior court (1859-), superior court of judicature (1693-1780), supreme judicial court (1780-), vital records (1714-85). Census: Pre-1800E, 1790R, 1800R, 1810R, 1820RI, 1830R, 1840RP, 1850RAIM, 1855S, 1860RAIM, 1865S, 1870RAIM, 1880RAIM, 1890C, 1900R, 1910R. Books: biography (1883/99, 1912/24), history (1858/83/99, 1924), probate (1687-1762). FHL microfilms (MSA): biography (1883/99, 1912/24), cemetery, courts of common pleas (1696-1859), courts of sessions (1702-30), deeds (1686-1956), history (1858/83/-99, 1924), marriage (1699-1799), probate (1687-1926). Deed repositories: Records 1685-1837 at Taunton, records 1837-92 for Northern District at Taunton, for Southern District at New Bedford, records 1892- for Northern District at Taunton, for Fall River District at Fall River, for Southern District at New Bedford. In the town/city listings which follow, the pertinent districts are indicated with capital letters (N for the Northern

District 1837–, S for the Southern District 1837–, S1 for the Southern District 1837–92, F for the Fall River District 1892–) placed at the ends of the listings.

7a. Town of Acushnet. Established 1860 from part of Fairhaven. Records to be sought: assessors, selectmen, town (1860–), vital (1860–). Copied vital records: see Fairhaven. Earliest church records: Baptist (1834–), Methodist (1807–), Quaker (1709–). Book: history. FHL microfilms (MSA): cemetery, history, town (1860–1920). Library: Russell Memorial Library, 88 Main St. (02743), 1–617–995–5414. S

7b. City of ATTLEBOROUGH. Established 1694 as a town from a part of Rehoboth which was called the North Purchase, made a city 1914. Split off North Attleborough 1887. Records to be sought: assessors, miscellaneous (1750–), proprietors (1666–1839), town (1697–), vital (1697–). Copied vital records: book, microfiche. Earliest church records: Baptist (1769–), Congregational (1686–), Catholic (1850–), Union (1828–), Universalist (1816–). Book: history. FHL microfilms (MSA): atlas, biography, cemetery, Civil War, Congregational (1740–1856), death (1856–1958), histories, jurors (1841–1918), land (1833–73), marriage (1694–1852), town (1699–1844), vital (up to 1850). Library: Attleborough Public Library, 74 N. Main St. (02703), 1–617–222–0157. Genealogy collection. N

7c. Town of Berkley. Established 1735 from parts of Dighton and Taunton. Records to be sought: assessors, miscellaneous (1735–), selectmen, town (1735–), vital (1735–). Copied vital records: manuscript in NEHGS. Earliest church records: Congregational (1820–). Book: history. FHL microfilms (MSA): town (1735–1867). Library: Berkley Public Library, Locust St. (02780), 1–617–822–3329. N

7d. Town of Dartmouth. Recognized 1652, established 1664 from land called Acushena, Ponagansett, and Coaksett, and known as Dartmouth. Split off New Bedford 1787, Westport 1787. Records to be sought: assessors, miscellaneous (1670–), proprietors, town, vital (1667–). Copied vital records: book. Earliest church records: Christian Connection (1780–), Quaker (1699–). Book: history. FHL microfilms (MSA): assessors (1842–50), church (1831–78), Congregational, land (1654–1846), marriage (1652–1850), mortgage (1838–59), Quaker (1698–1887), town (1647–1877), vital (1647–1877). S

7e. Town of Dighton. Established 1712 from part of Taunton. Town of Wellington split off in 1814, then absorbed 1828. Records to be sought: assessors, proprietors (1674–1740), selectmen, town (1712–), vital (1710–). Copied vital records: microfiche. Earliest church records: Baptist (1807–), Congregational (1826–), Unitarian (1797–). Books:

histories. FHL microfilms (MSA): birth (1713–90), Congregational (1798–1901), history, proprietors (1672–1795), town (1709–1884), treasury (1814–28), vital (1685–1855). Library: Dighton Public Library, 395 Main St. (02715), 1-617-669-6421. N

7f. Town of Easton. Established 1725 from part of a section of Norton which was called the Taunton North Purchase. Records to be sought: assessors (1767–), miscellaneous (1735–), proprietors (1668–), town (1726–), vital (1726–). Copied vital records: manuscript in NEHGS. Earliest church records: Congregational (1747–), Methodist (1810–), Catholic (1840–), Unitarian (1792–). Book: history. FHL microfilms (MSA): history, town (1725–1840), vital (1697–1847). N

7g. Town of Fairhaven. Established 1812 from part of New Bedford. Split off Acushnet 1860. Records to be sought: assessors, miscellaneous (1815–), town (1815–), all records 1812–5 lost in a fire. Copied vital records: none. Earliest church records: Congregational (1794–), Quaker (1849–), Methodist (1830–), Unitarian (1819–). Books: histories. FHL microfilms (MSA): cemetery, histories, school (1845–95), town meetings (1812–56), town records (1739–1863). Library: Millicent Library, Centre and William Sts. (02719), 1-617-992-5342. S

7h. City of FALL RIVER. Established 1803 as a town from part of Freetown, name changed 1804 to Troy, changed 1834 to Fall River, made a city 1854. Records to be sought: assessors, city (1854–), town (1803–53), vital (1803–). Copied vital records: microfiche. Earliest church records: Baptist (1781–), Christian Connection (1837–), Congregational (1816–), Quaker (1824–), Methodist (1827–), Presbyterian (1849–), Episcopal (1837–), Catholic (1840–), Unitarian (1839–). Books: histories. FHL microfilms (MSA): births and marriages (1840–1968), Catholic (1869–1979), cemetery, Central Church (1842–1905), death (1850–1968), deeds (1835–1904), Episcopal (1881–1926), histories, land (1686–1892), Presbyterian (1885–95), selectmen (1830–53). Library: Fall River Public Library, 104 N. Main St. (02720), 1-617-676-8541. S1, F

7i. Town of Freetown. Established 1683 from freemen's land at Fall River. Split off Fall River 1803. Records to be sought: assessors, miscellaneous, proprietors, town (1688–), vital (1686–). Copied vital records: book, microfiche. Earliest church records: Congregational (1807–), Quaker (1759–). Books: history, marriages (1686–1844). FHL microfilms (MSA): biography, births (1733–1853), histories, marriages (1686–1844), selectmen (1836–87), town (1688–), vital (1686–1855). Library: G. H. Hathaway Library, N. Main St., Assonet (02702), 1-617-644-2385. S1, F

7j. Town of Mansfield. Established 1770 as District of Mansfield from part of Norton, made a town 1775. Records to be sought: assessors, miscellaneous (1772-), town (1772-), vital (1731-). Copied vital records: book. Earliest church records: Baptist (1830-), Congregational (1838-), Quaker (1819-), Methodist (1811-), New Jerusalem (1846-), Unitarian (1734-). Books: histories. FHL microfilms (MSA): school (1830-83), town (1731-1856), vital (1703-1849). Library: Mansfield Public Library, Park Row (02048), 1-617-339-8803. N

7k. City of NEW BEDFORD. Established 1787 as a town from part of Dartmouth, made a city 1847. Records to be sought: assessors (1778-), miscellaneous (1787-), proprietors, town (1787-), vital (1787-). Copied vital records: book. Earliest church records: African Methodist Episcopal Zion (1840-), Baptist (1828-), Christian (1808-), Christian connection (1848-), Congregational (1807-), Quaker (1785-), Methodist (1820-), Episcopal (1933-), Unitarian (1731-). Books: histories, ship registers (1796-1850). FHL microfilms (MSA): assessors (1889), biography, Episcopal (1887-1900), passenger list (1902-54), Quaker (1698-1887), selectmen (1778-82), town (1812-41), vital (1650-1861). Library: New Bedford Free Public Library, 613 Pleasant St. (02740), 1-617-999-0291. Genealogy collections. S

7£. Town of Norton. Established 1711 from Part of Taunton called the North Purchase. Split off Easton 1725, Mansfield 1770. Records to be sought: selectmen and assessors, town (1715-60, 1769-), vital (1796-). Copied vital records: book. Earliest church records: Baptist (1761-), Congregational (1832-). Books: histories. FHL microfilms (MSA): assessors (1735, 1840-54), biography (1669-1859), Congregational (1714-1972), history, school (1846-1902), selectmen (1723-1859), town (1715-1866), treasury (1838-84), vital (1664-1882). Library: Norton Public Library, Mansfield Ave. (02776), 1-617-285-4761. N

7m. Town of Raynham. Established 1731 from part of Taunton. Records to be sought: assessors, town (1731-), vital (1731-). Copied vital records: in New England Historical and Genealogical Register. Earliest church records: Baptist (1831-), Congregational (1739-). Books: histories. FHL microfilms (MSA): assessors (1746), town (1731-1851). Library: Raynham Public Library, 760 S. Main St. (02767), 1-617-823-1344. N

7n. Town of Rehoboth. Established 1645 from land called Seacunck . Land split off to form part of Wannamoisett (Swansea) 1667, split off Seekonk 1812. Records to be sought: assessors, miscellaneous (1700-), proprietors, selectmen, town (1645-), vital (1645-). Copied vital records: book. Earliest church records: Baptist (1840-), Congregational (1721-), Methodist (1849-). Books: genealogical collection, histories. FHL microfilms (MSA): biography, birth (to 1690), cemetery, census (1755, 1775), Civil War, Congregational (1721-1950), earmarks (1795-1840), family history, fences (1825-1934), histories, inhabitants (to 1725), militia (1875-1916), mortgages (1846-70, 1888-1903), proprietors (1641-1849), rates (1671-1712), Revolutionary soldiers, town meetings (1636-1966) town miscellaneous records (1709-1856, 1871-87), town reports (1846-1914), vital (1642-1966), voter (1884-1966). Library: Blanding Public Library, Bay State Rd. (01769), 1-617-252-4236. N

7o. Town of Seekonk. Established 1812 from part of Rehoboth. Records to be sought: assessors, miscellaneous (1812-), selectmen, town (1812-), vital (1812-). Copied vital records: in Arnold Papers, book. Earliest church records: Baptist (1794-). FHL microfilms (MSA): history, miscellaneous (1811-53), town (1811-87), vital (1773-1883). Library: Seekonk Public Library, 410 Newman Ave. (02771), 1-617-336-8230. N

7p. Town of Somerset. Established 1790 from part of Swansea known as the Shewamet Purchase. Records to be sought: proprietors (1680-1830), selectmen and assessors, town (1790-), vital (1790-). Copied vital records: none. Earliest church records: Baptist (1803-), Christian Baptist (1841-), Quaker (1832-), Methodist (1802-). Books: histories. FHL microfilms (MSA): history, Quaker (1720-1891). Library: Somerset Public Library, 1464 County St. (02726), 1-617-675-1443. S1, F

7q. Town of Swansea. Established in 1667 as the Town of Wannamoisett from part of Rehoboth and some adjacent land, name changed 1668 to Swansea. Split off Barrington 1717 (Barrington annexed to Rehoboth and Swansea 1742), split off Somerset 1790. Records to be sought: assessors, miscellaneous (1681-), proprietors (1668-1769), soldiers, town (1667-), vital (1666-). Copied vital records: book. Earliest church records: Baptist (1663-), Christian Connection (1680-), Free Baptist (1843-), Episcopal (1846-). Books: histories, town records (1662-1705). FHL microfilms (MSA): birth (1662-1799), cemetery, histories, proprietors (1667-1725), Quaker (1720-1891), town (1661-1901), vital (1662-1858). Library: Swansea Free Public Library, 60 Main St. (02777), 1-617-674-9609. Genealogy collection. S1, F

7r. City of TAUNTON. Recognized 1639 with name changed from Cohannet to Taunton, made a city in 1864. Split off Norton 1711, Dighton 1712, Raynham 1731, land split off to form part of Berkley 1735. Records to be sought: assessors (1787-), city (1865-), proprietors (1638-), selectmen, town (1804-65), vital (1800-) with records 1660-1700 in proprietors. Copied vital records: book. Earliest church records: Baptist (1819-), Congregational (1792-), Methodist (1835-), Episcopal (1750-), Catholic (1832-), Unitarian (1637-), Universalist (1841-). Books: histories. FHL microfilms (MSA): assessors (1784-1855), biography, births and christenings (1639-1850), Congregational (1821-1901), deaths (1844-72), deed (1679-1794), directory (1869-70), Episcopal (1742-1921), histories, map (1881), marriages (1638-1939), proprietor (1638-1800), town (1642-1848), vital (to 1850). Library: Old Colony Historical Society Library, 66 Church Green (02780), 1-617-822-1622. Genealogy collection. N

7s. Town of Westport. Established 1787 from part of Dartmouth. Records to be sought: miscellaneous (1788-), selectmen and assessors, town (1787-), vital (1787-). Copied vital records: book. Earliest church records: Quaker (1766-), Methodist (1840-). Book: history. FHL microfilms (MSA): births and christenings (1675-1850), births and marriages (1740-1829), Quaker (1766-1887), town (1787-1842), vital (to 1850). Library: Westport Free Public Library, 408 Old County Rd. (02790), 1-617-636-4317. S

8. Dukes County

Dukes County established 1683 by NY, then taken over in 1695 by MA. County seat Edgartown (02539). Records to be sought: county quarter court (1665-1715), courts of common pleas (1722-1859), courts of sessions (1692-1827), deed (1641-), naturalization (1790-1857, 1890-), notary (1807-33), probate (1696-), superior court (1859-), superior court of judicature (1696-1780), supreme judicial court (held in Bristol County). Census: Pre-1800E, 1790R, 1800R, 1810R, 1820RI, 1830R, 1840RP, 1850RAIM, 1855S, 1860RAIM, 1865S, 1870RAIM, 1880RAIM, 1890C, 1900R, 1910R. Books: biography (1915), history (1908/15/25/35/85). FHL microfilms (MSA): cemetery, deed (1641-1895), history (1908/25/35/85), probate (1790-1938), proprietors (1641-1857). Deed repository: at Edgartown.

8a. Town of Chilmark. Recognized 1694, also called the Mannor of Tisbury in early years. Split off Gosnold 1864. Records to be sought: assessors, miscellaneous (1704-), selectmen, town (1704-), vital (1697-). Copied vital records: book. Earliest church records: Congregational (1797-), Methodist (1810-). Book: history. FHL microfilms (MSA): town (1697-1871), vital (to 1850). Library: Chilmark Library (02535), 1-617-645-3360.

8b. Town of Edgartown. Recognized 1671, formerly known as Great Harbour. Split off Cottage City (Oak Bluffs) 1880. Records to be sought: proprietors (1676-1827), town, vital (1656-) early ones in proprietors records. Copied vital records: book. Earliest church records: Congregational (1717-), Methodist (1787-), Baptist (1823-). Books: histories. FHL microfilms (MSA): assessors (1841-6, 1855), births and deaths and marriages (1843-1917), proprietor (1718-95), town (1657-1873), town finance (1830-48), vital (to 1850). Library: Dukes County Historical Society Library (02539), 1-617-627-4441.

8c. Town of Gay Head. Recognized 1855, called a district 1863, established 1870 as town. Records to be sought: assessors, general (1862-), selectmen, town (1862-), vital (1862-). Copied vital records: see other towns in Dukes County. Earliest church records: Baptist (1693-).

8d. Town of Gosnold. Established 1864 from part of Chilmark. Records to be sought: general (1865-), selectmen and assessors (1865-), vital (1865-). Copied vital records: see Chilmark. Earliest church records: Methodist (1875-). Books: histories. Library: Cuttyhunk Public Library, Cuttyhunk (02713), 1-617-996-9211.

8e. Town of Oak Bluffs. Established 1880 as Town of Cottage City from part of Edgartown, name changed 1907 to Oak Bluffs. Records to be sought: assessors, town (1880-), vital (1880-). Copied vital records: see Edgartown. Earliest church records: Baptist (1877-), Methodist (1877-). Library: Oak Bluffs Public Library (02557), 1-617-693-9433.

8f. Town of Tisbury. Recognized 1671, formerly known as Middletowne. Split off West Tisbury 1892. Records to be sought: assessors, general (1690-1800), proprietors (1750-), town (1838-), vital (1666-). Copied vital records: book. Earliest church records: Congregational (1701-), Baptist (1782-). Books: histories, town records (1669-1864). FHL microfilms (MSA): assessors (1826-50), births and deaths and marriages (1666-1905), town (1669-1884), vital (to 1850).

8g. Town of West Tisbury. Established 1892 from part of Tisbury. Records to be sought: see Tisbury. Copied vital records: see Tisbury. Earliest church records: see Tisbury. Book: history. Library: West Tisbury Free Public Library (02575), 1-617-693-3366.

9. Essex County

Essex County established 1643 from MA Bay Colony. County seat Salem (01970). Since 1869 deeds also registered at Lawrence. Records to be sought: county court (1636-92), courts of common pleas (1692-1859), courts of sessions (1692-1827), deed (1639-), Ipswich deeds (1640–94), justice of peace (1699–1841), marriage (1654–1795), naturalization (1859–), notary (1657–1883), Old Norfolk County records (1637–1714), probate (1635–), superior court (1859–), superior court of judicature (1693–1780), supreme judicial court (1780–), vital records (1636–1795). Census: Pre-1800E, 1790R, 1800R, 1810R, 1820RI, 1830R, 1840RP, 1850RAIM, 1855S, 1860RAIM, 1865S, 1870RAIM, 1880RAIM, 1890C, 1900R, 1910R. Books: biography (1888/98, 1907/22/35/74), history (1830/34/40/70/78/88/97, 1922), county quarterly court (1636–92), probate (1635–81). FHL microfilms (MSA): biography (1888, 1922/74), county court (1636–92), courts of common pleas (1692–1859), courts of sessions (1692–1796), deed (1639–1879), history (1870/78/88/97, 1922), probate (1635–1881), superior court (1859–65), supreme judicial court (1797–1826), vital records (1636–1795). Deed repositories: Records 1639–1869 at Salem, records 1869– for Southern District at Salem, for Northern District at Lawrence. Ipswich records (Ipswich, Newbury, Rowley 1640–94) at Salem. In the town/city listings which follow, the pertinent districts are indicated with capital letters (N for Northern District, S for Southern District, I for Ipswich records) placed at the end of the listings.

9a. Town of Amesbury. Established 1666 as Salisbury-New-Towne from part of Salisbury, name changed 1668 to Amsbury, 1675 to Amesbury. Split off Merrimac 1876. Records to be sought: general (1642–), selectmen and assessors, town (1642–), vital (1642–). Copied vital records: book. Earliest church records: Quaker (1701–), Congregational (1832–), Episcopal (1833–), Universalist (1833–). Books: histories. FHL microfilms (MSA): family records, histories, Quaker (1701–1901), town (1642–1861), vital (1637–1849). Library: Amesbury Public Library, 149 Main St. (01903), 1-617-388-0312. S

9b. Town of Andover. Established 1646 from land formerly called Cochichawick. Land split off to form part of Middleton 1728, land split off to form part of Lawrence 1847, split off North Andover 1855. Records to be sought: assessors, general (1643–), miscellaneous (1704–), selectmen, town (1643–), vital (1649–). Copied vital records: book. Earliest church records: Congregational (1708–), Episcopal (1835–). Books: histories. FHL microfilms (MSA): assessor (1678–1865), Congregational (1711–1859), Episcopal (1833–1915), histories, mortgage (1832–54), proprietors (1714–1824), selectmen (1715–1970), soldiers (1861–5), town (1660–1872), treasurer (1767–1874), vital (1647–1850), voter (1841–3). Library: Andover Historical Society, Underhill Research Library, 97 Main St. (01810), 1-617-475-2236. N

9c. City of BEVERLY. Established 1668 as a town from part of Salem called Basse River, made city 1894. Records to be sought: assessors, general (1665–), parish (1667–1830), proprietors (1698–

1817), vital (1665–). Copied vital records: book. Earliest church records: Unitarian (1668–), Congregational (1715–), Baptist (1801–). Books: baptisms (1667–1710), histories. FHL microfilms (MSA): assessors (1754–1849), Congregational (1667–1862), history, Episcopal (1861–1914), proprietors (1728–1817), selectmen (1792–1856), soldiers (1861–5), town (1685–1845), vital (1652–1890). Library: Beverly Historical Society, Galloupe Memorial Library, 117 Cabot St. (01905), 1-617-922-1186. Historical collection. S

9d. Town of Boxford. Recognized 1694. Land split off to form part of Middleton 1728. Records to be sought: assessors (1711–), miscellaneous (1825–), selectmen, town (1685–), vital (1685–). Copied vital records: book. Earliest church records: Congregational (1702–). Book: history. FHL microfilms (MSA): assessors (1711–1851), Congregational (1702–1907), history, town and vital (1681–1859). Library: Boxford Town Libraries, 10 Elm St. (01921), 1-617-887-7323. S

9e. Town of Bradford. Recognized 1675, annexed by Haverhill 1897. Records located in Haverhill. Split off Groveland 1850. Records to be sought: assessors (1861–97), miscellaneous (1858–68), selectmen (1796–1897), soldiers, town (1668–), vital (1669–). Copied vital records: book. Earliest church records: Congregational (1682–). Books: see Haverhill. FHL microfilms (MSA): civil (1853–78), history, town (1668–1883), town officers (1775–83), vital (1669–1860). Library: see Haverhill.

9f. Town of Danvers. Established 1752 as a district from part of Salem called Village and Middle Parishes, called a town 1772, made a town 1775. Split off South Danvers (Peabody) 1855. Records to be sought: miscellaneous (1752–), proprietors (1772–1841), selectmen and assessors, town (1752–), vital (1752–). Copied vital records: book. Earliest church records: Congregational (1672–), Baptist (1781–), Universalist (1815–). Books: histories. FHL microfilms (MSA): assessor (1766–1856), census (1837), Congregational (1689–1800), Episcopal (1857–1936), highway tax (1838–46), histories, militia (1840–58), people coming in (1766–90), strays (1765–1804), town (1752–1853), Village Parish (1670–1735), vital (1652–1884), war tax (1779–82), warnings out (1752–70), welfare (1774–92). Library: Peabody Institute Library, 15 Sylvan St. (01923), 1-617-774-0554. Historical collection. S

9g. Town of Essex. Established 1819 from part of Ipswich. Records to be sought: miscellaneous (1818–), proprietors (1722–47), selectmen and assessors (1818–), town (1818–), vital (1818–). Copied vital records: book. Earliest church records: Congregational (1665–), Universalist (1829–). Books: histories. FHL microfilms (MSA): assessors (1802–56), history, proprietors (1721–47), town (1819–52), treasury

(1819-85), vital (to 1850). Library: T. O. H. P. Burnham Public Library, Martin St. (01929), 1-617-768-7410. S

9h. Town of Georgetown. Established 1838 from part of Rowley. Records to be sought: selectmen and assessors (1838-), town (1838-), vital (1838-). Copied vital records: book. Earliest church records: Congregational (1732-), Baptist (1785-). Books: histories. FHL microfilms (MSA): town (1838-63), vital (to 1850). Library: Georgetown Peabody Library, Lincoln Park (01833), 1-617-352-8428. Historical collection. S

9i. City of GLOUCESTER. Recognized 1639 as Cape Ann, set apart 1642, name changed 1642 to Gloucester, made city 1873. Split off Rockport 1840. Records to be sought: assessors, board of alderman (1874-), common council (1874-), miscellaneous, parish, proprietors (1707-1820), selectmen (1699-1781, 1800-73), town (1642-1873), vital (1716-). Copied vital records: book. Earliest church records: Unitarian (1702-), Congregational (1716-), Universalist (1716-). Books: histories, ship registers. FHL microfilms (MSA): Congregational (1703-1839), deeds (1708-1914), Episcopal (1862-1907), histories, proprietors (1707-1820), selectmen (1699-1874), town (1642-1851), vital (1640-1861). Library: Cape Ann Historical Association Library, 27 Pleasant St. (01930), 1-617-283-0455. Genealogical collection. S

9j. Town of Groveland. Established 1850 from part of Bradford (Bradford annexed by Haverhill 1897). Records to be sought: miscellaneous (1850-), selectmen and assessors, town (1850-), vital (1850-). Copied vital records: see Bradford. Earliest church records: Congregational (1726-), Methodist (1831-). Book: history. FHL microfilms (MSA): births and christenings (1848-75), cemetery, inhabitants (to 1856), military. Library: Langley-Adams Library, Main St. Complex (01834), 1-617-372-1732. S

9k. Town of Hamilton. Established 1793 from part of Ipswich called Ipswich Hamlet. Records to be sought: selectmen and assessors (1793-), soldiers, town (1793-), vital (1793-). Copied vital records: book. Earliest church records: Congregational (1712-). Books: histories. FHL microfilms (MSA): assessors (1807-27), cemetery, Congregational (1714-1886), history, selectmen (1819-35), town (1712-1865), treasury (1793-1897), vital (1794-1849). S

9ℓ. City of HAVERHILL. Established 1641 as a town, made a city 1869, annexed Bradford 1897. Land split off to form part of Methuen 1725. Records to be sought: assessors, city (1870-), general (1643-1869), miscellaneous (1828-85), proprietors (1713-63), vital (1642-). Copied vital records: book. Earliest church records: Congregational

(1735–), Unitarian (1790–), Baptist (1793–). Books: biography, histories, magistrate and court records (1682–5). FHL microfilms (MSA): cemetery, history, selectmen (1840–69), town (1654–1861), vital (1654–1860). Library: Haverhill Public Library, 99 Main St. (01830), 1–617–373–1586. Genealogy collection. S

9m. Town of Ipswich. Established 1634 from land formerly called Aggawam. Split off Hamilton 1793. Records to be sought: assessors, proprietors (1638–80), town (1634–), vital (1664–). Copied vital records: book. Earliest church records: Congregational (1720–), Methodist (1822–). Books: histories, town records (1634–50). FHL microfilms (MSA): assessors (1780–1854), cemetery, Congregational (1665–1872), deeds and mortgages and wills (1639–1965), early inhabitants (1633–1700), Episcopal (1867–1917), histories, old records (1634–50), poor (1841–64), proprietors (1634–1905), school (1636–1869), town (1634–1864), treasury (1699–1867), vital (1635–1871), war records (1776–9). Library: Ipswich Public Library, 25 N. Main St. (01938), 1–617–356–4646. Genealogy collection. S, I

9n. City of LAWRENCE. Established 1847 as a town from parts of Andover and Methuen, made a city 1853. Records to be sought: assessors (1847–), city (1853–), miscellaneous (1847–), selectmen, town (1847–52), vital (1847–). Copied vital records: book. Earliest church records: Congregational (1846–), Baptist (1847–), Methodist (1847–), Episcopal (1846–), Unitarian (1847–), Universalist (1847–), Catholic (1849–). Books: biography, histories. FHL microfilms (MSA): Episcopal (1846–67), histories, vital (to 1850). Library: Lawrence Public Library, 51 Lawrence St. (01841), 1–617–682–1727. Historical collection. N

9o. City of LYNN. Recognized 1631 as a plantation called Saugus, recognized 1635 as Town of Saugus, name changed 1637 to Lynn, made a city 1850. Split off Reading 1644, Lynnfield 1782, Saugus 1815, Swampscott 1852, Nahant 1853. Records to be sought: assessors (1850–), city (1850–), miscellaneous (1800–), town (1691–1849), vital (1675–). Copied vital records: book. Earliest church records: Quaker (1677–), Congregational (1763–), Methodist (1794–). Books: histories. FHL microfilms (MSA): assessors (1818–34), Bible and family (1600–1936), cemetery, Congregational (1763–1929), Episcopal (1846–1905), histories, marriage (1715–1846), town (1691–1868), treasury (1698–1772), vital (1635–1868). Library: Lynn Historical Society Museum Library, 125 Green St. (01902), 1–617–592–2465. Genealogy collection. Lynn Public Library, 5 N. Common St. (01902), 1–617–595–0567. Genealogical collection. S

9p. Town of Lynnfield. Established 1782 as a district from part of Lynn, made a town 1814. Records to be sought: assessors, soldiers, town (1757-), vital (1757-). Copied vital records: book. Earliest church records: Unitarian (1720-), Congregational (1833-). Books: histories. FHL microfilms (MSA): assessors (1810-24), Congregational (1720-1850), histories, mortgage (1837-51), school (1828-49), town (1711-1808), treasury (1788-1853), vital (1763-1849). Library: Lynnfield Public Library, 18 Summer St. (01940), 1-617-334-5411. Genealogy collection. S

9q. Town of Manchester. Established 1640 as Village of Jeffryes Creek from part of Salem, established 1645 as Town of Manchester. Records to be sought: miscellaneous (1645-), proprietors (1718-69), selectmen and assessors, town (1654-), vital (1654-). Copied vital records: book. Earliest church records: Congregational (1837-). Books: histories. FHL microfilms (MSA): history, town (1624-1915), vital (to 1850). Library: Manchester Public Library, Union St. (01944), 1-617-526-7711. S

9r. Town of Marblehead. Recognized 1633 as a plantation, again 1635, established 1649. Records to be sought: assessors (1770-), selectmen (1770-), town (1648-), vital (1653-). Copied vital records: book. Earliest church records: Congregational (1684-), Episcopal (1714-), Unitarian (1716-), Methodist (1794-). Books: histories. FHL microfilms (MSA): assessors (1734-1839), cemetery, Congregational (1684-1857), Episcopal (1715-1915), histories, inhabitants (1794-1841), proprietors (1703-1842), town (1648-1851), vital (1653-1899). Library: Marblehead Historical Society Library, 161 Washington St. (01945), 1-617-631-1069. Genealogy collection. S

9s. Town of Merrimac. Established 1876 from part of Amesbury. Records to be sought: miscellaneous (1876-), selectmen and assessors (1876-), town (1876-), vital (1876-). Copied vital records: see Amesbury. Earliest church records: Congregational (1726-). FHL microfilms (MSA): history. Library: Merrimac Public Library, 34 W. Main St. (01860), 1-617-346-9441. Historical collection. S

9t. Town of Methuen. Established 1725 from part of Haverhill and adjoining lands. Land split off to form part of Lawrence 1847. Records to be sought: assessors, general (1725-), miscellaneous (1725-), selectmen, town (1725-), vital (1725-). Copied vital records: book. Earliest church records: Congregational (1781-), Baptist (1815-). Books: histories. FHL microfilms (MSA): assessors (1733-1860), cemetery, Congregational (1730-1855), Episcopal (1832-3, 1904-49), history, marriage (1713-1840), militia (1842-73), mortgage (1835-7), school (1827-55), selectmen (1733-1860), town (1725-1876), vital (1716-1876). Library: Nevins Memorial Library, 305 Broadway (01844), 1-617-686-4080. N

9u. Town of Middleton. Established 1728 from parts of Andover, Boxford, Salem, and Topsfield. Records to be sought: miscellaneous (1729–), selectmen and assessors, soldiers, town (1728–), vital (1728–). Copied vital records: book. Earliest church records: Congregational (1728–), Universalist (1829–). Books: histories. FHL microfilms (MSA): assessors (1728–99), Congregational (1729–1854), history, town (1782–1884), vital (1703–1884). Library: Flint Public Library (01949), 1-617-774-8132. S

9v. Town of Nahant. Established 1853 from part of Lynn. Records to be sought: assessors, miscellaneous (1853–), selectmen, town (1853–). Copied vital records: see Lynn. Earliest church records: Methodist (1850–). Books: histories. FHL microfilms (MSA): history. Library: Nahant Public Library, 15 Pleasant St. (01908), 1-617-581-0306. Historical collection. S

9w. Town of Newbury. Recognized 1635, formerly called Wessacucon. Split off Newburyport 1764, Parson (West Newbury) 1819. Records to be sought: miscellaneous (1635–), proprietors (1635–), selectmen (1635–), town (1635–), vital (1635–). Copied vital records: book. Earliest church records: Congregational (1674–), Methodist (1827–). Books: biography, histories. FHL microfilms (MSA): Congregational (1635–1935), ear marks (1715–1880), histories, mortgages (1833–47), proprietors (1635–1828), selectmen (1821–55), town (1635–1860), vital (1635–1886). Library: Newbury Town Library, Main St. (Byfield 01922), 1-617-465-0538. S, I

9x. City of NEWBURYPORT. Established 1764 as a town from part of Newbury, made a city 1851. Records to be sought: assessors (1764–), city (1851–), general (1764–1851), miscellaneous (1764–), selectmen (1764–), vital (1764–). Copied vital records: book. Earliest church records: Episcopal (1714–), Presbyterian (1764–), Congregational (1767–). Books: church records (1745–1862), Civil War servicemen (1861–5), GAR roster, histories, ships registers. FHL microfilms (MSA): assessors (1780–1851), Congregational (1745–1862), Episcopal (1714–1930), histories, mayor and alderman (1851–7), Presbyterian (1745–1971), soldiers (1861–5), town (1764–1851), treasurer (1783–92), vital (1740–1875), welfare (1808–54). Library: Newburyport Public Library, 94 State St. (01950), 1-617-462-4031. S

9y. Town of North Andover. Established 1855 from part of Andover. Records to be sought: assessors, town (1854–), vital (1854–). Copied vital records: see Andover. Earliest church records: Unitarian (1686–), Congregational (1834–). Books: histories. FHL microfilms (MSA): Episcopal (1880–1909), history. Library: Stevens Memorial

Library, 345 Main St. (01845), 1-617-682-6160. Historical collection. N

9z. City of PEABODY. Established 1855 as a Town of South Danvers from part of Danvers, name changed 1868 to Town of Peabody, made a city 1916. Records to be sought: assessors (1855-), miscellaneous (1855-), selectmen (1855-), town (1855-), vital (1855-). Copied vital records: microfiche. Earliest church records: Congregational (1793-), Unitarian (1826-), Universalist (1832). Book: history. FHL microfilms (MSA): cemetery, Episcopal (1875-1908), histories. Library: Peabody Institute Library, 82 Main St. (01960), 1-617-531-0100. S

9aa. Town of Rockport. Established 1840 from part of Gloucester. Records to be sought: selectmen and assessors (1840-), town (1840-), vital (1840-). Copied vital records: book. Earliest church records: Congregational (1755-), Baptist (1808-), Methodist (1808-). Books: histories. FHL microfilms (MSA): Episcopal (1872-1907), histories, vital (to 1850). Library: Rockport Public Library, 2 Cleave St. (01966), 1-617-546-6934. Historical collection. S

9bb. Town of Rowley. Established 1639 from land formerly called Rogers Plantation. Split off Georgetown 1838. Records to be sought: assessors (1788-1860), miscellaneous (1731-), proprietors (1643-), selectmen (1758-1864), selectmen and assessors (1860-), soldiers, town (1639-) vital (1639-). Copied vital records: book. Earliest church records: Congregational (1639-), Baptist (1830-). Books: histories, town records (1639-72). FHL microfilms (MSA): assessors (1817-50), cemetery, Congregational (1665-1838), early settlers (before 1700), fences (1756-1910), freeholders (1643-1870), history, militia (1804-39), poor (1821-65), proprietors (1674-1852), school (1796-1869), town (1638-1883), treasurer (1731-1820), vital (1636-1909). Library: Free Public Library, 17 Wethersfield St. (01969), 1-617-948-2850. S, I

9cc. City of SALEM. Recognized 1630 as a town, made a city 1836. Split off Manchester 1645, Marblehead 1649, Beverly 1668, land split off to form part of Middleton 1728, split off Danvers 1752. Records to be sought: assessors (1837-), city (1836-), miscellaneous (1636-), proprietors (1713-39), selectmen, soldiers, town (1636-), vital (1658-). Copied vital records: book. Earliest church records: Quaker (1677-), Episcopal (1735-), Congregational (1743-), Unitarian (1772-). Books: Civil War servicemen (1861-5), histories, town records (1634-91). FHL microfilms (MSA): assessors (1689-1850), commoners (1713-39), Congregational (1629-1819), Episcopal (1738-1942), histories, notary (1696-1722), Quaker (1709-1828), soldiers (1861-5), town (1634-1836), vital (1644-1865). Library: Essex Institute Library, 132 Essex St.

(01970), 1-617-744-3390. Excellent genealogy and historical collections. S

9dd. Town of Salisbury. Recognized 1639 as Town of Colechester, renamed 1640 as Salisbury. Split off Salisbury-New-Towne (Amesbury) 1666. Records to be sought: assessors (1775-), miscellaneous (1638), proprietors (1638-1733), soldiers, town (1733-), vital (1637-). Copied vital records: book. Earliest church records: Congregational (1718-), Baptist (1780-), Methodist (1793-). Book: history. FHL microfilms (MSA): assessors (1777-1850), Congregational (1752-1805), family records, town (1638-1858), vital (1598-1900). Library: Salisbury Public Library, Elm St. (01950), 1-617-465-5071. Genealogy collection. S

9ee. Town of Saugus. Established 1815 from part of Lynn. Do not confuse with the fact that Lynn was first called Saugus 1631-7. Records to be sought: assessors, town (1815-), vital (1815-). Copied vital records: book. Earliest church records: Universalist (1738-), Congregational (1739-). Books: histories. FHL microfilms (MSA): cemetery, Episcopal (1885-1917), history, town (1815-60), vital (1815-51). Library: Saugus Public Library, 295 Central St. (01906), 1-617-233-0530. S

9ff. Town of Swampscott. Established 1852 from part of Lynn. Records to be sought: assessors (1852-), miscellaneous (1852-), selectmen (1852-), town (1852-), vital (1852-). Copied vital records: see Lynn. Earliest church records: Congregational (1846-). Book: history. FHL microfilms (MSA): biography, history. Library: Swampscott Public Library, 61 Burrill St. (01907), 1-617-593-8380. Historical collection. S

9gg. Town of Topsfield. Recognized 1648 as a village in Ipswich, established 1650 as a town. Land split off to form part of Middleton 1728. Records to be sought: assessors (1744-), miscellaneous (1811-), parish (1684-), proprietors (1792-1804, 1816-50), selectmen, soldiers, town (1675-), vital (1645-). Copied vital records: book. Earliest church records: Congregational (1663-), Methodist (1824-). Books: histories, town records (1659-1778). FHL microfilms (MSA): assessors (1744-79), Congregational, histories, historical periodical, military (1811-41), poor (1821-62), town (1659-1889), treasury (1810-85), vital (to 1899). Library: Topsfield Town Library, S. Common St. (01983), 1-617-887-2914. S

9hh. Town of Wenham. Established 1643 from land called Enon. Records to be sought: assessors, miscellaneous (1841-), selectmen, town (1642-), vital (1695-). Copied vital records: book. Earliest church records: Congregational (1682-), Baptist (1831-). Books: histories, town records (1642-1810). FHL microfilms (MSA): assessors (1731-1840), cemetery, Congregational (1644-55), histories, town (1643-1960), vital (1654-1844). Library: Wenham Public Library, 138 Main St. (01984), 1-617-468-4062. Genealogy collection. S

9ii. Town of West Newbury. Established 1819 as Town of Parsons from part of Newbury, renamed 1820 as West Newbury. Records to be sought: selectmen and assessors, town (1819-), vital (1819-). Copied vital records: book. Earliest church records: Congregational (1698). Book: history. FHL microfilms (MSA): Congregational (1731-1869), history, Quaker (1701-1901), town (1819-56), vital (to 1850). Library: GAR Memorial Library, 490 Main St. (01985), 1-617-363-2952. S

10. Franklin County

Franklin County established 1811 from Hampshire County. County seat Greenfield (01310). Deed records date back to 1787 when Deerfield became a registry for Hampshire County. In 1812 the Deerfield deed records were transferred to adjacent Greenfield. Records to be sought: courts of common pleas (1812-59), courts of sessions (1812-28), deed (1787-), justice of peace (1790-2, 1816-96), naturalization (1859-), notary (1859-75), probate (1812-), superior court (1859-), supreme judicial court (1816-), vital records (1811-39). Census: 1820RI, 1830R, 1840RP, 1850RAIM, 1855S, 1860RAIM, 1865S, 1870RAIM, 1880RAIM, 1890C, 1900R, 1910R. Books: biography (1895, 1951), history (1855/79). FHL microfilms (MSA): biography (1895, 1951), cemetery, commissioners (1732-1867), court of common pleas (1812-59), deed (1787-1867), history (1855/79), justice of peace (1790-2, 1816-38), probate (1812-1971), superior court (1859-67), supreme judicial court (1816-88). Deed repository: At Greenfield.

10a. Town of Ashfield. Established 1765 from land formerly known as the Plantation of Huntstown. Records to be sought: miscellaneous (1762-), proprietors (1738-1802), selectmen and assessors, town (1776-), vital (1765-). Copied vital records: book. Earliest church records: Congregational (1763-), Episcopal (1830-). Books: histories. FHL microfilms (MSA): assessors (1817-50), Congregational (1786-1897), history, proprietors (1736-1808), town (1762-1854), treasurer (1813-79), vital (to 1850). Library: Belding Memorial Library, Main St. (01330), 1-413-628-4414.

10b. Town of Bernardston. Established 1762 from land formerly known as the new plantation called Falltown. Split off Leyden 1784. Records to be sought: proprietors (1735-1819), selectmen and assessors, town (1762-), vital (1762-). Copied vital records: manuscript in

NEHGS. Earliest church records: Baptist (1808-), Unitarian (1817-), Universalist (1820-). Book: history. FHL microfilms (MSA): assessors (1792-1855), Congregational (1817-68), family records, history, Methodist (1831-1909), proprietors (1735-1835), school (1808-75), town (1743-1918), vital (1752-1882). Library: Cushman Library, Church St. (01337), 1-413-648-9595.

10c. Town of Buckland. Established 1779 from part of Charlemont and a plantation called No-town. Records to be sought: miscellaneous (1876-), selectmen and assessors, town (1876-), vital (1876-). Copied vital records: book. Earliest church records: Congregational (1820-), Methodist (1849-). Book: history with genealogies. FHL microfilms (MSA): biography, family records, history, vital (to 1850). Library: Buckland Public Library (01338), 1-413-625-9412.

10d. Town of Charlemont. Established 1765 from a plantation called Charlemont. Land split off to form part of Buckland 1779, land split off to form part of Heath 1785. Records to be sought: assessors, town (1765-), vital (1765-). Copied vital records: book. Earliest church records: Baptist (1767-), Congregational (1791-). Books: histories. FHL microfilms (MSA): history, town (1749-1864), treasurer (1767-1866), vital (1749-1864). Library: Tyler Memorial Library, Main St. (01339), 1-413-339-4335.

10e. Town of Colrain. Established 1761 from a plantation called Colrain. Records to be sought: assessors (1824-), town (1741-98, 1803-), vital (1741-). Copied vital records: book. Earliest church records: Baptist (1780-), Congregational (1820-). Books: histories, one with genealogies. FHL microfilms (MSA): family records, histories, vital (1741-1859). Library: Griswold Memorial Library, Main St. (01340), 1-413-624-3619.

10f. Town of Conway. Established 1767 as a district from part of Deerfield, made a town 1775. Records to be sought: assessors, miscellaneous (1767-), town (1767-), vital (1767-). Copied vital records: book. Earliest church records: Baptist (1820-), Congregational (1767-). Books: histories. FHL microfilms (MSA): assessors (1780-1850), cemetery, Congregational (1767-1821), family records, history, town (1752-1868), vital (1750-1868). Library: Field Memorial Library, Elm St. (01341), 1-413-369-4646.

10g. Town of Deerfield. Plantation mentioned 1677, 1678, boundaries defined 1712, grant of land confirmed 1717. Split off Conway 1767, Shelburne 1768. Records to be sought: assessors, miscellaneous, proprietors (1699-1858), selectmen, town (1683-), vital (1683-). Copied vital records: book. Earliest church records: Congregational (1818–), Unitarian (1820–). Books: histories, Pocumtuck Valley series. FHL microfilms (MSA): assessors (1769–1850), cemetery, family records, historical periodical, histories, Methodist (1848–74), proprietors (1733–1866), treasurer (1737–1807), vital (to 1850). Library: Memorial Libraries (01342), 1-413-774-5581.

10h. Town of Erving. Established 1838 from land called Ervings Grant. Records to be sought: assessors, miscellaneous, town (1816–), vital (1816–). Copied vital records: microfiche. Earliest church records: Congregational (1832–). Book: history. FHL microfilms (MSA): Congregational (1832–1952). Library: Erving Public Library, 3 E. Main St. (01344), 1-617-544-2312.

10i. Town of Gill. Established 1793 from part of Greenfield. Records to be sought: assessors, miscellaneous (1793–), town (1793–), vital (1793–). Copied vital records: book. Earliest church records: Congregational (1806–). Books: histories. FHL microfilms (MSA): assessors (1826–50), family records, history, vital (to 1850). Library: Carnegie Library, Ave. A, Turners Falls (01376), 1-413-863-4484.

10j. Town of Greenfield. Established 1753 as a district from part of Deerfield, made a town 1775. Split off Gill 1793. Records to be sought: assessors, general (1756–), miscellaneous, vital (1755–). Copied vital records: book. Earliest church records: Congregational (1813–), Episcopal (1812–). Books: histories. FHL microfilms (MSA): assessors (1810–50), cemetery, family records, histories, town (1772–1865), vital (to 1850). Library: Greenfield Public Library, 402 Main St. (01301), 1-413-772-6305.

10k. Town of Hawley. Established 1792 from a plantation called Number Seven. Records to be sought: assessors (1861–), miscellaneous (1797–), town (1797–), vital (1795–). Copied vital records: manuscript in NEHGS. Earliest church records: Congregational (1777–). Books: histories, one with genealogies. FHL microfilms (MSA): biography, birth (1730–1835), Congregational (1777–1818), family records, history, marriage (1793–1834), town (1730–1855), vital (1727–1854).

10ℓ. Town of Heath. Established 1785 from part of Charlemont and a tract called Green and Walkers Land. Records to be sought: assessors (1785–), selectmen (1785–), town (1785–), vital (1785–). Copied vital records: book. Earliest church records: Congregational (1785–). Books: histories. FHL microfilms (MSA): Baptist (1800–89), Congregational (1785–1892), town (1785–1852), vital (1735–1900). Library: Heath Public Library, Main St. (01346), 1-413-337-4934.

10m. Town of Leverett. Established 1774 from part of Sunderland. Records to be sought: assessors, selectmen, town (1774–), vital (1774–). Copied vital records: microfiche. Earliest church records: Baptist (1767–), Congregational (1784–). Book: history. FHL microfilms (MSA): Congregational (1784–1860), family records, history, town (1727–1916), vital (1705–1843). Library: Field Memorial Library, E. Leverett Rd. (01054), 1-413-548-9220.

10n. Town of Leyden. Established 1784 as a district from part of Bernardston, made a town 1809. Records to be sought: assessors, miscellaneous, town (1808–), vital (1808–). Copied vital records: microfiche. Earliest church records: Methodist (1860), Universalist (1867–). Book: history. FHL microfilms (MSA): birth (1748–1842), history, town (1776–1834), vital (1777–1848). Library: Robertson Memorial Library, Leyden Rd. (01301), 1-413-773-7542.

10o. Town of Monroe. Established 1822 from part of Rowe and land called The Gore. Records to be sought: assessors, miscellaneous, town (1822–), vital (1822–). Copied vital records: none. Earliest church records: Baptist (1884–). FHL microfilms (MSA): history, town (1793–1868), vital (1793–1855). Library: Monroe Public Library, Monroe Bridge (01350), 1-413-424-5272.

10p. Town of Montague. Established 1754 as a district from part of Sunderland, made a town 1775. Records to be sought: assessors, general (1754–), miscellaneous (1865–), proprietors, vital (1754–). Copied vital records: book. Earliest church records: Unitarian (1825–), Congregational (1828–). Book: history. FHL microfilms (MSA): assessors (1784–1856), cemetery, histories, town (1719–1859), treasurer (1783–1810), vital (1715–1866).

10q. Town of New Salem. Established 1759 as a district, formerly township of New Salem with additional grant, made a town 1775. Land split off to form part of Prescott 1822 (absorbed by New Salem and Petersham 1938). Records to be sought: assessors (1861–), town (1855–), vital (1855–). Copied vital records: book. Earliest church records: Unitarian (1743–), Congregational (1779–). Book: history. FHL microfilms (MSA): Congregational (1743–1833), vital (to 1850). Library: New Salem Public Library, S. Main St. (01355), 1-617-544-6437.

10r. Town of Northfield. Established 1714 from plantation called Squakeag, reaffirmed 1723. Records to be sought: assessors, proprietors (1685–1723), selectmen, soldiers (1861–5), town (1766–), vital (1717–). Copied vital records: manuscript in NEHGS. Earliest church records: Congregational (1753–), Unitarian (1826–). Books: histories. FHL microfilms (MSA): assessors (1827–49), birth (1713–1839), family records, histories, marriage (1799–1829), vital (1713–1839). Library: Dickinson Memorial Library, Main St. (01360), 1-413-498-2455.

10s. Town of Orange. Established 1783 as a district from parts of Athol, Royalston, Warwick, and land called Ervingshire, made a town 1810. Records to be sought: assessors, miscellaneous (1783–), selectmen, town (1783–), vital (1783–). Copied vital records: microfiche. Earliest church records: Congregational (1843–), Universalist (1851–). Book: history. FHL microfilms (MSA): birth (1767–1819), town (1783–1820), vital (1770–1850). Library: Wheeler Memorial Library, 49 E. Main St. (01364), 1-617-544-2295.

10t. Town of Rowe. Established 1785 from land called Myrifield and adjoining land. Land split off to form part of Monroe 1822. Records to be sought: assessors, miscellaneous (1785–), town (1785–), vital (1785–). Copied vital records: microfiche. Earliest church records: Congregational (1804–), Baptist (1810–). Books: histories. FHL microfilms (MSA): history, town (1785–1866), vital (1774–1848). Library: Rowe Town Library, Zoar Rd. (01367), 1-413-339-4761.

10u. Town of Shelburne. Established 1768 as a district from part of Deerfield, made a town 1775. Records to be sought: assessors, miscellaneous, selectmen, town (1768–), vital (1768–). Copied vital records: book. Earliest church records: Congregational (1770–), Baptist (1833–). Book: history. FHL microfilms (MSA): assessors (1812–40), Congregational (1772–1880), financial (1786–1822), town (1768–1849), vital (1756–1883). Library: Shelburne Free Public Library, Sanger St. (01770), 1-617-653-0770.

10v. Town of Shutesbury. Established 1761 from a plantation called Roadtown. Land split off to form part of Wendell 1781. Records to be sought: assessors, miscellaneous (1798–), proprietors (1760–1805), town (1761–), vital (1763–). Copied vital records: microfiche. Earliest church records: Congregational (1804–), Baptist (1835–). Books: commemorative history. FHL microfilms (MSA): assessors (1826–50), mortgage (1772–1851), proprietors (1735–1805), town (1761–1857), vital (to 1891). Library: Spear Memorial Library, Cooleyville Rd. (01072), 1-413-259-1213.

10w. Town of Sunderland. Established 1714 as Town of Swampfield from plantation land, name changed 1718 to Sunderland. Split off Montague 1754, Leverett 1774. Records to be sought: assessors, miscellaneous (1730–), proprietors (1673–1718), town (1713–), vital (1714–). Copied vital records: microfiche. Earliest church records: Congregational (1718–), Baptist (1820–). Book: history. FHL microfilms (MSA): Baptist (1821–41), Congregational (1749–1850), family records, history, militia (1841–1912), town (1673–1855), treasurer (1762–1860), vital (1686–1858). Library: Graves Memorial Library (01375), 1-413-665-2642.

10x. Town of Warwick. Established 1763 from plantation called Roxbury Canada and lands belonging to it. Land split off to form part of Orange 1783. Records to be sought: assessors (1802–), proprietors (1735–72), town (1763–), vital (1763–). Copied vital records: microfiche. Earliest church records: Unitarian (1760–), Congregational (1829–). Books: histories. FHL microfilms (MSA): histories.

10y. Town of Wendell. Established 1781 from part of Shutesbury and land called Ervingshire. Records to be sought: assessors, miscellaneous, selectmen, town (1781–), vital (1781–). Copied vital records: microfiche. Earliest church records: Congregational (1774–), Baptist (1797–). FHL microfilms (MSA): assessors (1843–4), death (1816–39), selectmen (1793–1883), town (1781–1864), vital (1760–1890).

10z. Town of Whately. Established 1771 from part of Hatfield. Records to be sought: assessors (1800–), miscellaneous (1771–), town (1771–), vital (1771–). Copied vital records: book. Earliest church records: Congregational (1771–). Books: histories. FHL microfilms (MSA): Baptist (1789–1850), Congregational (1771–1875), deed (1717–1884), family records, histories, roads (1717–1884), town (1771–1878), treasurer (1838–67), vital (1749–1856). Library: Dickinson Memorial Library, 116 Chestnut Plain Rd. (01093), 1-413-665-2170.

11. Hampden County

Hampden County established 1812 from Hampshire County. County seat Springfield (01103). Springfield was county seat for Hampshire County 1662–1812, and before that during 1643–62 Springfield was in Middlesex County, and before 1643 in MA Bay Colony. Deed records for the region from 1636 are at Springfield. Records to be sought: courts of common pleas (1812–59), courts of sessions (1783–1827), deed (1636–), naturalization (1840–), notary (1837–73), probate (1812–), superior court (1859–), supreme judicial court (1816–). Census: 1820RI, 1830R, 1840RP, 1850RAIM, 1855S, 1860RAIM, 1865S, 1870RAIM, 1880RAIM, 1890C, 1900R, 1910R. Books: biography (1895. 1924/36), history (1855/79, 1902/36). FHL microfilms (MSA): biography (1895), cemetery, courts of common pleas (1812–59), courts of sessions (1783–1812), deed (1636–1902), divorce (1831–1936), history (1855/79, 1902), naturalization (1812–1986), probate (1812–1919), superior court (1859–1915). Deed repository: At Springfield.

11a. Town of Agawam. Established 1855 from part of West Springfield. Records to be sought: assessors, miscellaneous (1855-), parish (1758-1836), proprietors, town (1855-), vital(1855-). Copied vital records: See West Springfield. Earliest church records: Congregational (1758-), Baptist (1790-). FHL microfilms (MSA): cemetery, midwife (1827-82), WPA record inventory. Library: Agawam Public Library, 750 Cooper St. (01000), 1-413-789-1550.

11b. Town of Blandford. Established 1741 from Suffield Equivalent Lands commonly called Glasgow. Records to be sought: assessors (1816-), miscellaneous (1834-), town (1742-), vital(1844-). Copied vital records: microfiche. Earliest church records: Congregational (1799-), Methodist (1814-). Books: brief histories. FHL microfilms (MSA): Congregational (1799-1877), family records, histories, town (to 1800), vital (1737-1890). Library: Porter Memorial Library, Main St. (01008), 1-413-848-2853.

11c. Town of Brimfield. Mentioned 1714 and 1722, established 1731. Land split off to form part of Western (Warren) 1742, split off Monson 1760, South Brimfield (Wales) 1762. Records to be sought: assessors, miscellaneous (1808-), proprietors (1731-1824), selectmen, soldiers, town (1730-), vital(1730-). Copied vital records: book. Earliest church records: Congregational (1748-). Book: history. FHL microfilms (MSA): history, proprietors (1731-1824), vital (1720-1890). Library: Brimfield Public Library, Main St. (01010), 1-413-245-3518.

11d. Town of Chester. Established 1765 as Town of Murrayfield from plantation called Murrayfield, name changed 1783 to Chester. Land split off to form part of Middlefield 1783. Records to be sought: miscellaneous (1790-), proprietors, selectmen and assessors, town (1790-), vital (1765-). Copied vital records: book. Earliest church records: Congregational (1769-). Book: history. FHL microfilms (MSA): cemetery, Congregational (1769-1814), history, proprietors (1667-1830), town (1762-1864), vital (1762-1864). Library: Hamilton Memorial Library (01011), 1-413-354-7808.

11e. City of CHICOPEE. Established 1848 as a town from part of Springfield. Records to be sought: assessors (1848-), miscellaneous (1848-), selectmen (1848-), soldiers, town (1848-), vital (1848-). Copied vital records: microfiche. Earliest church records: Congregational (1824-), Baptist (1828-). Book: history. FHL microfilms (MSA): history, town (1741-1840), vital (1636-1871), WPA record inventory (1939). Library: Chicopee Public Library, Market Square (01013), 1-413-594-6679.

11f. Town of East Longmeadow. Established 1894 from part of

Longmeadow. Records to be sought: assessors (1894–), miscellaneous (1894–), selectmen (1894–), town (1894–), vital (1894–). Copied vital records: See Longmeadow. Earliest church records: See Longmeadow. Books: histories. FHL microfilms (MSA): See Longmeadow. Library: East Longmeadow Public Library, 60 Center Square (01028), 1-413-525-7813.

11g. Town of Granville. Established 1754 as district from land called Bedford, made a town 1775. Split off Tolland 1810. Records to be sought: selectmen and assessors, town (1737–), vital (1737–). Copied vital records: book. Earliest church records: Congregational (1747–), Baptist (1790–). Book: history. FHL microfilms (MSA): Congregational (1739–1861), family records, history, town (1751–1858), vital (1733–1890). Library: Granville Public Library, Granby Rd. (01034), 1-413-357-8531.

11h. Town of Hampden. Established 1878 from part of Wilbraham. Records to be sought: assessors (1878–), miscellaneous (1878–), selectmen (1878–), town (1878–), vital (1878–). Copied vital records: See Wilbraham. Earliest church records: Congregational (1788–), Baptist (1794–). Book: history. FHL microfilms (MSA): cemetery. Library: Hampden Public Library, Main St. (01036), 1-413-566-3047.

11i. Town of Holland. Established 1783 as district from part of South Brimfield (South Brimfield name changed 1828 to Wales), made a town 1835. Records to be sought: miscellaneous (1825–), selectmen and assessors, town (1775–), vital (1774–). Copied vital records: microfiche. Earliest church records: Congregational (1765–). Book: history. FHL microfilms (MSA): history, town (1783–1854), vital (1771–1854.

11j. City of HOLYOKE. Established as a town 1850 from part of West Springfield, made a city 1873. Records to be sought: assessors, city (1874–), miscellaneous (1850–), town (1850–73), vital (1850–). Copied vital records: See West Springfield. Earliest church records: Congregational (1799–), Baptist (1803–). Books: histories. FHL microfilms (MSA): Catholic (1869–89), history. Library: Holyoke Public Library, 335 Maple St. (01040), 1-413-534-2211.

11k. Town of Longmeadow. Established 1783 from part of Springfield. Records to be sought: genealogical (1700–1813), miscellaneous, proprietors, selectmen and assessors, town (1783–), vital (1783–). Copied vital records: microfiche. Earliest church records: Baptist (1807–), Congregational (1820–). Books: histories. FHL microfilms (MSA): cemetery, Congregational (1741–1923), genealogy, mortgages (1836–74), soldiers (1861–5), town (1842–76), vital (1774–

1882). Library: Storrs Library, 693 Longmeadow St. (01106), 1-413-567-5500. Genealogical collection.

11ℓ. Town of Ludlow. Established as a district 1774 from part of Springfield called Stony Hill, made a town 1775. Records to be sought: general (1774-), selectmen and assessors, vital (1774-). Copied vital records: microfiche. Earliest church records: Methodist (1793-), Congregational (1850-). Book: history. FHL microfilms (MSA): histories, town (1774-1882), vital (1774-1882). Library: Hubbard Memorial Library, 24 Center St. (01056), 1-413-583-3408.

11m. Town of Monson. Established as a district 1760 from part of Brimfield, made a town 1775. Records to be sought: assessors (1803-), miscellaneous (1830-), town (1762-), vital (1760-). Copied vital records: manuscript at NEHGS. Earliest church records: Congregational (1807-). Book: history. FHL microfilms (MSA): assessors (1805-50), Congregational (1762-1864), town (1788-1897), vital (1755-1837). Library: Monson Free Library, 2 High St., (01057), 1-413-267-3866. Genealogical collection.

11n. Town of Montgomery. Established 1780 from a part of Westfield called the New Addition and parts of Norwich (later called Huntington) and Southampton. Land split off 1792 to form part of Russell. Records to be sought: assessors, miscellaneous (1780-), selectmen, town (1780-), vital (1780-). Copied vital records: book. Earliest church records: Methodist (1847-). FHL microfilms (MSA): cemetery, history, vital (1780-1850). Library: Hall Memorial Library, Main Rd. (01085).

11o. Town of Palmer. Established as a district 1752 from a plantation called The Elbows, made a town 1775. Land split off to form part of Ware 1761. Records to be sought: proprietors (1716-50), selectmen and assessors, town (1732-), vital (1746-). Copied vital records: book. Earliest church records: Congregational (1733-), Baptist (1825-). Books: histories. FHL microfilms (MSA): assessors (1791-1814, 1824-46), cemetery, history, genealogy, proprietors (1732-1824), town (1781-1857), vital (1746-1849). Library: Palmer Public Library, 455 N. Main St. (01069), 1-413-283-3330. Genealogical collection.

11p. Town of Russell. Established 1792 from a part of Westfield called the New Addition and a part of Montgomery. Records to be sought: miscellaneous, selectmen and assessors (1828-), town (1804-), vital (1776-). Copied vital records: microfiche. Earliest church records: Baptist (1816-). Book: brief history. FHL microfilms (MSA): assessors (1831-66), Baptist (1800-71), Congregational (1801-33), selectmen (1800-48), town (1792-1864), treasurer (1804-62), vital (1792-1864).

Library: Russell Public Library, Main St. (01071), 1-413-862-4554.

11q. Town of Southwick. Established as a district 1770 from part of Westfield, made a town 1775. Records to be sought: miscellaneous (1834-), selectmen and assessors, soldiers, town (1777-1819, 1834-), vital (1771-1810, 1845-). Copied vital records: microfiche. Earliest church records: Congregational (1773-), Baptist (1805-). FHL microfilms (MSA): Congregational (1773-1895). Library: Southwick Public Library, 477 College Highway (01077), 1-413-569-6612.

11r. City of SPRINGFIELD. Mentioned as a town 1641 and 1647, made a city 1852. Split off Westfield 1669, Wilbraham 1763, West Springfield 1774, Ludlow 1774, Longmeadow 1783, Chicopee 1848. Records to be sought: assessors, city (1852-), miscellaneous, proprietors (1650-1813), selectmen, town (1636-1852), vital (1640-). Copied vital records: microfiche. Earliest church records: Congregational (1735-), Methodist (1815-), Baptist (1817-), Episcopal (1821-). Books: histories, church vital records (1736-1809), official town records (1636-1736). FHL microfilms (MSA): Baptist (1804-50), biography, Congregational (1736-1878), genealogy, histories, newspaper (1838-1946), selectmen (1636-1857), soldiers (1861-5), town (1636-1859), vital (1636-1940). Libraries: Springfield City Library, 220 State St. (01103), 1-413-739-3871. Genealogical collection. CT Valley Historical Museum Library, 194 State St. (01103), 1-413-732-3080.

11s. Town of Tolland. Established 1810 from part of Granville. Records to be sought: assessors, miscellaneous (1810-), town (1810-), vital (1810-). Copied vital records: none. Earliest church records: Congregational (1853-). FHL microfilms (MSA): Congregational (1793-1890), genealogy.

11t. Town of Wales. Established as a district called South Brimfield 1762 from part of Brimfield, made a town 1775, name changed to Wales 1828. Split off Holland 1783. Records to be sought: miscellaneous (1790-), selectmen and assessors (1790-), town (1790-), vital (1751-). Copied vital records: microfiche. Earliest church records: Baptist (1736-), Methodist (1830-). Books: soldiers (1861-5). FHL microfilms (MSA): biography, genealogy. Library: Wales Public Library, Main St. (01081), 1-413-245-9072.

11u. Town of West Springfield. Established 1774 from part of Springfield. Split off Holyoke 1950, Agawam 1855. Records to be sought: assessors, miscellaneous (1774-), town (1774-), vital (1774-). Copied vital records: book. Earliest church records: Congregational (1707-). Books: histories. FHL microfilms (MSA): cemetery, history, midwife (1827-82), vital (1774-1926). Library: West Springfield Public

Library, 200 Park St. (01089), 1-413-736-4561.

11v. City of WESTFIELD. Established as a town 1669 from part of Springfield called Woronoake, made a city 1920. Split off Southwick 1770, land split off 1780 to form part of Montgomery, land split off 1792 to form part of Russell. Records to be sought: assessors, miscellaneous (1823-), proprietors (1667-1830), selectmen, town (1675-), vital (1857-). Copied vital records: microfiche. Earliest church records: Congregational (1679-), Methodist (1795-). Books: histories. FHL microfilms (MSA): cemetery, Congregational (1679-1836), histories, proprietors (1667-1830), vital (1669-1915). Library: Westfield Athenaeum, 6 Elm St. (01085), 1-413-568-7833.

11w. Town of Wilbraham. Established 1763 from part of Springfield. Split off Hampden 1878. Records to be sought: assessors, miscellaneous (1740-), selectmen, town (1740-), vital (1740-). Copied vital records: microfiche. Earliest church records: Congregational (1741-), Methodist (1791-). Books: histories. FHL microfilms (MSA): assessors (1814-43), Congregational (1735-1800), genealogy, histories, town (1740-1862), vital (1740-1904). Library: Wilbraham Public Library, Crane Park Dr. (01095), 1-413-596-6141.

12. Hampshire County

Hampshire County established 1662. County seat Northampton (01060). County seat 1662-1812 was Springfield (now in Hampden County). Deeds registered at Springfield 1662-1812, also at Northampton for 1787- and Deerfield (now in Franklin County) for period 1787-1812. Those deeds registered at Deerfield were transferred to the adjacent town Greenfield in 1812. Probate records from 1660- in Northampton. Records of several types for 1651-62 are to be found in the court records of the Towns of Springfield and Northampton. Records to be sought: county court (1664-92), courts of common pleas (1677-1859), courts of sessions (1677-1827), deed (1662-), justice of peace (1787-1881), marriage (1758-89), naturalization (1849-), notary (1813-83), probate (1660-), superior court (1859-), superior court of judicature (1716-80), supreme judicial court (1797-). Census: Pre-1800E, 1790R, 1800R, 1810R, 1820RI, 1830R, 1840RP, 1850RAIM, 1855S, 1860RAIM, 1865S, 1870RAIM, 1880RAIM, 1890C, 1900R, 1910R. Books: biography (1896), history (1855/79, 1932/64). FHL microfilms (MSA): biography (1896), cemetery, county court (1677-92), courts of common pleas (1677-1859), courts of sessions (1677-1827), deed (1662-1869), divorce (1790-1960), gazetteer (1886), history (1855/79, 1932), naturalization (1849-1986), probate (1660-1869), superior court (1859-1986), supreme judicial court (1812-87). Deed repositories: Records 1662-1812 in Springfield, records 1787- at Northampton.

12a. Town of Amherst. Established 1759 as a district from part of Hadley, made a town 1775. Records to be sought: assessors (1777-), town (1735-), vital (1735-). Copied vital records: microfiche. Earliest church records: Congregational (1735-), Baptist (1827-). Books: histories, town records (1735-88). FHL microfilms (MSA): assessors (1759-1860), biography, histories, town (1650-1850), vital (to 1891). Library: Jones Library, 43 Amity St. (01002), 1-413-256-0246.

12b. Town of Belchertown. Established 1761 from a plantation called Cold Spring. Land split off 1927 to form part of new town of Enfield. Records to be sought: assessors (1797-), miscellaneous (1841-), town (1740-), vital (1732-). Copied vital records: microfiche. Earliest church records: Baptist (1795-), Congregational (1834-). Books: histories. FHL microfilms (MSA): genealogy, vital (to 1891). Library: Clapp Memorial Library, 19 S. Main St. (02109), 1-617-966-1660.

12c. Town of Chesterfield. Established 1762 from plantation called New Hingham. Land split off 1781 to form part of new town of Goshen. Records to be sought: assessors, miscellaneous (1762-), parish (1847-65), selectmen, town (1762-), vital (1762-). Copied vital records: microfiche. Earliest church records: Congregational (1828-). Books: histories, genealogies. FHL microfilms (MSA): Congregational (1764-1913), genealogy, town (1762-1805). Library: Chesterfield Public Library, Main Rd. (01012), 1-413-296-4735.

12d. Town of Cummington. Established 1779 from plantation called Number Five. District of Plainfield split off 1785. Records to be sought: assessors, miscellaneous (1762-), parish (1833-45), proprietors (1762-1804), selectmen, town (1762-), vital (1762-). Copied vital records: book. Earliest church records: Congregational (1840-), Universalist (1840-). Books: histories. FHL microfilms (MSA): proprietors (1762-84), town (1762-1804), vital (1750-1900). Library: Bryant Free Library, Route 9 (01026), 1-413-634-8884.

12e. Town of Easthampton. Established as a district 1785 from parts of Northampton and Southampton, made a town 1809. Records to be sought: selectmen and assessors, soldiers (1862-4), town (1785-), vital (1785-). Copied vital records: microfiche. Earliest church records: Congregational (1785-). Books: histories. FHL microfilms (MSA): genealogy, histories, town (1785-1865), vital (1764-1822). Library: Easthampton Public Library, 9 Park St. (01027), 1-413-527-1031.

12f. Town of Enfield. Established 1816 from parts of Belchertown and Greenwich, Enfield dissolved 1938 with parts going to Belchertown, New Salem, Pelham, and Ware. Records to be sought: assessors, miscellaneous (1816–), selectmen (1844–), town (1816–), vital (1844–). Copied vital records: microfiche. Earliest church records: Congregational (1787–), Methodist (1849–). Books: see towns into which it was dissolved. FHL microfilms (MSA): history. Library: see towns into which it was dissolved.

12g. Town of Goshen. Established 1781 from part of Chesterfield and the plantation called Chesterfield Gore. Records to be sought: general (1781–), miscellaneous (1781–), selectmen and assessors, vital (1795–). Copied vital records: microfiche. Earliest church records: Congregational (1828–). Books: histories. FHL microfilms (MSA): cemetery, genealogy, history, tax (1793–1854), town (1762–1857).

12h. Town of Granby. Established 1768 from part of South Hadley. Records to be sought: assessors (1850–), proprietors, town (1769–), vital (1768–). Copied vital records: manuscript in NEHGS. Earliest church records: Congregational (1820–). Book: history. FHL microfilms (MSA): genealogy, midwife (1827–82), proprietors (1719–1835), tax (1794–1849), town (1745–1870), vital (1745–1844). Library: Granby Free Public Library, Library Lane (01033), 1-413-467-3320.

12i. Town of Greenwich. Established 1754 from a plantation called Quabin, land split off 1801 to form part of new Town of Dana, land split off 1816 to form part of new Town of Enfield, Greenwich dissolved in 1938 with parts going to Hardwick, New Salem, Petersham, and Ware. Records to be sought: assessors, parish (1749–82), proprietors (1733–83), town (1805–), vital (1754–). Copied vital records: microfiche. Earliest church records: Congregational (1760–). Books: see towns into which it was dissolved. FHL microfilms (MSA): see towns into which it was dissolved. Library: see towns into which it was dissolved.

12j. Town of Hadley. Established 1661 from a new plantation near Northampton. Hatfield split off 1670, District of South Hadley split off 1753, District of Amherst split off 1759. Records to be sought: assessors, proprietors (1689–1702), town (1661–), vital (1661–). Copied vital records: manuscript in NEHGS. Earliest church records: Congregational (1766–). Books: histories. FHL microfilms (MSA): Congregational (1832–1900), genealogy, history, proprietors (1665–1779), town (1659–1719), vital (1660–1891). Library: Goodwin Memorial Library, Middle St. (01035), 1-413-584-7451.

12k. Town of Hatfield. Established 1670 from part of Hadley. Whately split off 1771, land split off 1771 to form part of new District of Williamsburg. Records to be sought: proprietors (1671–1767), selectmen and assessors, town (1662-), vital (1655-). Copied vital records: manuscript in NEHGS. Earliest church records: Congregational (1772-). Books: histories, genealogy. FHL microfilms (MSA): Congregational (1771-1869), genealogy, history, proprietors (1672-1767), town (1660-1848), vital (1655-1844). Library: Hatfield Public Library, Main St. (01038), 1-413-247-9097.

12£. Town of Huntington. Established 1773 as District of Norwich from part of Murrayfield, made Town of Norwich 1775. Land split off 1780 to form part of new Town of Montgomery, name changed to Huntington 1855. Records to be sought: miscellaneous (1773-), selectmen and assessors, town (1773-), vital (1773-). Copied vital records: none. Earliest church records: Congregational (1778-). Books: history. FHL microfilms (MSA): vital (1786-1844). Library: Huntington Public Library, East Main St. (01050), 1-413-667-3018.

12m. Town of Middlefield. Established 1783 from parts of Becket, Chester, Partridgefield (later called Peru), Washington, and land called Prescott's Grants. Records to be sought: assessors, miscellaneous (1783-1854), town (1783-), vital (1783-). Copied vital records: book. Earliest church records: Congregational (1783-), Baptist (1817-). Books: histories. FHL microfilms (MSA): genealogy, history, tax (1833-60), town (1783-1854), vital (1783-1854).

12n. City of NORTHAMPTON. Town recognized 1656. Split off District of Southampton 1753, split off Westhampton 1778, land split off 1785 to form part of new District of Easthampton, made a city 1883. Records to be sought: assessors, city (1884-), miscellaneous (1654-), proprietors (1653-), town (1653-1883), vital (1653-). Copied vital records: manuscript in NEHGS. Earliest church records: Unitarian (1825-), Congregational (1826-), Baptist (1826-), Episcopal (1826-). Books: Congregational (1661-1891), histories. genealogy. FHL microfilms (MSA): biography, cemetery, Congregational (1661-1924), genealogy, history, midwife (1827-82), newspaper (1786-1937), proprietors (1653-1731), town (1650-1820), vital (1653-1880). Library: Forbes Library, 20 West St., (01060), 1-413-584-8399. Genealogy collection.

12o. Town of Pelham. Established 1743 from land called New Lisburn. Land split off 1822 to form part of new Town of Prescott (annexed to Petersham and New Salem 1938). Records to be sought: assessors, miscellaneous (1738-), proprietors (1738-67), selectmen (1862-), town (1738-), vital (1738-). Copied vital records: book. Earliest church records: Methodist (1831-). Books: histories. FHL microfilms (MSA): history, proprietors (1738-67), town (1738-1830), vital (1738-1891). Library: Pelham Free Public Library, Rhodes Bldg. RD2 (01002), 1-413-253-7129. Local history collection.

12p. Town of Plainfield. Established 1785 as a district from part of Cummington, made a town 1807. Records to be sought: assessors, miscellaneous (1863-), soldiers (1861-5), town (1785-), vital (1785-). Copied vital records: microfiche. Earliest church records: Congregational (1786-). Books: histories. FHL microfilms (MSA): Congregational (1786-1850), history, vital (1779-1875). Library: Shaw Memorial Library, Main St. (01070), 1-413-635.2252.

12q. Town of Prescott. Established 1822 from parts of Pelham and New Salem, Prescott dissolved in 1938 with parts going to Petersham and New Salem. Records to be sought: miscellaneous (1822-), selectmen and assessors, town (1822-), vital (1822-). Copied vital records: microfiche. Earliest church records: Congregational (1825-). Books: see towns into which it was dissolved. FHL microfilms (MSA): histories, vital (1822-1930). Library: see towns into which it was dissolved.

12r. Town of South Hadley. Established 1753 as a district from part of Hadley, split off Granby 1768, made a town 1775. Records to be sought: assessors, miscellaneous (1753-), proprietors, town (1753-), vital (1753-). Copied vital records: microfiche. Earliest church records: Congregational (1733-), Methodist (1833-). Books: histories. FHL microfilms (MSA): cemetery, genealogy, histories, midwife (1827-82), militia (1825-67), proprietors (1762-1815), town (1730-67), vital, (1730-1847). Library: South Hadley Library, Bardwell St. (01075), 1-413-538-5045.

12s. Town of Southampton. Established 1753 as a district from part of Northampton, made a town 1775, land split off 1780 to form part of new Town of Montgomery, land split off 1785 to form part of new District of Easthampton. Records to be sought: assessors, miscellaneous (1758-), selectmen, soldiers (1861-5), town (1758-), vital (1750-). Copied vital records: microfiche. Earliest church records: Congregational (1743-), Methodist (1840-). Books: histories. FHL microfilms (MSA): Congregational, genealogy, Methodist (1842-1924), proprietors (1730-80), tax (1821-50), town (1741-1864), vital, (1740-1940). Library: Edwards Public Library, 225 College Hwy. (01073), 1-413-527-9480. Local history.

12t. Town of Ware. Established 1761 as a district from Ware River Parish (boundaries defined 1750) and some land from Palmer, made a town 1775. Records to be sought: assessors, miscellaneous (1837-73), selectmen, town (1742-), vital (1742-). Copied vital records:

microfiche. Earliest church records: Congregational (1751-), Methodist (1843-), Unitarian (1846-). Books: early grants, early settlers, genealogy, histories. FHL microfilms (MSA): history, town (1742-1864), vital, (1735-1844). Library: Young Men's Library Association, 37 Main St. (01082), 1-413-967-5491.

12u. Town of Westhampton. Established 1778 from part of Northampton. Records to be sought: assessors, miscellaneous (1841-), town (1778-), vital (1753-). Copied vital records: microfiche. Earliest church records: Congregational (1779-). Books: histories. FHL microfilms (MSA): Congregational (1779-1874), early settlers (1763-96), genealogy, town (1778-1868), Union Church (1829-50), vital, (1770-1851). Library: Westhampton Memorial Library, South Rd. (01017), 1-413-527-5386.

12v. Town of Williamsburg. Established 1771 as a district from part of Hatfield and some adjoining land, made a town 1775. Records to be sought: assessors (1800-), miscellaneous (1773-), town (1771-), vital (1765-). Copied vital records: microfiche. Earliest church records: Congregational (1771-). Books: histories. FHL microfilms (MSA): history, tax (1771-1849), town (1736-1858), vital (1753-1851). Library: Meekins Library, Main St. (01096), 1-413-268-7472.

12w. Town of Worthington. Established 1768 from a new plantation called Number Three, land split off 1783 to form part of the new Town of Middlefield. Records to be sought: assessors (1785-), miscellaneous (1768-), town (1768-), vital (1768-). Copied vital records: book. Earliest church records: Congregational (1771-). Books: histories. FHL microfilms (MSA): Congregational (1771-1850), history, proprietors (1762-72), vital (to 1850). Library: Frederick Sargent Huntington Memorial Library, Huntington Rd. (01098), 1-413-238-5565.

13. Middlesex County

Middlesex County established 1643 from MA Bay Colony. County seat Cambridge (02141). Since 1855 deeds also registered at Lowell. Records to be sought: county court (1649-99), courts of common pleas (1699-1859), courts of sessions (1681-1828), deed (1649-), justice of peace (1789-1809), marriage (1733-93), naturalization (1809-), notary (1869-84), probate (1648-), superior court (1859-), superior court of judicature (1693-1780), supreme judicial court (1780-), vital records (1632-1745, 1778-93). Census: Pre-1800E, 1790R, 1800R, 1810R, 1820RI, 1830R, 1840RP, 1850RAIM, 1855S, 1860RAIM, 1865S, 1870RAIM, 1880RAIM, 1890C, 1900R, 1910R. Books: biography (1890/98, 1905/08/27), history (1835/74/80/90, 1908/27), probate (1648-1871). FHL microfilms (MSA): biography, county court

(1649-99), courts of common pleas (1699-1847), courts of sessions (1686-1831), deeds (1649-1950), genealogies, histories, probate (1648-1924), supreme judicial court (1797-1850), vital (1651-1793). Deed repositories: Records 1649-1855 at Cambridge, records 1855- for Southern District at Cambridge, for Northern District at Lowell. In the town/city listings which follow, pertinent districts are indicated with capital letters (N for Northern District, S for Southern District) placed at the ends of the listings.

13a. Town of Acton. Established 1735 from part of Concord, land split off 1780 to form part of new District of Carlisle. Records to be sought: assessors, miscellaneous (1803-85), selectmen, town (1735-), vital (1735-). Copied vital records: book. Earliest church records: Congregational (1738-), Baptist (1846-). Books: histories. FHL microfilms (MSA): assessors (1777-1821), Congregational (1738-1932), history, militia (1810-23), town (1735-1862), vital (1735-1857). Library: Acton Memorial Library, 486 Main St. (01720), 1-617-264-9642. S

13b. Town of Arlington. Established 1807 as Town of West Cambridge from part of Cambridge, land split off 1850 to form part of new Town of Winchester, land split off 1859 to form part of new Town of Belmont, name changed 1867 to Arlington. Records to be sought: assessors, selectmen, town (1807-), vital (1807-). Copied vital records: book. Earliest church records: Unitarian (1732-), Baptist (1781-). Books: histories. FHL microfilms (MSA): Episcopal (1898-1914), genealogy, history, vital (to 1850). Library: Robbins Library, 700 Massachusetts Ave. (02174), 1-617- 641-4884. S

13c. Town of Ashby. Established 1767 from parts of Ashburnham, Fitchbury, and Townsend. Records to be sought: assessors, town (1767-), vital (1767-). Copied vital records: microfiche. Earliest church records: Congregational (1776-), Unitarian (1841-). Book: history. FHL microfilms (MSA): assessors (1769-1853), Bible, cemetery, mortgage (1809-59), poor (1810-32), selectmen (1848-1931), town (1750-1884), treasurer (1768-1897), turnpike (1806-26), vital (1754-1876), voter (1789-1838). Library: Ashby Free Public Library, Main St. (0143-1), 1-617-386-5377. S

13d. Town of Ashland. Established 1846 from parts of Framingham, Holliston, and Hopkinton. Records to be sought: assessors (1846-), miscellaneous (1846-), selectmen (1885-), town (1846-), vital (1846-). Copied vital records: see parent towns. Earliest church records: Congregational (1835-), Baptist (1843-). Book: history. FHL microfilms (MSA): histories, Library: Ashland Public Library, 66 Front St. (01721), 1-617-881-2490. S

13e. Town of Ayer. Established 1871 from parts of Groton and Shirley. Records to be sought: miscellaneous (1871–), selectmen and assessors (1871–), town (1871–), vital (1871–). Copied vital records: see Groton and Shirley. Earliest church records: Baptist (1851–), Unitarian (1855–). Book: history. FHL microfilms (MSA): history, WPA inventory. Library: Ayer Public Library, 26 E. Main St. (01432), 1-617-772-2257. Many special collections. S

13f. Town of Bedford. Established 1729 from parts of Billerica and Concord. Records to be sought: assessors, miscellaneous (1836–), selectmen, soldiers, town (1729–), vital (1729–). Copied vital records: book. Earliest church records: Congregational (1730–), Unitarian (1730–). Books: histories. FHL microfilms (MSA): assessors (1761–1830), genealogy, histories, selectmen (1794–1851), town (1729–1956), vital (1700–1850). Library: Bedford Free Public Library, Mudge Way (01730), 1-617-275-9440. S

13g. Town of Belmont. Established 1859 from parts of Waltham, Watertown, and West Cambridge (now Arlington). Records to be sought: assessors (1860–), general (1859–), miscellaneous, selectmen, vital (1859–). Copied vital records: see parent towns. Earliest church records: Unitarian (1856–), Congregational (1861–). Books: biography, history. Library: Belmont Public Library, 336 Concord Ave. (02178), 1-617-489-2000. S

13h. Town of Billerica. Recognized 1655/6, land split off 1729 to form part of new Town of Bedford, split off Tewksbury in 1734, land split off 1780 to form part of new District of Carlisle. Records to be sought: miscellaneous, selectmen and assessors, town (1655–), vital (1655–). Copied vital records: book. Earliest church records: Unitarian (1663–), Baptist (1828–). Books: histories. FHL microfilms (MSA): assessors (1822–50), Congregational (1663–1870), histories, selectmen (1678–1786), town (1653–1848), vital (1627–1854). Library: Billerica Public Library, Concord Rd. (01821), 1-617-671-0948. N

13i. Town of Boxborough. Established 1783 as District of Boxborough from parts of Harvard, Littleton, and Stow, made a town 1835. Records to be sought: assessors, miscellaneous (1785–), selectmen, town (1783–), vital (1783–). Copied vital records: book. Earliest church records: Congregational (1783–), Evangelical Congregational (1833–). Books: histories. FHL microfilms (MSA): genealogy, history, town (1783–1866), vital (to 1850). S

13j. Town of Burlington. Established 1799 from part of Woburn. Records to be sought: assessors, selectmen, town (1799–), vital (1799–). Copied vital records: book. Earliest church records: Congregational

(1730–). Book: brief historical addresses. FHL microfilms (MSA): assessors (1822–50), selectmen (1799–1885), town (1799–1856), vital (1736–1877). Library: Burlington Public Library, 22 Sears St. (01803), 1-617-272-2520. S

13k. City of CAMBRIDGE. Recognized 1631 as Newe Towne, name changed 1638 to Town of Cambridge, split off Lexington in 1713, split off Brighton in 1807, split off West Cambridge 1807, made a city 1846. Records to be sought: assessors, city (1846–), miscellaneous (1700–), proprietors (1634–1829), selectmen (1769–1846), soldiers, town (1632–), vital (1632–). Copied vital records: book. Earliest church records: Congregational (1636–), Unitarian (1696–). Books: biographies, histories, Baptist members, Congregational members, town records (1630–1703), Church of Christ vital records (1632–1830), proprietors (1634–1829), cemetery records, genealogical register, 1635 land owners. FHL microfilms (MSA): assessors (1794–1847), biography, cemetery, Congregational (1632–1830), genealogy, histories, Methodist (1834–1871), proprietors (1635–1841), selectmen (1704–1853), town (1630–1703), vital (1632–1886). Libraries: Cambridge Public Library, 449 Broadway (02138), 1-617-498-9080; Harvard University Libraries, (02138), 1-617-495-3650. S

13ℓ. Town of Carlisle. Established 1780 as District of Carlisle from parts of Acton, Billerica, Chelmsford, and Concord, made a town 1805. Records to be sought: selectmen and assessors, town (1755–), vital (1755–). Copied vital records: book. Earliest church records: Congregational (1830–), Unitarian (1842–). Books: histories. FHL microfilms (MSA): Congregational (1780–1943), genealogy, histories, town (1754–1861), vital (to 1850). Library: Gleason Public Library, 22 Bedford Rd. (01741), 1-617-369-4898. N

13m. Town of Chelmsford. Established 1655, split off Westford 1729, land split off 1780 to form part of District of Carlisle, split off Lowell 1826. Records to be sought: assessors, miscellaneous (1867–), parish (1741–1872), town (1655–), vital (1655–). Copied vital records: book. Earliest church records: Unitarian (1741–), Baptist (1771–). Books: histories. FHL microfilms (MSA): Congregational (1727–1901), histories, proprietors (1645–1750), town (1645–1869), vital (to 1850). Library: Chelmsford Public Library, Boston Rd. (01824), 1-617-256-5521. N

13n. Town of Concord. Established 1635 from a plantation called Musketequid, land split off 1729 to form part of new Town of Bedford, land split off 1735 to form part of new Town of Acton, land split off 1754 to form new Town of Lincoln, split off District of Carlisle 1754, District of Carlisle annexed 1756, land split off 1780 to form part of new District of

Carlisle. Records to be sought: assessors (1796–), miscellaneous, selectmen (1855–), town (1635–), vital (1635–). Copied vital records: book. Earliest church records: Unitarian (1738–), Congregational (1826–). Books: biography, histories, Civil War servicemen. FHL microfilms (MSA): assessors (1826–60), genealogy, histories, military, selectmen (1860–1962), town (1650–1930), vital (1635–1857). Library: Concord Free Public Library, 129 Main St. (01742), 1-617-369-5324. S

13o. Town of Dracut. Established 1702 from tract of land of the same name. Records to be sought: proprietors (1715–33), selectmen and assessors (1769–1857), town (1711–1819, 1831–), vital (1711–). Copied vital records: book. Earliest church records: Congregational (1765–). Books: early land grants, history. FHL microfilms (MSA): genealogy, history, proprietors (1710–21), town (1792–1858), vital (1792–1858). Library: Moses Greeley Parker Memorial Library, 28 Arlington St. (01826), 1-617-454-5474. N

13p. Town of Dunstable. Recognized 1673 and 1680, split off Nottingham 1733, land split off 1734 to form part of new Town of Litchfield, part of Nottingham annexed 1747, rest of Nottingham annexed 1754, land split off 1789 to form part of new Town of Tyngsborough. Records to be sought: miscellaneous, selectmen and assessors, town (1743–), vital (1743–). Copied vital records: book. Earliest church records: Congregational (1757–), Universalist (1818–). Books: histories, genealogy. FHL microfilms (MSA): genealogy, histories, town (1679–1890), vital (1679–1890). Library: Dunstable Free Public Library, Main St. (01827), 1-617-649-7830. N

13q. City of EVERETT. Established 1870 from part of Malden, made a city 1892. Records to be sought: assessors (1870–), city (1892–), miscellaneous (1897–) selectmen (1870–92), town (1870–92), vital (1870–). Copied vital records: see Malden. Earliest church records: Congregational (1861–), Methodist (1870–). Book: history. Libraries: Frederick E. Parlin Memorial Library, 410 Broadway (02149), 1-617-387-2550; Shute Memorial Library, 781 Broadway (02149), 1-617-387-3612. S

13r. Town of Framingham. Recognized 1675, established 1700, land split off 1846 to form part of new Town of Ashland. Records to be sought: assessors, miscellaneous (1701–), selectmen, town (1701–), vital (1701–). Copied vital records: book. Earliest church records: Baptist (1812–), Congregational (1827–). Books: histories, church members (1701–1930), genealogy. FHL microfilms (MSA): Episcopal (1861–1924), genealogy, history, vital (to 1850). Library: Framingham Public Library, 49 Lexington St. (01701), 1-617-879-3570. S

13s. Town of Groton. Established 1655 from a plantation called Petapawoge, land split off 1732 to form part of new Town of Harvard, split off Districts of Shirley and Pepperell in 1753, land split off 1871 to form part of new Town of Ayer. Records to be sought: miscellaneous (1805-), proprietors (1683-1829), selectmen, town (1662-), vital (1662-). Copied vital records: book. Earliest church records: Unitarian (1815-), Congregational (1825-). Books: early land grants, biographies, early records (1662-1707), histories. FHL microfilms (MSA): Congregational (1704-1880), early records, histories, proprietors (1716-1829), town (1662-1873), Union Church (1829-1913), vital (to 1850). Library: Groton Public Library, 99 Main St. (01450), 1-617-448-6761. S

13t. Town of Holliston. Established 1724 from part of Sherborn, land split off 1846 to form part of new Town of Ashland. Records to be sought: assessors, miscellaneous (1724-), town (1724-), vital (1724-). Copied vital records: book. Earliest church records: Congregational (1728-), Methodist (1833-). Books: histories. FHL microfilms (MSA): Episcopal (1864-1917), genealogy, history, town (1724-1896), vital (to 1850). Library: Holliston Public Library, 752 Washington St. (01746), 1-617-429-6070. S

13u. Town of Hopkinton. Established 1715 from tract called Moguncoy, land split off 1735 to form part of new Town of Upton, land split off 1846 to form part of new Town of Ashland. Records to be sought: assessors, proprietors, town, vital. Copied vital records: book. Earliest church records: Congregational (1724-), Episcopal (1817-). Books: histories. FHL microfilms (MSA): cemetery (1725-1966), Congregational (1724-1880), deeds (1743-1833), Episcopal (1735-1957), history, vital (to 1850). Library: Hopkinton Public Library, 13 Main St. (01748), 1-617-435-3450. S

13v. Town of Hudson. Established 1866 from parts of Marlborough and Stow. Records to be sought: assessors (1866-), miscellaneous (1866-), town (1866-), vital (1866-). Copied vital records: see Marlborough and Stow. Earliest church records: Baptist (1852-), Unitarian (1865-). Books: histories. Library: Hudson Public Library, Wood Square (01749), 1-617-562-7521. S

13w. Town of Lexington. Established 1713 from part of Cambridge, land split off 1754 to form part of new Town of Lincoln. Records to be sought: assessors, miscellaneous (1749-), selectmen, town (1692-), vital (1677-). Copied vital records: book. Earliest church records: Unitarian (1696-), Baptist (1830-). Books: histories. FHL microfilms (MSA): assessors (1729-1852), biography, cemetery, Congregational (1690-1844), histories, town (1692-1861), vital (to 1898). Library: Cary Memorial Library, 1874 Massachusetts Ave. (02173), 1-

617-862-6288. S

13x. Town of Lincoln. Established 1754 from parts of Concord, Lexington, and Weston. Records to be sought: assessors, miscellaneous (1754-), proprietors (1747-), town (1754-), vital (1754-). Copied vital records: book. Earliest church records: Congregational (1830-), Unitarian (1841-). Books: biography, history. FHL microfilms (MSA): assessors (1760-1860), Congregational, Episcopal (1873-1911), genealogy, history, town (1746-1878), treasurer (1755-1859), vital (to 1850). Library: Lincoln Public Library, Bedford Rd. (01773), 1-617-259-8465. S

13y. Town of Littleton. Mentioned 1698 as a tract of land called Nashoba, made Town of Nashoba 1714, name changed to Town of Littleton 1715, land split off 1783 to form part of new District of Boxborough. Records to be sought: assessors, proprietors, town (1715-), vital (1715-). Copied vital records: book. Earliest church records: Baptist (1822-), Unitarian (1830-). Book: history. FHL microfilms (MSA): deeds (1827-95), genealogy, town (1715-1898). Library: Reuben Hoar Library, Rogers St. (01460), 1-617-486-4046. S

13z. City of LOWELL. Established 1826 as Town of Lowell from part of Chelmsford, made a city 1836. Records to be sought: assessors (1826-), city (1836-), miscellaneous (1826-), town (1826-36), vital (1826-). Copied vital records: book. Earliest church records: Congregational (1797-), Episcopal (1824-), Baptist (1826-), Universalist (1827-), Unitarian (1829-). Books: histories, French Canadians. FHL microfilms (MSA): alderman (1836-47), assessors (1826-50), Episcopal (1860-1913), histories, Methodist (1861-94), St. Anne's Church (1824-1983), tax (1826-50), town (1826-36), vital (1640-1876). Library: Pollard Memorial Library, 401 Merrimack St. (01852), 1-617-454-8821. N

13aa. City of MALDEN. Town established 1649, split off Melrose in 1850 and Everett in 1870, made a city 1881. Records to be sought: assessors, city (1882-), miscellaneous, parish (1758-87), selectmen, town (1678-), vital. Copied vital records: book. Earliest church records: Congregational (1770-), Baptist (1803-). Books: histories. FHL microfilms (MSA): assessor (1812/25/34), Congregational (1747-1887), Episcopal (1862-1919), genealogy, histories, treasurer (1769-1820), town (1764-1845), vital (1649-1868). Library: Malden Public Library, 36 Salem St. (02148), 1-617-324-0218. S

13bb. City of MARLBOROUGH. Town established 1660, split off Westborough in 1717 and Southborough in 1727, land split off 1784 to form part of new District of Berlin, land split off 1866 to form part of new

Town of Hudson, made a city 1890. Records to be sought: city (1890-), miscellaneous (1861-), parish (1808-23), proprietors (1699-1795), selectmen and assessors, town (1656-1890), vital (1663-). Copied vital records: book. Earliest church records: Congregational (1700-), Unitarian (1804-). Books: histories, genealogy. FHL microfilms (MSA): assessors (1844), cemetery, genealogy, histories, poor (1811-28), proprietors (1637-1803), school (1803-24), selectmen (1760-1913), town (1666-1847), Unitarian (1804-1904), vital (1660-1860). Library: Marlborough Public Library, Main St. (01752), 1-617-485-0494. S

13cc. Town of Maynard. Established 1871 from parts of Stow and Sudbury. Records to be sought: assessors, miscellaneous (1872-), selectmen, town (1872-), vital (1872-). Copied vital records: see Stow and Sudbury. Earliest church records: Congregational (1851-). Books: histories. FHL microfilms (MSA): histories. Library: Maynard Public Library, Main St. (01754), 1-617-897-1010. S

13dd. City of MEDFORD. Recognized as a town 1630, land split off 1850 to form part of new Town of Winchester, made a city 1892. Records to be sought: assessors, city (1892-), miscellaneous (1835-), selectmen, town (1670-1892), vital (1673-). Copied vital records: book. Earliest church records: Unitarian (1712-), Universalist (1831-). Books: histories, Revolutionary War servicemen. FHL microfilms (MSA): Congregational (1712-1823), Episcopal (1848-1929), genealogy, histories, selectmen (1794-1843), town (1673-1864), vital (1718-1851). Libraries: Medford Historical Society Library, 10 Governor's Ave. (02155), 1-617-396-2091; Medford Public Library, 111 High St. (02155), 1-617-395-7950. S

13ee. City of MELROSE. Established as a town in 1850 from part of Malden, made a city 1899. Records to be sought: assessors (1850-), city (1899-), miscellaneous (1850-), selectmen, soldiers, town (1850-99), vital (1850-). Copied vital records: see Malden. Earliest church records: Methodist (1813-), Congregational (1848-). Books: histories. FHL microfilms (MSA): Episcopal (1856-1952), histories. Library: Melrose Public Library, 69 W. Emerson St. (02176), 1-617-665-2313. S

13ff. Town of Natick. Recognized as a plantation 1650, established as district 1762, made a town 1781. Records to be sought: assessors, miscellaneous (1720-), proprietors (1702-90), selectmen, town (1745-), vital (1745-). Copied vital records: book. Earliest church records: Congregational (1820-), Unitarian (1830-). Books: histories. FHL microfilms (MSA): Episcopal (1857-1930), history, mortgages (1838-53), miscellaneous (1700-1919), state census (1855/65), town (1745-1967), vital (to 1969). Library: Morse Institute Library, 14 E.

Central St. (01760), 1-617-651-7300. S

13gg. City of NEWTON. Established 1691 as a town from tract called Cambridge Village or New Cambridge, made a city 1873. Records to be sought: assessors (1790-), city (1874-), miscellaneous (1824-), selectmen, town (1706-1873), vital (1669-). Copied vital records: book. Earliest church records: Congregational (1770-), Baptist (1780-). Books: histories, genealogy, church members. FHL microfilms (MSA): biography, Episcopal (1812-1944), genealogy, histories, vital (1626-1892). Library: Newton Free Library, 414 Centre St. (02158), 1-617-527-7145. S

13hh. Town of North Reading. Established 1853 from part of Reading. Records to be sought: assessors, miscellaneous (1853-), selectmen, town (1853-), vital (1853-). Copied vital records: see Reading. Earliest church records: Universalist (1713-), Congregational (1802-). Book: history. FHL microfilms (MSA): genealogy, histories. Library: Flint Memorial Library, 21 Bow St. (01864), 1-617-664-4942. S

13ii. Town of Pepperell. Established 1753 as a district from part of Groton, made a town 1775. Records to be sought: miscellaneous, selectmen and assessors (1837-), town (1742-), vital (1727-). Copied vital records: microfiche, book. Earliest church records: Congregational (1832-), Unitarian (1833-). Books: histories. FHL microfilms (MSA): Congregational (1742-1861), genealogy, histories, town (1655-1919), vital (to 1850). Library: C. F. Lawrence Memorial Library, Main St. (01463), 1-617-433-6962. S

13jj. Town of Reading. Established 1644 from part of Lynn, land split off 1730 to form part of new Town of Wilmington, split off South Reading in 1812, split off North Reading in 1853. Records to be sought: assessors, proprietors, selectmen, town (1644-), vital (1644-). Copied vital records: book. Earliest church records: Congregational (1771-), Baptist (1837-). Books: histories, early settlers, colonial soldiers. FHL microfilms (MSA): assessors (1663-1811), Congregational (1648-1845), deeds and mortgages (1818-49), genealogy, histories, town (1638-1852), treasurer (1745-1855), vital (to 1850). Library: Reading Public Library, 64 Middlesex (01867), 1-617-944-0840. S

13kk. Town of Sherborn. Established 1674 from land at or near Boggestow, split off Holliston 1724. Records to be sought: assessors (1808-), miscellaneous, proprietors (1681-1730), town (1677-), vital (1663-). Copied vital records: book. Earliest church records: Unitarian (1734-), Congregational (1830-). Books: histories. FHL microfilms (MSA): Congregational (1830-76), genealogy, histories, town (1674-

1861), vital (to 1866). Library: Sherborn Library, Sanger St. (01770), 1-617-653-0770. S

13££. Town of Shirley. Established 1753 as District of Shirley from part of Groton, made a town 1775, land split off 1871 to form part of new Town of Ayer. Records to be sought: assessors (1753-), town (1753-), vital (1784-). Copied vital records: book. Earliest church records: United Society Shakers (1792-), Universalist (1812-), Unitarian (1822-). Books: histories, genealogy. FHL microfilms (MSA): genealogy, histories, proprietors (1721-1800), town (1750-1900), vital (to 1850). Library: Hazen Memorial Library, Lancaster Rd. (01464), 1-617-425-9645. S

13mm. City of SOMERVILLE. Established 1842 as a town from part of Charlestown, made a city 1871. Records to be sought: assessors (1842-), city (1872-), miscellaneous (1842-), selectmen (1842-), town (1842-71), vital (1842-). Copied vital records: see Charlestown. Earliest church records: Unitarian (1844-), Baptist (1852-). Books: histories, biography. FHL microfilms (MSA): church, histories, maps. Library: Public Library of the City of Somerville, 79 Highland Ave. (02143), 1-617-623-5000. S

13nn. Town of Stoneham. Established 1725 from part of Charlestown. Records to be sought: assessors, miscellaneous (1835-), selectmen (1859-), town (1725-), vital (1725-). Copied vital records: book. Earliest church records: Congregational (1729-). Books: histories, church members. FHL microfilms (MSA): assessors (1799-1840), biography, histories, military (1725-1861), town (1725-1861), vital (1714-1853). Library: Stoneham Public Library, 431 Main St. (02180), 1-617-438-1324. S

13oo. Town of Stow. Established 1683 from a plantation called Pompposittient, land split off 1732 to form part of new Town of Harvard, land split off 1732 to form part of new Town of Harvard, land split off 1783 to form part of new District of Boxborough, land split off 1866 to form part of new Town of Hudson, land split off 1871 to form part of new Town of Maynard. Records to be sought: assessors (1683-), miscellaneous (1759-), proprietors (1722-), selectmen (1846-), town (1683-), vital (1713-). Copied vital records: book. Earliest church records: Methodist (1823-), Unitarian (1833-). Books: histories. FHL microfilms (MSA): church, genealogy, history, military, town (1660-1911), vital (to 1969). Library: Randall Library, Common Rd. (01775), 1-617-897-8572. S

13pp. Town of Sudbury. Established 1639 from a new plantation adjacent to Concord, split off East Sudbury (Wayland) in 1780, land split off 1871 to form part of new Town of Maynard. Records to be sought: assessors, miscellaneous (1640-), proprietors (1700-80), town (1640-), vital (1640-). Copied vital records: book. Earliest church records: Unitarian (1785-), Methodist (1830-). Books: histories. FHL microfilms (MSA): cemetery, church, histories, proprietors (1705-1805), military, town (1638-1903), vital (1639-1857). Library: Goodnow Library, 21 Concord Rd. (01776), 1-617-443-9113. Genealogy. S

13qq. Town of Tewksbury. Established 1734 from part of Billerica. Records to be sought: assessors, miscellaneous (1829-), town (1734-), vital (1734-). Copied vital records: book. Earliest church records: Congregational (1736-), Baptist (1843-). Books: histories. FHL microfilms (MSA): history, town (1734-1860), treasurer (1793-1845), vital (to 1850). Library: Harold J. Patten Public Library, Town Hall Ave. (01876), 1-617-851-6071. N

13rr. Town of Townsend. Established 1732 from part of tract called Turkey Hills, land split off 1767 to form part of new Town of Ashby. Records to be sought: assessors (1700-), miscellaneous, proprietors, selectmen (1734-), town (1734-), vital (1734-). Copied vital records: microfiche. Earliest church records: Baptist (1818-), Congregational (1830-). Book: history. FHL microfilms (MSA): cemetery, history, proprietors (1719-1822), town (1732-1822), vital (1732-1882). Library: Townsend Public Library, 276 Main St. (01469), 1-617-597-2817. S

13ss. Town of Tyngsborough. Established 1789 as a district from part of Dunstable, made a town 1809. Records to be sought: assessors, town (1755-), vital (1780-). Copied vital records: book. Earliest church records: Unitarian (1834-), Universalist (1841-). Books: histories. FHL microfilms (MSA): history, vital (to 1850). Library: Littlefield Library, 252 Middlesex Rd. (01879), 1-617-649-7361. N

13tt. Town of Wakefield. Established 1812 as Town of South Reading from part of Reading, name changed to Town of Wakefield 1868. Records to be sought: assessors, miscellaneous (1852-), town (1812-), vital (1812-). Copied vital records: book. Earliest church records: Congregational (1722-), Baptist (1800-). Books: histories. FHL microfilms (MSA): church, genealogy, history, vital (to 1850). Library: Lucius Beebe Memorial Library, Main St. (01880), 1-617-245-0790. S

13uu. City of WALTHAM. Established 1738 from part of Watertown, land split off 1859 to form part of new Town of Belmont, made a city 1884. Records to be sought: assessors, city (1884-), miscellaneous (1828-), proprietors (1636-1742), town (1737-), vital (1737-). Copied vital records: book. Earliest church records: Congregational (1820-),

Methodist (1837–), Unitarian (1837–). Books: histories. FHL microfilms (MSA): assessors (1738–1820), church, genealogies, histories, town (1720–1875), vital (1720–1874). Libraries: Waltham Public Library, 735 Main St. (02154), 1-617-893-1750; American Jewish Historical Society, 2 Thornton Rd. (02154), 1-617-891-8110. S

13vv. Town of Watertown. Established 1630, split off Weston in 1713, split off Waltham 1738, land split off 1859 to form part of new Town of Belmont. Records to be sought: assessors, proprietors (1634–1742), soldiers, town (1630–), vital (1630–). Copied vital records: book. Earliest church records: Unitarian (1686–), Baptist (1830–), Methodist (1837–). Books: genealogy, histories, colonial and Revolutionary soldiers, town records (1635–). FHL microfilms (MSA): biography, cemetery, church, genealogies, histories, town (1630–1829), vital (1630–1851). Library: Watertown Public Library, 123 Main St. (02172), 1-617-924-5390. S

13ww. Town of Wayland. Established 1780 as Town of East Sudbury from part of Sudbury, name changed to Wayland in 1835. Records to be sought: assessors (1780–), miscellaneous, town (1780–), vital (1780–). Copied vital records: book. Earliest church records: Unitarian (1803–), Congregational (1818–). Books: histories, Civil War servicemen. FHL microfilms (MSA): assessors (1778–1854), cemetery, histories, town (1638–1908), treasurer (1845–66), vital (1676–1860). Library: Wayland Free Public Library, 5 Concord Rd. (01778), 1-617-358-2311. S

13xx. Town of Westford. Established 1729 from part of Chelmsford. Records to be sought: assessors, miscellaneous (1805–), town (1726–), vital (1728–). Copied vital records: book. Earliest church records: Unitarian (1727–), Congregational (1828–). Books: histories. FHL microfilms (MSA): assessors (1722–83), cemetery, church, genealogy, history, military, school (1750–1872), town (1726–1879), treasurer (1796–1835), vital (1701–1879). Library: J. V. Fletcher Library, 50 Main St. (01886), 1-617-692-5555. N

13yy. Town of Weston. Established 1713 from part of Watertown, land split off 1754 to form part of new Town of Lincoln. Records to be sought: assessors (1820–), miscellaneous (1784–), selectmen (1754–), soldiers, town (1746–), vital (1713–). Copied vital records: book. Earliest church records: Unitarian (1709–), Baptist (1784–). Books: histories, town records (1707–1900). FHL microfilms (MSA): assessors (1757–1859), biography, church, genealogies, histories, town (1683–1882), vital (1703–1900). Library: Weston Public Library, 356 Boston Post Rd. (02193), 1-617-893-3312. S

13zz. Town of Wilmington. Established 1730 from parts of Reading and Woburn. Records to be sought: assessors, miscellaneous, town (1730-), vital (1730-). Copied vital records: book. Earliest church records: Congregational (1733-). Books: histories. FHL microfilms (MSA): assessors (1731-1872), town (1766-1876), vital (1716-1898), voters (1789-1838). Library: Wilmington Memorial Library, Middlesex Ave. (01887), 1-617-658-2967. N

13aaa. Town of Winchester. Established 1850 from parts of Medford, West Cambridge (Arlington), and Woburn. Records to be sought: assessors (1850-), miscellaneous, selectmen, town (1849-), vital (1849-). Copied vital records: see parent towns. Earliest church records: Congregational (1840-), Baptist (1852-). Books: histories, church members, war records. FHL microfilms (MSA): biography, histories, military. Library: Winchester Public Library, 80 Washington St. (01890), 1-617-721-7171. S

13bbb. City of WOBURN. Established 1642 from tract called Charlestowne Village, land split off 1730 to form part of new Town of Wilmington, split off Burlington in 1799, land split off 1850 to form part of new Town of Winchester, made a city 1888. Records to be sought: assessors, miscellaneous (1640-), proprietors (1738-65), selectmen (1640-), town (1640-), vital (1640-). Copied vital records: book. Earliest church records: Congregational (1732-), Baptist (1781-). Books: histories, colonial soldiers, deeds (1649-1700). FHL microfilms (MSA): cemetery, church, genealogy, history, military, selectmen (1673-1775), town (1673-1853), vital (1641-1922). Library: Woburn Public Library, 45 Pleasant St. (01801), 1-617-933-0148. Genealogy, S

14. Nantucket County

Nantucket County established 1695 from area that was previously Dukes County, NY. County seat Nantucket (02554). Records to be sought: courts of common pleas (1721-1859), courts of sessions (1721-1827), deed (1659-), marriage (1766-90), naturalization (1889-), notary (1840-80), probate (1680-92, 1706-), superior court (1859-), superior court of judicature (1695-1780), supreme judicial court (in Bristol County). Census: Pre-1800E, 1790R, 1800R, 1810R, 1820RI, 1830R, 1840RP, 1850RAIM, 1855S, 1860RAIM, 1865S, 1870RAIM, 1880RAIM, 1890C, 1900R, 1910R. Books: biography (1941), history (1856/71/75/80/82/95, 1914/15/24/36/ 44/49/70). FHL microfilms (MSA): cemetery, courts of common pleas (1721-1859), courts of sessions (1721-1816), deeds (1657-1875), genealogy, histories, probate (1706-1867), proprietors (1716-1887). Deed repository: at Nantucket.

14a. Town of Nantucket. Mentioned in NY records 1687 as Sherborn, granted by NY to MA 1692, name changed 1795 to Nantucket. Records to be sought: proprietors (1716–), selectmen and assessors, town (1699–), vital (1662–). Copied vital records: book. Earliest church records: Quaker (1708–), Congregational (1767–). Books: Congregational Church members, histories, genealogies. FHL microfilms (MSA): Episcopal (1842–84), genealogy, histories, Quaker (1642–1899), selectmen (1784–1855), town (1695–1852), vital (1662–1875). Libraries: Nantucket Athenaeum Library, India St. (02554), 1-617-228-1110; Nantucket Historical Association (02554), 1-617-228-1655.

15. Norfolk County

Norfolk County established 1793 from Suffolk County. County seat Dedham (02026). Do not confuse with Old Norfolk County which was in existence 1643–80. Records to be sought: courts of common pleas (1793–1859), courts of sessions (1793–1822), deed (1793–), marriage (1793–5), notary (1849–81), probate (1793–), superior court (1859–), supreme judicial court (1793–). Census: Pre-1800E, 1800R, 1810R, 1820RI, 1830R, 1840RP, 1850RAIM, 1855S, 1860RAIM, 1865S, 1870RAIM, 1880RAIM, 1890C, 1900R, 1910R. Books: biography (1884/98, 1918), history (1884, 1919). FHL microfilms (MSA): biography, courts of common pleas (1793–1858), deeds (1793–1901), histories, probate (1793–1929), supreme judicial court (1793–1859). Deed repository: at Dedham.

15a. Town of Avon. Established 1888 from part of Stoughton. Records to be sought: assessors (1888–), miscellaneous (1888–), selectmen (1888–), town (1888–), vital (1888–). Copied vital records: see Stoughton. Earliest church records: see Stoughton. Books: see Norfolk County histories. FHL microfilms (MSA): town archives inventory. Library: Avon Public Library, 280 W. Main St. (02322), 1-617-583-0378.

15b. Town of Bellingham. Established 1719 from parts of Dedham, Mendon, and Wrentham. Records to be sought: assessors, general (1720–), miscellaneous (1802–), proprietors (1713–1813), selectmen, vital (1716–). Copied vital records: book. Earliest church records: Baptist (1737–). Books: histories. FHL microfilms (MSA): assessors (1811–58), cemetery, church, history, poor (1831–51), selectmen (1835–55), town (1774–1860), town archives inventory, treasurer (1753–1824), vital (1716–1860). Library: Bellingham Public Library, Common St. (02019), 1-617-966-1660.

15c. Town of Braintree. Established 1640 from part of Boston, land split off 1792 to form part of new town of Quincy, Randolph split off in 1793. Records to be sought: assessors (1792-), miscellaneous (1792-), selectmen (1688-), town (1641-), vital (1640-). Copied vital records: book. Earliest church records: Congregational (1825-). Books: histories. FHL microfilms (MSA): biography, church, genealogy, histories, town (1640-1850), vital (1640-1848). Libraries: Thayer Public Library, 798 Washington St. (02184), 1-617-848-0405; Braintree Historical Society Library, 786 Washington St. (02184), 1-617-848-1640.

15d. Town of Brookline. Established 1705 from part of Boston. Records to be sought: assessors, selectmen, town (1686-), vital (1686-). Copied vital records: book. Earliest church records: Baptist (1828-), Unitarian (1834-). Books: records (1634-1838), histories, maps, genealogy. FHL microfilms (MSA): assessors (1763-1857), vital (1634-1857). Library: Public Library of Brookline, 361 Washington St. (02146), 1-617-730-2360.

15e. Town of Canton. Established 1797 from part of Stoughton. Records to be sought: general (1797-), miscellaneous (1797-), selectmen, soldiers, town (1797-), vital (1797-). Copied vital records: book. Earliest church records: Unitarian (1717-), Baptist (1814-), Universalist (1819-). Books: histories. FHL microfilms (MSA): assessors (1801/20/29), histories, selectmen (1813-44), town (1797-1850), vital (1758-1900). Library: Canton Public Library, 786 Washington St. (02021), 1-617-828-0177.

15f. Town of Cohasset. Established 1770 as a district from part of Hingham, made a town 1775. Records to be sought: assessors, miscellaneous (1853-), proprietors (1636-), selectmen (1882-), town (1770-), vital (1770-). Copied vital records: book. Earliest church records: Unitarian (1721-), Congregational (1824-). Books: histories, genealogy. FHL microfilms (MSA): genealogy, history, land grants and mortgages (1635-1869), school (1849-94), selectmen (1812-57), town (1717-1864), treasurer (1814-59, 1891-8), vital (1732-1857). Library: Paul Pratt Memorial Library, 106 S. Main St. (02025), 1-617-383-1348.

15g. Town of Dedham. Recognized in 1636 as a plantation above the falls of the Charles River, Medfield split off 1650, Needham split off 1711, land split off 1719 to form part of new Town of Bellingham, Walpole split off 1724, Dover split off 1784, land split off 1868 to form part of new Town of Hyde Park, land split off 1872 to form part of new Town of Norwood, Westwood split off 1897. Records to be sought: general (1636-), miscellaneous (1832-), proprietors (1636-), selectmen and assessors (1738-), vital (1636-). Copied vital records: book. Earliest church records: Unitarian (1638-), Congregational (1820-). Books: early town records, births and deaths (1844-96), land grants

(1636-1876), histories. FHL microfilms (MSA): cemetery, church, histories, land (1636-1961), town (1636-1813), vital (1635-1961). Libraries: Dedham Public Library, 43 Church St. (02026), 1-617-326-0583; Dedham Historical Society Library, 612 High St. (02026), 1-617-326-1385.

15h. Town of Dover. Established 1784 as a district from part of Dedham, made a town 1836. Records to be sought: general (1784-), miscellaneous (1866-), selectmen and assessors, town (1784-), vital (1784-). Copied vital records: book. Earliest church records: Unitarian (1832-), Congregational (1838-), Baptist (1838-). Books: biography, military lists, early deeds, history. FHL microfilms (MSA): biography, genealogy, histories, vital (to 1850). Library: Dover Town Library, 56 Dedham St. (02030), 1-617-785-0953.

15i. Town of Foxboro. Established 1778 from parts of Stoughton, Stoughtonham (later called Sharon), Walpole, and Wrentham. Records to be sought: assessors, miscellaneous (1778-), selectmen, soldiers, town (1777-), vital (1777-). Copied vital records: book. Earliest church records: Universalist (1809-), Baptist (1816-). Books: histories. FHL microfilms (MSA): town (1778-1849), vital (1753-1856). Library: Boyden Library, 10 Bird St. (02035), 1-617-543-8882.

15j. Town of Franklin. Established 1778 from part of Wrentham, land split off 1870 to form part of new Town of Norfolk. Records to be sought: assessors (1825-), miscellaneous, parish (1737-78), selectmen, soldiers, town (1778-), vital (1778-). Copied vital records: book. Earliest church records: Congregational (1738-), Methodist (1854-), Universalist (1856-). Books: histories, vital (1778-1872). FHL microfilms (MSA): biography, early settlers, histories, vital (1778-1872). Library: Franklin Public Library, School and Main Sts. (02039), 1-617-528-0371.

15k. Town of Holbrook. Established 1872 from part of Randolph. Records to be sought: assessors, selectmen, town (1872-), vital (1872-). Copied vital records: see Randolph. Earliest church records: Congregational (1856-). Books: histories. FHL microfilms (MSA): town archives inventory. Library: Holbrook Public Library, 2 Plymouth St. (02343), 1-617-767-3644.

15ℓ. Town of Medfield. Made a village 1650 from part of Dedham, made a town 1651, Medway split off in 1713. Records to be sought: assessors (1829-), miscellaneous (1831-), proprietors (1719-), selectmen, town (1649-), vital (1651-). Copied vital records: book. Earliest church records: Unitarian (1652-), Baptist (1776-). Books: histories. FHL microfilms (MSA): genealogy, history, town (1649-1788), vital

(1651–1876). Library: Memorial Public Library, 468 Main St. (02052), 1–617–359–4544.

15m. Town of Medway. Established 1713 from part of Medfield, land split off 1870 to form part of new Town of Norfolk, Millis split off 1885. Records to be sought: assessors, miscellaneous, selectmen, town (1713–), vital (1713–). Copied vital records: book. Earliest church records: Congregational (1748–), Baptist (1819–). Books: biography, genealogy, histories. FHL microfilms (MSA): biography, Congregational (1750–1860), genealogy, histories, town (1714–1869), vital (1713–1849). Library: Medway Public Library, 26 High St. (02053), 1–617–533–2461.

15n. Town of Millis. Established 1885 from part of Medway. Records to be sought: assessors (1885–), miscellaneous (1885–), town (1885–), vital (1885–). Copied vital records: see Medway. Earliest church records: Congregational (1648–). Book: history. FHL microfilms (MSA): vital (1885–1965). Library: Millis Public Library, Auburn Rd. (02054), 1–617–376–8282.

15o. Town of Milton. Established 1662 from part of Dorchester, land split off 1868 to form new Town of Hyde Park (later annexed to Boston). Records to be sought: miscellaneous, selectmen and assessors, town (1668–), vital (1668–). Copied vital records: book. Earliest church records: Unitarian (1678–), Congregational (1839–). Books: vital (1662–1843), town (1662–1729), biography, histories, tax (1674–1800). FHL microfilms (MSA): assessors (1775–1859), cemetery, histories, mortgages and deeds (1785–1857), town (1662–1859), vital (1662–1856). Library: Milton Public Library, 476 Canton Ave. (02186), 1–617–698–5707.

15p. Town of Needham. Established 1711 from part of Dedham, Wellesley split off 1881. Records to be sought: assessors, miscellaneous (1832–), selectmen, soldiers, town (1711–), vital (1711–1801, 1854–). Copied vital records: microfiche. Earliest church records: Unitarian (1778–), Baptist (1854–). Books: histories. FHL microfilms (MSA): Episcopal (1894–1917), history, selectmen (1799–1850), town (1711–1862), treasurer (1769–84), vital (1702–1863). Library: Needham Free Public Library, 1139 Highland Ave. (02194), 1–617–455–7559.

15q. Town of Norfolk. Established 1870 from parts of Franklin, Medway, Walpole, and Wrentham. Records to be sought: parish, selectmen and assessors, town (1870–), vital (1870–). Copied vital records: see parent towns. Earliest church records: Congregational (1796–), Baptist (1842–). FHL microfilms (MSA): history. Library: Norfolk Public Library, 139 Main St. (02056), 1–617–528–3380.

15r. Town of Norwood. Established 1872 from parts of Dedham and Walpole. Records to be sought: assessors (1872-), selectmen (1872-), town (1872-), vital (1872-). Copied vital records: see Dedham and Walpole. Earliest church records: Congregational (1730-), Universalist (1827-). Books: histories. Library: Morrill Memorial Library, Walpole St. (02062), 1-617-769-0200.

15s. Town of Plainville. Established 1905 from part of Wrentham. Records to be sought: assessors (1905-), selectmen (1905-), town (1905-), vital (1905-). Copied vital records: see Wrentham. Earliest church records: see Wrentham. Library: Plainville Public Library (02762), 1-617-695-1784.

15t. City of QUINCY. Established 1792 as a town from part of Braintree, made a city 1888. Records to be sought: city (1888-), parish (1643-1865), town (1792-1888), vital (1792-). Copied vital records: microfiche. Earliest church records: Episcopal (1728-), Universalist (1831-), Congregational (1841-). Books: histories. FHL microfilms (MSA): cemetery, Episcopal (1728-1921), histories, town (1792-1894), vital (1792-1970). Libraries: Thomas Crane Public Library, 40 Washington St. (02269), 1-617-471-2400; Quincy Historical Society Library, 8 Adams St. (02169), 1-617-773-1144.

15u. Town of Randolph. Established 1793 from part of Braintree, Holbrook split off 1872. Records to be sought: selectmen and assessors, town (1793-), vital (1793-). Copied vital records: microfiche. Earliest church records: Congregational (1728-), Baptist (1819-). Books: histories. FHL microfilms (MSA): town (1792-1961), vital (1795-1962). Library: Turner Free Library, Crawford Square (02368), 1-617-963-3000.

15v. Town of Sharon. Established 1765 as District of Stoughtonham, made a town 1775, land split off 1778 to form part of new Town of Foxborough, name changed to Sharon 1783. Records to be sought: assessors, miscellaneous (1832-), town (1740-), vital (1740-). Copied vital records: book. Earliest church records: Congregational (1740-), Baptist (1814-). Books: histories, church records. FHL microfilms (MSA): assessors (1740-1839), Congregational (1741-1928), town (1740-1856), vital (1754-1850). Library: Sharon Public Library, N. Main St. (02067), 1-617-784-5974.

15w. Town of Stoughton. Established 1726 from part of Dorchester, District of Stoughtonham (later Town of Sharon) split off 1765, land split off 1778 to form part of new Town of Foxborough, Avon split off 1888. Records to be sought: miscellaneous, selectmen and assessors, town (1726-), vital (1726-). Copied vital records: book. Earliest church records: Congregational (1743-), Universalist (1743-), Baptist (1785-). Books: vital (1727-1800), histories. FHL microfilms (MSA): assessors (1724-1823), town (1715-1886), vital (1717-1886). Library: Stoughton Public Library, 84 Park St. (02072), 1-617-344-2711.

15x. Town of Walpole. Established 1724 from part of Dedham, land split off 1778 to form part of new Town of Foxborough, land split off 1870 to form part of new Town of Norfolk, land split off 1872 to form part of new Town of Norwood. Records to be sought: miscellaneous (1724-), selectmen, town (1724-), vital (1724-). Copied vital records: book. Earliest church records: Unitarian (1724-), Congregational (1826-). Books: histories. FHL microfilms (MSA): assessors (1842-8), Episcopal (1887-1921), histories, Methodist, town (1724-1885), vital (to 1949). Library: Walpole Public Library, Common St. (02091), 1-617-668-5497.

15y. Town of Wellesley. Established 1881 from part of Needham. Records to be sought: assessors, miscellaneous (1881-), selectmen, town (1881-), vital (1881-). Copied vital records: see Needham. Earliest church records: Congregational (1798-). Books: histories. FHL microfilms (MSA): cemetery, Episcopal (1891-1913), histories. Library: Wellesley Free Library, 530 Washington St. (02181), 1-617-235-1610.

15z. Town of Westwood. Established 1897 from part of Dedham. Records to be sought: assessors (1897-), miscellaneous (1897-), selectmen, town (1897-), vital (1897-). Copied vital records: see Dedham. Earliest church records: see Dedham. Book: history. FHL microfilms (MSA): directory (1930-1). Library: Westwood Public Library, 668 High St. (02090), 1-617-326-7562.

15aa. Town of Weymouth. Established 1635 from tract of land called Wessaguscus. Records to be sought: miscellaneous (1642-), selectmen, soldiers (1642-), town (1642-), vital (1642-). Copied vital records: book. Earliest church records: Congregational (1723-), Methodist (1822-). Books: histories, church records. FHL microfilms (MSA): Episcopal (1867-1939), genealogy, histories, proprietors (1642-4), town (1636-1860), vital (to 1850). Library: Tufts Library, 46 Broad St. (02188), 1-617-337-1402.

15bb. Town of Wrentham. Established 1673 from tract of land called Wollonopaug as approved by Dedham, land split off 1719 to form part of new Town of Bellingham, Franklin split off 1778, land split off 1788 to form part of new Town of Foxborough, land split off 1870 to form part of new Town of Norfolk, Plainville split off 1905. Records to be sought: assessors, miscellaneous (1794-), proprietors (1662-), selectmen, town (1660-), vital (1660-). Copied vital records: book. Earliest church records: Congregational (1692-), Baptist (1823-). Books: histories. FHL microfilms (MSA): assessors (1663-1776, 1818-56), Episcopal (1865-1908), history, selectmen (1760-81), town (1656-1885), vital (1660-1850). Library: Fiske Public Library, East St. (02093), 1-617-384-2761.

16. Old Norfolk County

Old Norfolk County established 1643, disestablished 1679. Towns of Salisbury, Haverhill and Amesbury transferred to Essex County, all others to NH. Records now at Salem (in Essex County). Records to be sought: court (1654-79), deed (1637-1714), marriage (1654-91), probate (1637-1714). FHL microfilms (MSA): county court (1654-79), deed (1647-1714), probate (1647-1714).

17. Plymouth County

Plymouth County established 1685 from Plymouth Colony. County seat Plymouth (02360). Records prior to 1685 are to be found in the Plymouth Colony records, the originals of which are in Plymouth. Records to be sought: county court (1620-97), courts of common pleas (1687-1859), courts of sessions (1686-1827), deed (1620-), marriage (1726-37), naturalization (1812-), notary (1768-1884), probate (1633-), superior court (1859-), superior court of judicature (1693-1780), supreme judicial court (1780-), vital records (1620-97, 1724-88). Census: Pre-1800E, 1790R, 1800R, 1810R, 1820RI, 1830R, 1840RP, 1850RAIM, 1855S, 1860RAIM, 1865S, 1870RAIM, 1880RAIM, 1890C, 1900R, 1910R. Books: biography (1884/97), history (1867/84, 1986), church records (1620-1859), colony records (1620-92), court records (1686-1859), marriages (to 1650), marriages (1692-1746), probate (1620-91), probate (1686-1881), vital records (1633-89). FHL microfilms (MSA): biography, court orders (1702-1859), courts of sessions (1686-1817), deeds (1620-1900), marriages (1692-1823), probate (1633-1967), vital (1635-1825). Deed repository: at Plymouth.

17a. Town of Abington. Established 1712 from part of Bridgewater and some adjacent land, land split off 1727 to form part of new Town of Hanover, Rockland split off 1874, land split off 1875 to form new Town of South Abingdon. Records to be sought: assessors, general (1712-), miscellaneous (1824-), selectmen, soldiers, town (1767-), vital (1749-). Copied vital records: book. Earliest church records: Congregational (1720-). Books: histories. FHL microfilms (MSA): histories, town (1712-1860), vital (1712-1860).

17b. Town of Bridgewater. Established 1656, land split off 1712 to form part of new Town of Abington, North Bridgewater (later called

Brockton) split off 1821, West Bridgewater split off 1822, East Bridgewater split off 1823. Records to be sought: assessors, miscellaneous (1656–), proprietors (1675–1827), selectmen, town (1656–), vital (1656–). Copied vital records: book. Earliest church records: Unitarian (1716–), Episcopal (1747–). Books: genealogy, histories. FHL microfilms (MSA): assessors (1837–50), cemetery, Congregational (1747–1980), genealogy, histories, proprietors (1672–1834), selectmen (1703–1863), school (1826–55), town (1656–1853), treasurer (1775–1855), vital (1656–1853). Library: Bridgewater Public Library, 15 South St. (02324), 1-617-697-2525.

17c. City of BROCKTON. Established 1821 as Town of North Bridgewater from part of Bridgewater, name changed 1874 to Brockton, made a city 1881. Records to be sought: assessors, city (1882–), miscellaneous, town (1821–81), vital (1821–). Copied vital records: book. Earliest church records: Congregational (1737–). Books: biography, genealogies, histories. FHL microfilms (MSA): genealogy, histories, vital (to 1850). Library: Brockton Public Library System, 304 Main St. (02401), 1-617-587-2515.

17d. Town of Carver. Established 1790 from part of Plympton. Records to be sought: selectmen and assessors (1853–), soldiers, town (1790–), vital (1790–). Copied vital records: book. Earliest church records: Congregational (1780–), Baptist (1789–). Book: history. FHL microfilms (MSA): cemetery, history, treasurer (1820–70), vital (to 1850). Library: Carver Public Library, Route 58 Main St. (02330), 1-617-866-4038.

17e. Town of Duxbury. Established 1637, Bridgewater split off 1656, land split off 1717 to form part of new Town of Pembroke. Records to be sought: assessors, miscellaneous, proprietors (1709–), selectmen, soldiers, town (1686–), vital (1645–). Copied vital records: book. Earliest church records: Quaker (1702–), Unitarian (1739–). Books: histories, town (1642–1770). FHL microfilms (MSA): genealogy, histories, militia (1851–1939), proprietors (1702–71), town (1645–1826), vital (1645–1964). Library: Duxbury Free Library, 147 St. George St. (02332), 1-617-934-5682.

17f. Town of East Bridgewater. Established 1823 from part of Bridgewater, land split off 1875 to form part of new Town of South Abington (later called Whitman). Records to be sought: miscellaneous (1823–), proprietors (1675–1827), selectmen and assessors, town (1823–), vital (1823–). Copied vital records: book. Earliest church records: Unitarian (1724–). Books: histories. FHL microfilms (MSA): Congregational, town (1823–67), vital (1769–1870). Library: East Bridgewater Public Library, 32 Union St. (02333), 1-617-378-2821.

17g. Town of Halifax. Established 1734 from parts of Middleborough, Pembroke, and Plympton. Records to be sought: assessors, miscellaneous (1755–), selectmen, town (1735–), vital (1735–). Copied vital records: book. Earliest church records: Congregational (1824–). Books: histories. FHL microfilms (MSA): history, town (1734–1856), vital (1730–1856). Library: Holmes Public Library, 516 Plymouth St. (02338), 1-617-293-2271.

17h. Town of Hanover. Established 1727 from parts of Abington and Scituate. Records to be sought: miscellaneous, selectmen and assessors, town (1727–), vital (1727–). Copied vital records: book. Earliest church records: Congregational (1728–), Episcopal (1782–). Books: histories, vital (1727–1857), Congregational (1727–1865), cemetery (1727–1894). FHL microfilms (MSA): Episcopal (1725–1905), genealogy, history, militia (1841–1907), soldiers (1861–5), town (1727–99), vital (1712–1857). Library: John Curtis Free Library, Hanover St. (02339), 10617-826-2972.

17i. Town of Hanson. Established 1820 from part of Pembroke. Records to be sought: general (1820–), miscellaneous (1820–), selectmen and assessors, vital (1820–). Copied vital records: book. Earliest church records: Congregational (1746–). Book: history. FHL microfilms (MSA): soldiers (1861–5), town (1779–1941), vital (1779–1941). Library: Hanson Public Library, School St., RFD, South Hanson (02351), 1-617-293-2151.

17j. Town of Hingham. Established 1634 as Town of Barecove, name changed 1635 to Hingham, District of Cohasset split off 1770. Records to be sought: miscellaneous, proprietors (1635–), selectmen and assessors, town (1635–), vital (1635–). Copied vital records: manuscript in NEHGS. Earliest church records: Unitarian (1720–), Episcopal (1818–). Books: histories, early settlers. FHL microfilms (MSA): biography, Episcopal (1880–1937), genealogy, history, soldiers (1861–5), vital (1635–1963). Library: Hingham Public Library, 66 Leavitt St. (02043), 1-617-749-0907.

17k. Town of Hull. Established 1644 from tract called Nantascot. Records to be sought: assessors (1860–), proprietors, town (1657–), vital. Copied vital records: book. Earliest church records: Episcopal (1816–). Book: history. FHL microfilms (MSA): Congregational (1725–66), town (1657–1841), vital (to 1850). Library: Hull Public Library, Main St. (02045), 1-617-925-2295.

17ℓ. Town of Kingston. Established 1726 from part of Plymouth. Records to be sought: miscellaneous, selectmen and assessors, town (1719–), vital (1719–). Copied vital records: book. Earliest church records: Unitarian (1720-), Baptist (1805-). Books: histories. FHL microfilms (MSA): assessors (1830-47), cemetery, Congregational (1720-1880), town (1717-1850), vital (1695-1885). Library: Frederick C. Adams Public Library, Summer St. (02364), 1-617-585-2557.

17m. Town of Lakeville. Established 1853 from part of Middleborough. Records to be sought: assessors, miscellaneous (1853-), selectmen (1853-), soldiers, town (1853-), vital (1853-). Copied vital records: see Middleborough. Earliest church records: Congregational (1719-). Book: history. FHL microfilms (MSA): cemetery. Library: Lakeville Public Library, 241 Main St. (02346), 1-617-947-9028.

17n. Town of Marion. Established 1852 from part of Rochester. Records to be sought: miscellaneous (1852-), selectmen and assessors (1880-), town (1852-), vital (1852-). Copied vital records: see Rochester. Earliest church records: Congregational (1703-). FHL microfilms (MSA): history. Library: Elizabeth Taber Library, 8 Spring St. (02738), 1-617-748-1252.

17o. Town of Marshfield. Established 1640 as Rexhame or Marshfield from a tract called Green Harbour, name Marshfield probably generally used by 1643, land split off 1712 to form part of new Town of Pembroke. Records to be sought: miscellaneous, proprietors, selectmen and assessors, town (1643-), vital (1643-). Copied vital records: book, microfiche. Earliest church records: Quaker (1692-), Congregational (1696-), Unitarian (1738-), Baptist (1788-). Books: biography, histories. FHL microfilms (MSA): Congregational (1696-1920), genealogy, histories, town (1631-1875), vital (1631-1875). Library: Ventress Memorial Library, Library Plaza (02050), 1-617-837-5035.

17p. Town of Mattapoisett. Established 1857 from part of Rochester. Records to be sought: assessors (1857-), miscellaneous (1857-), selectmen (1857-), town (1857-), vital (1857-). Copied vital records: see Rochester. Earliest church records: Quaker (1702-), Congregational (1736-). Books: histories. FHL microfilms (MSA): history. Library: Mattapoisett Free Public Library, Barstow St. (02739), 1-617-758-2213.

17q. Town of Middleborough. Established 1669 from a tract called Namassaket, land split off 1734 to form part of new Town of Halifax, Lakeville split off 1853. Records to be sought: assessors, miscellaneous (1708-), proprietors (1675-), town (1669-), vital (1669-). Copied vital records: book. Earliest church records: Congregational (1694-), Baptist (1756-). Books: histories. FHL microfilms (MSA): cemetery, Congregational (1710-1820), genealogy, histories, proprietors (1661-1887), selectmen (1736-1825), town (1658-1900), treasurer (1794-1850), vital (1674–1854). Library: Middleboro Public Library, North Main St. (02346), 1-617-974-0613.

17r. Town of Norwell. Established 1849 as Town of South Scituate from part of Scituate, name changed 1888 to Norwell. Records to be sought: assessors (1849–), selectmen (1849–), town (1849–), vital (1849–). Copied vital records: see Scituate. Earliest church records: Unitarian (1797–). Book: history. FHL microfilms (MSA): history. Library: Norwell Public Library, 64 South St. (02061), 1-617-659-2105.

17s. Town of Pembroke. Established 1712 from part of Duxbury and other adjacent land, land split off 1734 to form part of new Town of Halifax, Hanson split off 1820. Records to be sought: miscellaneous (1834–), selectmen and assessors, town (1711–), vital (1711–). Copied vital records: book. Earliest church records: Quaker (1708–), Unitarian (1764–). Book: history. FHL microfilms (MSA): history, proprietors (1702–71), Quaker (1676–1876), soldiers, town (1711–1841), Unitarian (1711–1899), vital (1711–1850). Library: Pembroke Public Library, Center St. (02359), 1-617-293-6771.

17t. Town of Plymouth. Established 1620, Plympton split off 1707, Kingston split off 1727, land split off 1739 to form part of new Town of Wareham. Records to be sought: miscellaneous, proprietors (1702–13), selectmen and assessors, town, vital. See Chapter 2, section 10. Copied vital records: book, microfiche. Earliest church records: Congregational (1620–), Unitarian (1620–). Books: see Chapter 2, section 10, histories. FHL microfilms (MSA): cemetery, Congregational (1620–1859), colony (1636–95), genealogies, histories, probate (1636–95), proprietor (1702–13), notary (1741–1830), town, Unitarian (1749–1824), vital (1620–1965). Libraries: Plymouth Public Library, 11 North St. (02360), 1-617-647-1927, genealogy; Pilgrim Society, Pilgrim Hall Library, 74 Court St. (02360), 1-617-746-1620.

17u. Town of Plympton. Established 1707 from part of Plymouth, land split off to form part of new Town of Halifax, Carver split off 1790. Records to be sought: assessors, general (1707–), vital (1689–). Copied vital records: book. Earliest church records: Congregational (1695–). Book: history. FHL microfilms (MSA): assessors (1783–1850), cemetery, Congregational (1780–1858), genealogy, histories, school (1831–55), town (1695–1863), treasurer (1796–1872), vital (1695–1924), voter (1812–53). Library: Plympton Public Library, 248 Main St. (02367), 1-617-585-4551.

17v. Town of Rochester. Established 1686 from tract called Scippican, land split off 1739 to form new Town of Wareham, Marion split off 1852, Mattapoisett split off 1857. Records to be sought: miscellaneous (1697–), proprietors (1679–), selectmen and assessors, town (1697–), vital (1697–). Copied vital records: book. Earliest church records: Congregational (1780–). FHL microfilms (MSA): history, Quaker (1646–1850), town (1673–1893), vital (1673–1866). Library: Joseph H. Plumb Memorial Library, New Bedford Rd. (02770), 1-617-763-8600.

17w. Town of Rockland. Established 1874 from part of Abington. Records to be sought: miscellaneous (1874–), selectmen and assessors, town (1874–), vital (1874–). Copied vital records: see Abington. Earliest church records: Congregational (1812–). Book: history. FHL microfilms (MSA): history. Library: Rockland Memorial Library, 366 Union St. (02370), 1-617-878-1236.

17x. Town of Scituate. Recognized 1633, land split off 1727 to form part of new Town of Hanover, South Scituate (later called Norwell) split off 1849. Records to be sought: miscellaneous (1665–), proprietors (1648–), selectmen and assessors, town (1665–), vital (1639–). Copied vital records: book. Earliest church records: Congregational (1634–), Unitarian (1695–). Books: histories. FHL microfilms (MSA): Episcopal (1725–1905), genealogy, histories, militia (1841–80), soldier, town (1640–1847), vital (to 1850). Libraries: Scituate Historical Society Library, 43 Cudworth Rd. (02066), 1-617-545-1083; Scituate Town Library, 85 Branch Rd. (02066), 1-617-545-6707.

17y. Town of Wareham. Established 1739 from parts of Rochester and Plymouth. Records to be sought: assessors, miscellaneous (1739–), town (1739–), vital (1739–). Copied vital records: book, microfiche. Earliest church records: Congregational (1739–). Books: histories. FHL microfilms (MSA): Christian (1831–48), Congregational (1739–1891), Episcopal (1882–1924), history, vital (1739–1833). Library: Wareham Free Library, 78 High St. (01571), 1-617-295-2343.

17z. Town of West Bridgewater. Established 1822 from part of Bridgewater. Records to be sought: miscellaneous (1823–), selectmen and assessors, town (1823–), vital (1822–). Copied vital records: book. Earliest church records: Unitarian (1721–). FHL microfilms (MSA): vital (to 1850). Library: West Bridgewater Public Library, 159 W. Center (02379), 1-617-583-2067.

17aa. Town of Whitman. Established 1875 as Town of South Abington from parts of Abington and East Bridgewater, name changed 1886 to Whitman. Records to be sought: miscellaneous (1875–), selectmen and assessors (1875–), town (1875–), vital (1875–). Copied vital records: see Abington and East Bridgewater. Earliest church records: Unitarian (1797–). FHL microfilms (MSA): history. Library: Whitman Public Library, South St. (02382), 1-617-447-2052.

18. Suffolk County

Suffolk County established 1643 from MA Bay Colony. County seat Boston (02108). Records before 1643 are in MA Bay Colony records which run into the Suffolk County records. Records to be sought: admiralty (1718-72), county court (1629-92), courts of common pleas (1692-1855), courts of sessions (1702-1822), deed (1629-), justice of peace (1787-1806), municipal court (1800-59), naturalization (1790-1888), notary (many), probate (1636-), Suffolk files of many courts (1618-1800), superior court (1855-), superior court of judicature (1693-1780), supreme judicial court (1780-). Census: Pre-1800E, 1790R, 1800R, 1810R, 1820RI, 1830R, 1840RP, 1850RAIM, 1855S, 1860RAIM, 1865S, 1870RAIM, 1880RAIM, 1890C, 1900R, 1910R. Books: biography (many volumes, see Chapter 2, section 3), history (Boston: 1824/48/56/61/71/81/82/84/92, 1903/12/16/29/47/66/70/74), county court (1671-80), court of assistants (1630-92), deeds (1629-97), early church records (1630-1868), early records (1630-99), governor and company records (1628-86), inferior court of pleas (1680-98), MA Bay Colony records (1628-41), notary (1644-51), probate index (1636-1894), superior court of judicature (1761-72), vital records (1630-1800), vital record index (1630-99). FHL microfilms (MSA): biography, county court (1629-92), court of admiralty (1718-22), courts of common pleas (1692-1855), courts of general sessions (1702-80), deed (1639-1920), genealogy, history, notary, probate (1636-1912), supreme judicial court (1686-1870), vital (1637-1774). Deed repository: at Boston.

18a. City of BOSTON. Established 1630, Braintree split off 1640, Brookline split off 1705, Chelsea split off 1739, made a city 1822, Roxbury annexed 1868, Dorchester annexed 1870, Charlestown annexed 1874, Brighton annexed 1874, West Roxbury annexed 1874, Hyde Park annexed 1912. Records to be sought: assessors (1780-), board of aldermen (1822-), church, common council (1822-), miscellaneous (1706-), proprietors (1634-1728), selectmen (1701-1822), town (1674-1822), vital (1630-). Records of annexed towns/cities are in Boston, and are listed below. See sections 18a1-18a6. Copied vital records: books, also in reports of Record Commissioners of Boston, Volumes 9, 24, 28, 30, microfiche. Earliest church records: Unitarian (1630-), Baptist (1665-), Congregational (1669-)., Episcopal (1686-). Books: histories, biographies, also see Chapter 2, Sections 10, 11, 15. FHL microfilms (MSA): Baptist (1665-), biography, birth (1630-1955), cemetery, Congregational (1630-), death (1630-1970), early town records (1634-1822), Episcopal (1703-), genealogies, histories, marriage (1646-1890), Methodist (1736-), obituaries (1704-1840), passenger lists (1820-91), Presbyterian (1730-), selectmen (1701-1822). Libraries: NEHGS; BPL; SLM; MHS; Congregational Library, 14 Beacon

St. (02108), 1-617-523-0470; Ancient and Honorable Artillery Company Library, Faneuil Hall (02109), 1-617-227-1638; Archives of the Society for the Preservation of New England Antiquities, 141 Cambridge St. (02114), 1-617-227-3956; Boston Athenaeum, 10 1/2 Beacon St. (02108), 1-617-227-0270; Bostonian Society Library, 15 State St. (02109), 1-617-242-5614; Boston University School of Theology Library (Methodist Collection), 745 Commonwealth Ave. (02215), 1-617-353-3034; Episcopal Diocese of MA, Diocesan Library and Archives, One Joy St. (02108), 1-617-742-4720; Grand Lodge of MA Ancient Free and Accepted Masons Library, 186 Tremont St. (02111), 1-617-426-6040; Unitarian Universalist Association Archives Library, 25 Beacon St. (02108), 1-617-742-2100.

18a1. Annexed Town of Brighton. Established 1807 from part of Cambridge, annexed by Boston 1874. Records to be sought: assessors, miscellaneous (1817-73), selectmen (1816-74), town (1807-74), vital (1787-1873). Look in Boston. Copied vital records: microfiche. Earliest church records: Unitarian (1772-), Congregational (1827-). Book: history. FHL microfilms (MSA): Episcopal (1872-1967), town (1807-74), vital (1771-1874). Libraries: see Boston; Archdiocese of Boston Archives, 2121 Commonwealth Ave. (02135), 1-617-254-0100.

18a2. Annexed City of CHARLESTOWN. Established 1630, Malden split off 1649, Stoneham split off 1725, Somerville split off 1842, made a city 1847, annexed by Boston 1874. Records to be sought: assessors (1721-1873), city (1847-74), miscellaneous (1628-1874), selectmen (1795-1847), soldiers, town (1629-1847), vital (1629-1873). Look in Boston. Copied vital records: book, microfiche. Earliest church records: Congregational (1632-), Baptist (1801-), Unitarian (1817-). Books: genealogies (1638-1802), Congregational (1632-1787), histories. FHL microfilms (MSA): Congregational (1632-1789), Episcopal (1820-1923), genealogy, histories, Methodist (1819-99), town (1629-1847), vital (1629-1880). Libraries: see Boston.

18a3. Annexed Town of Dorchester. Established 1630 from tract called Mattapan, Milton split off 1662, Stoughton split off 1726, land split off 1868 to form part of new Town of Hyde Park (later annexed by Boston), annexed by Boston 1870. Records to be sought: assessors, miscellaneous (1827-69), proprietors (1713-93), selectmen (1825-69), town (1633-), vital (1646-1869). Look in Boston. Copied vital records: book, also see Reports of Record Commissioners of Boston, Volumes 21, 36, microfiche. Earliest church records: Unitarian (1636-), Congregational (1804-). Books: Congregational (1636-1734), histories, biography. FHL microfilms (MSA): Congregational (1636-1845), Episcopal (1847-1919), genealogy, histories, proprietors, town (1632-1870), vital (1631-1869). Libraries: see Boston.

18a4. Annexed Town of Hyde Park. Established 1868 from parts of Dedham, Dorchester, and Milton, annexed by Boston 1912. Records to be sought: assessors, miscellaneous (1868–1912), selectmen, town (1868–1912), vital (1868–1912). Look in Boston. Copied vital records: see parent towns. Earliest church records: Episcopal (1860–), Congregational (1861–). Book: history. FHL microfilms (MSA): selectmen (1868–1912), town (1868–1912). Libraries: see Boston.

18a5. Annexed City of ROXBURY. Established 1630, made a city 1846, West Roxbury split off 1851, annexed by Boston 1868. Records to be sought: assessors, city (1849–67), miscellaneous (1806–46), selectmen (1783–84), town (1647–1849), vital (1630–1849). Look in Boston. Copied vital records: book, microfiche. Earliest church records: Unitarian (1641–), Baptist (1819–), Universalist (1820–). Books: histories, biography. FHL microfilms (MSA): Baptist (1821–84), cemetery, Congregational (1771–1860), Episcopal (1833–1970), history, miscellaneous (1787–1846), selectmen (1787–1846), town (1648–1846), vital (1630–1867). Libraries: see Boston.

18a6. Annexed Town of West Roxbury. Established 1851 from part of Roxbury, annexed by Boston 1874. Records to be sought: assessors, town (1851–73), vital (1851–73). Copied vital records: see Roxbury. Earliest church records: Unitarian (1712–), Congregational (1833–). Books: histories. FHL microfilms (MSA): Congregational (1712–1837), selectmen (1851–72), town (1851–73), vital (1851–73). Libraries: see Boston.

18b. City of CHELSEA. Established 1739 from part of Boston, North Chelsea (later called Revere) split off 1846, made a city 1857. Records to be sought: assessors, city (1857–), miscellaneous (1738–), selectmen (1843–57), town (1738–1857), vital (1738–). Copied vital records: book. Earliest church records: Unitarian (1838–), Baptist (1836–), Methodist (1839–). Books: histories. FHL microfilms (MSA): Episcopal (1841–1917), histories, militia (1849–64), soldiers, town (1738–1840), vital (to 1850). Library: Chelsea Public Library, 569 Broadway (02150), 1-617-884-2335.

18c. City of REVERE. Established 1846 as Town of North Chelsea from part of Chelsea, Winthrop split off 1852, name changed 1871 to Revere, made a city 1914. Records to be sought: city (1914–), selectmen and assessors, town (1846–1914), vital (1846–). Copied vital records: see Chelsea. Earliest church records: Unitarian (1715–), Congregational (1828–). Book: history. FHL microfilms (MSA): Episcopal (1885–1929), genealogy, history. Library: Revere Public Library, 179 Beach St. (02151), 1-617-284-0102.

19. Worcester County

Worcester County established 1731 from Suffolk and Middlesex Counties, County seat Worcester (01608). Since 1884 deeds also registered at Fitchburg. Records to be sought: courts of common pleas (1731-1859), courts of sessions (1731-1827), deed (1731-), justice of peace (1777-1836), marriage (1746-96), naturalization (1809-), notary (1831-84), probate (1731-), superior court (1859-), superior court of judicature (1731-80), supreme judicial court (1780-). Census: Pre-1800E, 1790R, 1800R, 1810R, 1820RI, 1830R, 1840RP, 1850RAIM, 1855S, 1860RAIM, 1865S, 1870RAIM, 1880RAIM, 1890C, 1900R, 1910R. Books: biography (1889/99, 1907/09/24), history (1793, 1879/89, 1924/34), court of general sessions (1731-7), probate index (1731-1881), warnings (1737-88). FHL microfilms (MSA): biographies, cemeteries, courts of common pleas (1731-1859), courts of sessions (1731-1862), deeds (1722-1889), genealogy, histories, militia (1781-1840), probate (1731-1920). Deed repository: Records 1731-1884 at Worcester, records 1884- for Southern District at Worcester, for Northern District at Fitchburg. In the town/city listings which follow, the pertinent districts are indicated with capital letters (N for Northern District, W for Worcester District) placed at the end of the listings.

19a. Town of Ashburnham. Established 1765 from tract called Dorcester-Canada, land split off 1767 to form part of new Town of Ashby, land split off 1785 to form part of new Town of Gardner. Records to be sought: assessors, miscellaneous (1736-), proprietors (1736-80), town, vital. Copied vital records: book. Earliest church records: Congregational (1824-), Methodist (1831-). Books: histories. FHL microfilms (MSA): genealogy, histories, vital (to 1850). Library: Stevens Public Library, 30 Main St. (01430), 1-617-827-4404. N

19b. Town of Athol. Established 1762 from tract called Payquage, land split off 1783 to form part of new District of Orange, land split off 1786 to form part of new Town of Gerry. Records to be sought: miscellaneous (1762-), proprietors (1749-1824), selectmen and assessors, town (1762-), vital (1843-). Copied vital records: book. Earliest church records: Unitarian (1750-), Baptist (1810-). Books: biographies, histories. FHL microfilms (MSA): biography, genealogy, histories, soldiers, town (1737-1844), vital (1737-1850). Library: Athol Public Library, 568 Main St. (01331), 1-617-249-9515. W

19c. Town of Auburn. Established 1778 as Town of Ward from parts of Leicester, Oxford, Sutton, and Worcester, name changed 1837 to Auburn. Records to be sought: assessors, miscellaneous (1832-), selectmen, soldiers, town (1740-), vital (1779-). Copied vital records: book, microfiche. Earliest church records: Congregational (1776-).

Book: history. FHL microfilms (MSA): cemetery, Congregational (1824-71), town (1761-1867), vital (1761-1867). Library: Auburn Public Library, 369 Southbridge St. (01501), 1-617-832-2081. W

19d. Town of Barre. Established 1753 as District of Rutland from part of Town of Rutland, made Town of Hutchinson in 1774, name changed 1776 to Barre. Records to be sought: assessors, miscellaneous (1762-), selectmen, soldiers, town (1762-), vital (1762-). Copied vital records: book. Earliest church records: Unitarian (1818-), Congregational (1827-), Baptist (1832-). Books: histories. FHL microfilms (MSA): cemetery, Congregational (1827-56), histories, miscellaneous (1637-1919), military (1775-1900), proprietors (1686-1770), town (1763-1927), vital (1752-1855). Library: Barre Town Library (02005), 1-617-355-2533. W

19e. Town of Berlin. Established 1784 as District of Berlin from parts of Bolton and Marlborough, made a town in 1812. Records to be sought: assessors, miscellaneous (1808-), selectmen (1861-), soldiers, town (1784-), vital (1739-). Copied vital records: book. Earliest church records: Congregational (1769-). Books: biography, histories. FHL microfilms (MSA): cemetery, Congregational (1778-1882), genealogy, histories, military (1775-1942), mortgages (1833-71), proprietors (1722-92), town (1779-1886), vital (to 1850). Library: Berlin Public Library, Carter St. (01503), 1-617-838-2812. W

19f. Town of Blackstone. Established 1845 from part of Mendon, Millville split off in 1916. Records to be sought: assessors, miscellaneous, selectmen, town (1845-), vital (1845-). Copied vital records: see Mendon. Earliest church records: Quaker (1812-83), Free Baptist (1822-), Congregational (1841-). Book: brief history. Library: Blackstone Public Library, Saint Paul St. (01504), 1-617-883-1931. W

19g. Town of Bolton. Established 1738 from part of Lancaster, land split off 1784 to form part of new District of Berlin. Records to be sought: assessors (1852-), miscellaneous, soldiers, town (1738-), vital (1738-). Copied vital records: book. Earliest church records: Quakers (1799-), Baptist (1833-), Unitarian (1834-). Books: histories. FHL microfilms (MSA): assessors (1788-1850), Baptist (1828-99), Congregational (1782-1927), history, miscellaneous (1765-1869), Quaker (1799-1884), Revolutionary soldiers, town (1771-1848), vital (1738-1917). Library: Bolton Public Library, 738 Main St. (01740), 1-617-778-2839. W

19h. Town of Boylston. Established 1786 from part of Shrewsbury, land split off 1808 to form part of new Town of West Boylston. Records to be sought: assessors (1797-), miscellaneous (1809-), selectmen (1863–), soldiers, town (1786–), vital (1786–). Copied vital records: book. Earliest church records: Congregational (1743–). Books: histories. FHL microfilms (MSA): Congregational (1776–1856), history, town (1786–1862), vital (to 1850). Library: Boylston Public Library, 695 Main St. (01505), 1-617-869-2371. W

19i. Town of Brookfield. Authorized 1673 from tract called Quobange, established 1718 as a town, land split off 1730 to form part of new Town of Western (later called Warren), land split off 1742 to form new District of New Braintree, North Brookfield split off in 1812, land split off 1848 to form West Brookfield, East Brookfield split off in 1920. Records to be sought: assessors, miscellaneous (1771–), proprietors (1702–67), town (1771–), vital (1771–). Copied vital records: book. Earliest church records: Unitarian (1755–), Baptist (1818–). Books: histories. FHL microfilms (MSA): Congregational (1755–1869), history, proprietors (1687–1804), town (1719–1853), vital (to 1850). Library: Merrick Public Library, Common (01506), 1-617-867-6339. W

19j. Town of Charlton. Established 1755 as a district, made a town in 1775, land split off 1816 to form part of new Town of Southbridge. Records to be sought: assessors, miscellaneous (1830–), soldiers, town (1780–1813, 1830–), vital (1750–). Copied vital records: book, microfiche. Earliest church records: Congregational (1761–). Books: brief histories. FHL microfilms (MSA): Congregational (1761–1836), history, town (1714–1865), vital (1714–1869). Library: Charlton Public Library, Main St. (01507), 1-617-248-7876. W

19k. Town of Clinton. Established 1850 from part of Lancaster. Records to be sought: assessors, miscellaneous (1850–), town (1850–), vital (1850–). Copied vital records: see Lancaster. Earliest church records: Congregational (1844–), Catholic (1845–), Baptist (1847–). Books: histories. FHL microfilms (MSA): history, record inventory. Library: Bigelow Free Public Library, 54 Walnut St. (01510), 1-617-365-5052. W

19ℓ. Town of Dana. Established 1801 from parts of Greenwich, Hardwick, and Petersham, absorbed 1927 by Petersham. Records to be sought: assessors (1801–), miscellaneous (1801–), selectmen (1866–), soldiers, town (1801–), vital (1801–). Copied vital records: book, microfiche. Earliest church records: Congregational (1852–), Methodist (1853–). Books: histories. FHL microfilms (MSA): see Petersham. Library: see Petersham.

19m. Town of Douglas. Recognized 1742 as the District of New Sherburn, established 1746, name changed to District of Douglas later in 1746, made a town 1775. Records to be sought: miscellaneous

(1749-), selectmen and assessors, town (1749-), vital (1749-). Copied vital records: book, microfiche. Earliest church records: Congregational (1747-). Book: history. FHL microfilms (MSA): genealogy, history, vital (to 1850). W

19n. Town of Dudley. Established 1732 from part of Oxford and some other land, land split off 1816 to form part of new Town of Southbridge, land split off 1832 to form part of new Town of Webster. Records to be sought: assessors (1840-), miscellaneous (1620-), selectmen, town (1732-), vital (1732-). Copied vital records: book. Earliest church records: Congregational (1744-). Books: histories. FHL microfilms (MSA): histories, mortgages (1832-65), town (1732-1878), vital (to 1850). Library: Pearle L. Crawford Memorial Library, Village St. (01570), 1-617-943-5333. W

19o. Town of East Brookfield. Established 1920 from part of Brookfield. Records to be sought: assessors, miscellaneous, selectmen, town, vital. Copied vital records: see Brookfield. Earliest church records: see Brookfield. Books: histories. FHL microfilms (MSA): see Brookfield. Library: East Brookfield Public Library, Depot Square (01515), 1-617-867-7928. W

19p. City of FITCHBURG. Established 1764 as a town from part of Lunenburg, land split off 1767 to form part of new Town of Ashby, made a city in 1872. Records to be sought: assessors, city (1873-), miscellaneous (1774-), proprietors, town (1764-1872), vital (1764-). Copied vital records: book. Earliest church records: Unitarian (1805-), Congregational (1823-). Books: biography, histories, older town records, military. FHL microfilms (MSA): histories, proprietors, soldiers, town (1719-), vital (1751-1873). Library: Fitchburg Public Library, 610 Main St. (01420), 1-617-345-9635. N

19q. City of GARDNER. Established 1785 as a town from parts of Ashburnham, Westminster, and Winchendon, made a city in 1921. Records to be sought: assessors, town (1785-), vital (1785-). Copied vital records: book. Earliest church records: Congregational (1828-), Baptist (1828-). Books: histories. FHL microfilms (MSA): biography, genealogy, histories, town (1785-1855), vital (1769-1879). Library: Levi Heywood Memorial Library, 57 City Hall Ave. (01440), 1-617-632-5298. W

19r. Town of Grafton. Established 1735 from tract called Hassanamisco. Records to be sought: assessors, miscellaneous (1735-), proprietors (1728-), selectmen, town (1735-), vital (1735-). Copied vital records: book. Earliest church records: Congregational (1731-), Baptist (1800-). Books: histories. FHL microfilms (MSA): Congregational

(1731-74), genealogy, history, proprietors (1728-1861), vital (1735-1872). Library: Grafton Public Library, Central Square (01509), 1-617-839-4649. W

19s. Town of Hardwick. Established 1739 from tract called Lambstown, land split off 1751 to form part of new District of New Braintree, land split off 1801 to form part of new Town of Dana (later absorbed by Petersham). Records to be sought: assessors (1825-), miscellaneous (1734-), proprietors (1734-), town (1734-), vital (1734-). Copied vital records: book. Earliest church records: Congregational (1736-). Books: genealogy, histories. FHL microfilms (MSA): Congregational (1736-86, 1833-1915), genealogy, history, selectmen (1818-97), Universalist (1841-52), vital (to 1850). W

19t. Town of Harvard. Established 1732 from parts of Groton, Lancaster, and Stow, land split off 1783 to form new District of Boxborough. Records to be sought: assessors (1726-), miscellaneous (1732-), town (1732-), vital (1732-). Copied vital records: book. Earliest church records: Unitarian (1733-), Baptist (1776-), Shakers (1791-). Books: histories. FHL microfilms (MSA): cemetery, Congregational (1773-1909), histories, vital (1732-1850). Library: Harvard Public Library, Harvard Common (01451), 1-617-456-3924. W

19u. Town of Holden. Established 1741 from part of Worcester, land split off 1808 to form part of new Town of West Boylston. Records to be sought: assessors (1787-), miscellaneous (1741-), proprietors (1722-), selectmen, town (1741-), vital (1741-). Copied vital records: book. Earliest church records: Congregational, Baptist (1804-). Books: histories. FHL microfilms (MSA): biography, histories, town (1741-1850), vital (1741-1850). Library: Gale Free Library, 23 Highland St. (01520), 1-617-829-4988. W

19v. Town of Hopedale. Established 1886 from part of Milford. Records to be sought: assessors, miscellaneous, town, vital. Copied vital records: see Milford. Earliest church records: see Milford. Book: history. FHL microfilms (MSA): histories. Library: Bancroft Memorial Library, 50 Hopedale St. (01747), 1-617-473-7692. W

19w. Town of Hubbardston. Established 1767 as a district from part of Rutland, made a town in 1775. Records to be sought: assessors, miscellaneous, soldiers, town (1767-), vital (1767-). Copied vital records: book. Earliest church records: Unitarian (1770-), Congregational (1810-). Books: histories. FHL microfilms (MSA): town (1767-1856), vital (1746-1886). Library: Hubbardston Public Library, Main St. (01452), 1-617-928-4775. W

19x. Town of Lancaster. Established 1654, land split off 1732 to form part of new Town of Harvard, Bolton split off in 1738, Leominster split off in 1740, Sterling split off in 1781, Clinton split off in 1850. Records to be sought: assessors, miscellaneous, proprietors (1653-1818), selectmen, town (1653-), vital (1653-). Copied vital records: book. Earliest church records: Unitarian (1836-), Congregational (1839-). Books: histories, military, town (1643-1725). FHL microfilms (MSA): cemetery, Congregational (1744-1813, 1839-1950), histories, proprietors (1649-1913), town (1649-1913), Unitarian (1644-1951), vital (1643-1969). Library: Lancaster Town Library, Main St. (01523), 1-617-365-2008. W

19y. Town of Leicester. Established 1714 from tract called Towtaid, Spencer split off in 1753, land split off 1765 to form part of new District of Paxton, land split off to form part of new Town of Ward (later called Auburn) in 1778. Records to be sought: assessors, proprietors (1714-76), town (1713-), vital (1713-). Copied vital records: book, microfiche. Earliest church records: Baptist (1737-), Congregational (1797-). Books: histories. FHL microfilms (MSA): genealogy, histories, vital (to 1850). Library: Leicester Public Library, 1136 Main St. (01524), 1-617-892-8236. W

19z. City of LEOMINSTER. Established 1740 from part of Lancaster, made a city in 1915. Records to be sought: assessors, miscellaneous (1701-), proprietors (1701-1847), selectmen, town (1740-), vital (1740-). Copied vital records: book. Earliest church records: Unitarian (1743-), Congregational (1822-), Methodist (1823-). Books: histories. FHL microfilms (MSA): biography, Congregational (1743-1907), histories, proprietors (1701-1847), vital (to 1850). Library: Leominster Public Library, 30 West St. (01453), 1-617-537-4811. N

19aa. Town of Lunenburg. Established 1728 from parts of Woburn and Dorchester and tracts called Turkey Hills and Boardman's Farm, Fitchburg split off in 1764. Records to be sought: miscellaneous (1728-), proprietors (to 1728), selectmen and assessors, soldiers, town (1728-), vital (1728-). Copied vital records: book. Earliest church records: Methodist (1805-), Congregational (1835-). Books: proprietors, town (1719-64). FHL microfilms (MSA): assessors (1761-70), biography, cemetery, deeds (1828-1946), genealogy, histories, proprietors (1729-1833), town (1719-1877), vital (1707-1877). Library: Ritter Memorial Library, 960 Massachusetts Ave. (01462), 1-617-582-7817. N

19bb. Town of Mendon. Established 1667 from tract called Qunshapage, land split off 1719 to form part of new Town of Bellingham, Uxbridge split off in 1727, land split off 1735 to form part of new Town of Upton, Milford split off in 1780, Blackstone split off in 1845. Records to be sought: assessors, miscellaneous, proprietors (1708-1815), selectmen, soldiers, town (1662-), vital (1662-). Copied vital records: book. Earliest church records: Quaker (1727-1841), Unitarian (1728-), Methodist (1741-). Books: genealogy, history, town records (1659-1880). FHL microfilms (MSA): biography, Congregational (1785-1866), genealogy, history, proprietors, town (1663-1862), vital (to 1878). Library: Taft Public Library, Main St. (01756), 1-617-473-3259. W

19cc. Town of Milford. Established 1780 from part of Mendon, Hopedale split off in 1886. Records to be sought: assessors, selectmen, town (1780-), vital (1758-). Copied vital records: book. Earliest church records: Congregational (1741-), Unitarian (1785-). Books: biography, history. FHL microfilms (MSA): biography, genealogy, histories, town (1777-1861), vital (to 1850). Library: Milford Town Library, 80 Spruce St. (01757), 1-617-473-2145. W

19dd. Town of Millbury. Established 1813 from part of Sutton. Records to be sought: assessors (1813-), town (1813-), vital (1813-). Copied vital records: book. Earliest church records: Congregational (1743-), Baptist (1836-). Books: history, vital statistics (1850-99). FHL microfilms (MSA): biography, Congregational (1718-1898), genealogy, property valuations (1813-53), treasurer (1832-89), town (1813-62), vital (1790-99). Library: Millbury Public Library, 128 Elm St. (01527), 1-617-865-1181. W

19ee. Town of Millville. Established 1916 from part of Blackstone. Records to be sought: assessors, miscellaneous, town, vital. Copied vital records: see Mendon. Earliest church records: see Blackstone. Book: brief history. W

19ff. Town of New Braintree. Established 1751 as a district from parts of Hardwick and Brookfield and some other land, made a town in 1775. Records to be sought: assessors, miscellaneous (1800-), selectmen, town (1751-), vital (1751-). Copied vital records: book. Earliest church records: Congregational (1779-). Book: history. FHL microfilms (MSA): vital (to 1850). Library: New Braintree Public Library (01531), 1-617-867-2071. W

19gg. Town of North Brookfield. Established 1812 from part of Brookfield. Records to be sought: assessors, miscellaneous (1862-), proprietors (1750-1812), selectmen, town (1862-), vital (1842-). Copied vital records: microfiche. Earliest church records: Congregational (1752-). Books: biography, histories, military. FHL microfilms (MSA): genealogy, history. Libraries: Merriam-Gilbert Public Library, Main St. (01585), 1-617-867-8784; Haston Free Public Library (01535), 1-

617-867-7978. W

19hh. Town of Northborough. Established 1766 as a district from part of Westborough, made a town in 1775. Records to be sought: assessors, selectmen, town (1744-), vital (1744-). Copied vital records: book. Earliest church records: Baptist (1827-), Congregational (1830-), Unitarian (1830-). Books: histories. FHL microfilms (MSA): cemetery, histories, town (1744-1843), vital (1761-1887). Library: Northborough Free Library, 34 Main St. (01532), 1-617-393-2401. W

19ii. Town of Northbridge. Established 1772 as a district from part of Uxbridge, made a town in 1775. Records to be sought: assessors, miscellaneous (1788-), selectmen, town (1772-), vital (1760-). Copied vital records: book. Earliest church records: Quaker (1730-), Congregational (1782-). Books: military records. FHL microfilms (MSA): Quaker (1783-1898), town (1733-1935), vital (1748-1850). W

19jj. Town of Oakham. Established 1762 as a district from part of Rutland, made a town 1775. Records to be sought: assessors, miscellaneous (1759-), selectmen, town (1759-), vital (1759-). Copied vital records: book. Earliest church records: Congregational (1773-). Books: histories, military records. FHL microfilms (MSA): biography, cemetery, Congregational (1773-1919), genealogy, histories, selectmen (1813-91), soldiers, town (1761-1954), vital (1751-1954). Library: Forbes Memorial Library, Maple St. (01068), 1-617-882-3372. W

19kk. Town of Oxford. Mentioned 1693 as a existing town, land split off 1732 to form part of new Town of Dudley, District of Charlton split off in 1754, land split off to form part of new town of Ward (later called Auburn) in 1778, land split off 1832 to form part of new Town of Webster. Records to be sought: assessors, miscellaneous, selectmen, town (1713-), vital (1713-). Copied vital records: book, microfiche. Earliest church records: Congregational (1720-), Universalist (1785-). Books: genealogy, histories, town records. FHL microfilms (MSA): financial (1796-1815), genealogy, histories, town (1800-62), vital (1714-1874). Library: Oxford Free Library, Main St. (01540), 1-617-987-2882. W

19££. Town of Paxton. Established 1765 from parts of Leicester and Rutland, made a town in 1775. Records to be sought: assessors (1821-), miscellaneous (1818-), selectmen (1881-), town (1765-), vital (1765-). Copied vital records: microfiche. Earliest church records: Congregational (1767-). Books: histories. FHL microfilms (MSA): cemetery, Congregational (1830-92), town (1749-1852), vital (1749-1852). Library: Richards Memorial Library, Richards Ave. (01612), 1-617-754-0793. W

19mm. Town of Petersham. Established 1754 from tract called Nichewoag, land split off 1801 to form part of new Town of Dana, Dana absorbed 1927. Records to be sought: assessors, miscellaneous (1832-), proprietors, selectmen (1841-), town (1780-), vital (1754-). Copied vital records: book. Earliest church records: Unitarian (1738-). Books: biography, histories. FHL microfilms (MSA): biography, cemetery, Congregational (1739-1961), history, town (1733-1888), Universalist (1837-48), vital (to 1850). Libraries: Petersham Historical Society Library, N. Main St. (01366), 1-617-724-3380; Petersham Memorial Library, Common (01366), 1-617-724-3405. W

19nn. Town of Phillipston. Established 1786 as Town of Gerry from parts of Athol and Templeton, name changed 1814 to Phillipston. Records to be sought: assessors, miscellaneous (1794-), selectmen, town (1794-), vital (1794-). Copied vital records: book. Earliest church records: Methodist (1829-), Congregational (1830-). Books: brief histories. FHL microfilms (MSA): assessors (1832-41), treasurer (1794-1817), vital (1764-1851). Library: Phillips Free Public Library, Athol (01331), 1-617-249-6828. W

19oo. Town of Princeton. Established 1759 as a district from part of Rutland and some adjacent land, made a town in 1771. Records to be sought: assessors, miscellaneous (1796-), proprietors (1714-70), selectmen, town (1761-), vital (1757-). Copied vital records: book. Earliest church records: Congregational (1767-). Books: histories. FHL microfilms (MSA): Baptist (1817-51), cemetery, Congregational (1764-1851), genealogy, histories, town (1762-1964), vital (to 1850). Library: Princeton Public Library, Mountain Rd. (01541), 1-617-464-2839. W

19pp. Town of Royalston. Established 1765 from tract called Royalshire, land split off 1783 to form part of new District of Orange. Records to be sought: assessors, miscellaneous (1765-), proprietors (1752-87), selectmen, soldiers, town (1765-), vital (1765-). Copied vital records: book. Earliest church records: Congregational (1766-), Baptist 1768-). Books: histories. FHL microfilms (MSA): histories, military, vital (1772-1849). Library: Phinehas S. Newton Library (01368), 1-617-249-3572. W

19qq. Town of Rutland. Established 1714 from tract called Naquag, Rutland District split off 1753, land split off 1759 to form part of new District of Princeton, Oakham split off in 1762, land split off 1765 to form part of new Town of Paxton, Hubbardston split off in 1767. Records to be sought: assessors (1832-), miscellaneous (1811-70), proprietors (1720-97), selectmen (1832-59), town (1720-), vital (1720-). Copied vital records: book. Earliest church records: Congregational (1727-). Books: biography, histories. FHL microfilms (MSA):

biography, histories, land (1720-99), mortgages (1832-63), miscellaneous (1770-99), town (1719-1860), vital (1720-1874). Library: Rutland Free Public Library, 246 Main St. (01543), 1-617-886-6266. W

19rr. Town of Shrewsbury. Boundaries defined in 1720, mentioned in 1722, established 1727, Boylston split off in 1786. Records to be sought: assessors, miscellaneous, proprietors (1718-1811), town (1719-), vital (1717-). Copied vital records: book, microfiche. Earliest church records: Congregational (1742-). Books: family register, histories. FHL microfilms (MSA): genealogy, histories, town (1717-1890), vital (1717-1890). Library: Shrewsbury Public Library, 609 Main St. (01545), 1-617-842-0081. W

19ss. Town of Southborough. Established 1727 from part of Marlborough. Records to be sought: assessors, miscellaneous (1768-), soldiers, town (1727-), vital (1731-). Copied vital records: book. Earliest church records: Baptist (1823-), Congregational (1831-). Books: history, military. FHL microfilms (MSA): assessors (1740-1887), Congregational (1791-1835), town (1723-1939), vital (to 1850). Library: Southborough Public Library, 25 Main St. (01772), 1-617-485-5031. W

19tt. Town of Southbridge. Established 1816 from parts of Charlton, Dudley, and Sturbridge. Records to be sought: assessors (1857-), miscellaneous (1816-), selectmen (1816-), town (1816-), vital (1816-). Copied vital records: book. Earliest church records: Baptist (1816-), Congregational (1816-). Books: histories. FHL microfilms (MSA): histories, town (1816-50), vital (to 1850). Libraries: Jacob Edwards Library, 236 Main St. (01550), 1-617-764-2544; Holland Public Library, RR2 (01550), 1-413-245-3607. W

19uu. Town of Spencer. Established 1753 as a district from part of Leicester, made a town in 1775. Records to be sought: assessors (1800-), miscellaneous (1800-), town (1744-), vital (1744-). Copied vital records: book, microfiche. Earliest church records: Baptist (1819-77), Congregational (1832-), Methodist (1843-). Books: histories. FHL microfilms (MSA): Congregational (1744-1819), histories, vital (to 1850). Library: Richard Sugden Public Library, Pleasant St. (01562), 1-617-885-3336. W

19vv. Town of Sterling. Established 1781 from part of Lancaster, land split off 1808 to form part of new Town of West Boylston. Records to be sought: assessors (1795-), miscellaneous (1828-), town (1795-), vital (1794-). Copied vital records: book. Earliest church records: Congregational (1745-). Books: histories. FHL microfilms (MSA): town

(1794-1849), vital (to 1850). Library: Conant Free Public Library, 4 Meetinghouse Hill Rd. (01564), 1-617-422-6409. W

19ww. Town of Sturbridge. Established 1738 from a tract called New Medfield, land split off 1816 to form part of new Town of Southbridge. Records to be sought: assessors, miscellaneous (1700-), proprietors, town (1738-), vital (1738-). Copied vital records: book. Earliest church records: Congregational (1736-), Baptist (1785-). Books: brief histories. FHL microfilms (MSA): history, vital (1734-1861). Library: Joshua Hyde Public Library, Maple St. (01566), 1-617-347-3735. W

19xx. Town of Sutton. Recognized 1714, land split off 1735 to form part of new Town of Upton, land split off 1778 to form part of new Town of Ward (later called Auburn), Millbury split off in 1813. Records to be sought: assessors, miscellaneous, proprietors (1714-1809), selectmen, soldiers, town (1715-), vital (1715-). Copied vital records: book, microfiche. Earliest church records: Congregational (1720-), Baptist (1785-). Books: brief histories. FHL microfilms (MSA): Congregational (1718-1898), history, proprietors (1704-1809), selectmen (1787-1810), town (1732-1835), treasurer (1731-1824), vital (1710-1877). Library: Sutton Free Public Library, Uxbridge Rd. (01527), 1-617-865-6939. W

19yy. Town of Templeton. Established 1762 from tract of land called Narragansett Number Six, land split off 1785 to form part of new Town of Gardner, land split off 1786 to form new Town of Gerry (later called Phillipston). Records to be sought: miscellaneous, proprietors (1733 ff), selectmen and assessors (1763-), town (1762-), vital (1762-). Copied vital records: book. Earliest church records: Unitarian (1756-), Baptist (1783-). Books: histories. FHL microfilms (MSA): histories, town (1733-1822), vital (1747-1850). Library: Boynton Public Library, Common St. (01468), 1-617-939-5582. W

19zz. Town of Upton. Established 1735 from parts of Hopkinton, Mendon, Sutton, and Uxbridge. Records to be sought: assessors, miscellaneous (1735-), town (1735-), vital (1735-). Copied vital records: book. Earliest church records: Congregational (1751-). Books: biography, histories. FHL microfilms (MSA): deeds (1743-1833), financial (1754-1850), soldiers, school (1841-68), vital (1736-1854). Library: Upton Town Library, Main St. (01568), 1-617-529-6272. W

19aaa. Town of Uxbridge. Established 1727 from part of Mendon, land split off 1735 to form part of new Town of Upton, land split off 1772 to form part of new Town of Northbridge. Records to be sought: assessors (1821-), miscellaneous (1805-), selectmen (1773-), town (1727-), vital (1730-). Copied vital records: book. Earliest church records:

Congregational (1730–), Unitarian (1797–). Books: histories. FHL microfilms (MSA): cemetery, Congregational (1797–1885), genealogy, Quaker (1783–1898), Revolutionary soldiers, town (1782–1848), treasurer (1768–1868), vital (1741–1858). Library: Uxbridge Free Public Library, 25 N. Main St. (01569), 1-617-278-3505. W

19bbb. Town of Warren. Established 1742 as Town of Western from parts of Brimfield and Brookfield, and land called Kingsfield, name changed to Warren in 1834. Records to be sought: assessors (1788–), miscellaneous (1741–), town (1741–), vital (1742–). Copied vital records: book. Earliest church records: Congregational (1824–). Books: histories. FHL microfilms (MSA): vital (to 1850). Library: Warren Public Library, Main St. (01083), 1-413-436-7690. W

19ccc. Town of Webster. Established 1832 from parts of Dudley and Oxford and some other land. Records to be sought: general (1832–), selectmen and assessors, vital (1832–). Copied vital records: book, microfiche. Earliest church records: Baptist (1814–), Methodist (1834–), Congregational (1838–). Books: histories, military. FHL microfilms (MSA): assessors (1832–40), town (1832–63), vital (1799–1908). Library: Chester C. Corbin Public Library, 1 Lake St. (01570), 1-617-943-0131. W

19ddd. Town of West Boylston. Established 1808 from parts of Boylston, Holden, and Sterling. Records to be sought: assessors, miscellaneous (1808–), selectmen, town (1808–), vital (1808–). Copied vital records: book. Earliest church records: Baptist (1818–), First Liberal (1830–). Books: genealogy, histories. FHL microfilms (MSA): genealogy, history, town (1808–61), vital (1752–1850). Library: Beaman Memorial Public Library, 8 Newton St. (01583), 1-617-835-3711. W

19eee. Town of West Brookfield. Established 1848 from part of Brookfield. Records to be sought: assessors (1848–), miscellaneous (1848–), selectmen (1848–), town (1848–), vital (1848–). Copied vital records: see Brookfield. Earliest church records: Congregational (1754–). Book: history.

19fff. Town of Westborough. Established 1717 from part of Middleborough, Northborough split off in 1766. Records to be sought: assessors, miscellaneous (1722–), town (1722–), vital (1717–). Copied vital records: book. Earliest church records: Congregational (1724–). Books: histories. FHL microfilms (MSA): Congregational (1808–1904), histories, vital (1694–1864). Library: Westborough Public Library, 55 West Main St. (01581), 1-617-366-0725. W

19ggg. Town of Westminster. Established 1759 as District of Westminster from tract of land called Narragansett Township Number Two, made a town 1770, land split off 1785 to form part of new Town of Gardner. Records to be sought: assessors, miscellaneous (1740-), proprietors (1728-59), selectmen, town (1759-), vital (1759-). Copied vital records: book. Earliest church records: Congregational (1820-), Unitarian (1820-), Baptist (1830-). Books: biographical, histories. FHL microfilms (MSA): genealogy, histories, town (1763-1874), vital (to 1850). Library: Forbush Memorial Library, Main St. (01473), 1-617-874-2172. N

19hhh. Town of Winchendown. Established 1764 from tract of land called Ipswich-Canada, land split off 1785 to form part of new Town of Gardner. Records to be sought: assessors (1859-), miscellaneous (1783-), proprietors (1737-97), selectmen (1859-), town (1764-), vital (1795-). Copied vital records: book. Earliest church records: Methodist (1796-), Advent Baptist (1798-), Congregational (1800-). Books: histories. FHL microfilms (MSA): justice of peace (1792-1805), genealogy, history, town (1735-1859), vital (to 1850). Library: Beals Memorial Library, 50 Pleasant St. (01475), 1-617-297-0300. W

19iii. City of WORCESTER. Established 1684 as a town from tract of land called Quansigamond, Holden split off in 1741, land split off to form part of new Town of Ward (later called Auburn), made a city 1848. Records to be sought: assessors, city (1848-), miscellaneous (1790-), proprietors (1667-1788), town (1722-1848), vital (1714-). Copied vital records: book, microfiche. Earliest church records: Congregational (1717-), Quaker (1735-), Unitarian (1785-). Books: biography, genealogy, histories, proprietors, Revolutionary soldiers, town records. FHL microfilms (MSA): biographies, cemetery, Congregational (1747-1892), genealogy, histories, military (1803-1922), proprietors, Quaker (1783-1898), town (1753-1848), vital (1714-1849). Libraries: American Antiquarian Society Library, 185 Salisbury St. (01069), 1-617-755-5221; Worcester Historical Museum Library, 39 Salisbury St. (01609), 1-617-753-8278; Worcester Public Library, Salem Square (01608), 1-617-799-1655. W

20. Extinct names, towns, and districts

Presented below is a listing of town and district names which have later been changed and of towns and districts which have been absorbed by other towns, districts, or cities. This list is given to facilitate your search in case you run into a town or district name which you cannot readily locate in the previous sections of this chapter.

Bethlehem, District of: See Otis in Berkshire County.
Boston Corner, District of: Established 1838, ceded to NY 1853.
Carlisle, District of: See Concord in Middlesex County.
East Sudbury, Town of: See Wayland in Middlesex County.
Gageborough, Town of: See Windsor in Berkshire County.
Gerry, Town of: See Phillipston in Worcester County.
Hutchinson, Town of: See Barre in Worcester County.
London, Town of: See Otis in Berkshire County.
Murrayfield, Town of: See Chester in Hampden County.
Nawsett, Town of: See Eastham in Barnstable County.
Newtowne, Town of: See Cambridge in Middlesex County. (Do not confuse with present Town of Newton in Middlesex County).
North Bridgewater, Town of: See Brockton in Plymouth County.
North Chelsea, Town of: See Revere in Suffolk County.
Norwich, Town of: See Huntington in Hampshire County.
Parsons, Town of: See West Newbury in Essex County.
Partridgefield, Town of: See Peru in Berkshire County.
Prescott, Town of: See Lancaster in Worcester County.
Rexhame, Town of: See Marshfield in Plymouth County.
Richmont, Town of: See Richmond in Berkshire County.
Rutland, District of: See Barre in Worcester County.
Saugust, Town of: See Lynn in Essex County.
Sherburn, Town of: See Nantucket in Nantucket County. (Do not confuse with present Town of Sherborn in Middlesex County).
South Brimfield, Town of: See Wales in Hampden County.
South Danvers, Town of: See Peabody in Essex County.
South Reading, Town of: See Wakefield in Middlesex County.
Southfield, District of: See Sandisfield in Berkshire County.
Stoughtonham, Town of: See Sharon in Norfolk County.
Troy, Town of: See FALL RIVER in Bristol County.
Ward, Town of: See Auburn in Worcester County.
Wellington, Town of: See Dighton in Bristol County.
West Cambridge, Town of: See Arlington in Middlesex County.
Western, Town of: See Warren in Worcester County.
West Towne, Town of: See Lancaster in Worcester County.

Key to Abbreviations

A	=	Agricultural census records
AGLL	=	American Genealogical Lending Library
BPL	=	Boston Public Library
C	=	Civil War Union veterans census
DAR	=	Daughters of the American Revolution
E	=	Early census-like lists
FHC	=	Family History Center(s)
FHL	=	Family History Library
FHLC	=	Family History Library Catalog
I	=	Industrial census records
IGI	=	International Genealogical Index
LGL	=	Large genealogical libraries
LL	=	Local library(ies) in MA
M	=	Mortality census records
MD	=	Mayflower Descendant
MHS	=	MA Historical Society
MSA	=	MA State Archives
NA	=	National Archives
NABB	=	National Archives, Boston Branch
NAFB	=	National Archives, Field Branch(es)
NEHGS	=	New England Historic Genealogical Society
P	=	Revolutionary War pensioner census
R	=	Regular census records
RL	=	Regional library(ies) in MA
S	=	MA state census records
SASE	=	Long, self-addressed, stamped envelope
SLM	=	State Library of MA

Books by George K. Schweitzer

CIVIL WAR GENEALOGY. A 78-paged book of 316 sources for tracing your Civil War ancestor. Chapters include I: The Civil War, II: The Archives, III: National Publications, IV: State Publications, V: Local Sources, VI: Military Unit Histories, VII: Civil War Events.

GEORGIA GENEALOGICAL RESEARCH. A 235-paged book containing 1303 sources for tracing your GA ancestor along with detailed instructions. Chapters include I: GA Background, II: Types of Records, III: Record Locations, IV: Research Procedure and County Listings (detailed listing of records available for each of the 159 GA counties).

HANDBOOK OF GENEALOGICAL SOURCES. A 155-paged book describing all major and many minor sources of genealogical information with precise and detailed instructions for obtaining data from them.

KENTUCKY GENEALOGICAL RESEARCH. A 154-paged book containing 1191 sources for tracing your KY ancestor along with detailed instructions. Chapters include I: KY Background, II: Types of Records, III: Record Locations, IV: Research Procedure and County Listings (detailed listing of records available for each of the 120 KY counties).

MASSACHUSETTS GENEALOGICAL RESEARCH. A 279-paged book containing 1709 sources for tracing your MA ancestor along with detailed instructions. Chapters include I: MA Background, II: Types of Records, III: Record Locations, IV: Research Procedure and County-Town-City Listings (detailed listing of records available for each of the 14 MA counties and the 351 cities-towns).

NEW YORK GENEALOGICAL RESEARCH. A 240-paged book containing 1426 sources for tracing your NY ancestor along with detailed instructions. Chapters include I: NY Background, II: Types of Records, III: Record Locations, IV: Research Procedure and NY City Record Listings (detailed listing of records available for the 5 counties of NY City), V: Record Listings for Other Counties (detailed listing of records available for each of the other 57 NY counties).

NORTH CAROLINA GENEALOGICAL RESEARCH. A 190-paged book containing 1233 sources for tracing your NC ancestor along with detailed instructions. Chapters include I: NC Background, II: Types of Records, III: Record Locations, IV: Research Procedure and County Listings (detailed listing of records available for each of the 100 NC counties).

PENNSYLVANIA GENEALOGICAL RESEARCH. A 225-paged book containing 1309 sources for tracing your PA ancestor along with detailed instructions. Chapters include I: PA Background, II: Types of Records, III: Record Locations, IV: Research Procedure and County Listings (detailed listing of records available for each of the 67 PA counties).

REVOLUTIONARY WAR GENEALOGY. A 110-paged book containing 407 sources for tracing your Revolutionary War ancestor. Chapters include I: Revolutionary War History, II: The Archives, III: National Publications, IV: State Publications, V: Local Sources, VI: Military Unit Histories, VII: Sites and Museums.

SOUTH CAROLINA GENEALOGICAL RESEARCH. A 190-paged book containing 1107 sources for tracing your SC ancestor along with detailed instructions. Chapters include I: SC Background, II: Types of Records, III: Record Locations, IV: Research Procedure and County Listings (detailed listing of records available for each of the 47 SC counties and districts).

TENNESSEE GENEALOGICAL RESEARCH. A 136-paged book containing 1073 sources for tracing your TN ancestor along with detailed instructions. Chapters include I: TN Background, II: Types of Records, III: Record Locations, IV: Research Procedure and County Listings (detailed listing of records available for each of the 96 TN counties).

VIRGINIA GENEALOGICAL RESEARCH. A 187-paged book containing 1273 sources for tracing your VA ancestor along with detailed instructions. Chapters include I: VA Background, II: Types of Records, III: Record Locations, IV: Research Procedure and County Listings (detailed listing of records available for each of the 100 VA counties and 41 major cities).

WAR OF 1812 GENEALOGY. A 69-paged book of 289 sources for tracing your War of 1812 ancestor. Chapters include I: History of the War, II: Service Records, III: Bounty Land and Pension Records, IV: National and State Publications, V: Local Sources, VI: Military Unit Histories, VII: Sites and Events.

All of the above books may be ordered from Dr. George K. Schweitzer at the address given on the title page. Or send a long SASE for a FREE descriptive leaflet on any or all of the books.